Technology of Object-Oriented Languages

TOOLS 28

The design of the TOOLS book series was adapted from one of the thousands of plates of d'Alembert and Diderot's Encyclopedie, also known as the Great Encyclopedia. The eighteenth century masterpiece — the result of collaborative work by dozens of the greatest experts in science, engineering, literature, art and philosophy — is one of the major intellectual achievements of the modern age. It played a key role in stating and promoting the ideas of the Enlightenment, and provided generations of students and professionals worldwide with a superb introduction to the technology of the time.

The quality, precision, depth and practicality of this work, and the sheer beauty of its illustrations depicting the great and small tools of all trades, serve as an inspiration to the TOOLS conference and book series in their effort to develop and improve one of the most challenging fields of research of our time: the art and science of software development, which object-oriented methods and tools are poised to affect

Mosaïque de Palestrine.

Proceedings

Technology of Object-Oriented Languages
TOOLS 28

November 23-26, 1998

Melbourne, Australia

Edited by

Christine Mingins and Bertrand Meyer

Sponsored by

Interactive Software Engineering (ISE) Inc., USA

IEEE
COMPUTER
SOCIETY

Los Alamitos, California

Washington • Brussels • Tokyo

1184007 2

IEEE Computer Society Order Number PR00053
ISBN 0-7695-0053-6
ISBN 0-7695-0055-2 (microfiche)
IEEE Order Plan Catalog Number 98TB100271
Library of Congress Number 98-89186

Learning Resources
Centre

Additional copies may be ordered from:

IEEE Computer Society
Customer Service Center
10662 Los Vaqueros Circle
P.O. Box 3014
Los Alamitos, CA 90720-1314
Tel: + 1-714-821-8380
Fax: + 1-714-821-4641
E-mail: cs.books@computer.org

IEEE Service Center
445 Hoes Lane
P.O. Box 1331
Piscataway, NJ 08855-1331
Tel: + 1-732-981-1393
Fax: + 1-732-981-9667
mis.custserv@computer.org

IEEE Computer Society
Ooshima Building
2-19-1 Minami-Aoyama
Minato-ku, Tokyo 107
JAPAN
Tel: + 81-3-3408-3118
Fax: + 81-3-3408-3553
Tokyo.ofc@computer.org

Editorial production by Regina Spencer Sipple
Cover art production by Joseph Daigle/Studio Productions
Printed in the United States of America by The Printing House

IEEE
COMPUTER
SOCIETY

IEEE

Table of Contents

Conference Committee

Conference Series Chair
Bertrand Meyer, *ISE*

Conference Chair
Christine Mingins, *Monash University*

Program Co-Chairs

John Potter
Microsoft Research Institute,
Macquarie University

Christine Mingins
Monash University

Organizing Committee Chair
Damien Watkins, *Monash University*

Tutorial Chair
Damien Watkins, *Monash University*

Conference Coordinator
Michelle Riseley, *Monash University*

Organizing Committee

Martin Dick
Jason Ceddia
Stephen Giles
Jason Lowder
Christine Mingins
Michelle Riseley
Monique Spence
Damien Watkins

Program Committee

Jean Bezivin, *University of Nantes, France*
Julian Edwards, *Object Oriented Pty Ltd., Australia*
Doug Grant, *Swinburne University of Technology, Australia*
Richard Helm, *IBM Global Services, Australia*
Brian Henderson-Sellers, *Swinburne University of Technology, Australia*
John Hosking, *Auckland University, New Zealand*
Shaoying Liu, *Hiroshima City University, Japan*
Ian Mathieson, *CSIRO, Australia*
James McKim, *Hartford Graduate Center, USA*
Bertrand Meyer, *ISE, Santa Barbara, USA*
Christine Mingins, *Monash University, Australia*
James Noble, *Microsoft Research Institute, Australia*
Sita Ramakrishnan, *Monash University, Australia*
Heinz Schmidt, *Monash University, Australia*
Diane Smith, *Ballarat University, Australia*
Paul Strooper, *University of Queensland, Australia*
Paul Swatman, *Swinburne University of Technology*
Paul Taylor, *Simsion Bowles & Associates*
Richard Thomas, *Queensland University of Technology, Australia*

Session 1

Patterns, Frameworks

Towards a Pattern Language for Object Oriented Design

James Noble
Microsoft Research Institute
Macquarie University
Sydney, Australia
kjx@mri.mq.edu.au

Abstract

Since the publication of the Design Patterns book, a large number of design patterns have been identified and codified. Unfortunately, these patterns are mostly organised in an ad hoc fashion, making it hard for programmers to know which pattern to apply to any particular problem. We have organised a large number of existing object oriented design patterns into a pattern language, by analysing the patterns and the relationships between them. Organising patterns into languages has the potential to make large collections of patterns easier to understand and to use.

1: Introduction

A object oriented design pattern is a *"description of communicating objects and classes that are customised to solve a general design problem in a particular context"* [12, p.3]. Designers can incorporate patterns into their programs to address general problems in the structure of their programs' designs.

Before they can apply a pattern to solve their design problem, programmers must select an appropriate design pattern. An expert programmer may have learnt tens or hundreds of patterns, and will intuitively select the correct pattern. Novice programmers will know far fewer patterns, and will have to search pattern catalogues such as *Design Patterns* [12], *Patterns of Software Architecture* [7], or the *Pattern Languages of Program Design* series [9, 24, 14] to select a pattern. We call the problem of selecting the pattern to apply to a given design problem the *pattern selection problem*.

The first collection of patterns was made by an architect, Christopher Alexander, and these patterns described building design rather than software design [1, 2]. Alexander solved the pattern selection problem by organising his patterns into a *pattern language*. A pattern language is organised from the most general large-scale patterns to the most specific small-scale patterns, based on the relationships between the patterns. Applying the patterns in a language should assist a programmer (or architect) to generate a design, with the appropriate pattern to apply next being indicated by the organisation of the patterns in the language, that is, by the interrelationships between them [8]. In effect, the patterns in a pattern language simultaneously solve design problems and pattern selection problems.

In this paper, we describe how the patterns from the *Design Patterns* can be organised into a pattern language. Section 2 briefly reviews patterns, pattern catalogues, and pattern languages, and discusses why catalogues such as *Design Patterns* do not form pattern languages. Section 3 then outlines the organisation of the *Found Objects* pattern language which we have constructed, based upon *Design Patterns*, presenting first the large scale structure of the whole language and the small scale structure of several of the more important fragments of the language. Section 4 compares pattern catalogues and pattern languages, and Section 5 presents our conclusions.

2: Patterns, Catalogues, and Languages

A design pattern is an abstraction from a concrete recurring solution that solves a problem in a certain context [12, 7]. Typically, a design pattern has a name, a description of problems for which the pattern is applicable, an analysis of the *forces* (the important considerations and consequences of using the pattern) the pattern addresses, a sample implementation of the pattern's solution, a disussion of how this solution resolves the forces, references to known uses, and a list of patterns which are related to this pattern. To use a design pattern, a designer must first recognise a problem within their design, locate a design pattern which resolves the problem, and then design (or redesign) their program to incorporate the pattern.

Design patterns were first applied to software by Kent Beck and Ward Cunningham [5]. They were popularised by the *Design Patterns* catalogue, which described twenty-three general purpose patterns for object oriented design. Since the publication of *Design Patterns* a large number of other patterns have been identified [9, 24, 14].

2.1: Pattern Catalogues and Systems

A single design pattern generally addresses a single design problem. To provide a greater coverage of the problems faced in software development, patterns are often collected into catalogues or systems. For example, *Design Patterns* is structured as a pattern catalogue. The patterns are placed into three chapters, containing creational patterns, structural patterns, and behavioural patterns, based on the patterns' scope. Other pattern catalogues have different organisational structures. For example, *Patterns of Software Architecture* structures patterns into a system with three main categories (architecture patterns, design patterns, and programming patterns) based on the scale of the patterns. Patterns have also been catalogued based on the roles objects play in the patterns [21], patterns' internal structure [28], and the purpose of the patterns [23].

However they may be organised, pattern catalogues do not really address the pattern selection problem. First, a programmer needing to use a pattern must understand the classification scheme used by the catalogue. Second, they must search that part of the catalogue to find the pattern(s) which are applicable to their problem. Finally, although the patterns within the catalogue may point the programmer to other possible patterns which could be applied next, or could be alternatives to a particular pattern, this guidance is only at the level of the patterns, and is not part of the structure of the catalogue itself.

2.2: Pattern Languages

A pattern catalogue contains a collection of patterns which provide solutions to a collection of problems. In contrast, a *pattern language* is a collection of interrelated patterns organised into a coherent whole, which provides a detailed solution to a large-scale design problem [8, 1]. In a pattern language, the patterns are organised by the relationships between the patterns, whereas in a pattern catalogue the patterns are organised by classification schemes originating outside the patterns themselves.

The structure of a pattern language is a rooted, directed graph, generally with few cycles, where nodes represent patterns and links the relationships between patterns. The *initial pattern* at the root of the graph addresses the large-scale problem addressed by the whole language, and broadly outlines the solution the language provides. This pattern provides a partial solution to the problem, resolving some of the forces acting on the problem, but leaving some forces unresolved and exposing smaller-scale subproblems. The initial pattern is related to (it *uses* or contains) smaller-scale patterns in the language, in particular, it will use those patterns which address the subpatterns and forces exposed by the initial pattern. These patterns will in turn provide solutions, exposing further subproblems, and use smaller-scale patterns to solve them.

This organisation gives a pattern language its overall shape and is why pattern languages may provide more leverage than single patterns or pattern catalogues in addressing the pattern selection problem. Unlike a catalogue, a pattern language can be traversed by following the *uses* relationship from larger-scale to smaller-scale patterns, with each pattern both describing a solution to a subproblem, and indicating subsequent applicable patterns. In Alexander's terminology, traversing the pattern language *generates* a design [2, 1, 8]. Because of this organisation, it is more difficult to compile a pattern language than a pattern catalogue.

The progression from larger to smaller scale patterns defines the large scale structure of a pattern language, with the *uses* relationship between patterns defining the small scale structure. Larger pattern languages also have medium scale structure. Alexander's pattern language [1] is actually made up of thirty-six *pattern language fragments* — groups of between four and ten patterns which are tightly interrelated. Also, *A Pattern Language* is subtitled "*Towns · Buildings · Construction*", as the patterns (and pattern language fragments) are organised at three different scales — town planning, architecture and construction and interior decoration.

A number of pattern languages have been written for software development [9, 24, 14], but these mostly apply to particular application domains. Only a few of these "languages" contain more than ten or twelve patterns, that is, they would be better described as pattern language fragments rather than full pattern languages. To the best of our knowledge, no substantial pattern language organising object-oriented software design patterns exists.

3: Towards A Pattern Language for Object Oriented Design

We are engaged in a long-term project called "*Found Objects*" that aims to organise patterns for object-oriented design [16, 17, 18, 19]. As part of this project, we are organising a pattern language for object oriented design derived from the twenty three patterns from *Design Patterns*, and including a number of other patterns drawn from the general patterns literature [7, 4, 9, 24, 14]. The current version of the pattern language, called *Found Objects*, contains over 90 patterns. Although this is approximately three times as many patterns as the *Design Patterns* catalogue, the language is not three times as complex, because the patterns in the language are smaller than those in *Design Patterns*. As part of organising the patterns into a language, we have subdivided the larger patterns, so that each pattern focuses on addressing one particular problem, and to explicate latent information in the pattern descriptions.

Because of the size of the pattern language, space does not permit us to present it in full detail here. To give the flavour of the language, we begin by presenting an overview of the language's large scale structure. We then present the structure of some of the more important fragments of the language in detail, to illustrate how patterns can be organised into pattern langauge fragments and then pattern languages. Also for space reasons, and since we have built the language primarily by organising well-known patterns from the pattern literature, we do not describe individual patterns in detail.

3.1: Large Scale Structure

The *Found Objects* pattern language is constructed out of a number of *pattern language fragments*. Each pattern language fragment contains a number of related patterns, and the relationships between the patterns in different language fragments determines the structure of the language as a whole. Figure 1 illustrates the structure of the fragments in the language, and shows how the fragments can be loosely organised into three main categories — architectural patterns, design patterns, and programming idioms — following *Patterns of Software Architecture* [7]. The links between the language fragments in Figure 1 represent the major dependencies between the patterns in the fragments — patterns in the higher level fragments use the patterns in the lower-level fragments. Most fragments contain between five and ten patterns, although some (in particular, Interpreter) contain only a single pattern. Figure 2 gives an overview of the patterns in each fragment.

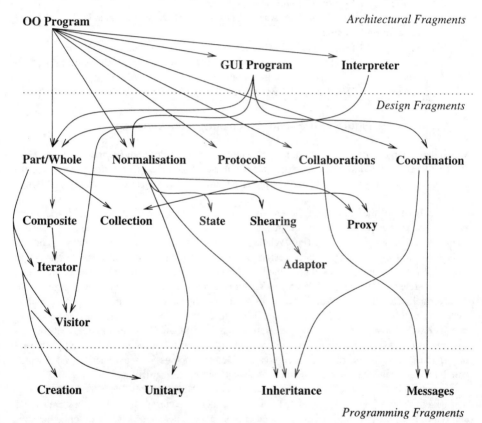

Figure 1. The Structure of the Pattern Language

The language has three architectural pattern fragments. The most important fragment is the OO Program fragment. This is the initial fragment, and it contains the initial pattern which is also called OO Program. The other architectural fragments describe architectural composite patterns

Fragment	Patterns
Architectural Fragments	
OO Program	OO program, Objects, Responsibilities, Collaborations [25]
GUI Program	MVC, View Handler, Command Processor [7]
Interpreter	Interpreter [12]
Design Fragments	
Part/Whole	Aggregation, Composition, Sharing [7]
Normalisation	Type Object [13], Method Object [4], State [10]
Protocols	Patterns on protocol design [17]
Collaborations	Patterns on relationship design [18]
Coordination	Chain of responsibility, Observer, Mediator [12]
Collection	Patterns on collections [4, Chapter 5]
Shearing	Facade, Bridge, Adaptor, Decorator, Strategy, Extension [11]
Programming Fragments	
Creation	Factory method, Abstract factory, Prototype, Builder [12]
Unitary	Singleton, Memento, Flyweight [12], What If [3], Null Object [27]
Inheritance	Abstract class [26], Template method, Hook method [12]
Messages	Delegation, OO Recursion [3], Double Dispatch [12]

Figure 2. The Major Fragments of the Language

which define large parts of a program's architecture — the GUI Program fragment contains high-level patterns for building user interfaces based on the Model-View-Controller pattern, and the Interpreter fragment contains only the Interpreter pattern, the sole larger-scale pattern from *Design Patterns*.

The majority of the patterns in the language address problems in OO design. This is unsurprising, since we are developing the language to organise the *Design Patterns*. The design section begins with five major fragments (Part/Whole, Normalisation, Protocols, Collaborations, and Coordination) containing patterns about designing objects' structures, interfaces, and relationships. The Part/Whole fragment is based upon the Part/Whole pattern [7], and leads to separate fragments which describe the Composite, Iterator, and Visitor patterns and their commonly occurring variants. The Normalisation fragment contains patterns about decomposing objects into subobjects, such as State, Type Object [13], and Method Object [4]. The Protocol and Collaboration fragments contain patterns about objects' interfaces and relationships [17, 18], the Coordination fragment contains patterns such as Mediator and Observer which coordinate or distribute control over multiple objects in programs, and the Shearing fragment contains patterns such as Strategy, Facade, and Adaptor, which help programs handle multiple rates of change within their structure.

The pattern language also includes a number of other OO design fragments named after a particular pattern. These fragments are related to the larger design patterns after which they are named, and typically contain that pattern, plus a number of smaller-scale patterns which describe how that design pattern can be implemented or alternative ways it can be used. For example, the Composite, Iterator, Visitor, and Adaptor fragments include several variants of each pattern, and the Collections fragment contains patterns which describe how collection classes can be used [4, Chapter 5].

Finally, the programming fragment contains lower level patterns which are used by many other patterns in the language, including patterns which rest solely upon inheritance, the creational patterns, and patterns which relate to unitary, self contained objects. The most interesting fragment here is the Creation fragment, which organises the Creational patterns from *Design Patterns*, in addition to other creational patterns like Product Trader [22].

3.2: Small Scale Structure

The small scale structure of the pattern language is determined by the specific patterns organised into each fragment of the pattern language, and the relationships between the patterns in each fragment. We consider three relationships between patterns — one pattern *uses* another pattern, patterns can *conflict* in providing differing solutions to common problems, and one pattern can *refine*, or be a specialisation of, another pattern [19].

Uses   One pattern *uses* another pattern when the second pattern solves a sub-problem raised by the application of the first pattern. For example, the Abstract Factory pattern *uses* the Factory Method pattern because abstract factories are often implemented using factory methods. The *uses* relationship is the most important and most common relationship between the patterns. The *uses* relationship guides the programmer through the language, indicating which patterns may be applicable at any stage. The *uses* relationship is the only explicit relationship between patterns in *A Pattern Language* [1] (where it is called *containment*), and most software pattern forms also explicitly record this relationship — typically in a section titled *Related Patterns* [12] or *See Also* [7]. Some pattern forms, including Alexander's, also record the inverse *used-by* relationship to give the context of more general patterns within which a particular pattern is likely to be instantiated.

Conflicts   Two or more patterns can *conflict*, that is, provide mutually exclusive solutions to similar problems. For example, the Decorator pattern conflicts with the Strategy pattern in that both patterns can (and have been) be used to add graphical borders or icons to window objects in window systems [12, p.180]. Most pattern forms do not provide an explicit section to record this relationship, but it is often expressed in the related pattern section along with the *uses* relationship or it may be discussed elsewhere in the pattern form.

Refines   One pattern can *refine* another pattern, that is to say, one pattern can be a specialisation of another pattern. For example the **Factory Method** pattern *refines* the Hook Method pattern, and in *A Pattern Language* the Sequence of Sitting Spaces pattern refines the Intimacy Gradient pattern [1]. A specific pattern refines an abstract pattern if the specific pattern's full description is a direct extension of the abstract pattern. That is, the specific pattern must deal with a specialisation of the problem the general pattern addresses, must have a similar (but more specialised) solution structure, and must address the same forces as the more general pattern, but may also address additional forces. To make an analogy with object oriented programming, the *uses* relationship is similar to composition, while the *refines* relationship is similar to inheritance.

3.3: The Architectural Fragments

The pattern language proper begins with the initial pattern from the initial fragment of the pattern language (see Figure 3). This is the OO Program pattern, which describes the single largest artifact produced by the language, by analogy with the Independent Regions (1) pattern from *A Pattern Language*. The OO Program pattern leads to several conceptual patterns which describe how programs are built from objects, their collaborations, and their relationships, and which in turn lead to more specific patterns. The OO Program pattern also leads to the composite patterns Model-View-Controller and Interpreter (in the GUI Program fragment and the Interpreter fragment respectively) to generate the overall structure of the program.

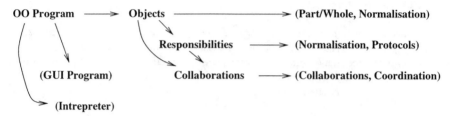

Figure 3. The OO Program fragment

Although the OO Program fragment is the capstone of the pattern language, it was one of the last parts of the language we completed, and it was the only fragment where we had to compile all the patterns specifically for the language. Once the other patterns were organised, the language needed an initial fragment as a starting point for reading or working through the patterns, so we introduced the OO Program pattern to fill this need, and the Objects, Responsibilities, and Collaborations patterns to fill it out. These patterns describe the basics of *Responsibility Driven Design* [25]. Together, these patterns provide an object oriented context in which the rest of the language can operate, and lead the reader into the more detailed design patterns.

This section also includes some composite architectural patterns. The GUI Program fragment (see Figure 4) is based around the Model-View-Controller composite pattern [7, 20], and includes the Command Processor and View Handler patterns [7]. The Model-View-Controller pattern also uses a number of smaller-scale patterns from other fragments in the language — these are shown parenthesised in the figure.

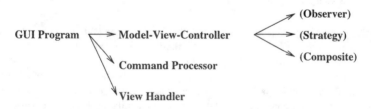

Figure 4. The GUI Program Fragment

The last architectural pattern langauge fragment contains only one pattern, Interpreter. We have placed this pattern into the architectural level of the language because it is at a higher level than the other patterns in *Design Patterns* — in particular, it can be described as a composite pattern which uses the Composite and Visitor patterns.

3.4: The Design Fragments

The Part/Whole fragment of the pattern language, illustrated in Figure 5, is the first fragment of the design patterns, and describes how larger objects can be composed from smaller parts. This fragment is based around the Part/Whole pattern from *Patterns of Software Architecture*, and is a complex fragment, because the patterns it contains have complex interrelationships. The main Part/Whole pattern is refined by three other patterns. The Assembly pattern [7] describes how aggregate objects can be assembled from smaller objects. The Collection pattern describes how collection (or container) objects can be used to hold groups of objects, and it refers the reader to a pattern language fragment describing a particular Collection library — Beck [4, Chapter 5] provides a good set for Smalltalk. The OO Trees pattern [3] describes how trees of objects can be assembled recursively using the very common Composite pattern, and also other patterns like Decorator and Visitor. Finally, the Sharing pattern [3, 7] describes how one Whole may share its Parts with other Wholes, and leads to its common specialisation, Flyweight, which is part of the Unitary programming fragment.

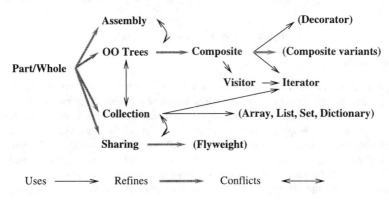

Figure 5. The Part/Whole fragment

The Part/Whole fragment illustrates how abstract patterns (such as the Part/Whole pattern) can be incorporated into a larger pattern language. The abstract Part/Whole pattern *refines* the more specific patterns it generalises, and proceeds these in the language. The Assembly, OO Trees, and Collection patterns *conflict* with each other, because, in refining Part/Whole, each provides a different solution to the general problem of decomposing an object.

3.4.1: Shearing Fragment

The Shearing Fragment organises a number of the *Design Patterns*, plus a number of patterns identified more recently. All the patterns in this fragment provide ways help programs remain flexible when different parts of their structure much change at different rates — the fragment takes its name from the *Shearing Layers* identified in buildings in *How Buildings Learn* [6]. Although other patterns also have this effect, the Shearing patterns address this problem most directly.

The fragment begins with an abstract pattern, also called Shearing, which identifies the general problem, and is refined by two conflicting patterns (Skin and Guts) which capture the dynamics of the two main solutions — *"Changing the skin of an object versus changing its guts"* [12, p. 179], that is, changing an objects interface versus changing its implementation. These two patterns are refined by more detailed patterns which provide concrete solutions in particular contexts, including the Bridge pattern, which allows both Skin and Guts to vary independently.

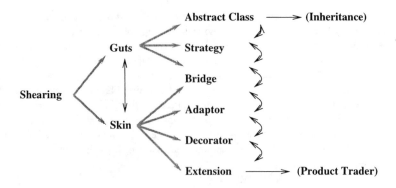

Figure 6. The Shearing Fragment

3.4.2: State Fragment

The State fragment incorporates Dyson and Anderson's *State Patterns* pattern language fragment [10] directly into our larger pattern language (see Figure 7). In this fragment, the State pattern captures the core of the State pattern from *Design Patterns*, and the other patterns act as *subpatterns* of State, describing how to apply it in more detail. In particular, the State Member and Exposed State patterns describe how to design the subsidiary state objects, the Owner Driven Transitions and State Driven Transitions patterns describe two alternative design for managing transitions between states, and the Pure State pattern describes how and when state objects can be shared. Because it is quite self-contained, this fragment can be directly incorporated into our pattern language — the patterns and their relationships are taken directly from the original description [10].

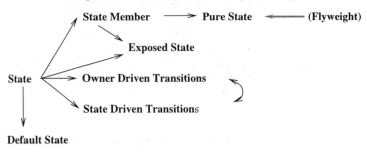

Figure 7. The State Fragment

The state fragment illustrates two points about building pattern languages. First, subpatterns can be incorporated simply by organising the language so that the that the main pattern *uses* all the top-level subpatterns. Second, well-conceived pattern language fragments can sometimes be incorporated wholesale into larger pattern languages.

3.5: The Programming Fragments

The Creation fragment is the most interesting Programming fragment, so it is the only one we present here (see Figure 8). This fragment incorporates all the *Design Patterns* creational patterns, the Product Trader pattern [22], and two abstract patterns — Natural Creation and Direct Creation — which are introduced to structure the fragment [15]. Natural Creation address the design problem of how should objects be created, and Direct Creation refines patterns describing the two basic mechanisms for creating objects provided by programming languages — instantiating a class or cloning a prototype.

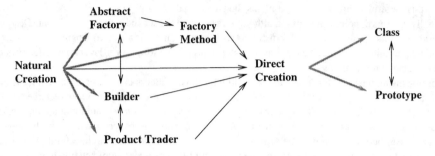

Figure 8. The Creation Fragment

4: Discussion

Design Patterns contains an analysis of why pattern catalogues are *not* pattern languages:

1. *People have been making buildings for thousands of years, and there are many classic examples to draw upon. We have been making software systems for a relatively short time, and few are considered classics.*

2. *Alexander gives an order in which his patterns should be used; we have not.*

3. *Alexander's patterns emphasise the problems they address, whereas design patterns describe the solutions in more detail.*

4. *Alexander claims his patterns will generate complete buildings. We do not claim that our patterns will generate complete programs.*

Design Patterns [12, p. 356], Gamma, Helm, Johnson, Vlissides.

In order to organise the *Design Patterns* into a language we must address these four points. We have not addressed the first point directly — there are still very few programs which are considered classics, and we have not tried to write or unearth any. In spite of this, the *Design Patterns* do seem to capture many of the important features of the design of those extant object oriented programs which are considered classics, and the patterns are becoming widely recognised as good software engineering practice.

The second point is the most important consideration for organising patterns into a language. *Design Patterns* is a pattern catalogue, so the patterns are organised into three chapters based on the pattern's scope, and within each section the sequence is alphabetical — essentially ad-hoc. In our pattern language, we have explicitly provided an order for the patterns, based on the relationships between the patterns, and the scale at which each pattern applies, to guide the programmer through the patterns.

The third point is also quite important, because although the bulk of the pattern descriptions we have drawn upon do concentrate upon the proposed solutions, all patterns include a description of the problem they solve — although in the *Design Patterns* form, it is split between the Intent, Motivation, and Applicability sections. In constructing our pattern language, we have analysed the patterns to identify the problems that each pattern solves, and where necessary decomposed monolithic patterns to highlight the problems the patterns address.

Finally, the fourth point is important, although less so than the second point. In particular, *Design Patterns* contains no larger-scale patterns to act as starting points for a pattern language, and there is certainly no initial pattern. The patterns also stop short of capturing lower-level knowledge about object oriented programming.

For organising a pattern language, the lack of higher-level patterns is more important, since they group the patterns into the whole language, and so we have introduced a number of large scale patterns to start the language. The pattern language we have constructed is an initial attempt, and is intentionally partial and open to extension. Although a complete pattern language in the sense that a path can be traced through the sequence of patterns from the initial architectural pattern to the lowest level programming pattern, the language will requires many more patterns to be able to generate designs for whole programs.

The pattern language is also incomplete in another sense, in that the we have described only the organisation or skeleton of a pattern language. This is because the language is made up mostly from existing patterns from the literature, so the body of the patterns are simply references into that literature. The complete language would be much more convenient to use if it included the full text of every pattern, but this would be a major undertaking. It is also not clear what kind of pattern form is best suited to this style of pattern language.

5: Conclusion

In this paper, we have described how the design patterns from *Design Patterns* can be organised into a pattern language, along with other patterns from the literature. We have described the large-scale structure of the resulting *Found Objects* pattern language, and outlined the contents and relationships within some of the main fragments in the language.

Practitioners and researchers need to experiment with the resulting pattern language, to evaluate the benefits and liabilities of presenting patterns using a pattern language vis-a-vis a pattern catalogue or pattern system. At this time, it is not clear whether pattern catalogues or pattern languages will prove to be the better approach for organising a practical handbook for software engineering. Organising the *Design Patterns* into a pattern language demonstrates that at least some kind of pattern language can be constructed for general, domain-independent software design patterns, and is an important step enabling more detailed comparisons to be carried out.

Acknowledgements

Thanks to Geoffrey Outhred, Ralph Johnson, and the anonymous referees, who kindly commented on drafts. This work was supported by Microsoft Australia Pty Ltd.

References

[1] Christopher Alexander. *A Pattern Language*. Oxford University Press, 1977.

[2] Christopher Alexander. *The Timeless Way of Building*. Oxford University Press, 1979.

[3] Sherman R. Alpert, Kyle Brown, and Bobby Woolf. *The Design Patterns Smalltalk Companion*. Addison-Wesley, 1988.

[4] Kent Beck. *Smalltalk Best Practice Patterns*. Prentice-Hall, 1997.

[5] Kent Beck and Ward Cunningham. Using pattern languages for object-oriented programs. Technical report, Tektronix, Inc., 1987. Presented at the OOPSLA-87 Workshop on Specification and Design for Object-Oriented Programming.

[6] Steward Brand. *How Buildings Learn*. Penguin Books, 1994.

[7] Frank Buschmann, Regine Meunier, Hans Rohnert, Peter Sommerlad, and Michael Stal. *Pattern-Oriented Software Architecture*. John Wiley & Sons, 1996.

[8] James O. Coplien. *Software Patterns*. SIGS Management Briefings. SIGS Press, 1996.

[9] James O. Coplien and Douglas C. Schmidt, editors. *Pattern Languages of Program Design*. Addison-Wesley, 1996.

[10] Paul Dyson and Bruce Anderson. State objects. In Martin et al. [14].

[11] Erich Gamma. Extension object. In Martin et al. [14].

[12] Erich Gamma, Richard Helm, Ralph E. Johnson, and John Vlissides. *Design Patterns*. Addison-Wesley, 1994.

[13] Ralph E. Johnson and Bobby Woolf. Type object. In Martin et al. [14].

[14] Robert C. Martin, Dirk Riehle, and Frank Buschmann, editors. *Pattern Languages of Program Design*, volume 3. Addison-Wesley, 1998.

[15] Gerard Meszaros and Jim Doble. A pattern language for pattern writing. In Martin et al. [14].

[16] James Noble. Found objects. In *EuroPLOP Proceedings*, 1996.

[17] James Noble. Arguments and results. In *PLOP Proceedings*, 1997.

[18] James Noble. Basic relationship patterns. In *EuroPLOP Proceedings*, 1997.

[19] James Noble. Classifying relationships between object-oriented design patterns. In *Australian Software Engineering Conference (ASWEC)*, 1998.

[20] Dirk Riehle. Composite design patterns. In *ECOOP Proceedings*, 1997.

[21] Dirk Riehle. A role based design pattern catalog of atomic and composite patterns structured by pattern purpose. Technical Report 97-1-1, UbiLabs, 1997.

[22] Dirk Riehle. Product trader. In Martin et al. [14].

[23] Walter F. Tichy. A catalogue of general-purpose software design patterns. In *TOOLS USA 1997*, 1997.

[24] John M. Vlissides, James O. Coplien, and Norman L. Kerth, editors. *Pattern Languages of Program Design*, volume 2. Addison-Wesley, 1996.

[25] Rebecca Wirfs-Brock, Brian Wilkerson, and Lauren Wiener. *Designing Object-Oriented Software*. Prentice-Hall, 1990.

[26] Bobby Woolf. The abstract class pattern. In *PLOP Proceedings*, 1997.

[27] Bobby Woolf. Null object. In Martin et al. [14].

[28] Walter Zimmer. Relationships between design patterns. In *Pattern Languages of Program Design*. Addison-Wesley, 1994.

Designing Persistent Object-Oriented Software Architectures

Paul Taylor,
Senior Consultant,
Simsion, Bowles & Associates,
1 Collins St., Melbourne, 3000, Australia.
http://www.sba.com.au
prt@sba.com.au

Abstract

Conventional object-oriented analysis delivers a business object model, which is transformed during design into collaborating class clusters which implement the business model's intent in the chosen software technology. Object persistence provided by Objectstore (Object Design International 98), a leading object-oriented database product, significantly impacts the design phase, driving the definition of implementation classes and their responsibilities, relationships and their implementation in the physical schema. Further, it is not the static characteristics of the database, but the dynamic transaction model which most dramatically shapes the persistent class model. Different transaction models for the same business object clusters lead to very different implementation object models. Failing to appreciate these forces on the design of a persistent schema can result in persistent object-oriented applications with hot-spots of unacceptable and unworkable performance, and equally unacceptable scalability. This paper surveys the experiences of an object database development project, and recommends ways of designing an object database application to avoid these problems.

1. Purpose

This paper addresses how the use of an object database impacts the persistent software architecture, and the *design* activity of object-oriented software development in a high volume, multi-processing transaction oriented environment. It is motivated by the need to explore several perceptions about some object databases and persistence mechanisms—the perceptions that:

> *...persistence is transparent to the business model* (Kim 1990)(Cattell 91)

and, as a result,

> *...persistence costs (almost) nothing in terms of design and implementation effort.*

Our experience validates these perceptions for a class of simple persistent architectures, but strongly invalidates them for a more common class of more realistically complex architectures. In our experience, the use of persistence impacts the implementation class model significantly, and the design of a non-trivial persistent architecture must be recognised and managed as a separate design activity. This paper discusses these observations, and offers a grab bag of schema and class design techniques to address the specific problems which may be encountered.

In a paper with a strong 'experience report' flavour like this one, it is tempting to drop into highly specific solution mechanisms. This would necessitate a deep knowledge of the Objectstore database product, and some domain knowledge. Consequently, the issues and solutions covered · have been selected to be sufficiently generic and independent of product to be accessible to readers without object database experience and practicioners using other object database products.

1.1   Context

The experience recounted in this paper was assembled over two and a half elapsed years of work on a large object-oriented business application.   There are many dimensions of scale by which these systems are measured—statically, the software architecture consists of around seven hundred classes, about seventy percent of which are persistent. This code base contains three quarters of a million executable lines of C++ source. Dynamically, the database consists of hundreds of collections, some containing over a million persistent objects. The application process architecture has one client process per user or workstation (of which there may be up to eighty during a business day) with around ten to twenty concurrent database interrogations at any time, all with hard response requirements.

There were two reasons for the initial selection of an object database for this system, one historical and one based on the mapping of business domain problem type to technology. The project's technical architecture grew on a firm base of successful system implementation and deployment using the same suite of client software, language, development environment, and database.   Transfer of this environment from the previous project was straightforward and immediate.   The second driver for an object database came from the need to implement a significant network model in the business domain—an application which has historically driven object databases (Sengupta 91).   This network component was both large (it contains several million objects) and has complex relationships (any given object in the model participates in two hierarchical relationships, one downward hierarchy which extends to the lowest bandwidth channel, and one upward hierarchy which relates the object to its physical cables).   A further requirement necessitated extensive searching and traversal in both directions through this network model, from many concurrent user processes. It seemed reasonable to reject any form of relational database solution, given that these traversals would be frequently performed from the user interface in interactive time-frames.

2.   Evolving to a Schema

Schemas in object-oriented databases are designed as a result of two activities—up-front schema design, before detailed design and implementation of the architecture, and schema evolution.

Designing a schema is not an easy task, as it assumes considerable knowledge of the database product, the business domain, the system requirements, and the emerging business object model (Bancilhon 1992). The time in a project when a business model is being analysed and designed is typically a time of steep learning involving many significant assumptions, as critical elements of the problem settle, along with the team's understanding of them. When large chunks of detail are, by necessity, missing from the business object model, it is clearly not the best time to be laying a further layer of design interpretation on the emerging infrastructure (Chorafas 93). Because of the number and extent of unknowns early in an object database project, schemas evolve towards stability from their initial design, typically in parallel with the evolution of the business model.

2.1 Reasons for Schema Evolution

This evolution takes the individual developer and the team through a number of stages in their use of persistence. The role of persistence in a conventional object-oriented development lifecycle is approximately depicted in Figure 1. The downward arrows represent schema formation. Object database products make persistence trivial—in object-oriented application development, this allows early business models to be made persistent, implying that the first schemas are highly immature, and are subject to extensive evolution as the development proceeds. Schema evolution continues throughout the entire lifecycle, as described below.

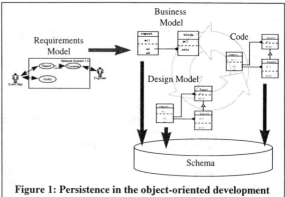

Figure 1: Persistence in the object-oriented development lifecycle.

2.2 Rates of Schema Evolution

Figure 2 presents our schema's evolution during development, drawn against the project phases which drove this evolution. This graph provides a relative indication of schema stability—it was drawn from a review of the project plans, and is not based on metrics from the source code control system. However, it provides an indication of the overall shape of the schema evolution graph.

Determination of what constitutes a schema change is product specific, and depends on what meta-data is stored by the product for runtime support and utilities. Objectstore allows the addition of a class or subclass (to an existing segment), the insertion of class or instance methods, and signature changes to an existing schema, but the addition of an attribute to a class, the addition of (some) virtual methods, and changing the type of an existing attribute all constitute a schema change. (Changing the type includes appending an enumeration to an existing enumerated type, a very limiting characteristic.) After any schema change, the client process cannot open an Objectstore database built to an earlier schema—changes must therefore me managed carefully at various times in the project.

Figure 2 indicates three peaks of schema change. The first schemas were largely driven by the team's initial implementation of the business model, and contained over-simplified collections of

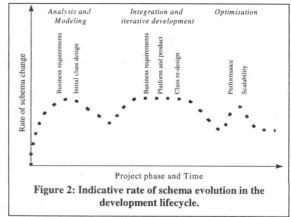

Figure 2: Indicative rate of schema evolution in the development lifecycle.

business objects and relationships. These persistent classes provided the vehicle for team familiarisation with the emerging business and design model, and allowed an early integration and release of the application to be demonstrated to users. The model was, however, naïvely business object focused, and lacked informed design input from both the database product domain, and the dimensions in which the application would scale. The discovery of these factors forced the second peak, which resulted in three more iterative integrations and user feedback releases. It was in this 'integration and iterative development' phase that some of the design idioms described later emerged (Section 0).

At this point, the application was viewed as functionally complete, and ready for performance modification and tuning (the driver for the last, most difficult and expensive peak). The critical performance issues, mostly concerning concurrency, were difficult to solve and necessitated significant but highly localised rework to both the application code and the schema. The remaining design solutions (Section 0) emerged in this phase.

2.3   Schema Access Patterns

During these last two project phases, we observed a sequence of schema development steps which most developers repeated. Persistence problems appeared to arise from a small number of database 'access patterns', which formed a basic classification of our use of persistence. Notice that the term 'access patterns' is being used here to refer to the recurring or stereotypical ways that application code accesses the schema, not design patterns, although the two are not unrelated (in an interesting way). These classifications of access patterns can be broadly applied to applications and architectures, and may help to anticipate the type and extent of persistence design effort to expect. Additionally, they help to organise the persistence design solutions discussed later in this paper. Our classification of persistence access patterns is illustrated in Figure 3.

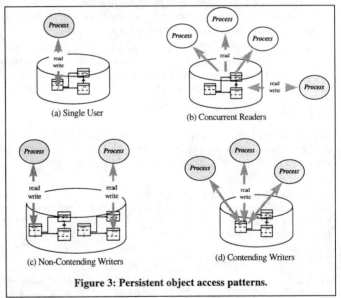

(a) Single User

(b) Concurrent Readers

(c) Non-Contending Writers

(d) Contending Writers

Figure 3: Persistent object access patterns.

2.3.1   Single User

The most basic form of persistence involves one user process with exclusive access to an object database segment. This elementary process architecture (Figure 3 (a)) is significant because every object database developer uses this model during their initial subsystem development. As well as being a passing development phase, a class of application architectures find this form of persistence perfectly adequate; their characteristics are:

- a single user or database client (either a single process, or a *logical* single process effected by some serialisation technique);
- no significant implications of long transactions.

Some examples of this access pattern are single-user data collection monitors or systems, simulators, machine or process controllers such as machine tool controllers, and single user computer aided design tools and consoles.

Single-User persistence is remarkably easy to use, and its suitability for an object database is very high —it is these access patterns which make 'seamlessness' a reality, because reliable persistence is often simply a matter of mixing in the object database persistence mechanism (however this needs to be done).

2.3.2   Concurrent Readers

The second category of persistence use involves many concurrent readers and a small number of distinct update processes (Figure 3 (b)). Since most object database locking systems support concurrent readers, this access pattern is contention free and efficient for readers. As a result, this pattern imposes no significant implications for the design of the schema.

Most applications have a need for concurrent readers. Two commonly occurring instances of this schema access pattern are:

- asynchronous utility processes: off-line processes, such as asynchronous application or database report generators;
- periods of application read-only application behaviour: during some parts of the application's execution, read-only access may be adequate database visibility—applications which move from read-only to update database modes during normal use explicitly change database open modes to exploit this form (this is expanded upon later).

Another common instance of this access pattern is an object cache which provides fast access to read-only data structures to off-load read transactions from a host database. This access pattern is used in web applications—airline timetables and route information is an example of heavily *read* information which changes infrequently.

2.3.3   Non-contending Writers

A third persistent object access pattern arises when multiple users access the same persistent objects without contention (Figure 3 (c)). Object databases provide physical segmentation to allow schema designers to distribute persistent objects across different physical database and paging to facilitate this.

An example of this schema access pattern is a data collection application which is comprised of processes which collect data from devices and write or update different database segments for subsequent batch analysis or reporting. As long as the writers can be kept separate, this access pattern presents no problems for schema design.

2.3.4   Contending Writers

The final persistent object access pattern arises when multiple users access the same persistent objects *with* contention (Figure 3 (d)). Although this access pattern appears to depict the classic concurrent database update problem underlying the majority of business and transaction applications, with careful schema design it can end up only representing a small region of an application's schema access.

3.   Mechanisms for Schema Evolution

The remainder of this paper is about how a persistent architecture is arrived at in an object database project during iterative development. It is suggested that without active management, schema design occurs as a reactive, somewhat haphazard series of transitions between the persistence access patterns generalised in the previous section. With conscious management, we can hope to structure the transitions by making them decisively, although this is not always possible or reasonable given the large number of influencing factors. To balance our observation that schemas are designed in a highly iterative fashion, we formed the opinion that:

...schema development is a process of moving from one access pattern to another,

where the typical first cut at a schema favours simplicity over complexity, and the transitions from simple to more complex schema access patterns are made only when the current access pattern breaks down in performance or concurrency. This approach helped us to view our schema development as more of a managed process than a haphazard Big Ball of Mud (Foote 97).

3.1 Transitions between Access Patterns

The most likely transitions between access patterns in response to contention are illustrated in Figure 4, which names some of the design techniques described in the following sections used to solve the accompanying problems.

Access patterns in a region of a persistent architecture change when concurrency reduces to the point of being unacceptable. This may manifest itself as long delays while processes accessing the same persistent objects serialise on database locks, or when two processes deadlock; this happens when a process acquires a lock on one persistent object's page and then (in the same transaction) attempts to acquire a lock on another persistent object

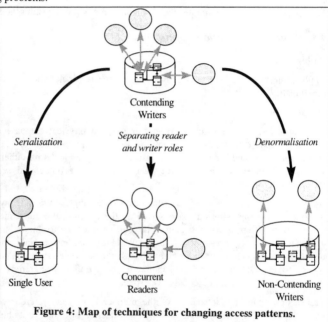

Figure 4: Map of techniques for changing access patterns.

which already locked by a second process which is attempting to lock the first processes' page. Databases detect deadlock and either fail one or both of the locking processes' transactions. Failed transactions can optionally be subsequently retried. In both cases, the use of Contending Writers may be judged as no longer appropriate.

Three possible transitions are illustrated. The left-most transition describes a set of design mechanisms which replaces update contention in a region of the software architecture with single user access, by serialising on business object locks or application semaphores. The middle transition turns contending writers into concurrent readers using design mechanisms which minimise update transactions and by reducing the time that the database is open for update. The third transition replaces contending writers with non-contending writers by physical schema design or de-normalisation of object relationships to separate update access. Some combinations of these techniques are possible for further reduction in contention and improvement in performance, such as the combination of shortened transactions and the physical separation of collections of business objects.

3.2 Mechanisms, Patterns and Pattern Instances

The solution mechanisms which follow are presented in simplified design pattern form, with 'problem' and 'solution' sections (Alexander 1977). Although they resemble a nascent design pattern language for persistent architectures, this is not the main emphasis of this paper—such a pattern language would need to draw on more expansive experience with a balanced mix of persistent architectures, products and domains. While some of the solutions appear to be excellent candidates for patterns, others look more like instances or applications of existing design patterns (Gamma 94) in the context of a persistent architecture, and some may simply be coding mechanisms. In the context of this paper, these distinctions are unimportant; it is enough to recognise each solution mechanism as a fragment of persistent architecture design. The solutions are presented in groups relating to the transitions between access patterns (Figure 4).

4. Serialisation

The following solution techniques address concurrency problems in schema design.

4.1 Small Transaction Spans

Problem

Application processes unnecessarily serialise or deadlock when executing basic application functionality.

Our Solution

Transaction 'span' refers to the spread around the physical database of the set of persistent objects referenced in a single transaction. Referencing an object typically refreshes its page in cache from disk, and for an update transaction, imposes locks on either the object, or its page. The schema developer has control over allocation of objects to segments, which directly influences the segment to page mapping.

An update transaction in a process which references objects across many pages effectively locks out other processes—the database serialises the second, and subsequent transactions. If the chosen transaction semantics cause the calling process to block, the user experiences an application freeze for no apparent reason. Wide transaction spans also increase the probability of deadlock, which can occur when two processes lock a page, then contend for an object on each other's pages. Optimistic locking schemes encourage this by upgrading transaction read locks to write locks only when an object changes state.

Transaction span is independent of the number of objects referenced in a transaction. For example, a transaction which iterates over a collection of a thousand objects on a single database page has a smaller span than a transaction which de-references pointers in single instances which are spread across ten pages.

The solution lies in finding the appropriate distribution of persistent objects around the database's physical segmentation model. The database products provide information about how to use segmentation, but the appropriate allocation must be determined for each application based on its transaction model. This can be done by superimposing segment boundaries over the persistent class model (the schema), and then drawing each (named) transaction over the resultant diagram. It then becomes possible to see the segment span of each named transaction, and by knowing which groups of transactions are likely to run concurrently, where they may contend. Careful segment design effort can then be focused on these areas of the schema.

4.2   Fast Transactions

Problem

Application processes unnecessarily serialise when executing basic application functionality.

Our Solution

Transactions in all database systems must be fast—in temporal terms. In object databases, the existence of the application code in the database makes it easy to inadvertently extend transaction times when adding extra application code.

We chose to make transactions fast by keeping all processing which did not require persistent object interactions outside transactions. Fast transactions reduce the probability of serialisation, and when it does occur, reduce the time blocked processes will wait. The most obvious example is to avoid adding code inside transactions which could be executed outside the transaction—any interactions with transient objects most likely fit this case. Some long transactions contain a code sequence which does not need to be in one transaction. Secondly, if a transaction's body is divisible, it should be separated into two or more fast transactions, using transient objects to preserve state over transaction boundaries. Clearly, the transaction must be divisible. Thirdly, some behaviour which runs out of a persistent object may legitimately run out of a transient copy outside a transaction (see Transient Clone).

4.3   Divisible Iterators

Problem

When persistent collections of persistent business objects get large, iterating over the collection creates a long update transaction.

Our Solution

Persistent collections of persistent business and design objects form a fundamental idiom in schema design, as does the corresponding use of a single iterator inside its own transaction in application code. We found that (previously fast) transactions for iterating over a business collection slowed, or caused unacceptable contention when the business collection grew (eg. a million objects) as a result of being loaded with real data (see 0 7.1   Real Data Early).   To address this problem, we noticed that some of these transactions could be interrupted. Using this property, we made the iterator persistent, so that the state of the iteration could be resumed over transactions, and broke up the complete iteration into repeating blocks of transactions, each of which iterated over a small number of collection objects.   This allowed other processes to interleave with the long transaction.

The creation and deletion of a persistent iterator should not be allowed to become expensive relative to the transaction length. An alternative to instantiation and destruction is to reset a permanent, common persistent iterator. Divisible Iterators may interleave with other transactions which perform deletions on business objects. Databases typically support deletion-safe iterators or cursors using a property of the iterator.

5.   Separating Readers from Writers

The following techniques address the design of read and update transactions on a persistent schema.

5.1 Readers or Writers

Problem

The process architecture of a multi-user application must be designed to support maximum concurrency.

Our Solution

Sometimes, a single application processes' requirement to apply read and write transactions to a region of a schema can be separated in time by taking a different view of how the application behaviour is allocated to processes. Most application's requirements include subsets which require read-only database access—if such a subset can be identified, they represent an opportunity to reduce contention.

We deliberately separated application read-only functionality and read-write functionality into different processes, and different regions of the same process. To implement this second case, we frequently switched between database open modes as the user process executed.

A variant of this solution is design a predominantly read-only region of an application's schema in separate physical database segments, or in an entirely separate database. This allows the predominant readers to have concurrent access, while the minority writers get access at a time convenient to the readers.

5.2 Transient Delegates

Problem

During a project, there will be periods when schema changes must be restricted. Once released, it may be impossible to change a schema without a significant schema migration effort. In this climate, changes to application behaviour implemented in persistent classes must be possible. While many simple changes to application code will not constitute a schema change, we frequently found that simple code changes became more involved upon investigation, and required the addition of attributes and changes to attribute types.

Our Solution

We used the rather obvious observation that transient objects are not subject to schema restrictions to work around the need for schema changes in some regions of the application architecture. Persistent business objects can delegate changeable or complex application behaviour into objects of a transient class—creating one or more Transient Delegates, which perform the required behaviour by collaborating with persistent objects. This allows areas of significant instability such as prototype algorithms, implementations of business rules, reporting logic, or process control logic to evolve independently of the released schema.

5.3 Transient Clones

Problem

In object database development, it is necessary to open a transaction to execute behaviour in a persistent object. This can lead to long transactions where a persistent object is de-referenced and its code executes independently of the schema for a period of time, before the transaction can be closed to commit the persistent object's final state. In highly concurrent regions of the schema, we found it necessary to eliminate or shorten these idle periods.

Our Solution

There are two examples of transactions made unnecessarily long by schema-independent processing—transactions involving interaction between the user interface and persistent objects, and transactions involving persistent objects and inter-process communication (using Unix sockets). In both cases, we created a Transient Clone, a class which contained behaviour to copy construct itself from its persistent source, the behaviour required to execute outside a transaction, and methods to perform the time-consuming business logic independent of the database.

Transient Cloning became a project idiom for shadowing persistent behaviour required to run outside of a transaction. The calling code which used transient clones typically used an initial transaction to instantiate the clone object, then executed application behaviour from the clone, and finally opened a short update transaction to allow the clone to copy changed attributes back to its persistent source object.

Transient Clones only need to copy those attributes needed to support the behaviour that will execute outside the transactions. The clone and persistent object pair must allow for interleavings (ie. another process running a concurrent Transient Clone), and the possibility of process termination or crashes between the transient copy and subsequent persistent update.

5.4 Transaction Proxy

Problem

Transient Clones provide methods to refresh the object's attributes from its persistent source during an initialisation transaction, and flush itself to its persistent source object inside an update transaction. The calling object's method code must manage transactions and Transient Clone states using these methods, even though in many cases, the caller does not need to know (and should not know) about the transience or persistence of the business object(s) being used.

Our Solution

We found that some areas of application code were manipulating a number of Transient Clones over common transaction boundaries. We also found a number of areas of the application which duplicated essentially similar transaction management code for using Transient Clones. Both forces were resolved by creating Transaction Proxy classes which encapsulated pointers (or references) to both transient and persistent objects, and which refreshed the transient clone on transaction boundaries. Some transaction proxies also managed the transactions themselves on behalf of the calling code. By using a Transaction Proxy, the calling code was not aware of the existence of a Transient Clone.

6. Denormalisation

6.1 Business Collections

Problem

Collections of business objects are a fundamental building block of schema design. Most schemas require a small number of (possibly large) collections of business objects, which can easily become a point of contention, particularly if new persistent object are being inserted and deleted in the collection during normal processing.

Our Solution

We decided to partition large collections of persistent objects on the basis of business or application-specific distinctions, such as the state of an object. In some cases, we defined Business Collections on the basis of use cases, and subsequently reorganised collections by patterns of user access. For example, our schema defined a large, changing collection of events, which cycled through a series of operational states. After this collection became a significant point of contention, we created independent collections for each event state (ie. a collection of all events in 'open' state, another for all events in 'closed' state, etc.). Business Collections contain pointers, so they can be added in parallel with a root collection.

Business Collections provided a simple way to distribute access paths to persistent business objects on demand. As contention increased around a specific persistent collection, it is straightforward to analyse the contenting processes' use of the existing collection, and farm off a subsets of accessors to use new Business Collections in separate database segments. Naturally, Business Collections must be kept consistent, which means adding insertion and deletion method calls around the instantiation and destruction of multiply indexed business objects.

Business collections can also used as an implementation mechanism for logical deletion. Many of our Business Collections had a second, identical collection added for deleted business objects. Logical deletion them simply becomes a matter of removing the business object from the 'active' collection and inserting it into the 'deleted' collection. The actual object destruction may be done at a later stage, when the database deletion overhead may be more palatable. Logical deletion has several advantages. Firstly, the fact that the objects are not destructed means any pointers or references to the object from other persistent objects in the database remain valid. Secondly, a 'deleted' Business Collection supports undelete.

6.2   Physical Locality of Collaborators

Problem

Object databases bring persistent objects in the scope of a transaction into memory (or cache) as they are referenced. Most databases bring objects from disk into memory in pages, in the same way that virtual memory managers and cache managers page between cache and disk. Cached pages are locked if they are written to during the transaction.

If two or more persistent objects which do not collaborate and are logically unrelated in the schema share a database segment, access to them may serialise due to page locking. This can mean that application processes serialise, even though the two processes are accessing apparently unrelated regions of the schema.

Our Solution

Persistent objects, like memory references in any cache, must be co-located in a working set. Object databases provide support for allocating persistent objects onto physical database structures, such as segments. While this sounds simple, it is not always straightforward to determine the optimal clustering strategy. To further confuse the picture, the coding techniques described in this paper change the schema access patterns, and other runtime parameters such as cache sizes and kernel tuning also impact, so static scenario or transaction analysis does not provide a prescriptive solution to the cluster optimisation problem.

We found that a static analysis of transactions needed to be balanced against timed, interactive load testing before the real performance of the segmentation model emerged. Fortunately, only the (three or four) most critical multi-processing business scenarios required this attention.

6.3   Stable Footprints and Lifecycles

Problem

Instantiation and deletion of persistent objects is expensive in most databases. Objects with very long persistent lifecycles (ie. classes which are infrequently instantiated and destructed) suit the persistence mechanisms of most object database products. Frequently changing the object's footprint in the database (the object's persistent size) can also be expensive.

Our Solution

Our experience suggested that objects should only be added to the schema when their footprint and lifecycle suited persistence. This meant avoiding persistent worker objects (such as controllers), buffers embedded in persistent objects, and frequent creation of persistent cursors and iterators (it is more efficient to reset iterators than instantiate/delete them). These lifecycle and size distinctions resulted in delegating some persistent object behaviour to Transient Delegates.

7. Development Process

Several schema evolution solutions were arrived at over time which use methodology and development process steps rather than software architecture as their solution medium. These are included here to illustrate some process issues.

7.1 Real Data Early

Problem

Performance blowouts and serious schema scalability problems must be detected early—ideally, when schema evolution is in its development peak.

Our Solution

In many projects, sourcing realistic, large scale data sets requires both personnel and software support from external systems which are outside the project's control. These dependencies make it easier to simulate rather than source test data. This can be dangerous—small, over-simplified test data sets in an object-oriented schema can mask performance and scaling problems which may invalidate aspects of the existing schema design.

Our experience suggests using real data early. Test data is 'real' if it contains a realistic number of instances of relationships, complexity, attribute sizes and collection sizes. If access to real data is not available, it is imperative to allocate project resources to identify schema scalability hot-spots (eg. large persistent collections, or deep object hierarchies) and drive them to realistic sizes with test suites. Experience with real data early can drive schema redesign at the appropriate phase of the project.

7.2 Transaction Walkthrough

Problem

Bad schema design and intrinsic database problems can creep into the project's schema and code base if the project's best knowledge of schema design practice is not effectively shared.

Our Solution

In an object database application, the binding of the business object model and the schema means that all application coders are schema developers—it is not possible to hide schema design complexities from application coders. For example, the detailed design and coding techniques which lead to small transaction spans and short transaction times represent project idioms which need to be developed, then communicated to all team members.

We recognised a need for 'transaction walkthroughs', in the spirit and style of code walkthroughs, which should become an integral element of the team's culture. All developers who write code which opens a database transaction of any kind must present their intended design in a walkthrough, involving (initially) the project's most experienced schema developer, so that the general design of the transactions and its overall sociability within the schema's existing transaction set can be checked. After a while, the reviewer's role can be rotated as the project idioms become engrained.

Transaction walkthroughs are not code walkthroughs, and vice-versa. In a code walkthrough, the focus should be on application code quality and correctness—trying to add a layer of schema design issues risks overloading the participants and compromising their primary objective. Also, the skill sets are not identical. Keeping the two separate reinforces the commitment to both application code and schema design quality.

8. Conclusions

As well as exploring a number of pragmatic object database schema design problems and solutions, two conclusions are claimed:

* on any reasonably sized persistent application, schema design will be highly evolutionary, and driven by a variety of diverse forces;
* we observed that persistence problems could be characterised by four basic access patterns, and we devised schema design and code solutions to effect transitions between these access patterns.

Subsequent projects going down a similar path must identify the areas of their persistent architectures which will suffer from contention, and devise their own schema design solutions (based on ours, if appropriate) early in the development.

9. Acknowledgements

Contributions to the design solutions outlined in this paper were made by a number of people, including Darren Allen, Paul Chapman, Joe Chioda, Alan McPharlane, and Nick Trevallyn-Jones. The environment was Objectstore v4.2 and later 5.0, on HP-UX 10.2.

10. References

Alexander, C. 1977. "A Pattern Language", Center for Environmental Structure, Berkeley, University of California. Oxford Press.

Bancilhon, F. 1992. "Building an Object-Oriented Database System: The Story of O_2", Morgan Kaufmann Publishers, San Mateo, California, 1992.

Foote, B. 1997. "Big Ball of Mud", Fourth Conference on Pattern Languages of Programs (PLoP '97), Monticello, Illinois, 1997.

Cattell, R. 1991. "Object Data Management", Addison-Wesley, Reading, Massachusetts, 1991.

Chorafas, D. 1993. "Object-Oriented Databases", Prentice Hall, Englewood Cliffs, New Jersey, 1993.

Kim, W. 1990. "Introduction to Object-Oriented Databases", MIT Press, Cambridge, Massachusetts, 1990.

Gamma, et.al. 1994. "Design Patterns–Elements of Reusable Object-oriented Software Architecture", Addison Wesley, 1994.

Object Design International. 1998. Object Design (Objectstore vendor), http://www.odi.com/.

Sengupta, S. 1991. "An Object-Oriented Model for Network Management", cited in Gupta, R. and Horowitz, E. (Ed). "Object-Oriented Databases with Applications to CASE, Networks and VLSI CAD", Prentice Hall Series in Data and Knowledge Based Systems, 1991.

From Interface to Persistence: A Framework for Business Oriented Applications

Lew Della   David Clark
School of Information Technology, Griffith University
l.della@gu.edu.au
Faculty of Information Sciences & Engineering, University of Canberra, ACT, 2601
davidc@ise.canberra.edu.au

Abstract

Since the coining of the term "Design Patterns" in the software engineering context, and specifically as related to object-oriented application, there has been an increasing emphasis placed on the relevance of patterns in successfully designing object-oriented software, by the recognition of patterns that can be applied for recurring problems. In this paper patterns are applied in a business-oriented environment, resulting in a framework that provides the core architecture suitable for use across a family of business applications. In designing this framework we take a "framework-centred design pattern" approach [Pree95, p63], with a number of patterns being applied as the application framework evolves. The language in which our framework is implemented is Java.

1 Introduction

A framework is a partially complete software system comprising abstract and concrete classes resulting in a generic reusable design which can be used to produce customised applications. The link between design patterns and frameworks is well established; "Frameworks can be viewed as concrete realisations of patterns that facilitate direct reuse of design and code" [Schmidt96, p39]. Current framework developments usually combine a number of design patterns, thereby helping in the design and reuse potential of the framework, as well as providing framework documentation. If they are developed with sufficient genericity, application frameworks can be applied across a family of related applications. In developing an application framework, we are actually providing a suitable "template" for customising by the user of the framework. This customising requires subclass derivation of the relevant abstract classes to create the specific application software. Thus at the core of framework design is a combination of abstract and derived concrete classes with the abstract classes defining the relationship that will exist between objects, while the derived classes implement the application specific implementation details. In this paper we develop a framework which can be used across a range of business oriented applications. As frameworks are *"semifinished software architectures"* [Pree95, p.vii] they are implemented in a particular language. We use Java as our language of implementation.

2 Business Requirements

In a business organisation, there are a number of functional requirements. These include marketing, production, personnel, inventory control. The developed model is the result of analysis of the requirements of the organisation. The various functions have specific data and processing requirements such as payroll, order entry, invoicing, entry and maintenance of customer details, entry and maintenance of the organisation's product lines. Traditionally, business applications have always been regarded as having heavy data handling or input-output (IO) requirements, with relatively simple algorithmic requirements. The requirements include a suitable front end user interface allowing ease of data input and display, and back end persistence storage.

The requirements of a typical business application can be summarised as the ability to:

- select a task and related sub-tasks
- select an object for activation
     from a list of objects
     via a key or identifier
- enter fields of related data on screen based form to
     create new data
     amend existing data
- display fields of related data
- save and retrieve data from persistent storage

2.1 The user interface

The IO requirements start with a suitable user interface, normally a graphical one (GUI) for ease of data entry, capture and display. This user interface is the main "connection" between the end user and the developed system. There is a requirement to present the user of the system with a suitable interface that allows selection from a number of tasks via matching macro (or top level) menu entries. Each of these top level options could provide a further breakdown of related subtasks for possible selection. The user of the system needs an easy to use interface to the system, with the options, choices and selections available being as intuitive as possible. This user interface is one crucial aspect of the developed system, since in a sense, to the user the interface *is* the system. A user interface to provide access to the sales, stock maintenance and accounting facilities for a sales organisation is shown below.

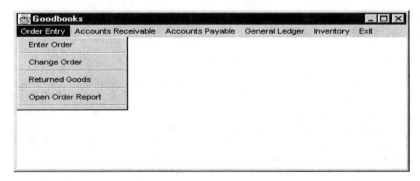

2.2 Persistence Requirements

As well as the "front end" user interface, business applications require a complementary "back end" to efficiently store persistent data, such as customer details, inventory information, order details. The state of the various attributes of these entities, at the end of any data processing, has to be stored by an efficient persistence storage engine, in an almost transparent manner, as far as the user is concerned. On subsequent processing, the details have to be retrieved quite readily.

3 A Business Oriented Framework

In this section we develop a framework suitable for a range of business oriented applications. A key consideration in developing the framework is the separation of responsibilities between components of a system. Coad and Yourdan [Coad+91, p26] identify four major components of an application. These include the human interaction component (HIC), the problem domain component (PDC) and the data management component (DMC).[1] Figure 1 shows the component structure.

Class design specifications	Human Interaction Component (HIC)	Problem Domain Component (PDC)	Data Management Component (DMC)

Figure 1. Coad & Yourdan's component

In designing software that reflects the above structure, the components have to be designed in such a way that allow them to be quite distinct, with the dual design goals of providing the particular functionality required and being reuseable in other applications. Thus, considering the human interface component, this has to be handled in a manner that provides the interface with a certain amount of independence from the actual problem domain, while at the same time being adaptable to the specific user interaction requirements. This separation of responsibilities simplifies the design of both the interface and the business domain application, and increases the reuse capabilities of both components.

3.1 Model / View / Controller Framework

The requirements of software which implements a human - computer interface can be satisfied by the use of the Model-View-Controller pattern, which can be depicted as shown in figure 2 below. This pattern was used in developing one of the earliest frameworks, the model-view-controller (MVC) approach used in the graphical user interface design of the Smalltalk-80 system.

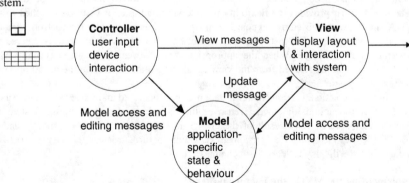

Figure 2. Model-View-Controller representation [Pree, 1995]

---

[1] The fourth, task management, applies mainly to real time systems and is not used in this framework.

The three main components of model (problem domain - Coad and Yourdon's PDC), view (the screen interface - Coad and Yourdon's HIC), controller (component that reacts to user input events) are associated in a way that provides a deal of decoupling between the components. The normal mode of operation with current graphical user interface applications is event-driven, allowing action selection via appropriate component selection. This is where the controller plays its part. When a component (menu item, button, icon) is selected by keyboard or mouse action, the appropriate event is triggered with the result that the controller sends a message, usually to the model. Since these controller components are such an integral part of the displayed view (the view and controller make up the user interface), we use the Model-View representation to include the Model-ControllerView structure. As one author puts it "nowadays the original MVC model triad often coalesces into an MV dyad" [Coplien+95, p59]. Thus a more realistic class diagram representation, combining the view and controller responsibilities, would be as shown in figure 3, with added flexibility provided by the the concrete model and view-controller classes being derived from base abstract classes. In this figure, we use an order entry application as the derived subclasses example

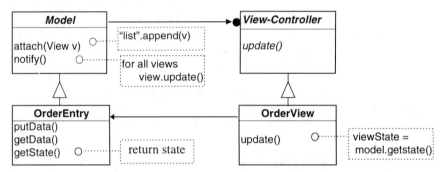

Figure 3. Modified Model/View/Controller class

There is a requirement for the view (or views) to be associated with the model. Thus after the model and view are instantiated, the view has to be attached to the model. The view is passed in as a parameter to the model; the model records the view passed to it, typically by appending to a list (The use of a list provides the flexibility for allowing multiple views to be attached to the model). An input event, caused by keyboard or mouse action, is handled by the controller via the appropriate action method. For instance, when capturing new data, the data has to be entered via the presented view interface. When the appropriate "save" event is triggered (usually by a button click), the data are relayed from the view to the model, and then from the model on to the data storage subsystem.

Actually, this a bidirectional arrangement. If data has to be accessed and retrieved, again usually triggered by button action, the model retrieves the data from the data storage system for presentation to the view. As a result of the change in state to the model, the model sends a message to the view/s via its `notify` method, which in turn, triggers the view's `update` method, so that the display reflects these changes..

3.2 Implementing the MVC - the Factory pattern

To create the class structure just described, it is natural to use one of the "creational" patterns, such as the Factory Method pattern [Gamma+95, p107]. We need to create model and view classes and provide the relevant association between them. The class details will vary depending on the particular application (order entry, order maintenance, back order) and it is left to the individual application to implement them. We can use the Factory Method pattern to "Define an interface for creating an object, but let the subclasses decide which class to instantiate" [Gamma+95, p107]. Thus, the overall structure would have an abstract application class from which the concrete application is derived, and abstract MVC classes (the model and view classes) from which the actual models and views are derived (figure 4).

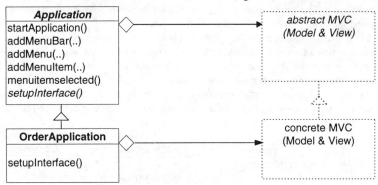

Figure 4. Application MVC creation

However the interaction of suitable patterns for this framework goes further. Within the abstract application class we define the simple algorithm necessary to set up the model - view matched pairs and start the application. This algorithm invokes the method *setupInterface* which is implemented in the derived application class. This is a natural use of the of the Template Method pattern whose purpose is to "define the skeleton of an algorithm in an operation, deferring some steps to subclasses. Template Method let subclasses redefine certain steps of an algorithm without changing the algorithm's structure" [Gamma+95, p325]. Gamma further observes that "Factory Methods are often called by template methods" [Gamma+95, p330]. This is quite understandable since the template method uses inheritance to customise part of an algorithm, and this customising often involves the subclass deciding which specific class to instantiate.

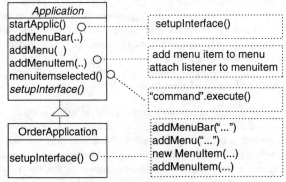

Figure 5. Factory Method handling of the application classes

3.3 Beyond the MVC - the Command pattern

One of the requirements of a business oriented application is the ability to provide the user with a selection from a number of tasks or sub-tasks. This needs to be implemented in a way which preserves loose coupling between the model and controller-view components. This can be achieved by using the Command pattern. Users are typically given choices of tasks and sub-tasks by menus. The application "creates these menus and menu items along with the rest of the user interface... The application configures each MenuItem with an instance of a concrete Command subclass" [Gamma+95, p233-234].

With the Command pattern the key aspect relates to the Command subclasses in that each subclass contains an `execute` operation. Each command subclass would be associated with a menu item so that the selection of a menu item would trigger the `execute` method of that command. The `execute` operation could contain a range of directives from a simple single operation to a full sequence of operations. As an example of a command subclass with an `execute` method consisting of a single operation, consider an exit command (figure 6).

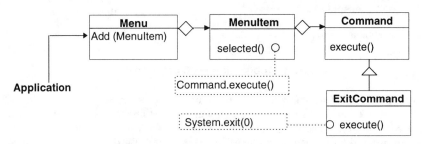

Figure 6. Exit Command subclassing

There are a number of ways in which we can implement the Command pattern in Java. We could, for example, have an array of MenuItems and a matching Command array, with each menu item's index value matching the index of the command with which it is associated. Then when the menu item is selected its associated command is invoked; that is the command's `execute` method is called. A more elegant way of implementing the Command pattern in Java is to create a subclass from MenuItem that implements a defined Command interface [Cooper98, p65]. The MenuItem subclass provides a relatively simple and convenient mechanism for association of a command with a menu item. Then the command's `execute` method is called when the menu item is selected.

3.4 Use of command pattern for model-view instantiation

When we consider the use of command subclassing to handle the model-view class instantiation which would often be a core necessity for a business oriented application, the requirements for the `execute` method become a little more demanding. What is required in this situation is an `execute` operation that handles the instantiation of the model object and the view object/s, and establishes the required association between the model and view/s as discussed previously. If we consider the order entry example again, the command subclassing will be as shown below.

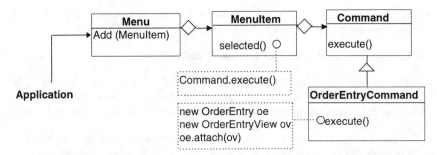

Figure 7. Order Entry Command subclassing

The MVC pattern and the Command pattern as implemented by the particular application form a vital cooperating structure creating a core component in the business application framework being developed. For this structure to be successfully developed it is necessary for the application to seamlessly combine the two patterns. The Command pattern menu item when initiating a particular subtask has to incorporate the Model-View separation of responsibilities. Using the structure depicted above, the merging of the Command pattern with the Model-View pattern will be as shown below in figure 8.

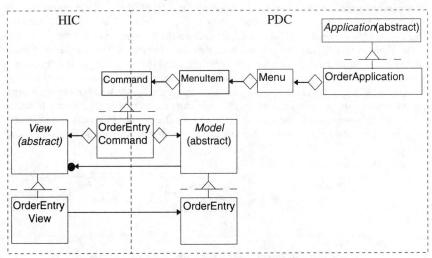

Figure 8. Combining Model-View and Command

One of the essential characteristics of the MVC framework, and patterns that evolved from MVC, and the other patterns just described, is the decoupling of the cooperating subsystems. This is an essential ingredient in enhancing the reuse capabilities of the individual classes, since tight coupling results in excess inbuilt interdependence between the coupled classes, which reduces their potential as standalone reuse classes and impairs the extensibility of the application. This decoupling or "separation of concerns" [Buschmann+96, p400] allows easier reuse of the developed components for the very reason that they do have this independence of action, and collaborate with other components via simple message passing requests.

3.5 Persistence management interface - the Facade pattern

In considering the persistence storage requirements of the framework, we apply the same separation of responsibilities, in that the data management component is loosely coupled to the problem domain component, again providing the structure which will allow reuse of the data management component in other related applications.

The requirements of business applications include the ability to access data via a key. This is beyond the basic capabilities provided by Java, per se. Java provides selectively comprehensive stream handling facilities, including sequential file input and output, simple random file access, as well as object serialization. The Java developers have also provided a library that allows Java Database Connectivity (JDBC). However, it does not provide for easy indexed access to file data via specified key values. This, of course, is a prime requirement for business data processing where there is a requirement to access data such as customer information or parts details via designated key values.

In our framework development, use is made of a the persistence storage engine (PSE) of Objectstore. This provides the ability to conveniently store data in a number of formats, and allows ready access via specified keys. The persistence storage (PS) backend consists of basic, low-level persistence managing classes, incorporating logic to handle database access and the basic read and write actions, for the various data types. For ease of access to the facilities provided by the persistence storage subsystem, it is advantageous to provide an interface to help reduce the complexity involved in low-level access to this subsystem. This acts as a Facade pattern, which is implemented to "provide a unified interface to a set of interfaces in a subsystem. Facade defines higher-level interface that makes the subsystem easier to use" [Gamma+95, p185]. The Interface (Facade) class serves as the bridge between the application domain (Model) and the persistence storage (PS), providing the capability for convenient access to the PS data, shown in simple form in figure 9. The construction of this class is such that it can serve as a generic storage interface for any class requiring persistence storage and access capabilities.

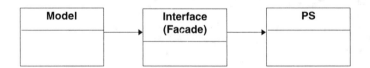

Figure 9. Persistence management structure

Expanding on the role provided by the Facade, there are a number of low-level operations at the PS level for which the Facade provides more convenient higher level commands. Thus from the Model perspective, it is shielded from having to issue commands to handle specific database operations, such as database creating and opening as well as transaction creation, which is handled by the Facade interface and its derived classes (figure10). This allows the user of the framework to operate at a higher level and also provides the potential to replace the persistence mechanism with another in the future. In figure 10 we show the persistence storage interface in the context of one of the derived applications, the order entry application.

Again the Template pattern is used in that the abstract class Facade contains the simple algorithm to handle database creation and opening. The steps of the algorithm are implemented in the concrete Facade class, InvFacade.

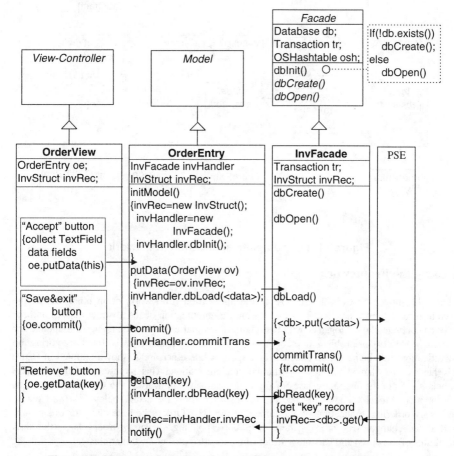

Figure10. IOFacade interface for persistence management

3.6 Merging the View-Model and the Model-Storage components

The above presentation has concentrated on framework design for business oriented applications. The core requirement is that the cooperating classes, toolkits, patterns work together to achieve the goals specified, as embodied in the described requirements. As can be seen in the class structures of figures 9, 10 and 11 the common thread linking these two sub-frameworks together is the concrete "Model". This is not surprising, since the model is the core entity around which other components are developed to achieve the required results. That being the case, with careful attention to detail in the design stage, it is a relatively simple matter to combine the above two sub-frameworks to achieve the complete business oriented framework. This merging is depicted in figure 11.

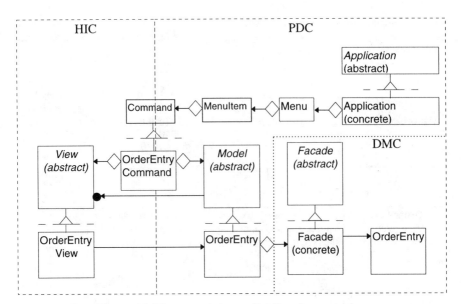

Figure 11. The complete application framework

4 Using the Framework

Figure 11 shows the overall structure of the application framework, or in other words, the architecture of the framework. This architecture, a combination of the abstract classes and the derived concrete classes together with the relationships that exist between them, is adaptable for use in a variety of problem domain areas. Part of the framework is fixed, requiring no modification, this being the so called frozen spots, while other areas, shown stippled in figure 11, have to be shaped to fit the particular implementation. This requires deriving concrete subclasses from the abstract classes of figure 11, namely Application, the Command subclass, one or more Model / View pairs and the Facade. We show the details below for (part of) an inventory ordering application. We assume that the class Order (the base class for order entry and order change) has been written, with corresponding InventoryStruct class (the data attributes of the class) and CustomerStruct (the data attributes of customer class).

4.1 Command subclassing

With regards the command subclasses. the order entry command (OrderEnt) would implement the interface provided by the abstract command interface. Each command subclass would be derived in this fashion

```
public abstract interface Command
    {abstract public void execute();
    }

class OrderEnt implements Command
    {public void execute()
        {OrderEntry oe = new OrderEntry();
```

```
OrderView ov = new OrderView(oe, "Order Entry");
oe.attach(ov);
oe.initModel();
ov.initView();
ov.setSize(500,340);
ov.show();
}
}
```

We extend Java's MenuItem class to allow passing in both the menu item title and the command to associate with this menu item, thereby creating a structure that when called provides this association .

```
class CommandMenuItem extends MenuItem implements Command
    {Command comd;
     public CommandMenuItem(String title, Command cmd)
        {super(title);
         comd = cmd;
        }
     public void execute()
        {comd.execute();
        }
    }
```

4.2 Customising the application

The individual requirement for our concrete application (order entry class) is the associating of the each required command with a matching menu item. This is handled by calling CommandMenuItem for each association required. Below we show the creation of an Exit command and the order entry command.

```
cmi = new CommandMenuItem("Enter Order", new OrderEnt());
addMenuItem(cmi);
cmi = new CommandMenuItem("Exit", new ExitCommand());
addMenuItem(cmi);
```

4.3 Concrete model

We abstract as many of the responsibilities as possible to the abstract model class, while the OrderEntry class handles the tasks specifically related to it. One of the responsibilities that the abstract model class handles is the attaching (appending) of each view, associated with the model, to a list. Thus, whenever the model changes state, each view can be accessed in turn, to be notified of this state change, and directed to update itself to the model's new state.

```
void attach(View vin)
    {Link ll=new Link(vin,null);
     ll.append(ll);
    }
void notify()
    {Enumeration e = ll.elements();
     View vl;
     while(e.hasMoreElements())
        {vl = (View)e.nextToken();
```

```
        v1.update(this);
     }
  }
```

The methods in the OrderEntry class which must be made concrete are initModel, putData, commit and getData. The initModel method creates an instance of the data structure to be used, in this case InventoryStruct, and an instance of the Inventory Facade and then invokes the database initialisation.

```
class OrderEntry extends Model
  { InventoryStruct invRec;
    InventoryFacade invHandler;
    • • •
    void initModel()
      { invRec = new InventoryStruct();
        invHandler = new InventoryFacade (" <dbname>" );
        invHandler.dbInit();
    }
```

Methods putData and getData simply provide commands to control the IO traffic to/from the persistence storage, while commit sends a message to the DMC to commit the transaction.

```
    void putData (View viewIn)
      { invRec = viewIn.invRec;
        invHandler.dbLoad(invRec);
    }
```

For any alteration to the state of the Order Entry model, such as when data is retrieved from persistence storage, the notify method is called, which as shown above, accesses each view in turn (in our case, there is just the one view), firing up the view's update method, which updates the view's state to that of the model.

```
  void getData(String key)
        {InvHandler.readdb(key);
         invRec = InvHandler.invRec;
         notify();
        }
```

4.4. Concrete view

The view class(es) will contain user interface components such as input boxes, pick lists, buttons, to support the particular user interaction required. Java's Abstract Windowing Toolkit (AWT) supplies classes to implement these components. The method *setupInterface* has to be made concrete.

```
class OrderView extends View
    {OrderEntry ordEnt;
     <declare various textfields and buttons>
     OrderView (Model modelIn, String s)
       { setTitle(s);
         ord = modelIn;  // ord declared in View - type Model
    }
```

Method setupInterface uses the declared components to create the data entry / data display interface for the particular implementation.

4.5 Concrete IOFacade

This class will have to make the methods dbCreate, dbOpen, dbLoad, and dbRead concrete. DbCreate creates a new database, dbOpen opens an existing database, dbLoad loads the database tables prior to committing the transaction, while dbRead reads the database row using the supplied key (dbCreate and dbOpen are selected, as appropriate, from the Template Pattern method, dbInit (figure 10), in the abstract IOFacade superclass).

```
void dbCreate()
  { db = Database.create (<filename>, Objectstore.ALL_READ |
                                       ObjectStore.ALL_WRITE);
    tr = transaction.begin (ObjectStore.UPDATE);
    db.createRoot( <rootname>);

  }
```

5 Conclusion

In this paper we have developed a framework, a semi-finished software system suitable for reuse, for business oriented applications. In developing this framework we have relied heavily on the use of design patterns as the building blocks for the framework architecture combining a number of patterns, thereby helping in the design and reuse potential of the framework, as well as providing framework documentation. The result is a software system suitable for reuse in a problem domain, in this case a business oriented domain, with the generic hot spots allowing ready adaptation of the framework to the application under development.

References

[Buschmann+96]   Buschmann, F., Meunier, R., Rohnert, H., Sommerlad, P., Stal, M., (1996) Pattern-Oriented Software Architecture - A System of Patterns John Wiley & Sons

[Coad+91]   Coad, P. and Yourdon, E., (1991) Object-Oriented Design, Prentice-Hall

[Cooper98]   Cooper, J.W., (1998) Using Design Patterns, Commun. ACM,41(6)

[Coplien+95]   Coplien, J.O. and Schmidt, D.C.(ed), (1995) Pattern :Languages of Program Design, Addison-Wesley

[Gamma+95]   Gamma, E., Helm, R., Johnson, R., Vlissides, J.,(1995) Design Patterns: Elements of Reusable Object Software, Addison-Wesley

[Pree95]   Pree, W.,(1995) Design patterns for Object-Oriented Software Development, Addison-Wesley

[Schmidt96]   Schmidt, D.C., Fayad, M., Johnson, R.E.(1996) Introduction to Software Patterns, Commun. ACM, 39(10)

Development of PDM Framework and Customization Environment

Jeong Ah Kim
Computer Education Department, Kwandong University
521 NaeKok–Dong, KangNung–City
KangWon–Do, 210–701, KOREA
Tel: +82–391–649–8091, Fax: +82–391–647–3152
E–mail:clara@kdccs.kwandong.ac.kr

Jin Hong Kim
SDS Software Research Institute, #1101 Samsung MultiCampus
718–5, YeokSam–Dong, KangNam–Ku, SEOUL, KOREA
Tel : +82–2–3429–5653, Fax : +82–2–3429–5997
E–mail :gopdm@samsung.co.kr

Namkyu Park
Advanced Manufacturing System Division, Korea Institute of Industrial Technology
35–3 Hong–Chon, Ib–Jang, Chon–An 330–820, KOREA
Tel : +82–417–560–8464, Fax : +82–417–560–8260
E–mail :namkyu@kitech.re.kr

Abstract

Framework is a template for working program since framework consists of related classes and wired–in interactions among those classes. Reuse by framework is a promising way for improving the productivity and reducing the learning curve of new domain. So far, many efforts for developing the frameworks have been begun and a few real frameworks like CIM framework and domain frameworks were announced. We have a project for developing a framework in PDM (Product Data Management) domain. PDM can be applied to several application domains, but there are some little differences in each application. Developing the framework is not easy. In this paper we want to talk about the current states and results of our project: 1) the phases of developing our framework, 2) applying design pattern, 3) supporting environments for customizing the framework, 4) the problems in developing a framework

Keywords:

Object-Oriented, Framework, Reuse,
Design Pattern, Hot Spot, Generalization,
Customizing

1. Introduction

Reusing the existing software may be a way of solving the current problems in software development. In order to reuse something, previous experiences and assets should be stored in the library. Software library is the collection of related components: functions in procedural programming and classes in object–oriented paradigm. Even the characteristics of components are little different, the way to reuse the library has been same. Identification of proper components from the library is the first step to reuse. And then, application developers put the identified components together into one program. As we know, it is not an easy job, especially for non–experts inthat domain. They should understand the components in the library and their application requirements and should write the codes for integrating the components.

Framework can change the way of reusing. Since framework already knows the architecture of a domain and defines the default behaviors in that domain, developers can easily understand what are necessary for developing new application. The reuse of the framework is different from the reuse of the library. It is not necessary to write control programs in which we define the control flow to integrate the components since framework already has them. But we can redefine the default behaviors of framework by subclassing mechanism. It is easier and more effective way for reuse [1,2,4].

0-7695-0053-6/98 $10.00 © 1998 IEEE

We have already used several frameworks such as MFC, ET++, other GUI framework. These are horizontal frameworks that we can use in the most application domains. But the requirements for the vertical frameworks have been increased. In Korea, we have several framework projects sponsored by gonvernment. Our project is the part of R&D proejcts, constructing the PDM framework. PDM domain is very large and complex so it is not easy to understand the PDM application. If you had PDM framework, then it could help the developers to understand the domain and deploy it into new application by customizing the framework [6]. Of course, we already had good commercial PDM framework such as Metaphase, WorkManager, Matrix so on. Since these are frameworks so that developers can customize them for their new requirements with well-defined customizing API (Application Programming Interface). But the problems to our small company were that those are too expensive and large system. Also learning and understanding them required so long time. There are the reason why we developed our small PDM framework and their customizing-supporting environment.

In this paper, we want to discuss our experiences and current states-of-art of our framework. It consists (1) the characteristics of our PDM framework in terms of framework (2) our process model to develop the PDM framework (3) the state-of-art of our design (4) current implementation of supporting environment (5) the problems and issues in development of framework

2. The Characteristics of Our Framework

2.1 The characteristics of our framework

Framework is a template for working program so framework defines the wired-in interactions among the classes. As well as related classes. Reusing the framework means the customizing the framework by subclassing the existing classes. In other words, framework has hot spot as well as frozen spot. The frozen spots are abstract classes and template methods, which provides the default behaviors of framework. Even framework is a template for working program, framework might not satisfy the whole requirements of real application. So, we should extend or refine the framework. The hot spots are the place where we should extend or refine for fitting with new requirements [5,9]. Framework can be classified as a black-box framework and a white-box framework [4,5]. Black-box framework

means that programmers don't need to write any code for customizing the framework since framework already provide the candidate components for hot spots. In the case, the way of reusing the framework could be the composition of these candidates. Reusing the white-box framework requires the programmers to write the codes for extending or refining the framework to refine the hot spots. Something specific to new application is up to application developer. Inheritance is a way to refine the framework and to define the hot spots.

Our PDM framework has the characteristics of white-box framework. In other words, we defined abstract classes as the template classes of our framework and hot spots that would be defined later when the real applications would be generated based on our framework.

2.2 The scope of our PDM framework

The challenges are to maximize the time-to-market benefits of concurrent engineering while maintaining the controls of data and distributing it automatically to the people who need it – when they need it. This is the reason why PDM is getting important. PDM can store the essential data in a secure 'vault' where its integrity can be assured and all changes to it monitored, controlled and recorded. These days, many manufacturing companies are interested in constructing their PDM system. Of course, in Korea, many companies reconzige the improtances of PDM for their productivity and maintainability. Many huge company such as Samsung or LG has constructed their PDM with Metaphase or WorkManager that are well-defined PDM frameworks [6]. But small-sized and medium-sizedcompanies have no enough budgets to buy those framework and no people to develop their PDM system.

In 1997, Korean government initiated new project, which developed PDM system for the small companies. We are involved in this project. At the beginning of this project, we focused on developing a PDM system for small company. After one year, we found every company has quite a few differences in data management and process management. For fitting with their working environments, we need customization, which might be more difficult if our system were not well designed or well structured software. Therefore, we decided to develop a PDM framework as flexible and extendible PDM system.

Good framework design requires the good scope definition [8]. As we know, PDM system is very large and complex domain. In our view of PDM, PDM system

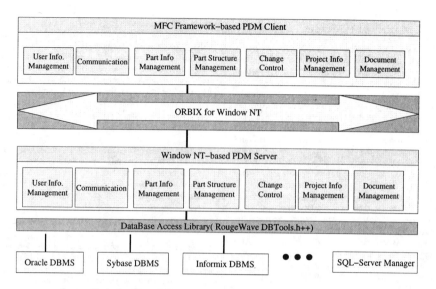

<Fig 1> Our Target Environment of PDM System

consists of 6 subsystems: user management, document management, BOM, project management, change control management, product structure management. In the first year of our project, development of the prototype for our framework was the goal. Our framework will have broad but thin scope, which can be broader and deeper when we will develop the actual framework. Fig 1. shows the configuration for our PDM systems. Our framework is based on Window NT system since our medium or small-sized companies were preffered Window NT solutions. We seperated stricktly client component from server component. We used orbix as middleware so that our server components are based on CORBA component model and out client components are based on MFC. We also used RougeWave library for database interoperability. Actually, we developed our framework based on Oracle database but can easliy be replaced with other databases.

3. Our Efforts for Developing the PDM Framework

In this section, our process model for developing the framework and results are described.

3.1 Domain analysis

Understanding the domain and the identifying the

common objects are the purposes of the domain analysis. When we started this project, we didn't have enough knowledge about the PDM domain so we analyzed several PDM applications and PDM general references to try to construct our PDM domain model. Our PDM domain model focuses on key abstractions of PDM and shows the logical view of the PDM systems.

When we started our project, there were two reference sites where PDM system already constructued but their functionalities were limited so that they tried to extend the existing thier PDM system. We analyzed these companies with their existing applications and their new requirements. For gethering more general requirements we referenced the PDM's buyer's guide. The PDM buyer's guide and several international standard documents were good sources for analyzing the PDM domain. PDM Buyer's guides classified the basic functionality of PDM like followings.

User Function	Utility Function
Data Vault & Document Management	Communication & Notification
Workflow & Process Management	Data Transport
Product Structure Management	Data Translation
Classification & Retrieval	Image Service
Program Management	Administration

<Table 1> Classification of the functionalities of PDM

During this step, we constructed the use case diagrams as the domain model for formulating the scope of the domain. For understanding the domain, we prepared the

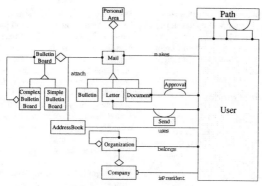

<Fig 2> the part of integrated object model

problem descriptions with use scenarios, which are narrative description for explaining one use case. Use case models are the result of domain analysis.

3.2 Requirement analysis

Based on identified use cases, we tried to find all requirements on the system during the requirement analysis. Since our purposes was the development of a framework, we analyzed two applications being used by different companies. Through these, we found a little differences and many commonalities between two applications. For validating our framework, we also analyzed existing PDM standard specification.

Our requirement model was constructed by applying the typical requirement analysis process. We defined the system boundary with use case diagram and wrote functional requirements captured from user interview and analyzing the current system. Also, we constructed logical object model in a view of PDM domain. It didn't include system−dependent objects like database or network or user interface objects. Since PDM systems were so large, we decomposed our system into 7 packages which are user management, communication, document management, BOM (Bill−Of−Material), project management, change control management, product structure management. These subsystems were decomposed based on categorized use cases. We classified related use cases into one category, which are tightly coupled. For each package, object model was constructed. Then we integrated these object models into one, showing our integrated concepts of PDM. As I explained ealier, we had two requirements. Each system analysist was assigned to each company to capture the basic functionalies of PDM system. As the result, two different integrated object models were constructed. Fig 2 shows the example that integrated user management and communication−related subsystems.

For each object model of one requirement, we also prepared the term glossary for each object, attribute, operation, and other technical terms. Our requirement model consisted of object model that captured the logical view of PDM application, OCD (Object collaboration Diagram) that shows the system behaviors and STD (State Transition Diagram) that shows the behavioral characteristics of object. We used ObjectTeam as CASE tools. which is developed by Cayenne. And we followed OMT(Object Modeling Techniques) for object modeling[10]. ObjectTeam produced CAD(Class Associated Diagram) for object model, MFD(Message Flow Diagram) and CCD (Class Collaboration Diagram), so on.

3.3 Generalization of requirement model

To develop a framework, we should know what are the common requirements in PDM domain and what are the specific requirements in a certain PDM application. We analyzed two applications and one standard. After then, we separated requirements into framework requirements and application requirements. In our concerns, framework requirements means what are the common among the several application so these might be the template classes for framework. Application requirements are the specific ones to a cetain application. These seperations of requirements were done by generalization concept. We tried to find the common domain object among the different object models.

Through this phase, we could find what parts are common, which will be template classes in PDM framework. These template classes define the domain structure and default behaviors. Also we identified what parts were different in each application, which would be the hook classes. These hook classes will be redefined or customized later when real application will be developed with this framework. This step resulted in constructing an integrated object model by generalizing three different object models that were represented two different applications and one PDM standard.

3.4 Abstracting the object model

After constructing the requirement model, we tried to identify the key abstractions of PDM domain. Of course, we found the general concepts, classes in PDM domain from requirement analysis and generalization phases. But, constructed model didn't seem enough for framework. If the framework counld be refined or extended, it couldn't be said good framework. The more extendible and general framework model was required. It was the reason why we needed abstraction process. From this phase, we considered design issues. So, in this step, we added more detail information to requirement model including system–dependent objects or algorithms, which were related to design issues.

Our strategy for finding abstraction is that abstraction will be helpful for the customizing or extending the framework. Abstraction can make our framework model to be more extendible. To abstract our model, there were several factors to be considered. Since our PDM system was based CORBA–based environment, client and server should be separately extendible. Until now, since we used RDBMS not OODBMS, our framework should not depend on database for later extension. These are the same with other software engineering issues for extendibility or reusability.

We captured the PDM abstraction based on the hot spots and MVC concepts. MVC model was applied to design the interaction among domain classes, user interface classes and persistent classes.

Our abstraction strategies are two layer. First is the concers of framework structure : it is our DUNP model for abstraction. The second is the concers of the strategy for abstracting the classes in one layer. Our DUNP model consists of 4 layes. These layers are followings :

(1) Domain layer
(2) User interface layer
(3) Network Interface layer
(4) Persisten layer

The goal of DUNP model is that we can easily replace the component of one layer without effecting the components of other layer.

User interface layers consists of front classes, which handle the user interactions and pass the user's events to domain classes. UserCreateDlg, TransferDlg, NotificationDlg are the examples of user interface classes. Persistent layers provide the data base scheme and operations for handling the specific database. The classes defined in this layer connect directly with database. Domain classes define what kinds of data should be maintained and how to manage these business data. User, Part, Drawing, Assembly, Process, Notification are the examples of domain classes. Network interface layer corresponds the interface classes between the client and server components.

For designing the domain classes, we apply hot spots for abstracting. It means that we find what parts are not changeable. We abstracted those parts as our abstract classes. Also we find what parts are changeable and which way to redefine them. We abstracted those parts as the hot spots. In this abstraction process, we focused on domain layer.

We abstracted PDM domain with three abstract classes : PDMData, PDMRelation, and PDMBehavior class. PDMData class defines that some classes should have several attributes and operations for handling their attributes. This class is data–centric. So many attribute are defined in these classes but their operations are not complex. So, PDMData class doesn't know how they interact to other classes and the behavior related with other classes. PDMData is a template classes so that it just knows that they should interact with other classes and they should perform many behaviors but they don't know what classes are related and how to do. Part, Drawing, Mail are the subclasses of PDMData. PDMRelation defines the association between PDMData. If the association had link attribute, then we made that association to PDMRelation class. When some behaviors are derived from the association, we also made it as PDMRelation. PDMRelation class is also template class what classes are necessary for making this relationship and which attributes and behaviors are required. Binary, Ternary, AttachTo, AssignTo are the subclasses of PDMRelation. PDMBehavior class is abstract class, which defines the algorithm being changeable later. So all operation in class should not be PDMBehavior. If operations were different in each application and need the attribute defined in other classes as well as self–contained attributes, we defined these operations as PDMBehavior. Transfer, Baseline, Validate are the subclasses of PDMBehavior. The reason why we defined three classes as key abstraction is these classes are the hot spots of

PDM domain. Through three abstract classes, we can easily extend classes without effecting other class hierarchy. For example, we can extend business item objects by inheriting PDMData and attach the existing the subclasses of PDMBehavior. Like this, we can easily extend other classes. <Fig 3> shows the part of abstract model for developing our PDM framework.

3.5 Documenting PDM framework with design patterns

It was not easy to document our framework design concepts. Design patterns are generic solutions to problems [3]. We identified hot spots, which can be refined later. We applied several design patterns to document our framework according to what kinds of hot spots are. The parts of our guidelines are following, in table 2.

We want to explain how to apply several design patterns for framework. The most important patterns were strategy, state, and collection. As described earlier, PDMBehavior, abstract class, specialized into several PDM-specific behaviors. But each PDM application should have different algorithm for performing its processes. PDMBehavior class hierarchy is an example of applying strategy pattern.

state determine the behaviors of each operation. The more important thing is that the classification of state is changeable according to the business rules. So we used state pattern to separate the state-dependent behaviors from self-defined behaviors. As a result, the state pattern was combined with the strategy pattern since the process also can be changeable depending on states. <Fig 4-b> shows the state pattern. PDM has the characteristic for managing the collection of several data. We needed so many kinds of collection classes for each being managed data. But the responsibilities of these collection classes were similar. So we designed the template class for these collection classes. This template class can manage the subclasses of PDMData. <Fig 4-c> shows the object model applied with collection pattern.

Also we wrote our own patterns : AnyCreator, Mapper, Validator, Manager. In this paper, we describe just the purpose of AnyCreator and Mapper patterns.

(1) AnyCreator : provides an interface and an implementation for creating the business item objects with their attribute description. This AnyCreator helps to extend the business data-related classes without coding.
The strcuture of AnyCreator is like the following:

Guideline	Pattern Name
Collection of Homogeneous Items	Collection – Member&iterator
Collection of Heterogeous Items that have same parent classes	Composite &iterator
Some attribute or related classes will be addes	Decorator Interpreter
New object type that is same concept with existing but has different policy for each operation will be added	State Strategy
New behavior will be added	Strategy & Adapter
New event will be added	Command
Interaction between user interface class and domain class	Memento & Prototype

<Table 2> Our guidelines for selecting a pattern

<Fig 4-a> shows the applied object model. We identified that BusinessItem class has the strict states so that these

```
class AnyCreator {
    struct attribute {
```

```
Cstring   szName;
TYPE      eType;
void      *pValue;
};
CarrayAtt<attribute, attribute> m_att;
void getAttribute(Cstring);
void      setAttribute(Cstring, void *);
PdmItem_var    m_pSrv;
PDMItem();
Create();
};
```

In designing any PDMData, we inherited this AnyCreator class for generating the PDMData class.

(2) Mapper : decouple an abstraction between the layer, between domain and user interface, between domain and persistent, between client and server. We suggested DUNP model for extendibility. To meet this, an abstraction of one model can be independent from an abstraction of the other model. Their dependency should be defined seperately in mapper classes. When an abstraction will be chagend but their related components will not be changed, we can just modify the mapping information between newly defined components and the other existing componets.

4. Constructing PDM Framework

We are constructing PDM framework now. Of course, before starting this process, we have designed user interface and database and so on. When we design the user interfaces, we defined each user interface as Dialog classes and controls contained in it. We applied composite pattern to user interface class. Dialog is the superclass and Composite dialog, Simple dialog and Control class are the subclass of Dialog class.

Control class is corresponding to text edit box or command button. Simple dialog class defines the control needed for performing the behavior defined in domain class. These controls are related with attributes required for one operation. Composite dialog is window for one domain class. So Composite dialog class consists of several simple dialogs.

As we mentioned earlier, we use relational database for storing the PDM data. But we constructed object model that has classes and inheritance. We can't map our model into RDB. We mapped concrete classes not abstract classes into DB Table. Each DB table has the attribute defined in every super classes of concrete class. The

following figure explains our structure of module for PDM framework.

We try to make the components independent. So, ViewClass just knows how to handle user interactions and what is the responsible class for them. It means that ViewClass makes a message to corresponding DocClass for processing. But the DocClass in client component can't know how to process the user event but can know what server component can make a result. The responsibilities of DocClass are following. 1) binding and maintaining the pointer to server component. 2) Send or adapt the user event to the interface define in server components.

We separated server components into two: one is implantation class that knows how to realize the business logic and business properties, the other is Tm (Table Manager) class that knows how to use RogueWave class library and how to interface with real data base. In our structure, client component can't interact with Tm class directly. Every processing can be done by ImpClass. In a result, only the ViewClass and DocClass are dependent on MFC framework. If the user interface framework would be changed, we just change client components. ImpClass is tightly related with business. If the business should be extended, these ImpClass were be revised. Of course we can easily change the DBMS or the way to interface with DB since we put all related with DB into TmClass.

5. Integrated Customization Toolkit

We also have developed the environment for customizing the framework. By reusing the framework, we can reuse the design concept as well as domain knowledge. But understanding the framework is much more difficult than that of library since framework is much larger that library. To understand the framework, we should understand the interactions and default behaviors as well as class structure. When we customize the framework, understanding is very important. So we just started to develop the integrated customization toolkit to support the understanding and customizing of framework when we started to implement our PDM framework. Our toolkit consists of three parts: Object modeler, UI Editor, Meta Repository. <Fig 6> shows the block diagram for subsystem and their interface. We can understand the domain knowledge with object modeler. Object modeler knows the component's behavior and structure. Also it knows the relationship between domain class and UI class and the relationship between domain class and data base class. We can redefine the domain class with object modeler. Then object modeler creates new subclass of existing UI class and persistent class. Using UI Editor, programmer can rearrange the user interface class that created from object modeler. Meta repository consists of core framework classes, mapping information among classes, and rules for customizing the framework. Our customization toolkit is an application generator based on our PDM framework.

6. Conclusion

We have developed PDM framework based on object technology. We generalized several PDM applications to capture the domain object model. With generalized object model, we apply to design patterns to document the framework showing what the hot spots are. It was based on our design of customization toolkit. Now, we are developing the framework and customizing toolkit.

We identified the several problems of developing the framework.

    1) There are no strict guidelines for abstracting the domain.

    2) It is very difficult to integrate independent framework. PDM application requires the user interface, data base management, and network management. So should integrated MFC, CORBA, RogueWave. It was not easy job.

    3) We have no validation strategy for our framework. The only way is to show that our framework is customizable and extendible

Currenlty we extend our framework and validate our framework to develop new PDM application by customizing our framework. Two small-sized company have their PDM requirements so that we customize our framework to satify their requirements. From this process, we find some limitations and advantages of our framework. Based on our framework, our customer easily image what will be delivered and what functionalities they need. So, framework is a good executable prototype. The more good thing is that we don't need to throw wasy our prototype since our framework can be customized. We need little customizer for developing new PDM applications. But some parts of requirments are difficults to refine since the component have no hot spot for them. From this results, we continue to refine our framework to be more extendible and more general in PDM domain.

References

1. Pree, W., Framework Patterns, SIGS Books, New your, NY, 1996

2. Pree,. W., Design Patterns for Object–Oriented Software Development, Addison–Wesley/ACM Press, Reading, MA, 1995

3. Gamma,E., Helm, R, Johnson, R., and Vlissides, J. Design Patterns : Elements of Reusable Object–Oriented Software, Addison–Wesley/ACM Press, MA, 1995.

4. R. Johnson, "Frameworks = (Components + Patterns) ," CACM Vol. 40., No. 10, Oct., 1997, pp39–42

5. Michael Mattsson, Object–Oriented Frameworks: A Survey of methodological issues, LU–CS–TR:96–167

6. HP Metapahase : Object Management Framework, PDM Manual

7. Mike Potel, "MVP : Model–View–Presenter , The Taligent Programming Model fo C++ and Java," Technical Report of Taligent, 1996

8. Paul Dustin Keefer, An Object Oriented Framework for Accounting Systems, MS Thesis of University of Illinois at Urbana–Champaign, 1994

9. Hans Albrecht Schmid, " Design patterns for constructing the hot spots of a manufacturing framework," JOOP June, 1996, pp 25 – 37

10. James Rumbaugh, et al, Object–Oriented Object Modeling and Design Techniques, Prentice–Hall, 1988

48

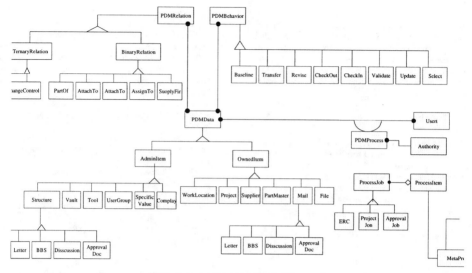

<Fig 3> Abstracted Object Model for PDM framework

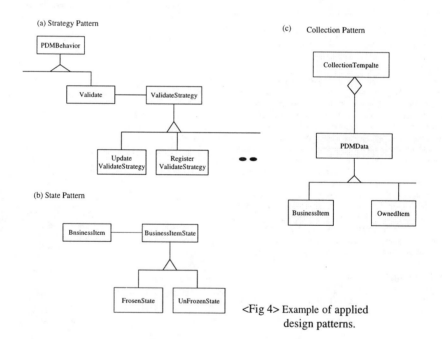

(a) Strategy Pattern

(c) Collection Pattern

(b) State Pattern

<Fig 4> Example of applied
design patterns.

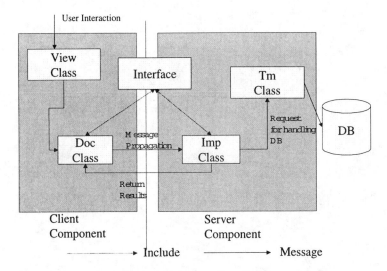

<Fig 5> our strategy for module structure

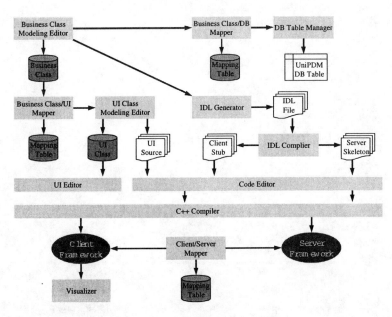

<Fig 6> Integrated Customization Toolkit

Object-Oriented Design
and Methodology

An Object-oriented Design Methodology
for Distributed Services

Marc Born, Andreas Hoffmann
GMD FOKUS Kaiserin-Augusta-Allee 31, D - 10589 Berlin
Tel. +49 30 3463 7 235, Fax. +49 30 3463 8 235
email: {born I a.hoffmann}@fokus.gmd.de

Abstract:

Due to the highly increasing complexity of new telecommunication services and the distributed nature of them on the one hand and the requirement to come up with a short time to market on the other hand, new methods, techniques and tools covering the whole service development process are needed.

This paper presents an integrated approach covering the fields of designing, validating and testing services and reusable service components. Therefore, a methodology which applies concepts from the Reference Model for Open Distributed Processing (ODP) is introduced. As an important part to bridge the gap from the design plane to the implementation plane a language mapping from ODL to C++ is described. ODL is an extension of CORBA-IDL and allows to specify objects with multiple interfaces. A CORBA based environment is assumed to be the execution platform.

To ensure that the service to be designed meets the requirements of a potential user, a validation stage has been included into the design methodology. Therefore an (abstract) behavior description based on a formal language is needed and provided by a combination of ODL and SDL. After the validation of the SDL model abstract TTCN test cases are derived from it semi-automatically. This paper also contains a new method for automated testing of distributed services through executing these test cases in a CORBA based target environment.

1. Introduction

In order to overcome the immense complexity of current telecommunication systems the Reference Model for Open Distributed Processing (RM-ODP) [5] [6] describes an architecture for the design of such services where the basic idea is to split the design concerns into several viewpoints. Each of them covers different aspects of the system which is to be designed. Though the RM-ODP itself does not define a concrete design methodology, there is a lot of ongoing work concerning this topic.

This paper presents an integrated approach not only covering the field of service design but also validation and testing of services and reusable service components. It proposes a methodology providing notations and usage guidelines to cover all stages during the development lifecycle of an arbitrary (telecommunication) service. This service development lifecycle describes all activities that are necessary to define a distributed service. It is a description of both, stages and steps involved in the analysis, design and implementation plane.

The process is not to be understood as a top-down approach, but it is more an iterative application of each of the stages from an abstract level down to a detailed specification and implementation. Repetition of steps is needed if errors are detected either by validation on the design plane or by testing the implementation. Since the testing step normally takes a lot of the overall development time, an approach to reduce this time via automation of test execution in a distributed Common Object Request Broker Architecture (CORBA) [11] environment is introduced in this paper, too.

The following figure shows the relation between the service development lifecycle and the viewpoint based methodology. As to be seen, there is no fixed one to one relation between the viewpoints and the planes of the lifecycle. Most viewpoints cover topics belonging to different planes.

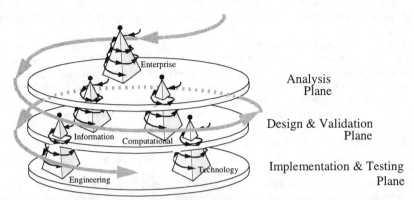

Figure 1: The overall development lifecycle

This paper focuses on the computational viewpoint as a part of the design and validation plane and on the connection to the implementation and testing plane.

To describe the components according to the computational viewpoint Object Definition Language (ODL) [4] is used.

Since ODL describes the structure of the service and the signatures only, there are two ways of covering the semantic of the service. The traditional one is to step directly into the implementation plane. For supporting this there is a need for a language mapping from ODL into the used implementation language in order to make use of the specified structure and signature information. Such a language mapping to C++ has been developed and is discussed in this paper. By applying this mapping, the time needed for the implementation can be reduced compared with using the IDL to C++ mapping provided by the Object Request Brokers (ORBs) only. The introduced mapping rules will be submitted to the ITU and the OMG to be standardized.

Though the way of directly mapping of ODL to the implementation language is the most common method, another approach is needed in order to allow validation of the component behavior before its implementation and to perform automated testing. That is to provide a computational behavior description for the components. This behavior description should be an abstract one since in most cases only the external visible behavior should be specified without prescribing any implementation details. In this paper it is shown, that SDL is a good candidate language to do that.

The overall methodology is mostly tool supported and has been applied to different projects dealing with the development of telecommunication services.

The paper is structured as follows:

Section 2 addresses briefly, how the requirements for a new service design task can be captured. Section 3 explains how different modelling languages can be combined to provide a computational model for service components. To increase the quality of the service a validation stage is included into the design plane. Section 4 describes the direct mapping of ODL to C++ and proposes a method to automate the process of testing an implementation in a CORBA based target environment.The

SDL based component behavior description is used for that purpose. Section 5 describes the tool chain supporting this method. Section 6 concludes this paper.

2. Analysis plane - requirement capturing

The task of capturing the requirements for a new service is not a main issue of this paper. However, it is not trivial and the result of requirement capturing plays an important role during the validation stage.

In order to capture the functional requirements, the proposed methodology follows the Use Case approach of Jacobsen which is also supported by the UML. An Use Case contains an abstract sequence of actions which is provided by the system to a certain user in a particular role. Following the enterprise viewpoint of ODP, we describe the actions in terms of policies. Each policy is either an obligation, a permission or a prohibition on the expected system behavior.

However, the main lack of the Use Case model is that Use Cases are only described informally by plain text. That means, they cannot serve as a basis for automated validation. To overcome this drawback, Use Cases are formalized here by attaching Message Sequence Charts (MSC) [9] on an high level of abstraction to them.

An example to illustrate this is the Access Session taken from the Service Architecture specification of the TINA-Consortium (TINA-C). It contains the description of a method to get uniform access to telecommunication services from different providers and retailers. This is a very practice related example. Due to the increasing amount of telecommunication services and their providers it is necessary to fix the interfaces between the consumers, the retailers and the providers of services. It is important, that this fixing does not only include signatures but behavior. Figure 2 contains one Use Case and its MSC.

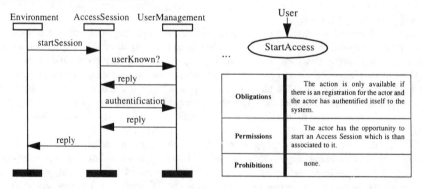

Figure 2: Formalization of use cases with MSCs

3. Service design and validation plane

3.1. The information model

The intention for having an information model in ODP is to provide a specification of the kind of information, which is processed by the system and of the relations between the information entities. Additionally, the information model can cover the state information and the state changing information of the whole system by defining static and dynamic schemes.

A well known notation for that purpose is the OMT object model notation, which is also part of the UML. In the tools introduced later on the OMT notation is integrated in order to be able to specify an information model. However, the practical experience in different projects shows, that the information model is often omitted depending on the kind of service which is to be produced. If the service to be designed makes use of a database, the information model is used to describe the data model. If there are only data types for the interface signatures to be described, the information model can be omitted and that information is contained in the computational viewpoint specification (ODL).

3.2. The Computational Model

In the Computational Viewpoint, the distributed service is described as a collection of interacting data processing entities, called computational objects (CO). The several COs interacting through their well defined computational interfaces. The service designer focuses on how a particular functionality can be provided without taking into account what kind of computing or network infrastructure is used, when the service is going to be implemented.

Hence, the task of a computational model is to define the object (or component) structure together with the interface signatures on the one hand and to describe the behavior provided at the interfaces on a high level of abstraction on the other hand.

The computational model plays an important role, because it is the basis for a validation of the system behavior against the requirements without implementing it on top of a real computing and networking architecture. However, it depends on the used description technique, how abstract the behavior specification can be kept and whether or not the model can be analyzed or validated.

We use a combination of ODL and SDL to describe the computational model. Object Definition Language (ODL) is a suitable notation to cover the task of defining the structures and signatures of the system. ODL was initially developed by the TINA- consortium.

Within the Access Session example the user communicates by the means of an appropriate user application via the provider agent with the user agent located in the retailer domain. The interface i_RetailerNamedAccess provided by the user agent has been chosen for the presented example and is shortened to four operations.

These operations are used to do initialization (setUserCtxt), to establish a TINA service (startService), to terminate a TINA service (endSession) and to close the connection to a service provider (endAccessSession). The detailed description of the operation's behavior is not of interest in the context of this paper and therefore it is not explained here. For reasons of simplicity the following specification example lacks the data type, exception and operation parameter definitions.

```
module Ret_RP {
interface i_RetailerNamedAccess{
    void setUserCtxt (// for the purpose of initialization...)
        raises (e_AccessError,e_UserCtxtError);
    void endAccessSession(// to close connection to the provider)
        raises (  e_AccessError,e_EndAccessSessionError);
    void startService (// to establish a service...)
        raises (  e_AccessError,e_ServiceError,e_PropertyError);
    void endSession (// to terminate a service...)
        raises (e_AccessError,e_SessionError);

    CO UA{
        supports i_RetailerNamedAccess;
    };
};
};
```

With the combination of ODL and a behavior definition language it is possible to provide the environment with information on how the component behaves. This behavior description should be abstract enough to ensure that concrete implementation details are hidden to the public when a vendor sells a component. However, even an abstract behavior description would allow to validate and test the component together with the environment into which it is to be embedded.

The ITU language SDL is chosen in our methodology to serve as a notation for certain aspects of behavior description. SDL allows to specify sequences of interactions at the interfaces using the extended finite state machine concept. An SDL specification serves also as a basis for validation, simulation and test case generation. Via simulation MSCs can be generated and validated against (possibly hand written) MSCs from the enterprise or computational viewpoint.

For applying the methodology it is not a must to use SDL, but practical reasons such as tool support for validation and test case derivation were important for making the choice. Alternatives would be other formal languages like Z or LOTOS.

One often hear the argument, that a combination of ODL and a behavior description technique like SDL is not useful since the information covered by the ODL specification can be described using the behavior description technique (especially in SDL) directly. However, there are good reasons for applying both languages:

- SDL does not allow to specify IDL datatypes and signatures. This information is needed for the implementation on top of a CORBA based execution environment,
- the structuring mechanisms in SDL are not intuitive enough and the model becomes often confusing,
- not all components will be fully described with SDL, instead they will be implemented directly. The ODL specification serves as a basis for both ways.
- computational specifications are often prescribed in terms of interfaces which have to be used, for instance TINA reference points or CORBA services. These specifications are given in ODL/IDL and have to be included in the design process.

It should be noted that there is ongoing work in the ITU to include IDL datatypes in SDL and to enhance the SDL structuring mechanisms. If this work will be finished, SDL can serve as the language for the computational viewpoint without a need for ODL. But for the time being the way of combing them seems to be the most suitable one.

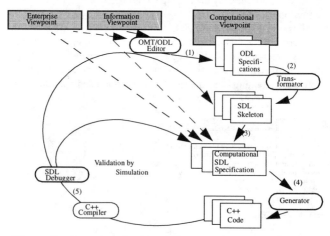

Figure 3: Computational modelling process Using SDL

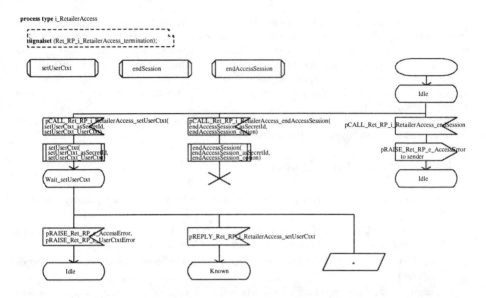

Figure 4: Example of behavior description in SDL

The most important steps of the methodology are (see Figure 3):

Step (1): Using the information and the enterprise specification, partially developed in OMT and Use Cases, a computational ODL specification has to be defined.

Step (2): The ODL specification is mapped into a structural equivalent SDL specification. This can be done automatically and is founded by a language mapping which is published in [2].

Step (3): The SDL inheritance feature is applied to enrich the SDL specification generated by step 2 with behavior descriptions for both the interface and object templates.

Step 3 can be repeated to achieve different levels of abstraction in the design of object composition and behavior. The result is an executable computational model which is not the engineering solution. It defines only a behavior model to observe and evaluate special aspects of object behavior which are visible from outside. Especially complex object configurations can be studied.

Step (4): With help of tool packages the SDL specification from the last step can be checked for correctness of syntax and static semantics. Additionally, it is possible to generate C++ code that can be linked with a simulation library. This leads to a simulator for the SDL system which represents the ODL specification and includes the computational behavior aspect and hence allows one to check the dynamics of the system.

Step (5): A simulation of the computational model is used to detect design errors prior to implementation. The components of the SDL simulator can be distributed using CORBA.

Another way of error detection is to explore the state space of the SDL model to find lifelocks or deadlocks. If design errors are detected, a repetition of the steps 1 to 4 could be necessary.

The result of applying this method is a computational model of either a complete telecommunication service or a single component or a set of components. The reusability of these components is supported by a so called computational database or repository (see Section 5 for details on tool support).

A part of the behavior description for the Access Session example is shown In Figure 4. It is a state machine, describing the behavior at the i_RetailerAccess interface. In the initial state Idle, there are 2 methods which are allowed: endAccessSession and setUserCtxt. If one of these invocations is received, the appropriate procedure is called. The method endSession is not allowed in this state, therefore, and exception signal is generated and the procedure is not called. This approach allows to model exceptions even in SDL'92 which is essential for specifying telecommunication services.

In the following section, it is described how the design information contained in the ODL and SDL specifications can be used for the implementation.

4. Implementation & testing plane

In this section the two ways, how the implementation can be derived from the design model are described:

- Either the ODL specification can be mapped to the implementation language (in that case C++) and the code for the behavior has to be added by hand or
- the SDL behavior specification serves as a basis for automatic implementation code generation.

It depends on the problem which way is selected, the methodology provides support for both ways and also tool support is available for both.

To increase the quality of the service implementation a testing step has been included in our methodology. This is needed since the properties of the service designed might not be fulfilled by the implementation of the service. Hence, it has to be checked whether the implementation behaves like specified during the design process. The testing step is shortly explained in this section too.

4.1. ODL to C++ mapping

4.1.1. Requirements to the mapping

Once the design of the service to be developed has been finished it has to be implemented using a common programming language such as C++. Of course, other languages like Pascal or Java are also possible, but in this paper we will concentrate on C++. To decrease the implementation effort implementation classes for client stubs and server skeletons are usually generated from the IDL part of the ODL specification. The major drawback of this approach is that a lot of design information is lost through this transition from the design stage to the implementation stage. That way all the information about the structure of the service is lost since only classes for interfaces are generated. Hence, it is no longer to be seen which object or component (object group) the generated interface classes belong to. To overcome this drawback and to automate the implementation process as much as possible we have developed language mapping from ODL to C++. This direct mapping of ODL specifications to C++ is one way to bridge the gap from the design to the implementation plane.

The mapping rules have to fulfill at least the following requirements:

- To be compatible with IDL to C++ mapping. That means, that no changes to existing ORB implementations have to be made and existing IDL tools can be re-used.
- To provide adequate representation of computational objects. The mapping should be as straightforward as possible so that the user has structural equivalence between the specification and the implementation.
- To preserve the separation of "Core"-object and its interfaces. This is a key issue and corresponds to the previous one.

- To distinguish between supported and required interfaces. This is one major advantage of the ODL. It allows to minimize the size of the code, since for the required interfaces only the client mapping is needed.
- To offer flexibility for implementation of interfaces and objects.
- To allow a distinction between interface and object related behavior. Interface related behavior can be state information like which operations have already been called at that interface instance and which operations are currently allowed to be executed.
- To support the management of interfaces and objects (lifecycle support). The user should concentrate on the object behavior he wants to implement but not on things like how to create additional instances of interfaces.

4.1.2. Mapping rules

Since ODL is a superset of OMG-IDL the language mappings contained in CORBA serve as guideline to define a language mapping for ODL. As stated in the previous section one goal is to map the IDL parts of ODL as defined there to be able to use the IDL compilers delivered with existing CORBA products. This will increase the expectance of the proposed mapping since a lot of current distributed platforms are CORBA-based.

However, from a general point of view the mapping rules are independent from CORBA and can be used for several kinds of Distributed Processing Environments (DPE). In the following sections, the mapping for only those concepts which are not part of IDL is explained.

4.1.2.1 Flows (stream interfaces)

ODL stream interface definitions consists of a set of data flow definitions. Such dataflows have a well-defined frame type and an attribute specifying the direction of the flow, i.e. whether the interface serves as a sink or source for the specific data flow.

There is no proposal for a mapping of flows currently. A possible solution might be to adopt the results from the OMG in the area of AV-streams.

4.1.2.2 Mapping for computational object templates

ODL CO definitions consists of a set of interface templates which are offered by the described object to its environment, a set of interface templates which ate needed by the CO to perform its service and an interface template, which is instantiated at the time where the CO itself is instantiated. This initial interface serves as a handle to the CO. It may contain operations to obtain other interfaces, to perform identity checks etc.

Computational object templates are mapped to C++ classes (CO classes). The main functionality which is provided by the generated classes is, that they contain methods for creation and deletion of the supported interfaces of the ODL CO definition.

Additional functionality such as checkpointing or migration can be provided but is not prescribed and depends on the platform on which the application should run. For that reason it might be useful to have a common base class similar to ::CORBA::Object, and let all generated classes inherit from it.

Required interface specification

Required interface templates are not mapped themselves. There is the CORBA client mapping for the interface template only.

However, the required interface information is needed, if a minimal server implementation (with respect to the number of generated classes) should be built. In that case only the client part of the CORBA mapping for those interfaces which are required and the server part for the interfaces which are supported has to be generated.

Supported interface specification

The interface templates announced in the list of supported interfaces on an arbitrary CO are mapped in the following way:

- There is a C++ class generated which implements the class generated according to the OMG-IDL mapping. This class contains implementations for all operations of the interface. The behavior is to delegate an incoming call to an implementation class.

  The programmer does not have to touch any of these delegation classes. An example of a delegation class is presented below. The class contains private member variables for the pointer to its „Core"-object and its implementation class, methods for getting and setting these pointers and the IDL operations are implemented to delegate an incoming call. The name of the base class is ORB specific, in that case for Orbix.

```
class i_RetailerNamedAccess__DEL: virtual i_RetailerNamedAccessBOAImpl {
   private:
     i_RetailerNamedAccess__IMPL *my_impl;
     CO *my_core;

   public:
     i_RetailerNamedAccess__DEL(i_RetailerNamedAccess__IMPL *impl=NULL, CO * object=NULL): my_impl(impl),
                                  my_core ( object ){
     };

     i_RetailerNamedAccess__IMPL* getImplClass() { return my_impl; };
     void setImplClass(i_RetailerNamedAccess__IMPL* impl) { my_impl=impl; };

   protected:
     virtual void setUserCtxt (
        ::TINAAccessCommonTypes::t_AccessSessionSecretId asSecretId,
        t_UserCtxt userCtxt,
        CORBA::Environment &IT_env=CORBA::IT_chooseDefaultEnv ()
     )
     throw (::TINAAccessCommonTypes::e_AccessError, e_UserCtxtError,::CORBA::SystemException){
        try {
           getImplClass()->setUserCtxt(asSecretId, userCtxt,IT_env);
        }
        catch(CORBA::SystemException&){
           throw;
        };
        catch(::TINAAccessCommonTypes::e_AccessError&){
           throw;
        };
        catch(e_UserCtxtError&){
           throw;
        };
        catch(...){
           throw;
        };
     };

     virtual void getUserCtxt ...;
     ...
} /*end opr interface delegation class */;
```

- The implementation class is generated for all interfaces listed somewhere as supported. The implementation class contains all operations as pure virtual methods. The programmer is responsible to provide implementations of these implementation classes.

- There is a possibility to make a reference to an instance of an implementation class known to the delegation class instance. This can be implemented either in the constructor of the delegation class or by a method __set_implementation.

The CO can create instances of its supported interface templates in the following way:

1. Create an instance of the delegation class.
2. Obtain a reference to an instance of the implementation class (can exist or be created).
3. Make the reference to the implementation class instance known to the delegation class instance.

A class for the UserAgent is presented below. It contains a method for the generation of its i_RetailerNamedAccess interface.

```
class UA : virtual CO{
    ...
protected:
    virtual i_RetailerNamedAccess__DEL* create_i_RetailerNamedAccess ( i_RetailerNamedAccess__IMPL* impl){
        return new i_RetailerNamedAccess__DEL(impl,this);
    };
    ...
} /*end object class */;
```

Initialization specification

The initial interface is mapped in the same way as supported interfaces. It is task of the used DPE to provide an instance of the initial interface to the instantiator of the CO. The way how to do this is not prescribed by this mapping.

Inheritance

Object template inheritance is realized as C++ inheritance between the generated C++ classes.

The programmer is free in the choice how to structure the application. He must only provide implementations for the implementation classes and possibly for the CO classes.

The following figure shows some examples how the implementation might be structured. It is assumed that there is one computational object which supports the interfaces i1, i2 and i3.

- There is the possibility to have one implementation for each interface implementation class. That normally happens when there is a lot of state information related to the interface. The synchronization and information exchange is handled via the CO class implementation.

- It is possible to have one implementation for a number of interface implementation classes.

- If there is no state information related to the interfaces, the implementation could be done directly in the CO class implementation.

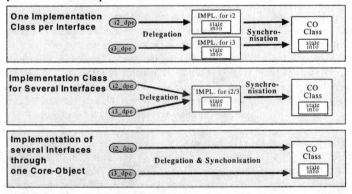

Figure 5: Implementation possibilities for generated classes

4.1.2.3   Mapping for object group templates

ODL Object group templates are sets of computational objects and computational groups which can be clustered together for any reason. This concept has been adopted from ODP. It is a structuring concept for a wide range of applications. The reason for grouping them is contained in the group predicate specification. Since the predicate specification can vary, there is no prescribed mapping for object groups. Examples for a group predicate can be that all members of the group belong to the same domain or that they provide together a particular service.

However, if the purpose of the group is to group its members for implementation reasons, the group can be mapped onto a class definition in the same way as COs. The contracts of the group (the supported and required interfaces) are than mapped in the same way as for computational objects.

4.1.3. Benefits of the mapping

The introduced mapping rules are extensions of the IDL to C++ mapping rules. That means, that existing ORB implementations can be used as well as all IDL tools. Full flexibility for the implementation is provided, since the implementation and linkage of generated classes for supported interfaces and objects is open. The programmer has not to touch the generated classes for interfaces any more, he can concentrate on the object behavior. Additionally he can make use of the generated methods which support the interface and object lifecycle like creation and deletion methods.

4.2. Code generation for SDL

It is possible to generate C++ code from an SDL specification. Depending on the used code generator this code can be executed on CORBA environments. It depends on the level of detail of the SDL specification whether the code has to be completed by hand or not.

Because of the usage of CORBA as the communication mechanism, there is no problem to connect components which are coded by hand using the ODL to C++ mapping and those components which are more or less completely generated from the SDL specification.

4.3. Automated testing

Once the implementation of the service to be developed has been finished a testing phase should be performed to increase the quality of the service implementation. Testing is a general method to determine that the implementation behaves like expected, i.e. it behaves like specified during the design phase. Hence, it has to be checked whether the service implementation is conform to the behavioral specification of the developed service. Furthermore testing can be used to increase the likelihood that the service developed works together with other services in the target environment. However, it should be noted that testing does not assure that the service, which has been validated and tested separately, works together with other services in a way expected. The validation and testing of services can only minimize the risk that the service developed does not interwork with other services in a multi-service environment.

The starting point for testing is the development of test cases. A suitable and standardized notation for the specification of test cases is TTCN (Tree and Tabular Combined Notation) [13]. Test cases may be developed either manually or derived from a behavioral specification in an automated manner. Following our methodology we derive test cases semi-automatically from the computational SDL specification. The derived test cases have to be completed by hand with timer and test suite operations to get an abstract test suite.

Since an abstract test suite is not executable it has to be implemented to obtain an executable test system. In order to automatize this implementation process and to bridge the gap between the abstract test suite (ATS) and the executable test suite (ETS) a test code generator (ETS generator) has been developed by GMD FOKUS. This generator is able to generate code for an abstract TTCN test suite which is ready for execution in a distributed CORBA environment by means of an adaption layer - the TTCN-CORBA-Gateway. The gateway is needed because the message-oriented implementation of the abstract TTCN test suite has to be integrated into an object-oriented system.

5. Summary of methodology and tool support

In order to get acceptance for new software development methods it is not enough to propose the method from a theoretical perspective only. Tools have to be provided to enable the usage of the method. In this section we will show how already existing tool packages and new developed tools can be combined and integrated to support the whole lifecycle of service development as introduced in Section 1.

Analysis plane

GMD FOKUS has developed a tool called Y.SCE [7] which provides graphical notations for the Use Case Model and an ODP based organizational model. The information is stored in a repository (database). High level MSCs can be captured using the TAU toolset from Telelogic. Both tools will be connected to allow that MSCs can be attached to the Use Cases and a navigation form one tool to the other is possible.

Design & validation plane

The Y.SCE tool provides a graphical notation for ODL and is able to import and export textual ODL and CORBA-IDL files. The ODL information is stored in the same repository as the Use Case information. It is possible to establish links between the Use Cases and the ODL model and to navigate along these links.

The Y.SCE tool is able to generate SDL files which afterwards can be imported into SDT from Telelogic. Navigation is again possible. The behavior information can be added using SDT. This tool provides also the functionality of simulation and validation of an SDL specification and the ability to check an SDL specification against the requirement specification of the enterprise model partially provided by enterprise-MSCs.

Implementation & testing plane

The generation of C++ code from ODL as described in this paper is supported by the Y.SCE tool. For the generation of C++ code from SDL, the TAU toolset can be used.

For the development of TTCN test cases the ITEX toolset supplies powerful means. Since both ITEX and SDT are integrated into the TAU toolset provided by Telelogic the derivation of test cases from an SDL specification is well-supported. Especially TTCNLink and AutoLink should be mentioned for semi-automated or automated derivation of test cases.

To bridge the gap between the abstract test suites and executable ones GMD FOKUS has developed a toolset to make abstract test suites executable in an distributed CORBA environment. The ETS generator generates code from the TTCN test suite which can be executed by means of the TTCN-CORBA gateway to test an implementation (SUT) automatically.

6. conclusion

Since distributed services are highly complex they are hard to develop. Hence, a powerful object-oriented methodology for the development of distributed services is needed. The ODP framework provides a lot of concepts and abstract notations for the development and specification of distributed services. The viewpoint concept allows to control the complexity of distributed services by splitting the design model into 5 different submodels. Each of them covers different aspects of the service to be developed.

This paper presents a methodology for the improved development of object-oriented distributed services according to the ODP viewpoint model. For the service design ODL has been selected as a suitable language since it is a small but powerful description language supporting multiple interfaces per object. In order to ease the implementation process of the service under development, mapping rules from ODL to C++ have been defined and implemented. Moreover, the implementation phase has been extended by a testing phase to proof that the service implementation behaves like specified in the design model, i.e. to check whether or not the service is ready for shipping.

The future work will concentrate on the development of deployment support for services and its integration into the methodology. Another research issue is the development and improvement of the ODL to C++ Mapping rules for streams and groups and the enhancement of the tools.

7. References

[1]. Born, M.; Fischer, J.; Winkler, M.: Formal Language Mapping from CORBA IDL to SDL'92 in Combination with ASN.1, Informatik-Bericht Nr. 44, Humboldt-University Berlin, 1995

[2]. Fischer J., Fischbeck N., Born M., Hoffmann A., Winkler M.: Towards a behavioral Description of ODL, TINA'97 conference

[3]. G. Booch, I. Jacobson, J. Rumbaugh: Unified Modeling Language 1.1

[4]. TINA-C: TINA Object Definition Language MANUAL, Version 2.3, 1997

[5]. ITU-T Rec. X.903 I ISO/IEC 10746-3: 1995, Open Distributed Processing - Reference Model Part 3

[6]. ITU-T Rec. X.904 I ISO/IEC 10746-4: 1995, Open Distributed Processing - Reference Model Part 4

[7]. GMD Fokus Berlin: Y.SCE Tool, 1997

[8]. CCITT: SDL - Specification Description Language, International Standard Recommendation Z.100, Genf,1992

[9]. CCITT: Message Sequence Charts, International Standard Recommendation Z.120, Genf, 1996

[10]. TINA-C Baseline Document: Service Architecture, Version 5.0. June 1997.

[11]. OMG: The Common Object Request Broker Architecture and Specification, Version 2.1. Aug. 1997.

[12]. Telelogic: The Tau 3.2 Toolset Guidelines, Telelogic, Malmö, Oct., 1997

[13]. ISO/IEC 9646: Part 3: The Tree and Tabular Combined Notation (TTCN), Edition 2, Nov. 1997.

Industry Experience in Migrating to Object Technology

Richard Thomas
School of Computing Science
Queensland University of Technology
GPO Box 2434
Brisbane, Qld 4001
Ph: (07) 3864 2961
Fax: (07) 3864 1801
Email: richard@fit.qut.edu.au

Abstract

Object oriented software engineering (OOSE) is becoming a common approach to software development. As third generation OOSE processes are established (eg. OPEN [1] and the Unified Software Development Process [2]) organisations will start to consider OOSE as a mature technology. This recognition will mean that more organisations will go through the process of changing their current software development processes. This paper will report on the experience of one team at a large technical firm as they adopted OOSE processes for a major project. The experience of this team confirms most of what has been previously reported in the literature, and adds two additional observations. The first observation is that other literature in this field does not consider team motivation as a factor that contributes to migration success. The second observation is that other literature does not consider the relative impact of some factors over other factors.

Introduction

The author of this paper became involved in this team's migration to object technology when he was approached by the company to provide an object oriented analysis and design training course. Following that course he has maintained contact with the team to monitor their progress in adopting object technology. He has subsequently provided a follow-up object oriented programming training course as the team started the detailed design phase of the project. He intends to continue monitoring the team over the remainder of the development of this system. He also plans to monitor the second project that this team undertakes, as well as monitoring the start of the maintenance phase of this system.

The author was not involved in planning the transition process for this team and is not a member of the company. This means that he can provide an unbiased critique of the transition plan. This critique is based on observations of the team and on interviews with team members and the project manager. As the author provided all the training that the team received during the transition process, some unintentional bias may be introduced in regards to the success of the training. The author will try to avoid bias by reporting the comments that the team members and project manager have made about the training.

This paper will provide a brief description of the type of company and the team that undertook the migration to object technology. This will be followed by a description of the type of project on which OOSE was applied. The paper will then discuss the reasons that the company had for adopting OOSE processes and the strategy that was followed in adopting OOSE. The successes and failure of the project will then be considered along with lessons learnt during this project. The paper will conclude with a summary of what was learnt and further issues that need to be explored as a result of this paper.

Company profile

TechCo1[1] is a large international firm that develops both software and hardware systems. The company specialises in developing technical real-time and concurrent systems. The company provides a range of services including application consulting, functional specification and design, custom software development, and systems integration.

Team profile

The software development team that is the focus of this paper is based at one of the Australian offices of TechCo1. All members of the software development team have either engineering or computing degrees. Several of the senior people on this team have engineering degrees and have moved into software development. The newer employees have computing science degrees, or combined engineering and computing degrees.

All developers have commercial experience developing software in C. Some have taken a subject at university that introduced C++. Only two developers have commercial experience using C++. All developers feel that they do not have adequate knowledge of object oriented software engineering processes.

Pilot project

The pilot project is a large complex computer based system called TechProj1[1]. TechProj1 is a distributed system with hard real-time constraints. The system also contains a large number of hardware devices that will be controlled by embedded software. TechProj1 will replace an existing computer based system that provides a subset of the required functionality. The project involves developing and supplying the necessary hardware as well as the control software. The main software system will run on Sun Ultra 30 servers. The servers will be configured as a primary server group and a backup server group. The backup server group will mirror the operations of the primary server group and take over control in case of emergencies. Each embedded system will be networked back to the servers.

The development team will consist of up to fifty engineers. The software team consists of sixteen software engineers within the development team. The development cost is estimated as forty million Australian dollars. The development time is estimated as fourteen months. The system is scheduled for delivery in late 1998. The team has had little experience on similar systems.

The client for this project represents an additional problem on top of the complex system being developed. The client is based overseas, limiting the amount of communication between the development team and the client. The client representatives have limited English skills and

---

[1] Due to the confidential nature of the system and the company's proprietary processes the name of the company and the project are fictitious.

the development team has no members fluent in the client's language. The client has also enforced a set of constraints on the development process. All of these issues have made the requirements gathering process difficult. Consequently, the requirements gathering phase of the project overran its estimated completion date by four months. The project manager estimates that the project will be four to six months late if development continues at the current rate. The development and delivery schedules have not been modified at this date.

Reasons for migrating to object technology

Object oriented software engineering processes have been adopted for this project for two reasons. The first, and primary, reason is that the framework that is used as the core for the majority of the company's software systems has been redeveloped using object oriented programming practices. The framework is written in C++ and implements an object oriented database. To use and extend the framework an object oriented software development approach is needed. The pilot project will not only use the framework but will require the team to make significant extensions to the framework.

The second reason is that the client has mandated that the software be developed using a specified set of development techniques. These techniques include data flow diagrams, flow charts, and an object oriented analysis and design method. The software development team is aware that this is a poor mix of development techniques, but are unable to change the client's requirements. Part of the reason for the client's inflexibility on this issue is that they are requiring the system to conform to a European Economic Community standard applicable to this development area. This standard requires that the software be documented using some of these techniques.

Migration strategy

The migration strategy being used for this team is a supported "sink or swim" approach. The project manager for the team is committed to using object oriented software engineering processes. The majority of team members are enthusiastic about applying object technology. Some training and a good tool set have been provided. However, no allowance has been made in the project schedule for the team to adjust to this new approach to software development.

Training and mentoring

A small amount of training has been provided for the majority of the software development team. A three day introduction to object oriented analysis and design course was arranged for the team. Twelve members of the team attended this course. The course was held two months after the start of the project. Mentoring was provided as a single day workshop held the day following the course. The workshop was led by the course presenter and applied some of the analysis techniques from the course to a problem in the pilot project. A small amount of e-mail support was also provided by the mentor.

Shortly after the start of the design phase of the project, a three day introduction to object oriented programming in C++ course was provided. This course concentrated on the standard features of C++, avoiding compiler or library specific issues. The course was customised for the team from a standard professional development course that is offered by the presenter. The main customisation was to provide extra material on the use of templates and exception handling in C++ and the performance penalties associated with these features [3].

When the analysis and design course was held the initial Software Requirements Specification (SRS) had been written and was going through its approval process. During the workshop, and subsequently during the approval process, it became apparent that the initial SRS lacked many important details. Following this course a prototyping process was undertaken for eight weeks. The prototyping was to develop the user interface for the monitoring sub-system. Two members of the team travelled to the client's location to conduct the prototyping. These team members also attempted to clarify some of the missing details from the SRS. Other team members visited the client during this period to work solely on the SRS problems.

Tool support

The team has a set of tools to support their software engineering process. The tools that they are using are:
- Continuous for configuration management.
- Requisite Pro to store and track the software requirements.
- Rational Rose for reverse engineering and for developing analysis and design models.
- The company's framework that provides the architecture and database support for the system.
- Microsoft's Visual C++ compiler for the MS Windows environment
- Sun's C++ compiler for the Unix environment.

The entire system, both code and documentation, is base-lined under Continuous. The team has discovered that Continuous does not work well with Rose and Requisite Pro. Neither tool interfaces easily with Continuous to automatically check documents in or out. They are also finding that requirements tracing is a serious problem that they need to confront. They have not found any tools that adequately support requirements tracing with the tool-set that they have.

Rational Rose provides support for drawing models of the system, some code generation and some reverse engineering. The team is using Rose as the main design tool for this project. Initially the team had intended to use the reverse engineering feature of Rose to document the framework. After experimenting with Rose, they have discovered that its reverse engineering feature is not practical for a large system.

At the start of the project another team, at another site, within the company was still completing the framework. This had the benefit that the project team could negotiate with the framework team to request features that would support this project. The drawback was that the requirements and project schedule had to be developed without knowing some of the details of the framework. The framework has almost no supporting documentation.

Microsoft's Visual C++ compiler version 5.0 is being used to develop the sub-system that will allow operators to monitor the entire system. Sun's C++ compiler version 4.2 is being used to develop the code for the rest of the system. A small problem is that these two compilers support different, and at times conflicting, features of C++. For example, Visual C++ 5.0 supports compressed header files and the new naming convention for the standard library; Sun C++ 4.2 does not support those features.

Management support

The company has made a commitment to adopting object technology by developing the latest version of their framework using object oriented practices. This will require all future projects based on this framework to use object technology. This project is the first project within the company to make use of the new version of the framework. This commitment, and interviews with the project manager, show that the company's management believes that object technology will provide benefits to the company in the long term. However, management provides limited practical support to successfully implement object technology within the company.

The support that management has provided is described above in the training and tools sections. In regards to the training, it should be noted that management did try to ensure that the entire team was able to attend all the training. The analysis and design training was provided two months after the project was started; though this was only partially management's fault. (The presenter was not available until a month and a half after the course was requested. However, the course was not requested until after the project had already started.)

The main area where management has not supported the migration to object technology is in project planning. No time has been built into the development schedule to accommodate a learning curve for the team. The project deadlines are tight without introducing new processes to the team. Also too many other risks are associated with the project. These risks include other new technologies with which the team has to become familiar and the amount the project contributes to this division's income.

The team that has developed the object oriented framework is considered the company's premier research and development team. As such there is a certain amount of prestige to be a member of this team. Management has decided that they will not use the object oriented expertise acquired building the framework to support other teams in the company. This means that members of the framework development team will not be used as mentors to other teams that are using the framework.

Successes

The project has not been completed at this stage. Therefore, final success of the project cannot be judged. Three things could be considered successes at this stage. They are the team's morale, tool support, and management "buy-in".

Despite the stress that the team is under, due to the tight project deadlines and due to having to learn a number of new technologies, the team has maintained good morale. The observation that the team has maintained good morale is subjectively judged from discussions with team members. The level of moral was judged was by observing how interested the team members' were in the project and in applying object technology. This level of moral can at least partially be attributed to management's ability to sell the team on the benefits of this project and learning the new technologies. Another factor contributing to morale is that the team members find this project interesting and see that participating in this project is likely to benefit their careers in the long term.

Good CASE tool support has been claimed to be essential for a successful first object technology project [4]. Not everyone may agree that CASE tools are essential for successful migration to object technology, but few would argue that CASE tools hinder migration. The team carefully evaluated the range of CASE tools available. As described above in the tool support section they chose a tool-set that provided the best mix of features. The team has encountered a number of difficulties in using the tools, but still believe that the tools are providing some benefit. The team claims that the most important tool is the use of Continuous to base line all documents and source code. As the team has derived some benefit from the use of CASE tools it will be claimed that this was a successful aspect of the migration strategy. Due to the difficulties the team had in integrating tools and the limited benefit that this team has observed from using tools, more work needs to be done to confirm whether Fayad's claim that CASE tools are essential to the migration process is correct or not [4].

Management support for migrating to object technology is considered critical. If an organisation's management does not believe that there are benefits to migrating to object technology there will be no support for staff to undertake the migration [4]. Management at TechCo1 has indicated their support for the migration process by allowing their core framework to be redeveloped using object oriented techniques. They have also indicated their support by providing a good supporting tool-set and by providing the training requested by the team. Another indication of management's support for the migration is how management has informed the team about the rationale for the project schedule. Management admitted that the project schedule is very tight and that the project deadlines were set for commercial reasons, not due to realistic project scheduling. Team members commented that this openness has helped to keep them from being discouraged about their progress on the project, thus contributing to the team's good morale. Following on from this, management has not blamed the project delays on the team or on particular technologies.

Failures

As the project has not been completed it is not possible to say that the migration process has been a failure. Some of the issues that have reduced the effectiveness of the migration process are discussed below.

Although training in object oriented analysis and design, and object oriented programming were provided a different training approach may have been more effective. "Just in time" training is advocated as the most appropriate form of training when adopting object technology [5]. The idea is that team members learn techniques just prior to when they need to apply them. Thus their work re-enforces the training. In this project the initial training was not held until two months after the start of the project. The requirements for the system were specified before the first training course. This meant that a large portion of the analysis of the system was completed before the team started applying object oriented processes. Another impact of the late training was that the team had to develop and apply the specific development process for the project immediately after completing the training. There was no time to consider options and to test different techniques. Additionally, as the requirements for the system were already specified, the first few stages of the project had been completed which meant that those stages did not follow the software development process that the team adopted. One problem that they encountered was in their approach to finding classes. They specified in their process that they would develop use cases for each sub-system. They then would identify classes from the use cases based on Jacobson's object oriented software engineering approach [6]. They found that developing use cases was beneficial in clarifying the requirements. However, they often found that the classes they identified did not work well with their framework. Consequently, they found that they were spending a lot of time reworking their class specifications. After three months they modified their process, to identify classes to interface with the framework first and then use a modified Jacobson approach to identify other classes from the use cases.

Making use of an object technology expert as a mentor is another well established approach to aid in the migration to object technology [4] [5]. The company's management has decided not to use mentors in its migration process. The team that has developed the new version of the framework has acquired some experience in applying object technology. Management has decided that it is more beneficial to keep that team intact to continue development of the framework than it would be to use members from that team to mentor other teams.

Management has also decided that they are not willing to spend the money that would be required to hire an expert or to hire a consultant. The trainer that provided the analysis and design course also ran a one day workshop with the software development team. The workshop allowed the team to see how the trainer, who was experienced in object oriented software development, would apply the techniques covered in the course to a problem from the project. Team members commented that the workshop was beneficial in seeing the techniques applied to a real problem, particularly seeing how the mentor overcame difficulties. But, a one day workshop meant that the mentor could only work on the analysis and high-level design of a single sub-system.

Learning to apply any new development process takes time. This applies to object technology as well as other techniques. Estimates on the amount of time it takes an average development team to effectively transition to object technology vary, but a common figure is approximately one year [4] [7]. It is usually recommended that the first project on which a team applies object oriented software development should have some slack built into the project schedule [5]. This project has a very tight schedule. No time has been put into the schedule to accommodate learning how to apply object technology. Even training time was not originally in the schedule. This resulted in putting the entire team under pressure that distracted them during the analysis and design course. The C++ course was scheduled for afternoons and evenings so that the team could work on the project in the morning. The schedule was set by the client and is based on when they want to start using the system, rather than being based on formal project scheduling techniques. TechCo1's project manager has said that the client representatives have informally indicated that they are aware that the project schedule is too short. The project manager said that TechCo1 agreed to the schedule to win the contract, rather than believing they could meet the schedule.

Migrating to object technology introduces extra risk to a project. It is usually recommended that a pilot project should be a low risk project [5]. This is a high risk project. The most obvious risk is the tight project schedule described above. Another risk is that the team consists of several new staff members who are unfamiliar with the general engineering domain in which the company works. This means that they are unaware of all the purposes for which the project framework is to be used. The existing staff members only have to learn how to use the new implementation of the framework, the new staff members also have to learn what support the framework provides. Another risk is that the project is mission critical, if the system does not perform to specifications it can cause the client to be liable for severe financial penalties. To some extent the system is also safety critical, in cases of extreme failure it is possible for there to be harm to or loss of human life. The team is working with an external consulting group who are experts in the area of safety critical system development. This alleviates some of the safety critical risk, but introduces other risks because the team is unfamiliar with the external group's processes. A final risk is that the project contributes a large amount to this division's income. Migration to object technology increases this project's risk further. This adds to the stress the team is under and could lead to team members using more familiar non-object oriented techniques in order to complete the project. So far, the team has avoided making short cuts to circumvent their object oriented processes.

Other authors have suggested that it is important that object technology be applied to all phases of a project [4] [5]. In this project the detailed development process was not established until after the initial requirements had been developed and high-level design had started. This meant that the majority of the analysis was done using structured techniques. The team had to redo much of the analysis work to be able to progress onto object oriented design.

A final failure was related to the team's general processes, rather than being specific to object technology migration. Documents were produced and reviewed, but were not considered closely in terms of the development process. Part of this problem was that several of the initial documents were produced before the detailed development process was established. This problem was highlighted when the team used the software requirements specification to start high-level design. They identified a large number of ambiguities in the document that meant that the requirements had to be respecified. Fortunately, the team also discovered that they had to redo much of the analysis work in order to perform a good object oriented design. This meant that the object oriented analysis could be used to help clarify the requirements.

Lessons learnt

Much of what has been learnt by observing this team reconfirms other work in this area. The factors that contribute to the success of the migration process that have been reconfirmed are:

- "just in time" training and appropriate training [4] [5] [8] [9] [10] [11]
- a complete object oriented process that is used for all stages of a project [4] [5] [8] [9] [10]
- time needs to be built into the project schedule to accommodate learning object technology [4] [5] [11]
- project risk needs to be assessed to see if it can accommodate the extra risk of adopting object technology [5] [9] [10] [11]
- management support for the adoption of object technology [4] [8] [9] [10] [11]

There are two additional observations that have been made during this transition process. These observations seem fairly intuitive but are not considered explicitly in other works in this field. Team motivation seems to be a critical factor that contributes to the success of the migration process. Another observation, which is not clearly considered in other works, is that some factors contribute more to the success of migration than other factors.

Team motivation seems to have been a critical factor for this team. Despite numerous difficulties, the team maintains a positive attitude towards the project and the migration process. Given the current state of the project it seems likely that it will be delivered late. However, the project manager believes that it is likely to be completed and to meet the project's specifications. During the project the team has shown that they are applying object technology and that they are becoming more sophisticated in their application of object technology. This indicates that the team will have successfully migrated to object technology by the end of the project, even if the project itself is not a complete success. This will be despite the fact that the migration plan failed to follow many of the published guidelines.

"Just in time" training is considered the best training approach to enhance individual's retention of the material [5]. The C++ course was presented when the team started detailed design and needed to be aware of implementation issues. The team members commented that the course was beneficial and timely. One team member who had commercial C++ experience commented that he learnt a lot from the course, both things he did not know about C++ and things that he had forgotten about C++.

Related to "just in time" training is that introductory training should be provided at the start of the transition process. Many of the problems that the team experienced in the analysis of the system are directly contributable to the fact no one on the team was very familiar with object technology and no training was provided at the start of the project.

The other problem that contributed to the poor initial analysis of the system was that the detailed development process was not established until the project had been running for over two months. The development process needs to be established before the team starts development. This requires either an object technology "guru" within the company to design the process, or for the company to bring in a consultant to work with the team leaders to develop an appropriate process. During the transition process it is expected that the process would be modified, as this team has done with their process. However, an initial process needs to be in place to guide the team at the start of their first object oriented project. As that is when they need the most guidance.

This project is four months behind schedule. A major contributor to the lateness of the project is that the migration process was not well planned. If training had been provided, and if a detailed development process had been established, before the start of the project it is likely that much of the analysis rework would not have needed to be done. It is likely that the requirements would still have needed to be clarified, but the analysis should have proceeded in a more iterative fashion. Scheduling for a pilot object oriented project needs to include time for the team to become familiar with the technology [4] [5].

Migrating to object technology adds risk to the first project to which it is applied. The risks for a project need to be assessed to determine if the project can accommodate the additional risk of being a pilot object technology project [5]. The pilot project in this report has several risks. Each of these risks has to be dealt with during the project development. The team members commented that they would be able to concentrate more on object technology if they did not have to deal with the other risks in the project. Another issue is that a high risk project puts the development team under additional pressure that is likely to reduce their overall effectiveness.

The team discovered severe problems in the software requirements specification for the system. This was despite the fact that the document and its lead up documents were reviewed by at least three team members and by the client. Part of the reason that this document had so many flaws was that the reviews were not conducted with a clear understanding of the development process. The course presenter quickly discovered some of the flaws in the document when trying to use the document in the analysis and design workshop. Having an expert review documents and designs can resolve a number of future difficulties.

Conclusions and further work

This research has been conducted as part of the initial stage of a project to develop a process framework to guide organisations as they adopt object technology. More work needs to be done to determine which factors contribute the most to the success of the migration process. This may lead to the discovery that different factors are more important for some types of teams and organisations. The observation that team motivation contributes to the success of the migration process is not surprising, but does need to be confirmed across several teams and organisations. Measures need to be established to determine the success of a particular migration project. This would also allow different projects to be compared against each other to consider their relative success. Related to this project a tool has been developed to collect design metrics from C++ source code. This tool will be used to collect data on the design of this project. This data will be used to attempt to determine the quality of the project's design. It is hoped that this will provide a quantifiable measure of the success of the team's migration to object technology. Finally, more work needs to be done to confirm, or disprove, that CASE tools are essential for the success of an initial object technology project [4].

74

Works cited

1. Graham, Ian, Brian Henderson-Sellers, and Houmann Younessi. *OPEN Process Specification*. Addison Wesley, 1997.
2. Jacobson, Ivar, Grady Booch and James Rumbaugh. *The Unified Software Development Process*. Addison Wesley, 1999 (to be published).
3. Coplien, James. *Advanced C++ – Programming Styles and Idioms*. Addison Wesley, 1992.
4. Fayad, Mohamed, Wei-Tek Tsai and Milton Fulghum. "Transition to Object-Oriented Software Development." *Communications of the ACM*. ACM, NY: February, 1996. Vol. 39, No. 2, pp 108 – 121.
5. Parkhill, Dave. "Object-Oriented Technology Transfer: Techniques and Guidelines for a Smooth Transition." *Object Magazine*. SIGS Publications: May/June, 1992. Vol. 2, No. 1, pp 57 – 59.
6. Jacobson, Ivar, Magnus Christerson, Patrik Jonsson and Gunnar Övergaard. *Object-Oriented Software Engineering: A Use Case Driven Approach*. Addison Wesley, 1992.
7. Fichman, Robert and Chris Kemerer. "Object Technology and Reuse: Lessons from Early Adopters." *Computer*. IEEE Computer Society, CA: October, 1997. Vol. 30, No. 10, pp 47 – 59.
8. Graham, Ian. *Migrating to Object Technology*. Addison Wesley, 1995.
9. Goldberg, Adele and Kenneth Rubin. *Succeeding with Objects: Decision Frameworks for Project Management*. Addison Wesley, 1995.
10. Meyer, Bertrand. *Object Success*. Prentice Hall, 1995.
11. Booch, Grady. *Object Solutions: Managing the Object-Oriented Project*. Addison Wesley, 1996.

Objects and Constraints

James Noble
Microsoft Research Institute
Macquarie University
Sydney, Australia
kjx@mri.mq.edu.au

Abstract

An object oriented program is a set of communicating encapsulated objects, while a constraint program is a set of variables linked by constraints. This difference in underlying models makes it difficult to combine objects and constraints in the same program. Message constraints are constraints that access objects by message sending and treat objects as abstractions. Message constraints can be attached directly to existing objects in object oriented programs without modifying those objects, seamlessly providing the benefits of constraint programming within object oriented programming languages.

1: Introduction

Object oriented programming and constraint programming have a shared origin and history. As early as 1963, Ivan Sutherland's Sketchpad [33] used both objects (sketches were made up of graphical objects) and constraints (graphical objects were linked by constraints). Both programming models also have application areas in common — interactive graphics (as in Sketchpad), financial modelling, and typesetting, to mention just three.

Object orientation and constraint programming view computation in quite different ways, in spite of their shared past. An object oriented program is a set of communicating objects [9, 29]. An object contains both data (variables) and procedures (methods). An object is *encapsulated* — an object's methods can only be accessed by sending messages to the object which contains them, and its variables accessed only from within its methods. An object is *abstract* — it is defined by its externally visible behaviour rather than its implementation, and can be thought of as modelling an entity from the program's problem domain. Every object has a unique *identity* by which two otherwise identical objects can be distinguished. In an object oriented program, computation consists of objects exchanging messages — when an object receives a message it can either invoke a method (thus sending further messages to itself or to other objects) or set or access one of its variables.

In contrast, a constraint program is essentially a set of *variables* linked by *constraints* [16]. A constraint is a declarative relationship between two or more variables — for example, two variables may be constrained to be equal, or a variable may be constrained to be the sum of two other variables. A constraint is *solved* (or satisfied) if the relationship between variables it describes actually holds in the system. Computation in constraint systems is seen as solving a set of constraints. In imperative constraint systems, external events or program actions change the values of variables while a constraint solving engine simultaneously changes other variables to ensure that the constraints are satisfied.

In this paper, we describe *Message Constraints*, a novel approach to integrating constraints and object oriented programming. Message constraints are attached directly to objects, and access those objects via message passing, and so they maintain object orientation's benefits of abstraction and encapsulation. Message constraints describe relationships between objects which can be maintained automatically, and so they also provide the major benefit of constraint programming. Our initial implementation of message constraints maintains constraints using naïve one-way dataflow propagation, however, message constraints can also be used to link objects to more powerful constraint solvers.

This paper begins by describing the relationships between objects, abstractions, and constraints, and then introduces message constraints. We then define message constraint formulas and describe their operation. Next, we demonstrate the utility of message constraints by discussing several applications including assertion checking and program visualisation, and describe how message constraints can provide access to a general purpose constraint solver. We conclude with a review of related work, a summary of this work, and our plans for the future.

2: Objects, Abstractions, and Constraints

Several programming languages have integrated constraint programming and object oriented programming, including ThingLab [2], Kaleidoscope [19], Amulet [26], and Garnet [25]. Constraints have also been made available via libraries or frameworks in traditional OO systems (such as the QOCA library for C++ [10] and the OTI/Solver library for Smalltalk [4]. Although they differ in detail, the architectures of these systems are fundamentally very similar — they integrate objects and constraints by unifying constraint variables and object variables. That is, variables inside objects are linked by constraints — for this reason, we call this approach the constrained-object-variable approach (COV). Depending upon the implementation style, constraints and the variables they can constrain may be implemented directly in a programming language, or themselves represented as objects which the programmer can incorporate into their programs.

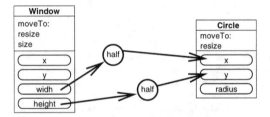

Figure 1. Constrained Objects Variables

Figure 1 sketches the general arrangement of the COV scheme. Constraints link the width and height slots of a Window object and the x and y slots of a Circle object. The constraints keep the circle centred in the window — when a new value is assigned to one of the window's slots, then constraint ensures the corresponding circle's slot set to half of the assigned value. When the circle is consequently redrawn, it will be centred in the window.

Within COV systems, the merging objects and constraints via variables is generally quite effective, and has been well tested in practice, however, the COV approach has several deficiencies. First, constraining an object's variables does not treat the object as an abstraction in the same way as object orientation. In standard object oriented programming an object's messages provide the interface to that abstraction, whereas in the COV approach, an object's constrained variables provide the interface to the object.

Second, attaching constraints to objects' variables breaks encapsulation, because the constrained variables are accessible from outside the object. In a traditional object oriented model, objects can only be changed by messages sent via their interface, while in the COV model objects can also be changed indirectly via constraints.

Third, COV constraints don't merge well with the imperative message sending typical of object oriented programming style. Because objects have mutable variables and identity, they have state, and messages are often sent to objects to invoke operations which change their state — for example to add or remove elements from a collection. These operations have a much larger granularity than the assigning of new values to variables which typifies constraint programming. In particular, if an operation needs to change a number of different variables while it is executing, the object containing those variables can be in inconsistent states during the execution of the operation [22]. A constraint system which accesses the objects' variables during a complex operation may well retrieve inconsistent values for those variables.

Finally, precisely because they need access to object's variables, COV constraints cannot be easily attached to pre-existing objects in traditional object oriented languages. Most COV systems either require that programming language variables are replaced by special *constrained variable* objects [7, 10] , or programs must be written in specialised programming languages [26, 24].

We have developed *Message Constraints* to integrate object oriented programming and constraint programming, while avoiding the problems of the COV approach. Figure 2 illustrates the basic message constraints scheme. Constraints are attached to whole objects, rather than object's variables. When an object changes, the constraints which depend upon those objects are executed. As a result of solving the constraints, other objects may be changed, but these objects are changed by message sending, rather than by changing their variables directly. For example, when the Window object in Figure 2 is resized, the moveTo message constraint will send the Circle object a moveTo message to ensure that the circle remains centred in the window.

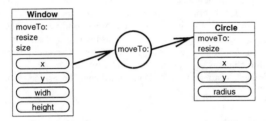

Figure 2. Message Constraints

Message constraints differ from COV constraints in several important ways. First, message constraints treat objects as abstractions — constraints are attached directly to objects, and communicate with objects via those objects' interfaces, rather than via variables contained within objects. Message constraints thus support the typical object oriented style of programming by sending messages to abstract objects — this is why we call them "message constraints".

Second, message constraints respect encapsulation, since they can be used without exposing objects' implementations. Rather, objects are accessed and changed only via messages that pass through objects' interfaces.

Third, being based on message sending, message constraints treat operations in the same way as object oriented programming. Message constraints integrate well with the imperative state based programming style typically used in object oriented programs — when an object changes (as the result of a message), any constraints attached to that object are examined and other objects changed as necessary as the constraints are executed. Inconsistent states are never visible outside an object, since, to an observer external observer, an object state is updated instantaneously by each message send.

Finally, because they treat objects as abstractions, message constraints can be attached to pre-existing objects (such as those provided by language libraries) without the objects' implementations having to be changed, although the programmer may need to provide some hints about the objects' properties to achieve best performance. Message constraints require no changes to a language's compiler or runtime system, so they can be incorporated into standard object systems with little effort. Being based on standard object systems, message constraints should impose no overhead if they are not used.

3: Message Constraints

A message constraint is an expression which establishes and maintains a long-term relationship between the objects in a program. A normal expression describes a short lived pattern of computation — an expression describes a series of messages to be sent to objects, and when the expression is executed, its constituent messages are sent. In contrast, a message constraint expression describes a long lived relationship, because, once the constraint has been executed, whenever particular objects involved in a constraint change, the constraint expression is automatically reevaluated.

This section begins by describing message constraint expressions (or *formulas*), then describes the stages in message constraint execution — gathering a constraint's dependencies, detecting abstract changes in objects, and constraint reevaluation.

3.1: Formulas

Syntactically, a message constraint *formula* is specialised kind of an expression in an object oriented programming language, that is, a description of one or more messages to send to one or more objects. One or more of the message send subexpressions in a message constraint formula are marked as *constraint message sends*. Constraint message sends distinguish message constraint formulas from standard expressions — when a formula is executed, the formula gathers dependency information about the objects which receive the constraint message sends it contains, as explained in the next subsection.

For example, the message constraint illustrated in Figure 2 could be written as the formula[1]:

circle moveTo: window **centre**

This formula looks very similar to a message expression which, when executed, would send centre to the window object, then pass the result as an argument to the moveTo: message sent to circle. In this formula, the message send of **centre** to the window is a constraint message send (in this paper, we write constraint sends in boldface). Because **centre** is a constraint message send, once the formula has been executed, it will be reevaluated whenever the window object changes.

A formula can involve more than one message send to more than one object. For example, the following formula ensures that a list of figure objects are always displayed in a window, by first clearing the window then drawing each figure in turn.

window clear.
listOfFigures **do:** [|:eachFigure| eachFigure **draw**]

This formula uses two constraint message sends. The **do:** message which iterates through the list is a constraint message send, so that whenever the list changes — if a new figure is added to the list, or an existing figure deleted — the formula will be reevaluated and the figures redrawn. The **draw** message sent to each figure is also a constraint message send, to ensure that whenever any individual figure in the list changes — for example, if a figure changes its position or size — the formula will also be reevaluated, again redrawing all the figures.

These examples illustrate several important points about message constraint formulas. First, the evaluation of one constraint can trigger the evaluation of another. For example, if the circle object referred to in the first constraint is a member of the listOfFigures in the second constraint, then when the first constraint moves the circle figure, the second constraint will ensure the circle is redrawn. Second, constraint message sends can depend upon other constraint message sends, that is, message constraints incorporate indirect constraints [37]. In the figure drawing example above, the actual objects to which the **draw** message is sent depends on the **do:** message which iterates through the list of figures. If the list is empty, the **draw** message will never be sent. Third, apart from the use of constraint message sends, formulas are no different from other expressions

---

[1]Since our prototype implementation of message constraints is written in Self [35], we use Self syntax to present the examples in this paper.

in object oriented programming languages. In particular, formulas can send messages to objects (which may cause side effects), perform I/O, and use loops or other control structures.

Message constraint formulas have some similarity to constraint formulas in imperative COV systems, and Amulet [26] and Garnet [25] in particular. Both of these systems express formulas as programming language expressions with some distinguished constraint subexpressions, however, COV formulas can depend only upon object's variables, whereas message constraints can depend upon any message send. Like the constraints in these systems, message constraints are one-way constraints — in the example above, changing the window reevaluates the constraint to update the circle, but changing the circle does not reevaluate the constraint to update the window. This is in contrast to the more powerful constraint systems, such as QOCA [10] or ThingLab [2, 20], which support two-way constraints where all variables (or objects) in a constraint may be used for both input and output.

3.2: Gathering Constraints' Dependencies

Once a message constraint has been created, it can be evaluated. Like a normal expression, when a formula is evaluated it will send messages to objects, so it may change those objects or produce output. More importantly, it must gather dependency information so that it can be reevaluated whenever the objects which received constraint message sends change. We use a simple version of the algorithm used in Amulet to gather this information dynamically [21].

In our prototype implementation, at runtime each instance of a constraint formula is enclosed in a constraint object. Whenever a constraint message send in a formula is executed, the formula's enclosing constraint object records the object to which the constraint message was sent. We call the recorded objects the constraint's *dependencies*.

Once a constraint's dependencies have been recorded, they are monitored, so that whenever a constraint's dependency object changes, the constraint object can reevaluate its formula. When a formula is reevaluated, the messages it contains (including its constraint messages) will be resent, changing objects to enforce the constraint. The constraint object constructs a new dependency list and adjusts the monitoring so that only the objects on the new dependency list are monitored.

For example, Figure 3 shows the listOfFigures containing three figure objects (a Circle, a Square, and a Rectangle). When the figure drawing formula is executed, the first constraint message send, **do:**, is sent to the list object, so the formula's associated constraint records a dependency on the list object. The list's do: method is then executed, causing the iterator block to be invoked for each of the figures contained in the list. Inside the block, the **draw** constraint message is sent to each of the figure objects, so the figures are also recorded in the constraint's dependencies.

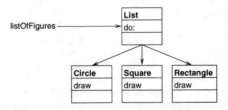

Figure 3. Constraint listOfFigures **do:** [| :eachFigure | eachFigure **draw**]

If one of the figures (say the circle) was removed from the list, the change to the list object would be detected and the constraint formula reevaluated. The constraint object would again record dependencies on objects which receive constraint message sends, so dependencies would be recorded for the list object and the two remaining figures. Since the constraint no longer depends upon the circle, the circle object is not included in the new dependency list, and it would no longer need to be monitored for this constraint.

3.3: Detecting Changes to Objects

Message constraints have to be reevaluated whenever their dependent objects change. An implementation of message constraints must therefore have some way to detect when objects change. COV constraint systems link constraints to variables, and it is quite easy to determine whenever a variable changes. Message constraints treat objects as abstractions, so an object should be considered to have changed when the abstraction represented by that object has changed. A change to an object cannot simply be equated with a change in the object's variables, rather, an object is considered to have changed whenever a message sent to the object would return a different value.

We have adopted our change detection scheme for aggregate objects to support message constraints [27]. This scheme detects changes in objects by monitoring the operations that objects execute, that is, by detecting the messages that objects receive. When an object completes executing any messages which can change it (*mutator messages*) the object is assumed to have changed, and any constraints which depend upon that object must be reevaluated. Messages which simply retrieve information from the object (*accessor messages*) and do not change the object to which they are sent, do not trigger constraint reevaluation, but delay any pending reevaluation until they have finished executing. Of course, in order for this scheme to work, the messages an object understands must be categorised as accessor messages or mutator messages.

The change detection scheme manages a number of subtleties related to scheduling constraint execution in the presence of reentrant and recursive programs. For example, an object is only considered to have changed when it has finished executing a complete mutator operation — i.e., a mutator operation executed in response to a message sent from outside the object. Messages sent internally within objects as part of external operations can never trigger constraint reevaluations, so do not need to be monitored. Similarly, an object is unlikely to be able to process an operation correctly (such as handling a message sent from a constraint) while simultaneously processing another operation. The change detection scheme therefore delays signalling changes for an object until that object is *quiescent* (not executing any operation) and so is capable of accepting a message to invoke a new operation.

This change detection scheme is also effective in the presence of inter-object aliasing [28]. If one of the components of an aggregate object can be accessed directly (that is, if the component object is *aliased*) the aggregate object can be changed even though no message was sent to its interface. Our change detection scheme manages aliases by allowing the programmer to associate a *shadow function* with each object. The shadow function returns any other objects upon which the original objects depends and which are accessible from outside the object's interface — that is, external objects which, if changed, will indirectly change the original object. When monitoring an object which supplies a shadow function, the monitoring is expanded to include the objects returned by the shadow function.

3.4: Constraint Reevaluation

Reevaluation is the simplest stage in the execution of message constraints. When a change is detected in an object depended upon by a constraint, and all the constraint's dependent objects are quiescent, the constraint is reevaluated by executing the constraint formula. The entire formula is reevaluated, even if only one dependency object (related to one of many constraint message sends) has changed. This evaluation can send messages (either normal message to objects or constraint messages) to change objects, to produce output, and to reestablish the relationship being maintained by the constraint — in the examples above, to re-centre a circle within a window, or to re-display a list of figures. As the formula is reevaluated, its dependencies are gathered, and then the object monitoring is updated, as described in the previous two subsections.

4: Applications

In this section, we describe some larger examples of message constraints — in particular, checking assertions about programs, visualising programs, building temporal constraints, and integrating a multi-way constraint solver with message constraints.

4.1: Assertion Checking

We have used message constraints to check invariants about the consistency of program's data structures and object structures, similarly to (but more powerfully than) the invariant checking supported by the Eiffel language [23]. For example, the following constraint checks the consistency of a hash table (Self's dictionary object) stored as two parallel arrays — in particular, the constraint checks whether the two arrays keys and values have the same size.

(aDictionary **keys size** = aDictionary **values size**)
iffalse: [error: 'Assertion Violation']].

This formula depends upon the two arrays **keys** and **values**. If either of the arrays change, the constraint is executed, whereupon the constraint checks whether the two arrays have the same size, and raises an error if they do not.

Because invariants only apply to an object that is not processing an operation [22] these formulas rely on message constraints' execution being delayed until their dependency objects are quiescent. For example, if many new elements are added to a Self dictionary, the hash table size must be expanded, so the two arrays will be updated. The arrays will be updated in series, so during the update the arrays will momentarily be of different sizes. Message constraints do not (and should not) detect this inconsistency, because it only exists during an update operation. Message constraints correctly detect the inconsistency if it remains once the update operation is complete.

Message constraints can also be used to monitor the consistency of more complex object structures — for example, to check data integrity rules found in object model designs and databases. For example, a stock portfolio system could include a constraint that the number of portfolios managed by agents must equal the number of portfolios held by clients.

$$\sum_{n=1}^{N_{agents}} |portfolios(agent_n)| = \sum_{n=1}^{N_{clients}} |portfolios(client_n)|$$

This integrity rule can be translated into the following message constraint involving portfolios, agents, and clients. This formula uses two loops which calculate the total number of portfolios held by all agents and clients respectively. The totals are compared when they have been computed and an exception raised if they differ.

| agentPortfolios ← 0. clientPortfolios ← 0. |
agents **do:** [|:eachAgent|
    agentPortfolios: agentPortfolios + eachAgent **portfolios size**].
clients **do:** [|:eachClient|
    clientPortfolios: clientPortfolios + eachClient **portfolios size**].
(agentPortfolios = clientPortfolios)
iffalse: [error: 'Assertion violation'].

This rule demonstrates the generality of message constraints. Unlike the dictionary constraint, this formula could not easily be expressed as an invariant in Eiffel, because it involves an invariant relationship across many objects, each of which may change independently. This formula relies on dynamic collection of dependencies (each loop iteration adds a new dependency on an agent or a client) and indirection (constraint messages are sent to the results of other constraint messages, for example, the size constraint message is sent to the result of sending portfolios to eachAgent). Most obviously, the constraint is expressed purely in terms of the interfaces of the objects involved — agents, clients, and portfolios presumably all have their own internal implementation structure.

A message constraint can record historical information that can be the subject of later constraints or queries. For example, one object may be constrained to equal the previous value of another object, or the result of a message send may be constrained to be monotonically increasing. The formula below creates a constraint which raises an exception if a new password entered in a dialog box is the same as any of the five previous passwords.

```
| buffer ← ringBuffer copySize: 5.
password ← ' ' |
```

```
password: changePasswordDialog passwordEntered.
buffer includes: password
    ifTrue: [changePasswordDialog error: 'Password used recently']
    False: [buffer add: password].
```

This formula uses two variables — buffer which stores the last five passwords, and password which caches the current password. When the change password dialog box changes, the constraint checks to see if the password entered is stored in the list of the last five attempts.

4.2: Program Visualisation

We have used message constraints to construct simple visualisations of programs. For example, Figure 4 shows simple display of a Quicksort algorithm, modelled after the dots view produced by Balsa [6]. This view plots array element values against their position in the array. About one third of the array has been sorted in the figure, and Quicksort's characteristic rectangular partitions are visible in the unsorted section. This view was produced by the following constraint formula:

```
| x. dotSize ← 3 |
window clear.
x: leftMargin.
array do: [ |:v |
    window drawDot: x @ (v * dotSize).
    x: x + dotSize. ].
```

The formula constrains the array (via the **do:** message) so that when the array is changed, the view is redrawn. Obviously, this formula is quite inefficient in practice, as it causes the whole view to be redrawn whenever even a single array element changes. The initial experiments we have carried out, however, indicate that the overhead of the constraint maintenance (rather than the graphics) is acceptable.

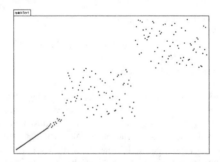

Figure 4. Quicksort

4.3: Temporal Constraints

Temporal constraints, introduced in Animus [3], depend upon time and have to be reevaluated periodically. For example, a graphical object can be animated by constraining it's position or appearance to be a function of the current time. Temporal constraints have to be reevaluated every time interval. Message constraints seamlessly incorporate temporal constraints, by treating temporal constraints as message constraints which depend upon time varying objects. We identify these time varying objects to the system, giving a time interval when these objects change, essentially assuming that an unnamed mutator message is periodically executed by the object. Since the object changes periodically, any constraints depending on the object will be automatically reevaluated periodically.

For example, Self provides a time object (called time) which responds to the message **current** with the current time. We have annotated this object with a hint that it is time-dependent with a period of once second. A constraint then can be attached to the time object to display it in a text view, and this constraint will be automatically reevaluated every second, resulting in the simple digital clock shown in Figure 5. No other programming is required in the window, the constraint, or the system-provided time object.

window drawString: (time **current** timeString)

Figure 5. Digital Clock

4.4: Integration with a Multiway Constraint Solver

A network of message constraints is solved by naïve one-way dataflow propagation. When one constraint is executed, it may change other objects in the program, thus triggering more constraints which may change more objects. While dataflow is easy to implement, and quite efficient for systems with a small number of mostly unrelated constraints, it is not suitable for larger systems of constraints. In particular, naïve dataflow can perform more computation than is necessary if objects are changed by many constraints, and can fail to satisfy all constraints or fail to terminate in the presence of cyclic constraints [31].

To address these problems, we have investigated using more powerful constraint solving algorithms with message constraints. Constraint algorithms solve networks consisting of constraints and constrained variables [8, 13, 10], and message constraints can be used to connect these variables directly to objects. Note that there is an important difference between using message constraints with constrained variables, and the COV approach discussed in Section 2 above which uses constrained variables alone. In the COV approach, the objects to be constrained must use constrained variables directly, which will require the objects to be modified, since most programs are not written to use constrained variables. If message constraints are used to link constrained variables to objects via those objects' interfaces, the objects are treated as abstractions and do not need to be modified. In effect, the message constraints treat the constraint solver as another object in the program.

We have experimented with attaching the DeltaBlue incremental constraint solver [8] to objects via message constraints. Figure 6 illustrates an interface to a simple temperature converter (modelled after ThingLab [20]) built using DeltaBlue.

DeltaBlue handles the conversion between Fahrenheit and Celsius temperatures, while message constraints link DeltaBlue's constrained variables to the graphical thermometers. Since DeltaBlue supports multi-directional constraints, the mercury in either thermometer can be dragged using the mouse, and the other thermometer's value will be updated appropriately. Because they are linked by message constraints, the thermometer objects do not have to be programmed to use DeltaBlue's constrained variables.

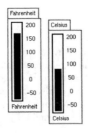

Figure 6. Fahrenheit-Celsius Converter

Although less intrusive than using constrained variables, linking constraint solvers to objects using message constraints still has some problems. First, the solver's variables and the program's objects usually need to be linked by two-way connections, while message constraints provide only one-way connections. A two-way connection can be modelled using two one-way constraints, but since the one-way constraints will form a cycle, they need to be programmed so that the naïve dataflow propagation will terminate — in practice, this has not been a problem. Second, most constraint solvers operate under a closed world assumption — the solver assumes it knows all the relationships between the constrained variables. When message constraints are used to link the solver's variables to objects in a program, two apparently independent constrained variables may in fact be related — they may belong to the same object, to objects which are related in the program, or they may be related by other message constraints, or even another external constraint solver. We have used DeltaBlue to maintain specialised constraints in small parts of the program, so this problem has not arisen in practice.

5: Related Work

Code annotation and data annotation are the most common approaches for connecting object oriented programs to constraint systems or other external systems such as user interfaces or databases. Code annotation requires the programmer to insert calls to *update event* routines to signal when an object has changed. Code annotation first came to prominence in Smalltalk-80's Model-View-Controller (MVC) framework [9, 15], but has since been used widely. Data annotation — the COV approach — involves modifying the program to use constrained variables instead of the variables provided by the programming language. Constrained variables have been used to add constraint solvers to several existing systems, including the Cooldraw [7] and Unidraw graphical editors [10].

ThingLab [2, 20] was the first system to combine constraints and a conventional object oriented programming language. Although ThingLab was built in Smalltalk, ThingLab objects differ substantially from standard Smalltalk objects, for example ThingLab objects use multiple inheritance, and refer to their subparts by named paths rather than object references. As a result, ThingLab could not attach constraints to standard Smalltalk objects. ThingLab II [20] reimplemented ThingLab based on the DeltaBlue hierarchical incremental constraint solver [8] but the integration mechanism for constraints and objects remained based on COV, although using object references to constrained variables rather than named paths.

New object oriented languages have been designed to link objects and constraints. Garnet [25], Amulet [26], Rendezvous [11], and Snart [24] are based on specialised object systems where constraints can be attached directly to object's variables. R++ [17] uses a preprocessor to provide constrained variables in C++. Our message constraints are similar to Amulet's constraints in some respects — for example, we have adopted a simplified version of Amulet's dynamic algorithm for calculating a formula's dependencies [21], and as in Amulet, message constraints' formulas may have side effects including creating and deleting other objects. Amulet's constraints are based on accessing values stored in objects' slots, however, whereas message constraints are based on sending messages via objects' abstract interfaces.

The constraint imperative programming (CIP) family of languages, which includes Kaleidoscope [18] and Siri [12], tightly integrates objects and constraints. Kaleidoscope distinguishes between methods which can cause side effects and *constraint constructors* which are used to build up composite constraints from the primitive constraints supplied by the language, but which may not cause side effects. Unlike message constraints, these composite constraints are translated by *constraint splitting* into more primitive constraints which are eventually attached to variables. In contrast, our message constraints are never split and are attached directly to objects.

The Equate constraint solver [38] supports constraints over objects expressed in terms of their interfaces. Equate is both more powerful and more limited than message constraints. Equate is more powerful because it uses a backtracking rule based planner to solve constraints rather than naïve dataflow. It is more limited because the programmer must write rules that describe how the operations provided by objects can be used to solve constraints, and must modify the program to explicitly call Equate to solve a set of constraints, to explicitly execute that solution, and to allow the solver to backtrack.

The Chiron UIMS [34] connects views to objects by automatically wrapping objects and then monitoring their mutator messages. Smalltalk encapsulators or message wrappers can perform the same function [30, 5]. Compared to message constraints, these systems lack a general model of constraints — they simply notify a set of dependent objects when a subject object has changed. These systems do not provide indirect or temporal constraints, nor do they deal with scheduling updates or aliasing. Mediators [32] or Observers [9] provide even less support, as both dependencies and change notifications must be programmed explicitly.

Some features of object oriented languages are also related to message constraints. The concurrent object oriented language Procol [36] includes constraint propagators which notify an object whenever another object receives a nominated message. Composition filters [1] are a more general mechanism which intercept all the messages an object sends and receives and have been used to implement constraints between objects. Even more generally, reflexive languages can redefine the semantics of message sends and receipts, and can also be used to detect message sends [14]. Eiffel includes assertions which define the permissible states of objects [22]. Eiffel assertions are checked automatically whenever a thread of control enters an object, but they cannot interact with the program other than to throw exceptions if they are violated. Unlike message constraints, Eiffel assertions are written in a very restricted subset of the language and are susceptible to aliasing problems [23].

6: Future Work

Several aspects of this work merit further attention. While the performance of the current prototype is just sufficient to support the examples described in this paper, a more efficient implementation would allow us to experiment with larger-scale examples. Our current implementation (written in the obsolete version 2.3.0 of Self) essentially interprets messages to trigger constraint evaluation. For example, the prototype intercepts every message an object receives, and then filters these messages dynamically. We plan to develop a more efficient implementation which will compile this information, so that only top level messages will be intercepted (i.e. message sends where a thread of control was finally leaving an object) by creating two entry points for every message. One entry point would be used by messages sent from outside the object (which may cause constraints to be reevaluated) and the second entry point used by messages sent within the object (which cannot trigger constraint evaluation).

Message constraints currently treat objects as monoliths — either an object has changed, or it has not. For example, a constraint accessing a single element of a large array will be reevaluated whenever any of the array's elements are reassigned. We plan to extend message constraints to support constraints on parts of objects by adopting the *aspects* used by Smalltalk's MVC framework [9]. An aspect is a logical partition of an object's interface. We will extend message annotations so that an aspect can be associated with each message, and then a mutator will only invalidate those constraints depending upon accessors which are associated with the mutator's aspect.

Message constraints only record dependencies on the receivers of constraint message sends; they do not record dependencies on the arguments of constraint message sends. This reflects the privileged position of message receivers in most forms of object oriented programming, although it does introduce an arbitrary asymmetry — a constraint will be evaluated if the receiver of a constraint message send changes, but not if an argument to a constraint send changes. Where necessary, dependencies can be established on arguments explicitly, by a constraint message send to the argument object, such as the identity message **yourself**, and this has been sufficient for every case with which we've experimented.

Perhaps more important is that message constraints only record dependencies for constraint messages sends: normal sends in formulas do not establish dependencies. The system could record dependencies for all message sends in formulas, effectively treating every send as a constraint message send. By requiring programmers to nominate constraint message sends, we follow Garnet [25] and Amulet [26], which require the programmer to nominate those variable accesses which establish dependencies. Recording only those dependencies programmers nominate does increase the efficiency of the system, but is certainly harder to use than most other constraint systems which treat all expressions in constraints uniformly.

Although message constraints allow existing objects to be used without modification, the change detection scheme [27] requires programmers to provide information about the properties of objects in the program. Methods must be categorised as accessors or mutators, shadow functions must be written for objects subject to aliasing, and temporal objects must be identified. We have not found supplying this information to be a large burden, however, programming languages should be able to provide much of this information directly. For example, Eiffel and C++ programmers distinguish accessor and mutator messages as a matter of course. Temporal and immutable objects could be similarly identified via annotations to their interfaces. Shadow functions require more support, but are no more complicated than the hash functions required ubiquitously by many languages [27].

7: Conclusion

Constraint programming and object oriented programming are two complementary models of programming. Message constraints integrate these two models, while combining their respective strengths. In particular, message constraints maintain the abstraction and encapsulation of object orientation, because the constraints communicate with objects via message sends rather than variables. Objects from existing applications or libraries do not need to be modified to be used with message constraints, because message constraints treat objects as abstractions.

Acknowledgements

We would like to thank John Potter and Bjorn Freeman-Benson, who commented on various drafts, the Self group at Sun Microsystems for their assistance with Self, and John Maloney for the implementation of DeltaBlue in Self. This work was supported by Microsoft Australia Pty Ltd.

References

[1] Mehmet Aksit, Ken Wakita, Jan Bosch, Lodewijk Bergmans, and Akinori Yonezawa. Abstracting object interactions using composition filters. In *Proceedings of the ECOOP '93 Workshop on Object-Based Distributed Programming*, LNCS 791, 1994.

[2] Alan Borning. The programming language aspects of ThingLab, a constraint-oriented simulation laboratory. *ACM Transactions on Programming Languages and Systems*, 3(4), October 1981.

[3] Alan Borning and Robert Duisberg. Constraint based tools for building user interfaces. *ACM Transactions on Graphics*, 5(4), October 1986.

[4] Alan Borning and Bjorn N. Freeman-Benson. The OTI constraint solver: A constraint library for constructing interactive graphical user interfaces. In *Proceedings of the First International Conference on Principles and Practice of Constraint Programming*, 1995.

[5] John Brant, Brian Foote, Ralph E. Johnson, and Donald Roberts. Wrappers to the rescue. In *ECOOP Proceedings*, 1998.

[6] Marc H. Brown. *Algorithm Animation*. ACM Distinguished Dissertation. MIT Press, 1988.

[7] Bjorn N. Freeman-Benson. Converting an existing user interface to use constraints. In *Proc. ACM Symposium on User Interface Software and Technology (UIST)*, 1993.

[8] Bjorn N. Freeman-Benson, John Maloney, and Alan Borning. An incremental constraint solver. *Communications of the ACM*, 33(1), January 1990.

[9] Adele Goldberg and David Robson. *Smalltalk-80: The Language and its Implementation*. Addison-Wesley, 1983.

[10] Richard Helm, Tien Huynh, Kim Marriott, and John Vlissides. An object-oriented architecture for constraint-based graphical editing. In *Third Eurographics Workshop on Object-Oriented Graphics*, 1992.

[11] Ralph D. Hill, Tom Brinck, Steven L. Rohall, John F. Patterson, and Wayne Wilner. The Rendezvous architecture and language for constructing multiuser applications. *ACM Transactions on Computer-Human Interaction*, 1(2), 1994.

[12] Bruce Horn. Constraint patterns as a basis for object-oriented programming. In *OOPSLA Proceedings*, October 1992.

[13] Scott E. Hudson. Incremental attribute evaluation: a flexible algorithm for lazy update. *ACM Transactions on Programming Languages and Systems*, 13(3):315–341, July 1991.

[14] Gregor Kiczales, Jim des Rivières, and Daniel G. Bobrow. *The Art of the Metaobject Protocol*. MIT Press, 1991.

[15] Wilf Lalonde and John Pugh. *Inside Smalltalk*, volume 2. Prentice-Hall, 1991.

[16] W. Leler. *Constraint Programming Languages: Their Specification and Generation*. Addison-Wesley, 1988.

[17] Diane Litman, Anil Mishra, and Peter F. Patel-Schneider. Modelling dynamic collections of interdependent objects using path-based rules. In *OOPSLA Proceedings*, 1997.

[18] Gus Lopez, Bjorn Freeman-Benson, and Alan Borning. Implementing constraint imperative programming languages: the Kaleidoscope'93 virtual machine. In *OOPSLA Proceedings*, 1994.

[19] Gus Lopez, Bjorn Freeman-Benson, and Alan Borning. Kaleidoscope: A constraint imperative programming language. In *Constraint Programming*, 1994.

[20] John H. Maloney, Alan Borning, and Bjorn N. Freeman-Benson. Constraint technology for user-interface construction in ThingLab II. In *OOPSLA Proceedings*, 1989.

[21] Rich McDaniel and Brad A. Myers. Amulet's dynamic and flexible prototype-instance object and constraint system in C++. Technical Report CMU-HCII-95-104, Human Computer Interaction Institute, Carnegie Mellon University, 1995.

[22] Bertrand Meyer. *Object-oriented Software Construction*. Prentice Hall, 1988.

[23] Bertrand Meyer. *Eiffel: The Language*. Prentice Hall, 1992.

[24] Warwick B. Mugridge, John G. Hosking, and S. Blackmore. Objects and constraints: a constraint based approach to plan drawing. In *TOOLS Pacific*, 1994.

[25] B. A. Myers, D. A. Guise, R. B. Dannenberg, B. Vander Zanden, D. S. Kosbie, E. Pervin, A. Mickish, and P. Marchal. Garnet: Comprehensive support for graphical, highly interactive user interfaces. *IEEE Computer*, 23(11), 1990.

[26] Brad A. Myers, Rich McDaniel, Rob Miller, Alan Ferrency, Patrick Doane, Andrew Faulring, Ellen Borison, Andy Mickish, and Alex Klimovitski. The Amulet environment: New models for effective user interface software development. Technical Report CMU-HCII-96-104, Human Computer Interaction Institute, Carnegie Mellon University, 1996.

[27] James Noble and John Potter. Change detection for aggregate objects with aliasing. In *Australian Software Engineering Conference (ASWEC)*, 1997.

[28] James Noble, Jan Vitek, and John Potter. Flexible alias protection. In *ECOOP Proceedings*, 1998.

[29] Geoffrey A. Pascoe. Elements of Object-Oriented Programming. *BYTE*, pages 137–144, August 1986.

[30] Geoffrey A. Pascoe. Encapsulators: A new software paradigm in Smalltalk-80. In *OOPSLA Proceedings*, 1986.

[31] M. Sannella, J. Maloney, B. Freeman-Benson, and A. Borning. Multi-way versus one-way constraints in user interfaces: Experience with the deltablue algorithm. *Software - Practice And Experience*, 23(5), May 1993.

[32] Kevin J. Sullivan and David Notkin. Reconciling environment integration and software evolution. *ACM Transactions on Software Engineering and Methodology*, 1(3):229–269, July 1992.

[33] Ivan E. Sutherland. Sketchpad: A man-machine graphical communication system. In *Proceedings AFIPS Spring Joint Computer Conference*, volume 23, pages 329–346, Detroit, Michigan, May 1963.

[34] Richard N. Taylor and Gregory F. Johnson. Separations of concerns in the Chrion-1 user interface development and management system. In *INTERCHI Conference Proceedings*, 1993.

[35] David Ungar and Randall B. Smith. SELF: the Power of Simplicity. *Lisp And Symbolic Computation*, 4(3), June 1991.

[36] Jan Van Den Bos and Chris Laffra. PROCOL: a parallel object language with protocols. In *OOPSLA Proceedings*, 1989.

[37] Bradley T. Vander Zanden, Brad A. Myers, Dario A. Guise, and Pedro Szekely. The importance of pointer variables in constraint models. In *Proc. ACM Symposium on User Interface Software and Technology (UIST)*, November 1991.

[38] Michael R. Wilk. Equate: An object-oriented constraint solver. In *OOPSLA Proceedings*, 1991.

Guiding Object-Oriented Design

Anthony MacDonald   David Carrington
Software Verification Research Centre
Department of Computer Science and Electrical Engineering
The University of Queensland
Brisbane 4072, Australia

email: {anti, davec}@csee.uq.edu.au

Abstract

In this paper we show how software architectural styles can be used to guide object-oriented design. Design guidance is important as the initial phases of software design significantly impact software quality. We use two different architectural styles to guide the design process from a formal specification to a design. Software architectural styles assist by providing a different level of reuse than currently practised in software design. A style provides a framework for top-level structure and guides selection of components and interfaces. In this paper we show the impact of software architectural styles on software design.

1: Introduction

We believe the initial phases of software design [4, 23] have significant impact on software quality. When considering these early phases of software design, we have two specific areas of interest: formal methods and software architecture. Firstly, we are interested in the impact of formal methods on the design process, especially the use of formal specifications to guide design. Secondly, we wish to investigate the effect of explicitly considering software architecture and how this impacts both the design process and quality.

The object-oriented community has been keen in their uptake of design patterns [9] for a level of reuse above the code reuse available through libraries, frameworks etc. Shaw [25], relates software architecture to patterns and shows how they both are seeking Alexander's [2] goal, "the quality without a name" [7]. Software architecture, while seeking the same goals as patterns, offers a different granularity of reuse to the software designer. Gamma et al. [8] say design patterns define something less than the complete application and are at best, micro-architectures. Monroe and Garlan [20] claim that software architecture offers a different granularity of reuse in their recent paper. They are interested in "(a) the use of components, connectors, and configurations as the basic vocabulary of reusable assets, and (b) the exploitation of architectural style to aid in the classification, retrieval, and instantiation of those assets". This guiding of design by software architecture could be called conceptual reuse, as opposed to concrete reuse.

In this paper we show how software architectural styles [1] can be used to guide object-oriented design. Meyer [16] states "Object-oriented design is the method which leads to software architectures based on objects [that] every system or subsystem manipulates". Software architectural styles enable software designers to improve seamlessness and traceability in design. This is achieved without sacrificing a clear separation of concerns between phases of the software life cycle.

In this paper, software architectural styles are used to guide the design and eventual implementation of two systems from a non-object-oriented formal specification. A controller for the production cell, a case study in safety-critical systems, was formally specified[1] in the Z notation [26, 3]. From this formal specification, two separate design paths are taken, each guided by a different software architectural style. The first is based on a standard abstract data type approach and the second is based on an event system. The software architectural style not only assists in guiding the design process, but also guides the designer to the relevant sections of the formal specification and hence helps bridge the gap between phases in the software lifecycle. The software architectural style assists the transition from a specification to a design. We aim to show that using architectural styles can give both conceptual reuse and design guidance.

Section 2 introduces the concept of software architecture and two architectural styles. Section 3 gives an overview of the production cell and the formal specification. The designs generated using each architectural style are discussed in Section 4. The paper summarises how explicit consideration of software architecture can aid the software designer in Section 5 and closes with conclusions.

2: Software architecture

The term, software architecture [10, 22], describes the high-level organisation of computational elements and the interactions between these elements, or simply the top-level structure of a software system. By abstracting to the architectural level, we can view the system as a graph consisting of a collection of components and connectors. Components are the primary computational elements of the system, while connectors are the interactions between these components. These interactions may be simple procedure calls, message passing, remote procedure calls, event-broadcasts, etc.

An architectural style defines a family of systems in terms of the top-level structure. Common architectural styles include abstract data type (ADT), event, blackboard, and pipe and filter architectures [10].

An individual system can be documented using its architecture to aid understanding and improve maintenance. An architectural style not only supports this aspect of software engineering, but it can also be used as a design guide. A style enables the designer to build a system around a defined and understood structure, improving understanding in all phases of the software lifecycle.

Design is a broadly used word; in this paper we are focusing on architectural design: the stage of design where both the connectors and components within the final system are chosen and the top-level structure is decided. The properties of an architecture can be viewed from two perspectives: at the system level where system-wide attributes are considered and at the module[2] level where module-specific attributes are considered. Using architectural styles, architectural design can be described as the process of mapping a particular specification onto an architectural style. This generates an instance of the architecture (a design) which meets the requirements captured in the specification.

Two architectural styles are used throughout this paper: an ADT-based architecture and, an event-based architecture. Each architecture is introduced and discussed in the following sections.

2.1: An ADT-based architecture

An architectural style is ADT-based when the core components are ADT modules and the connectors are routine calls (function and procedure calls).

---

[1] An alternative specification using Object-Z [6, 24] was also developed [15].
[2] Module is used here as a logical unit and is not programming- language-specific. In an Eiffel [18] context, *class* could be substituted.

The defining attribute of an ADT-based architectural style is at the module level and is the presence of encapsulated data. This data can only be accessed by procedure or function calls. The encapsulation of data is based on the principle of information hiding [21], as the physical representation and implementation of the module is irrelevant to users of the module (this includes the designer of the system containing the ADT initially). By encapsulating the data, the module is responsible for the integrity of the contained data.

At the system level, an ADT module can be viewed as an object containing state and operations to transform and query the state. A system based on an ADT architecture generally requires centralised control and all routines are explicitly invoked.

Object-oriented designs are generally based on ADT architectures. Meyer's [16] alternative definition for object-oriented design is "Object-oriented design is the construction of software systems as structured collections of abstract data type implementations".

Concrete reuse is possible at the individual module level. This type of reuse is generally as part as a library, like EiffelBase [19], or as part of a framework [11, 5].

2.2: An event-based architecture

An architectural style is event-based when the core components are modules (no particular defining features) and the connectors are events. The defining attributes of an event-based architectural style are at the system level and result from events being the predominant connectors.

The system can be viewed as a collection of events and registered responses to those events (there may be, and often are, multiple responses to a single event). The event manager is treated as part of the supporting system and hence the event-based system appears to have a decentralised or distributed control mechanism. This method of routine invocation is implicit and is the primary method of invocation in event-based systems. Explicit invocation still occurs, but is a result of events rather than a source of control. A consequence of implicit invocation is that modules cannot make assumptions about order of invocation or the state of other modules.

A module in an event-based system can be viewed as a collection of reactive routines. A characteristic of these routines is they must be independent and atomic, i.e., they can't rely on system state and expected behaviour, and they must leave the system in a stable state.

Event-based systems can be reused in two ways. The underlying event system (event manager and events) may be reused with new responses and overall behaviour, as is achieved with the X Window System. An event system can also be reused as a whole with event-based systems lending themselves to easy extension for new environments or extended behaviour.

3: A case study: the production cell

The original production cell is in a metal processing plant in Karlsruhe, Germany. Forschungszentrum Informatik (FZI), Karlsruhe, used the production cell as the basis for a study of formal methods for critical software systems [12]. The first step of the study generated a requirements document [12, Chapter 2] which attempts to capture, in plain language, the specification of a software controller for the production cell. To simplify the case study, the system specified is a simulation of the production cell and the simulator (see Figure 1) runs cyclically.

The production cell simulation (the system) takes a metal blank as input. The metal blank is transported by a conveyer belt (the feed belt) to an elevating rotary table. The elevating rotary table rotates and rises vertically to present the metal blank for the robot to pick up. The robot rotates and delivers the metal blank to the press. The press presses the metal blank and the robot retrieves the metal blank. The robot rotates and delivers the metal blank to a second conveyer belt (the deposit

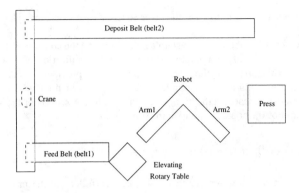

Figure 1. The production cell

belt). The deposit belt transports the metal blank to a crane. The crane picks up the metal blank and transports the metal blank to the feed belt and completes the cycle. Throughout this paper, the crane is used as an example to explain details of the specification, the design and the design process.

The system actions are further complicated by a desire for speed and efficiency. To accommodate these aims, the robot is fitted with two arms. The arms are placed at right angles to each other and rotate together. The arms can extend/retract and load/unload independently. A second consequence of the aim for speed and efficiency is that the system should be able to handle multiple metal blanks in different parts of the system concurrently.

3.1: Production cell specification overview

Our Z specification [14, 15] was developed in a bottom-up manner. To simplify the specification, we developed an abstract model of the system that involved:-

- hiding the vertical movement of the crane's arm,
- allowing only discrete movement of machines and completely hiding conveyor belt movement, and
- restricting the conveyor belts to hold a maximum of one metal blank each.

The first part of the specification specifies each component independently. The system is subdivided into the following components: feed belt, elevating rotary table, robot, press, deposit belt and crane. The independent specification of each component captures the local state information and the allowable operations on the state.

The independent component specifications do not take into account relationships between different components. For example, the crane cannot pick up a metal blank from the deposit belt if no metal blank is there; however this information is not relevant to the independent specification of either the crane or the deposit belt. The independent specifications, each with their own local state, are combined to give the overall state of the system. Operations from the independent specifications are promoted to apply to the total state and are adjusted to take into consideration the relationships between components.

The system is modelled by the overall state and the corresponding operations, but the operations are partial and are only guaranteed to succeed (i.e., have a specified behaviour) when their preconditions are satisfied. The final section of the specification extends the partial operations to total operations. This is achieved by specifying possible error cases for each partial operation as an error schema. Joining the partial operation and the error schema via the schema calculus generates the final operation.

The specification clearly captures the system's behaviour and the constraints for safe operation. It is however a specification of the complete system, not a specification of a possible controller implementation and while providing the safe, total operations, it provides no indication of the order of use (scheduling) of operations. The complete specification, which includes textual description for each piece of mathematical specification, is 26 pages long. A section of the specification that models the behaviour of the crane is provided in Appendix A.

4: Production cell controller designs

The design problem requires producing a software controller for the production cell. The following sections outline two possible designs for the production cell controller. The designs are guided by software architectural styles; the first an ADT-based architectural style and the second an event-based architectural style. The discussion includes a description of the designs, the process involved (the transition from formal specification to design), and the transition from design to implementation.

4.1: ADT-based design

Designing a controller for the production cell using the ADT-based architectural style as a guide requires breaking the system into two parts. The first is the collection of abstract data types (ADT library) that define this style. The second is the control centre (main program) which coordinates the system, in this case a scheduler. Following this initial separation of the system into policy(the scheduler) and mechanism (the ADT library), the major design effort is developing the ADT library for the production cell controller.

Developing an ADT library for a specific problem requires the system state to be logically partitioned into cohesive sections. Due to the nature of the production cell and the specification used as the starting point of the design, the choice of logical partitions is simplified. An ADT module is developed for each component (the crane, feed belt, elevating rotary table, robot, press, and deposit belt) as shown in Figure 2.

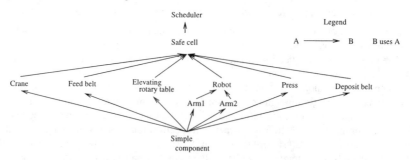

Figure 2. ADT-based design

As each module is responsible for the integrity of its encapsulated state, it is possible to schedule the production cell simulation using these modules as a collection. However, this ad hoc collection of modules does not consider inter-component interactions and hence makes scheduling difficult. To simplify the scheduler (and modification of the scheduling algorithm), the ADTs for each component are gathered into a subsystem, the *Safe_Cell*. The *Safe_Cell* provides an ADT interface to the scheduler[3]. The state encapsulated is the total system state and the operations are the allowable operations on the subsystem as a whole. The transitional operations in this interface are limited to the safe operations on the production cell, i.e., the inter-component interactions are captured. The inquisitive operations on each component are simply promoted to this level.

Using the crane as an example, the transformational operations needed (and defined in the specification) are *Move*, *Load*, and *Unload*. The inquisitive operations are *Loaded* and *Position*, which respectively return whether the crane is loaded and the current location of the crane.

From Figure 2, a subsidiary ADT has been included. This ADT, *Simple_Component*, provides basic state and behaviour required by each module.

The transition from this design to an Eiffel implementation was trivial. This transition was aided by the clarity of operation definition in the specification, especially the pre- and post-conditions when designing using "Design by Contract" [17].

Implementation in Eiffel forced a small, but unexpected change in the design. This resulted from the use of enumerated types in the specification and design. Enumerated types are not present in Eiffel and operations that rely on them must be changed. This affects both transformational and inquisitive operations and forces the use of several simple operations rather than one powerful operation. The transitional operation, *Move* was split into two smaller operations that performed specific moves. The inquisitive operation, *Position* was split into location-specific boolean operations. This implementation with a simple scheduler consists of 21 classes[4] and 1700 lines of code. The scheduler moves one metal blank sequentially through the system and is a single class consisting of 70 lines of code.

The ADT-based design provides an easy to understand/maintain system with a collection of simple ADTs composed into a subsystem. A side-effect of this compositional method is increasingly abstract and powerful transitional operations and many inquisitive operations to query the state.

The constraints of the ADT-based architectural style motivated the majority of the design decisions made. Though this relationship may seem trivial, with the specification structure mirroring the the design, it is not the case. This design can also be generated from a flat specification [13] of the system that focuses on the allowable transitions on a metal blank rather than focusing on the components in the production cell. With this alternative specification, the architecture provided invaluable guidance and traceability for the design process.

4.2: Event-based design

Designing a controller for the production cell using an event-based architectural style as a guide requires consideration of both events and the interactions between components in the system. Events are the defining attribute of this architectural style and designing routines (implicitly called) to handle events is the focus of design.

Partitioning the system into modules in an event-based system is not necessary for architectural reasons (as in the ADT-based architectural style), but is performed for software engineering reasons. The partitioning, as seen in Figure 3, is based on keeping related event handlers together. Related event handlers tend to share state and grouping them increases modular cohesion and decreases inter-module coupling. Due to the nature of the production cell, the modules chosen match the components present in the physical system.

Designing the interface (and hence the implicit state and behaviour) for each module is best explained using the crane as an example. The crane picks a metal blank up at the feed belt, retracts its arm, moves to the deposit belt, extends its arm, deposits the metal blank, retracts its

---

[3]The *Safe_Cell* accesses each module in the subsystem via its public interface.
[4]The short/flat form of the *CRANE* class is in Appendix B.1.

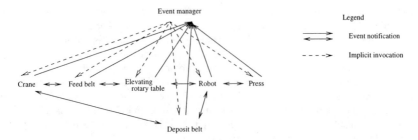

Figure 3. Event-based design

arm, returns to the feed belt and re-extends its arm ready for the next metal blank. A module for the crane must[5] respond to the events: *over_deposit_belt*, *arm_extended_db*, *arm_retracted_db*, *over_feed_belt*, *arm_extended_fb* and *arm_retracted_fb*. Designing handlers for these events cannot proceed in isolation as a constraint on an event-based architecture is that no assumptions can be made about the state of the system as a whole. In this case, the crane is dependent on whether the feed belt is ready to load or whether the deposit belt is ready to unload. If either component is not ready, the crane must stall until the component is ready. It is the interplay between the components and the events that enables the control, in this case the scheduling, to be implicitly distributed throughout the system.

The interface for the crane module contains eight routines; two to stop horizontal movement, two for stopping retraction and extension at the feed belt, two for stopping retraction and extension at the deposit belt, and two routines to advise the crane that an adjacent component is ready to interact. The first six routines are implicitly called via the event-manager, but the last two are explicitly called by an adjacent component. The primary purpose of the first six routines is to handle a stop event[6]; however they also initiate the next stage of system behaviour. This may be starting the movement of the crane and registering for the corresponding stop event, or stalling the crane. When stalled, the crane waits for an adjacent component to call one of the routines that restarts the crane. Modules register event-handlers dynamically by calling the event-manager. Many event-based systems register events at initialisation; however this is not possible in the production cell. The production cell events are only of interest when they first occur. For example, the extension of the crane's arm over the feed belt is stopped when an *arm_extended_fb* event occurs, i.e., the arm has reached a specified extension. We do not wish to continually handle this event while the arm stays at this extension, hence the event is only registered for when it is required.

The interactions between components are as important as the events themselves, but it is harder to ensure that all interactions are captured. The formal specification was invaluable for this phase of the design. The intermediate level of the specification, which promotes the individually specified components to the system level and adds constraints on their interactions, provided concise descriptions of the allowable interactions within the system. This included pre- and post-conditions on the interactions.

Translating this design to an Eiffel implementation was straight-forward, due largely to the quality and completeness of the design. The implementation of the underlying event management subsystem was a simple task. This subsystem was implemented using inheritance and polymorphism and is reusable (as a framework). The total system consists of 47 classes[7] and 1700 lines of code. The event subsystem is the major component of this with 39 classes and 1000 lines of code. As

---

[5]These are also the only events directly related to the crane.

[6]Each event is generated by a moving component and the first action is to stop the component, hence stop events.

[7]The short/flat form of the *Crane* class is in Appendix B.2.

part of the event subsystem, there is a class for each event to which a component responds, i.e., there are 6 event classes for the crane. These event classes inherit from an abstract class event and redefine *trigger* and *reaction* operations. The core of the event system, the abstract class *EVENT* and the class *EVENT_MANAGER*, consists of 150 lines of code. This system schedules 7 metal blanks, with multiple components active simultaneously.

Designing an event-based controller for the production cell required more effort than the ADT-based controller. However, the comparison is misleading as the event-based system and the ADT-based system differ in two important areas. Firstly, the event-based system does not require an explicit scheduler, while the ADT-based system does. Much of the extra design effort for the event-based system was due to this fact. Secondly, the event-based system allows concurrency of the physical components, i.e., multiple components can be in motion with their stop events handled when they are raised. The ADT-based system does not allow this as the routines are responsible for the integrity of the system they act on. High-level atomic (safe) routines are provided instead. This second point highlights a difference in the suitable targets for the architectures. The ADT-based architectural style (and the formal specification) assume an abstract world where operations are instantaneous, whilst the event-based architectural style is sensitive to this real world issue. An example of this difference is the ADT-based design ignoring the vertical movement of the crane's arm within a load/unload operation and the event-based design having to make this movement explicit.

5: Design benefits of software architecture

In the preceding sections of this paper, we gave two examples of design guided by software architectural styles. The discussion of each design focussed on using software architectural styles to drive the design process. A secondary topic in the discussion was the influence and assistance of a formal specification to architecturally-driven software design. In this section we summarise software architecture's contribution to design and then highlight future work which aims to improve software architecture's ability to guide the design process.

5.1: Current contribution

In the introduction (Section 1), we state that software architectural styles improve seamlessness and traceability in design. Likewise we stated that software architectural styles bring a higher level of conceptual reuse to design than is currently present. In this section, we abstract from the example and highlight how these aims are currently supported by software architectural styles.

Using a specific software architectural style to guide design means choosing an architectural style which suits the problem. In this manner, an architectural style is like a pattern and provides conceptual reuse. As with patterns, the specific choice of style provides guidance. The architectural style clarifies the top-level structure of the system enabling the designer to focus on specifics of the problem. For example, in choosing an event-based system, the designer can concentrate on meeting the constraints of such a system and ignore the underlying architectural subsystem. Design becomes a process of mapping the specification (requirements) onto a framework.

In a similar fashion, the constraints on an architecture guide the style of a module and the granularity of the module interface. In the ADT-based design, the constraints on design include encapsulated data and the integrity of that encapsulated data. These constraints force an interface that contains routines to transform the encapsulated data and routines to query the encapsulated data. This process of using the constraints on an architectural style to guide the style and interface of a module is ad hoc and is the focus of future work.

The architectural style not only guides structure and individual module design, but can help in the transition from specification to design. For example, the design of the event-based system used the specification to ensure all inter-component interactions are handled by the design. This relationship between software architectural styles and specifications is not well understood and is also an area of active research.

Guiding design is the major focus of this work, but software architectural styles can provide more than guidance to the software engineer. The explicit choice of an architectural style eases initial understanding by placing the design within a family group. The system can then be understood relative to previous experience with the style or at least relative to a description of the style (as seen in Section 2). Design decisions can be justified relative to constraints on the architectural style and this improves traceability. Likewise seamlessness between specification and design can be improved by using the relationship between specifications and the architectural style. This relationship can be used to link the specification and the design.

5.2: Future work

Two main areas of future work are raised in the previous section: using the constraints on an architectural style to guide design, and discovering relationships between specifications and architectural styles.

Current descriptions of architectural styles provide an overview of the style, its structure, and the constraints on the architecture. This style of description is useful for understanding the style, and hence a family of systems, but does not capture explicitly an architecture's impact on the design and design process. We believe architectural style descriptions should be extended by providing a designer's view of an architectural style. A designer's view should provide:-

- an architecturally-specific design process,
- a collection of architectural constraints with guidelines for meeting them, and
- a discussion of the module structure and module interfaces expected.

We believe this view can be extended to include the relationship between a formal specification and the architectural style, in particular, directing the designer to relevant sections of a specification. This has two important implications: firstly, formal specifications can become more useful to the average designer, by integrating them into the design process and secondly, a documented relationship between a specification and a style can be used to link the specification to the design and add traceability.

6: Conclusions

In this paper we have shown how software architectural styles can be used to guide object-oriented design. Using two different architectural styles, we showed how to guide the design process from a formal specification to a design (subsequently implemented). From this example, we highlighted how software architectural styles can guide the design process. In particular, we demonstrated how software architectural styles can give a different granularity of conceptual reuse than is currently practised in software design. Using software architectural styles also improves seamlessness and traceability in the design process.

7: Acknowledgements

We wish to thank Andrew Hussey for clarifying design issues during the writing of this paper, and Andrew Martin for his thorough review of the final draft.

References

[1] G. Abowd, R. Allen, and D. Garlan. Using style to understand descriptions of software architectures. In D. Notkin, editor, *SIGSOFT'93, Proceedings of the First ACM SIGSOFT Symposium on the Foundations of Software Engineering*, volume 18(5) of *Software Engineering Notes*, pages 9–20. ACM Press, December 1993.

[2] C. Alexander. *The Timeless Way of Building*. Oxford University Press, 1979.

[3] S. M. Brien and J. E. Nicholls. Z base standard version 1.0. Technical Monograph PRG-107, Programming Research Group, Oxford University Computing Laboratory, November 1992.

[4] D. Budgen. *Software Design*. Addison-Wesley, 1994.

[5] L. P. Deutsch. Design reuse and frameworks in the Smalltalk-80 system. In T. J. Biggerstaff and A. J. Perlis, editors, *Software Reusability, Volume II: Applications and Experience*, pages 57–71. Addison-Wesley, 1989.

[6] R. Duke, G. Rose, and G. Smith. Object-Z: a Specification Language Advocated for the Description of Standards. Technical Report 94-45, Software Verification Research Centre, Dept. of Computer Science, Univ. of Qld, Australia, 1994.

[7] R. P. Gabriel. The quality without a name. *Journal of Object-Oriented Programming*, 6(5):86–89, September 1993.

[8] E. Gamma, R. Helm, R. Johnson, and J. Vlissides. Design patterns: Abstraction and reuse of object-oriented design. In O. Nierstrasz, editor, *European Conference on Object-Oriented Programming*, number 707 in Lecture Notes in Computer Science, pages 406–431. Springer-Verlag, July 1993.

[9] E. Gamma, R. Helm, R. Johnson, and J. Vlissides. *Design Patterns: Elements of Reusable Object-Oriented Software*. Addison-Wesley, 1994.

[10] D. Garlan and M. Shaw. An introduction to software architecture. In V. Ambriola and G. Tortora, editors, *Advances in Software Engineering and Knowledge Engineering*, volume I. World Scientific Publishing Company, 1995.

[11] R. E. Johnson and B. Foote. Designing reuseable classes. *Journal of Object-Oriented Programming*, 1(2):22–25, June 1988.

[12] C. Lewerentz and T. Lindner. *Case Study Production Cell: A Comparative Study in Formal Software Development*. Number 891 in Lecture Notes in Computer Science. Springer-Verlag, 1995.

[13] A. MacDonald. A Transition-based specification of the Production Cell. Working paper, Dept. Computer Science, Univ. of Qld, Australia, June 1995.

[14] A. MacDonald and D. Carrington. Z specification of the Production Cell. Technical Report TR94-46, Software Verification Research Centre, Dept. Computer Science, Univ. of Qld, Australia, November 1994.

[15] A. MacDonald and D. Carrington. Structuring Z Specifications: Some Choices. In J.P. Bowen and M. G. Hinchey, editors, *ZUM'95*, number 967 in Lecture Notes in Computer Science, pages 203–223. Springer-Verlag, September 1995.

[16] B. Meyer. *Object-oriented Software Construction*. Prentice Hall, 1988.

[17] B. Meyer. Design by contract. In D. Manrioli and B. Meyer, editors, *Advances in Object-Oriented Software Engineering*, pages 1–50. Prentice Hall, 1991.

[18] B. Meyer. *Eiffel: The Language*. Prentice Hall, 1994.

[19] B. Meyer. *Reusable software - The base object-oriented component libraries*. Prentice Hall, 1994.

[20] R. T. Monroe and D. Garlan. Style based reuse for software architecture. In *Proceedings of the 1996 International Conference on Software Reuse*. IEEE, April 1996.

[21] D. L. Parnas. On the criteria to be used in decomposing systems into modules. *Communications of the ACM*, 15(12):1053–1058, December 1972.

[22] D. E. Perry and A. L. Wolf. Foundations for the study of software architecture. *ACM SIGSOFT Software Engineering Notes*, 17(4):40–52, October 1992.

[23] R. S. Pressman. *Software Engineering: A Practioneer's Approach*. McGraw-Hill, Inc, European edition, 1994. Adapted by D. Ince.

[24] G. Rose. Object-Z. In S. Stepney, R. Barden, and D. Cooper, editors, *Object Orientation in Z*, Workshops in Computing, pages 59–77. Springer-Verlag, 1992.

[25] M. Shaw. Patterns for software architectures. In J. O. Coplien and D. C. Schmidt, editors, *Pattern Languages of Program Design (PLOP'94)*. Addison-Wesley, August 1995.

[26] J. M. Spivey. *The Z Notation: A Reference Manual*. Prentice Hall, second edition, 1992.

A: Crane specification

When specifying the crane, only two crane positions are modelled: the crane is either over the deposit belt or over the feed belt. The crane's state has two variables. The first, $crane\_position$, records whether the crane is $over\_deposit\_belt$ or is $over\_feed\_belt$. The second, $crane\_loaded$, records whether the crane is $loaded$ or $unloaded$. Initially the crane is $unloaded$.

$Crane\_Position ::= over\_deposit\_belt \mid over\_feed\_belt$

$Component\_Loaded ::= loaded \mid unloaded$

```
┌─ Crane ──────────────────────────
│ crane_position : Crane_Position
│ crane_loaded : Component_Loaded
└──────────────────────────────────
```

```
┌─ Init_Crane ─────────────────────
│ Crane
├──────────────────────────────────
│ crane_loaded = unloaded
└──────────────────────────────────
```

The crane has three operations. $Load\_Crane\_0$ picks up a metal blank from the deposit belt. To pick up a metal blank, the crane must be both $over\_deposit\_belt$ and $unloaded$. When the crane has picked up the metal blank, the crane's position is unchanged but the crane is now $loaded$. $Unload\_Crane\_0$ is similar. The crane deposits a metal blank onto the feed belt. The precondition of the unload operation is the crane must be in position, $over\_feed\_belt$, and the crane must be $loaded$. The crane is not moved after the unload operation but the crane is now $unloaded$.

```
┌─ Load_Crane_0 ───────────────────
│ ΔCrane
├──────────────────────────────────
│ crane_position = over_deposit_belt
│ crane_loaded = unloaded
│ crane_position' = crane_position
│ crane_loaded' = loaded
└──────────────────────────────────
```

```
┌─ Unload_Crane_0 ─────────────────
│ ΔCrane
├──────────────────────────────────
│ crane_position = over_feed_belt
│ crane_loaded = loaded
│ crane_position' = crane_position
│ crane_loaded' = unloaded
└──────────────────────────────────
```

The third operation deals with moving the crane between the two possible positions and does not change the crane load state, $crane\_loaded$.

```
┌─ Move_Crane_0 ───────────────────────────────────────
│ ΔCrane
│ new_pos? : Crane_Position
├──────────────────────────────────────────────────────
│ crane_position' = new_pos?
│ crane_loaded' = crane_loaded
└──────────────────────────────────────────────────────
```

The independent component specifications do not take into account relationships between different components. For example, the crane cannot pick up a metal blank from the deposit belt if no metal blank is there; however this information is not relevant to the independent specification of either the crane or the deposit belt. The independent specifications, each with their own local state, are combined to give the overall state of the system, the $Cell$. Operations from the independent specifications are promoted to apply to the total state and are adjusted to take into consideration the relationships between components. To simplify the promotion process, sub-states of $Cell$ are declared. Equating a sub-state within an operation is equivalent to equating each of the state variables within the sub-state in the operation. In Z, state variables are equated when the operation does not change them. Sub-states are used purely for aesthetics, but highlight which state variables the operation changes. In the case below, only the state variables belonging to the deposit belt and the crane may be changed[8].

$$Cell\_7 \;\hat{=}\; Cell \setminus (Deposit\_Belt, Crane)$$

The crane picks up metal blanks from the deposit belt. To do this, the crane must perform a *Load_Crane_0* operation and the deposit belt must perform a *Unload_Deposit_Belt_0* operation. The resulting operation over the *Cell* state is called *Load_Crane_1*.

```
┌─ Load_Crane_1 ──────────────────────────────────────────────────
│ ΔCell
│ Unload_Deposit_Belt_0
│ Load_Crane_0
├─────────────────────────────────────────────────────────────────
│ θCell_7' = θCell_7
└─────────────────────────────────────────────────────────────────
```

The system is modelled by the overall state and the corresponding operations, but the operations are partial and are only guaranteed to succeed (i.e., have a specified behaviour) when their preconditions are satisfied. The final section of the specification extends the partial operations to total operations. This is achieved by specifying possible error cases for each partial operation as an error schema. Joining the partial operation and the error schema via the schema calculus generates the final operation.

Each operation outputs a value of type *Report*. If the operation is successful, the value is *ok*; however if the operation fails, i.e., satisfies one of the error conditions, the value explains the failure.

$$Report ::= ok \mid wrong\_crane\_position \mid component\_already\_loaded \mid deposit\_belt\_not\_ready \mid \cdots$$

The total operations take the form:- Total operation $\hat{=}$ (partial operation $\wedge$ *Success*) $\vee$ error
The *Success* schema provides the ok report value for the partial operations. The *Error* schema is included in the error schemas for each operation.

$$Success \;\hat{=}\; [r! : Report \mid r! = ok] \qquad\qquad Error \;\hat{=}\; [\Xi Cell;\; r! : Report]$$

The crane cannot pick up a metal blank when the crane is over the feed belt, the crane is already loaded, or the deposit belt has not delivered a metal blank.

```
┌─ Load_Crane_Error ──────────────────────────────────────────────
│ Error
├─────────────────────────────────────────────────────────────────
│ crane_position = over_feed_belt ⇒ r! = wrong_crane_position
│ crane_position = over_deposit_belt ⇒
│    (crane_loaded = loaded ⇒ r! = component_already_loaded ∧
│    crane_loaded = unloaded ⇒ (deposit_belt_loaded = unloaded ⇒ r! = deposit_belt_not_ready))
└─────────────────────────────────────────────────────────────────
```

$$Load\_Crane \;\hat{=}\; (Load\_Crane\_1 \wedge Success) \vee Load\_Crane\_Error$$

The other total operations involving the crane are *Move_Crane* and *Unload_Crane*.

---

[8] The hiding for *Cell_7* should actually contain the variables being hidden in brackets rather than the state schema to which the variables belong. However, this is messy and the hiding of the state is equivalent. This method of promotion is awkward and an alternate method is proposed in [15].

B: Eiffel short/flat crane interfaces[9]

These classes are from the implementation of the design developed in Sections 4.1 and 4.2.

B.1: ADT-based design

This class has been design and implemented following the principles of "Design by Contract" [17].

class interface *CRANE*
creation
    init
feature
    init
    is_loaded: *BOOLEAN*
    is_over_dep: *BOOLEAN*
    is_over_feed: *BOOLEAN*
    load
        require is_over_dep **and not** is_loaded
        ensure is_loaded
    move_to_dep
        ensure is_over_dep
    move_to_feed
        ensure is_over_feed
    unload
        require is_over_feed **and** is_loaded
        ensure not is_loaded
end -- class *CRANE*

B.2: Event-based design

The class has an initialisation routine that must be called after creation since creation routines cannot have parameters. The initialisation routine establishes object references to enable inter-object communication.

class interface *CRANE*
feature
    init(fb: *FEED_BELT*; db: *DEPOSIT_BELT*; e: *EVENT_MANAGER*)
    ready_to_load
        -- called by the *DEPOSIT_BELT*. crane can now load from waiting belt.
    ready_to_unload
        -- called by the *FEED_BELT*. crane can now unload to the waiting belt.
    stop_ext_over_dep
    stop_ext_over_feed
    stop_horizontal_over_dep
    stop_horizontal_over_feed
    stop_ret_over_dep
    stop_ret_over_feed
end -- class *CRANE*

---

[9]Most comments have been removed to conserve space.

Object Oriented Reuse through Algebraic Specifications

Liliana Favre
Isistan
Facultad de Ciencias Exactas
Universidad Nacional del Centro de la Pcia. de Buenos Aires
Argentina
lfavre@necsus.com.ar

Abstract

Most current approaches to object-oriented reusability are based on empirical methods. However, the formal specification of reusable components and the development of a rigorous method for their systematic reuse permit building "correct" and efficient object-oriented software.

This paper proposes the SRI model for the definition of the structure of a reusable component. This model integrates algebraic specifications and concrete classes in an object oriented language. A rigorous method for retrieval, adaptation and integration of SRI components is described.

Eiffel was chosen as the language to demonstrate the power of the model. In such a framework, an Eiffel application is produced semiautomatically from previously existing classes by applying specification building operators for extension, renaming, restriction and composition.

1: Introduction

Software reusability is a promising approach to increase software productivity. An ideal software reusability technology should facilitate a consistent system implementation, starting from the adaptation and integration of "implementation pieces" that exist in reusable component libraries.

In object-oriented programming, reusability is achieved by extending existing libraries. Abstract classes and inheritance are crucial for extensibility and reusability. Classification is the most widely accepted use of inheritance as it is the ideal mechanism for capturing commonalties between similar reusable components. A different use enables a class to inherit from another one for implementation purposes. To obtain flexibility, class hierarchies are structured through mechanisms of dynamic binding and polymorphism.

To facilitate code reuse, object-oriented programming languages, such as Eiffel, Smalltalk and C++, provide large reusable class libraries. By consulting these libraries, users can develop their own domain-specific reusable components. However, most object-oriented applications have inheritance hierarchies, which are imperfectly designed. Identification of components in a hierarchy and their adaptation to a particular context is therefore difficult.

Software reusability is difficult because it requires taking many different requirements into account, some of which are abstract and conceptual, whereas others, such as efficiency, are concrete. A good approach for reusability must reconcile the abstract concepts with their concrete implementations.

Considering the issues described above, we introduce the SRI model for the definition of the structure of a reusable component. The model makes it possible to describe object class hierarchies at different abstraction levels, which integrate algebraic specifications and concrete classes in an object-oriented language. It tries to take advantage of the power given by the algebraic formalism to describe behaviour in an abstract way and besides, to respect the taxonomy of classes for object oriented libraries.

Object classes can be formally specified through structured algebraic specifications. The specification language selected for this work is GSBL (Generic Specification Base Language)[3]. The outstanding characteristic of GSBL is that it allows incomplete specifications, which facilitate the description of class hierarchies in object-oriented languages. We have extended the language to increase its expressiveness. We call our extended language GSBL$^+$.

To facilitate component identification and code reuse, a reusable component consists of three different abstraction levels:

- Identification: hierarchies of incomplete algebraic specifications related by formal subtyping relations.
- Realisation: hierarchies of complete algebraic specifications related by formal realisation relations.
- Implementation: hierarchies of object-oriented class schemes related by implementation relations.

The letters S, R and I, which name the model, refer to the relations used to integrate specifications on the three levels: subtyping, realisation and implementation.

The manipulation of reusable components by means of specification building operators for extension, renaming, restriction and composition of other specifications is the basis for the semiautomatic generation of implementations.

The paper has the following structure. We start by looking at related work in section 2. In section 3 we describe how to specify reusable components. Section 4 introduces the SRI model. In section 5 we describe transformation operators. This is followed by a description of a rigorous reusability method in section 6. Section 7 describes how to bridge the gap between algebraic specifications and Eiffel classes. Finally, experimental results are discussed and conclusions are made.

2: Related work

A classical reference in this subject is the Larch family of specification languages [8]. A Larch specification has components written in two languages: one that is designed for a specific programming language and another that is independent of any programming language (Larch Shared Language).

Larch/Smalltalk was the first Larch interface specification language with subtyping and specification inheritance [4]. Other Larch interface languages with similar characteristics are Larch/Modula3 and Larch/C++. Larch/Smalltalk is notable for a clear separation of types from classes. The most interesting feature of Larch/C++ is that a class specification can have multiple interfaces.

Formal techniques, based on the algebraic formalism, for the reengineering of C programs, are described in [15].

Object-oriented extensions have been proposed for several specification languages (Z, VDM, etc) [16].

There is a wide range of research that proves that software reusability can be addressed from structured algebraic descriptions [7, 10, 11, 14].

Hennicker and Wirsing [9] introduce a model for the definition of reusable components. They define a reusable component as a tree of algebraic specifications with behavioural semantics: the root of the tree is the most abstract specification, nodes are related by implementation relations and the leaves correspond to different implementations of the root. In this model, an implementation is a formal specification. The realisation level subcomponents of the SRI model may be associated to the model described above.

Our current work makes its main contributions through the definition of the SRI model; a method based on this model and an application of the principles described by integrating algebraic specifications with the Eiffel language. The SRI model allows the identification of different types of relations between complete and incomplete specifications and classes, and permits the specification of incomplete behaviour and its association with deferred classes in the implementation level. The method separates the design strategy from the generated code, facilitates the automatic identification and retrieval of components, and extends building operators to the implementation level classes. The application is a particular case of our model and our method, which is based on the characteristics of the Eiffel language for operational class specification.

3: Specifying reusable components

Object classes can be specified in an implementation independent way by using structured algebraic specifications of data types. The basic idea of the algebraic approach consists of describing data structures by just giving the names of the different sets of data, the names of the basic functions and their properties, which are described by formulas (mostly equations). A (many sorted) signature Σ is a pair (S, F) where S is a set of sorts and F is a set of function symbols.

We have selected GSBL+ as the specification language. This language extends GSBL [2, 3] with mechanisms for error treatment, explicit parameterisation and restriction of specifications [5].

In GSBL+, we use two algebraic specification techniques for defining the set of values belonging to the sort associated with a type. The first technique is based on a set of first order formulae and the second one on a set of equations.

The first specification technique leaves much freedom to the specifier in the elaboration of a type specification. However, GSBL+ also supports another style of specification based on the "term generation principle "used in a more classical approach of algebraic specification based on equations. In this approach, it should be possible to associate a term with each value belonging to the sort. This style is sometimes difficult to adopt at the requirements level because of the identification of generators operations associated with the generation of all the values of a sort and the restriction on formulas to be equations between terms (equational logic).

The mechanism of the language that creates the new specification is the class definition. In GSBL$^+$ strictly generic components can be distinguished by means of explicit parameterisation. The EXPORT clause describes which names (of sorts and operations defined inside the class) are visible from outside.

GSBL+ specifications are considered structured objects. This structure is based on two relations associated to two specification building mechanisms. The OVER relation defines which specifications are considered components of a given specification. Similarly, the SUBCLASS relation defines which specifications must be considered subclass or superclasses of a given specification. Note that the SUBCLASS relation is conceptually linked to the inheritance relation in the object oriented level and the OVER relation to the client one.

The WITH clause declares new sorts, operations or equations that are incompletely defined, i.e. there are not enough equations to specify the new operations or there are not enough operations to "generate" all values of a given sort. A GSBL+ specification is implicitly parameterised in its incomplete parts.

The DEFINE clause either declares new sorts, operations or equations, that are completely defined, or completes the definition of some sort or operation, belonging to some superclass, that was not completely defined.

A class may introduce any number of new sorts; if one of them has the same name as the class, this sort is considered the *sort of interest* of the class.

The syntax of a class specified with the second technique includes the BASIC CONSTRUCTOR clause that refers to generator operations and does not contain WITH clause.

As examples, we propose an incomplete specification of a class *Traversable* and a complete specification of a class *Sequence*(Figure 1).

CLASS Traversable [G:ANY]	**CLASS** Sequence[element:ANY]
EXPORT first, rest, end	**EXPORT** emptyseq, put, empty?, first, rest,...
OVER Boolean	**BASIC CONSTRUCTORS** emptyseq, put
SUBCLASS-OF Container	**SUBCLASS-OF** Collection
WITH	**OVER** Boolean
SORTS Traversable	**DEFINE**
OPS first: Traversable -> G	**SORTS** Sequence
rest: Traversable-> Traversable	**OPS**
end: Traversable -> Boolean	emptyseq: -> Sequence
END-CLASS	put: Sequence x element -> Sequence
	empty? : Sequence-> Boolean
	first: Sequence(s) -> element
	pre: not empty?(s)
	rest:Sequence(s)->Sequence
	pre: not empty?(s)
	....
	EQS{c:Sequence; e:element}
	empty?(emptyseq) = TRUE
	empty?(put(c,e)) = FALSE
	first(put(c,e))= e
	rest(put(c,e))=c
	....
	END-CLASS

Figure 1. GSBL+ specifications

4: The SRI model

Considering the issues described in section 1., we introduce the SRI model for the definition of the structure of a reusable component. It describes object classes at three conceptual levels: identification, realisation and implementation.

The identification level describes a hierarchy of incomplete specifications in GSBL+ as an acyclic graph $G=(V,E)$, where V is a non-empty set of incomplete algebraic specifications in GSBL+ and $E \subseteq V \times V$ defines a subtype relation between specifications. In this context, it must be verified that if $P(x)$ is a property provable about objects x of type T, then $P(y)$ must be verified for every object y of type S, where S is subtype of T [11].

Every leaf in the identification level is associated with a subcomponent at the realisation level. A realisation subcomponent is a tree of complete specifications in GSBL+:
- The root is the most abstract definition.
- The internal nodes correspond to different realisations of the root.
- Leaves correspond to subcomponents at the implementation level.

If E and E1 are specifications, then E can be realised by E1 (written E~~~>E1) if E and E1 have the same signature and every model of E1 is a model of E [9]. Every specification at the realisation level corresponds to a subcomponent at the implementation level, which groups a set of implementation schemes associated with a class in an object oriented language. This level defines implementation relations denoted by the symbol " ≈≈≈>".

Eiffel was chosen as the language to prove the power of the model. It is used as a tool for the design and implementation of object-oriented code. It is reflected in the powerful "Design by Contract" principle, which is based on the protection of both sides of the contract. It protects the client by specifying how much should be done, and the contractor by specifying how little is acceptable. Contracts imply obligations and benefits for both parties, and are made explicit by the use of assertions. They allow us to integrate axioms of specification levels with the implementation level.

There is a relation between the other two levels and the implementation level:

- Every incomplete GSBL+ class in the identification level is associated with a deferred Eiffel class that matches the specified incomplete behaviour.
- Internal nodes of the realisation level components, including the root, correspond to an abstract class that defers implementation in the object-oriented level.
- Leaves in the realisation level correspond to complete Eiffel classes.
- The implementation level can contain classes that are not related to the specifications in the identification and realisation levels. They reflect implementation aspects.

Why the SRI model? Software reusability takes many different requirements into account, some of which are abstract and conceptual, whereas others are concrete and bound to implementation properties. Reusable components must be specified in an appropriate way. For example, at more abstract levels, we need descriptions satisfying three conditions [13]:

- "They should be precise and unambiguous.
- They should be complete or at least as complete as we want, in each case.
- They should not overspecify."

Identification level reconciles the need for precision and completeness in abstract specifications with the desire to avoid overspecification.

Adaptation of reusable components, which consumes a large portion of software cost, is penalized by overdependency of components on the physical structure of data. The realisation level in the SRI model allows us to distinguish design decisions related to the choice of physical structure data.

A reusable component CONTAINER appears in Figure 2. All specifications that describe "containers" are descendants of an incomplete specification (Container-I). Every leaf in the identification level is a complete specification, corresponding to a subcomponent at the realisation level. For example, Set-C is a leaf that links different realisations: Set-Tree and Set-List. They correspond to subcomponents at the implementation level that represent concrete classes.

5: Transformation operators

We describe the operators applied to specifications and their extension to reusable components.

5.1: Renaming

This transformation is based on the notion of signature morphism. Let $\Sigma=(S,F)$ and $\Sigma'=(S',F')$ be two signatures with sets of sorts S, S' respectively and sets of operation symbols F, F' respectively.

A signature morphism can be defined as a function $\rho: \Sigma \rightarrow \Sigma'$, where $\rho=(\rho_{sorts}, \rho_{oper})$ are the mappings $\rho_{sorts}: S \rightarrow S'$ and $\rho_{oper}: F \rightarrow F'$. ρ_{sorts} and ρ_{oper} are compatible with the functionality of the operations, i.e. $\forall f \varepsilon F: f: s_1, \ldots, s_n \rightarrow s$, ρ_{oper} has functionality $f:\rho_{sorts}(s_1),\ldots,\rho_{sorts}(s_n) \rightarrow \rho_{sorts}(s)$.

106

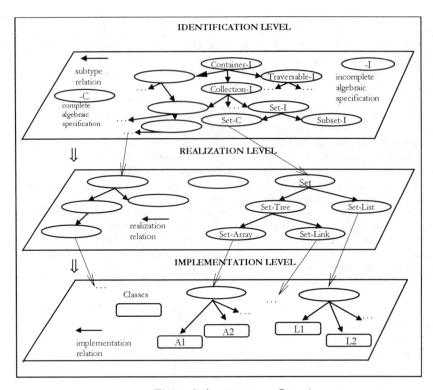

Figure 2. A component Container

Then, we can say that given a specification SP, a signature Σ' and a signature morphism ρ: sig(SP) -> Σ that represents a rename, *renaming(SP, ρ)* is a specification with signature Σ'. This means that all of its sorts and operations have been renamed [9].

5.2: Restriction

Restriction is a transformation operator that creates a new specification formed by a subset of the sorts and operations of other ones. Let SP be a specification with signature Σ=sig(SP), *restriction(SP, Σ')* is a specification with signature Σ', where Σ' ⊆ Σ. After the application of this operator, the resulting specification does not include the sorts and operations of Σ which do not belong to Σ' [9].

5.3: Extension

Let SP be a specification with a set of sorts S and a set of operations F, the extension operator creates a new specification that enriches SP. Then, *extension(SP,S',F',Eqs)*, where S', F' and Eqs are sets of sorts, operations and equations, results in a specification SP' where the set of sorts is S'∪S and the set of operations is F∪F' [9].

5.4: Composition

The composition operator combines two specifications SP1 and SP2 to form a new one. It intuitively denotes a specification whose signature is the union of the signatures of SP1 and SP2 and the axioms are the union of the axioms of SP1 and SP2.

The classes to be composed can belong to the same or to different reusable components. *composition(SP1,SP2)* results in a new specification whose signature and axioms are the unions of the ones of the composed specifications.

Building operators on specifications can be extended to manipulate subcomponents in the realisation level. Informally, this implies simultaneous application of an operator to every node of the subcomponent. Renaming of a component is defined as a renaming of its root and recursively all of its children. The restriction and extension operators are applied in the same way. Applying a renaming to Figure 3 yields the reusable component shown in Figure 4. A detailed description may be found in [6].

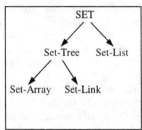 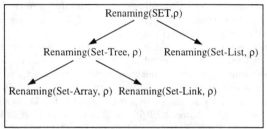

Figure 3. A component SET   **Figure 4. Renaming SET**

6: A rigorous reusability method

The following is the description of a rigorous method for the systematic reuse of components described by the SRI model. We want to construct an implementation for a goal specification E_g by reusing existing components. The method has the following steps: decomposition, identification, adaptation and composition.

Decomposition: Formalise the decomposition of a goal specification E_g into sub-specifications E_1, E_2,.....,E_n. The decomposition is expressed through a transformation pattern, which is based on GSBL$^+$ subspecifications. This specification relates classes through the OVER and SUBCLASS clauses.

Identification: For each sub-specification E_i identify a component C_i (in the identification level) and a sequence $s_1,s_2,....,s_n$ of GSBL$^+$ specifications that verify subtype relations. If s_n is complete, it is associated with the root of a subcomponent CR_j in the realisation level. If s_n is not complete, select a leaf in C_i (i.e. those specifications for which there is a path in the graph from s_n) as a candidate to be transformed.

Identification of a component is correct if renaming, restriction and extension operators can modify it to match the query E_i. The sorts and operations must be connected with E_i's by an appropriate rename. The renamed version must be extended with sorts, operations and axioms. The visible signature must be restricted to the visible signature of E_i. Let OP_1, OP_2, ...OP_K be the sequence of operators applied to these transformations.

Adaptation: Select a leaf (LEAF$_j$) in the subcomponent CR$_j$ and apply OP$_1$, OP$_2$, ...OP$_K$, i.e. construct the specification OP$_1$(........(OP$_K$(LEAF$_j$)....) verifying OP$_1$(.....(OP$_K$(Root(CR$_j$)......)~~~>OP$_1$(....OP$_K$(LEAF$_j$))...) is a realisation relation.

Select a class scheme ESQ$_m$ in the subcomponent of the implementation level whose root is LEAF$_j$.

Apply the sequence of operators OP$_1$, OP$_2$, ...OP$_K$ to ESQ$_m$, i.e. construct the specification OP$_1$(........(OP$_k$(ESQ$_m$)....) verifying OP$_1$(.....(OP$_K$(LEAF$_j$)......)≈≈≈>OP$_1$(....OP$_K$(ESQ$_m$))...) is an implementation relation.

Composition: Generate Eiffel classes for each E$_i$. Compose the sub-specifications E$_i$ and their implementations according to the matching pattern.

7: Integrating GSBL+ specifications and Eiffel classes

Having defined formal specifications, we need to generate the Eiffel classes that implement the desired behaviour. To achieve this we analyse every clause and relation present in a GSBL$^+$ class and translate it to Eiffel code.

GSBL+ bears explicit parameterisation. The parameters can be restricted to a specified class or to its subclasses. GSBL+ and Eiffel have the same syntax for the declaration of class parameters. Then, this transformation is reduced to a trivial translation.

The relation introduced in GSBL$^+$ using the clause OVER will be translated into a client relation in Eiffel. The relation expressed through the keyword SUBCLASS-OF in GSBL$^+$ will become a subtype relation in Eiffel. In both cases we have to identify a class from the library of reusable components. This cannot be any class, but one whose behaviour is the closest to the desired one. Once identified, the class will be transformed to obtain a new one that has exactly the specified characteristics.

Possible transformations are renaming, restriction, extension and composition. Renaming and restrictions will be applied to the identified class following the definition made for these operators in the identification and realisation levels. It is worth pointing that this is done above the class "text", not through mechanisms provided by the Eiffel language. The application of the extension operator involves the intervention of the programmer, who should analyse different representations and provide feature implementation. The SUBCLASS-OF clause may cause the application of the composition operator. When we give a list of superclasses on the algebraic level, we are just expressing that our class will have the same behaviour of several other classes. This can be solved as multiple inheritance or as a composition in the implementation level.

The construction of new classes by transformation of existing ones implies access redefinition for client classes and inherited features and, by this, the creation of an interface for the new client or superclass. Every specification pattern can contain functions and axioms that incorporate new behaviour. Every function given on the algebraic specification will be translated into a new feature on the Eiffel class. This translation will have to take into account that Eiffel has four categories of features: variables, constants, procedures and functions. The system will consult the user when it is not possible to decide automatically the feature category.

Eiffel provides an assertion language. Assertions are boolean expressions expressing semantic properties of the classes. They "serve to express the specification of software components: indications of *what* a component does rather than *how* it does it" [13]. They can play the following roles:

- Precondition: expresses the requirements the client must satisfy to call a routine.
- Postcondition: expresses the conditions that the routine guarantees on return.
- Class invariant: expresses the requirements that must be satisfied by every object of the class after its creation.

Axioms in a formal specification language represent the constraints that the class introduces on the operations. Analysing these axioms we can derive the assertions that will be included in the Eiffel classes. Preconditions and axioms of a function written in GSBL⁺ are used to generate preconditions and postconditions for routines and invariant for Eiffel classes.

A GSBL+ precondition is a well-formedness term defined over functions and constants of the global environment classes, and its translation to Eiffel precondition is automatic.

It is worth clarifying for the assertions generation that a basic functionality $f: s \times a1 \times a2 \times \dots \dots an{-}> ar$, where s is the sort of interest, it is translated into Eiffel syntax as $f(a1,a2,a3, \dots an)$. The sort of interest is associated to the key word *Current* in Eiffel. In like manner the axioms terms must be translated respecting the Eiffel syntax, for example *select(rest(s), minus(n,1))*, if s is the sort of interest, it is translated to *rest.select(n-1)*.

In the Figure 5, we show how to translate a GSBL+ precondition of the operation *top* (in the left column) into an Eiffel precondition (in the right column).

CLASS LINKED-STACK [G:ANY]	.....
....	top: G
DEFINE	**require**
SORTS LINKED-STACK	not isempty
OPS	....
isempty: LINKED-STACK → Boolean	
top: LINKED-STACK(s) → G	
pre: not isempty(s)	
....	
END-CLASS	

Figure 5. Precondition

The system can derive an invariant automatically if it can establish a correspondence between the functions in the axiom and class features that only depend on the state of the object. The obtaining of invariants for a class BOUNDED STACK is exemplified in Figure 6.

A postcondition can be generated automatically from one axiom if a term e(<list_of_arguments>), associated to an operation can be distinguished within itself in such a way that any other term of the axiom depends upon the <list_of_arguments> or constants. Then, the postcondition will associate itself with the method that reflects the term and will obviously depend only upon the previous state of the method execution, upon the state after its execution and upon the method arguments.

The obtaining of postconditions for a class SET is exemplified in Figure 7. The axiom (1) is translated to a post condition of the method *extend* and axiom (2) is translated to a postcondition of the method *has*. If the selected term is linked with a value belonging to the sort of interest, it is associated to *Current*, and the sort of interest in its own functionality to *old*. If the selected term is different from the sort of interest then it is associated to *Result*.

Any other type of situation cannot be derived automatically. These cases do not enable the system to build an assertion without the user's interventions. The programmer can also incorporate assertions that reflect purely implementation aspects.

CLASS BOUNDED-STACK [G:ANY]	class BOUNDED-STACK[G]
....	.....
DEFINE	capacity:INTEGER ....
SORTS BOUNDED-STACK	count:INTEGER...
OPS	full:BOOLEAN...
capacity: BOUNDED-STACK→ integer	empty:BOOLEAN...
count: BOUNDED-STACK→ integer	**invariant**
full: BOUNDED-STACK→ Boolean	full= (count=capacity);
empty: BOUNDED-STACK → Boolean	empty= (count =0)
......	.....
EQS {s: BOUNDED-STACK; s: G}	**end**
full(s) ≡ (capacity(s) = count(s))	
empty(s)≡ (count(s)=o)	
......	
END-CLASS	

Figure 6. Invariants

CLASS SET[G:ANY]	
....	**class** SET[G]
DEFINE	....
SORTS SET	empty:BOOLEAN
OPS	
.....	has(v:G):BOOLEAN
has: SET x G → BOOLEAN	....
count: SET→ INTEGER	**ensure**
extend: SET x G → SET	Result **implies not** empty
empty: SET → BOOLEAN	......
EQS{s:SET; v:G}	extend(v: G)
count(extend(s,v))= if has(s,v) then count(s) else	....
plus(count(s) ,1)	**ensure**
(1)	**old** has(v) **implies** count=old count
	not old has(v) **implies** (count=old count
has(s,v)⇒not empty(s)	+ 1)
(2)	....
......	
END-CLASS	

Figure 7. Postconditions

8: Experimental results

To demonstrate the feasibility of our approach, a prototype (HARLOO) was implemented [6]. A detailed description appears in [1]. The prototype offers facilities for handling reusable components and verifying the user's expectations. The prototype assists in:

- Specification editing.
- Analysis of specifications written in GSBL+
- Specification validation.
- Component reuse: The prototype assists in the creation of new applications by applying the

transformation operators to existing classes.
- Transformation of GSBL+ specifications to Eiffel code.
- Design maintenance

Results of experiments with the prototype reveal advantages of the reusability method as well as limitations. The object-oriented paradigm offers great potential for productivity improvements but it creates unfamiliar problems for maintainers. The various uses of inheritance, binding dynamics and polymorphism can make the dependencies between classes harder to find and analyse. Real design maintenance requires automation, which depends on formalisation.

The proposed method forces systematic reuse of behaviour from structured algebraic specifications. The application of building operators to SRI subcomponents and recording of the "design history" permits good maintenance.

In the object-oriented paradigm, changes are made incrementally to classes, and specialisation is achieved by means of the subclass mechanism. Access to objects that are instances of specialised classes may be inefficient due to dynamic binding. Inheritance can also waste memory space. The proposed method uses dynamic binding and polymorphism only where needed. Code is generated in its purest form, omitting such mechanisms as method redefinition, direct repeated inheritance, etc.

9: Concluding remarks

In this work we presented a rigorous method for the systematic reuse of object-oriented software. Eiffel was chosen as the object-oriented language of our implementation level classes because it offers a large class library that is classified in a clear and natural way.

This method was partially implemented by a prototype called HARLOO (Tool for Assisting on the Reusability with an Object-oriented Language). For the construction of this prototype we have specified a subset of the libraries provided by the language ISE Eiffel version 3 [12].

The integration of behaviour algebraic specifications and object-oriented code avoids dealing with the problems presented by dynamic binding and polymorphism to understand and maintain classes. With these mechanisms, the form that an object will take is only known at run time. Following the ideas proposed by the method based on the SRI model, the user is completely isolated from this and deals directly with the desired behaviour. It is the system the one in charge of maintaining the classes in a coherent way to make them work.

The fact that we build new applications and reusable components by transformation of existing ones guarantees that the generated code is correct and efficient, if we apply those transformations to a correct initial code. One class is produced from previously existing ones by applying semantic-preserving transformation rules. To justify this a model of computation was described in [5].

The informality of software classification schemes is an impediment to automate the reusability of a software component. The use of formal specifications to model and retrieve reusable components alleviates the informality, but it is worth considering the fact that the formal reasoning required for retrieval introduces questions of scalability.

References

1. Carbajo,M.; Diez,G.; Palomeque,C.; Undergraduate Thesis. Departamento de Computación. Facultad de Ciencias Exactas. Universidad Nacional del Centro de la Pcia. de Buenos Aires. Argentina. 1997.

2. Clérici,Silvia. PhD. Thesis LSI Department. Universidad Politécnica de Catalunya. España. 1989.

3. Clérici,S.; Orejas, F.; The Specification Language GSBL; Recent Trends in Data Type Specification;pp 17-20 April. 1990.

4. Cheon,Y.;Leavens,G.; The Larch/Smalltalk Interface Specification Language. ACM Trans. on Soft. Eng. and Meth. Vol 3, N° 3, July. pp 221-253. 1994.

5. Favre, L.; Formal Methods and Object-oriented Reusability. RR 35. Isistan. UNCPBA. Argentina. 1996.

6. Favre, L.; Diez, G.;Carbajo, M.; Palomeque, C.: Object-oriented Software Reusability: A Rigorous Method; SEKE'97 (The Ninth International Conference on Software Engineering and Knowledge Engineering") KSI. USA.pp 158-167. 1997.

7. Guerreri, E. editor.; Second International Workshop on Software Reusability; Lucca, Italy. 1993.

8 . Guttag, J.; Horning, J.; Larch: Languages and Tools for Formal Specification. Springer-Verlag. 1993.

9. Hennicker, R. , Wirsing, M.; A Formal Method for the Systematic Reuse of Specification Components; Lecture Notes in Computer Science 544; Springer-Verlag; Berlin. 1992.

10. Krueger, C.;Software Reuse; ACM Computing Surveys, Vol. 24, N° 2, pp. 131-183. 1992.

11. Liskov, B.; Wing, J.; A Behavioral Notion of Subtyping; ACM Trans. on Programming Languages and Systems, Vol 16, N° 6, November. 1994.

12. Meyer, B.; Reusable Software: The Base Object-oriented Libraries; Prentice Hall Object-oriented Series. 1994.

13. Meyer, B.; Object Oriented Software Construction.; Prentice Hall Object-oriented Series. 1997.

14. Schafer, W., Prieto-Díaz, R. , Matsumoto, M.; Software Reusability; Ellis Horwood. 1994.

15. Tan, Y.; Formal Specification Techniques for Engineering Modular C Programs. Kluwer Academic Publishers. 1996.

16. Wirsing, M.; Algebraic Specification Languages: An Overview. In E. Astesiano, G. Reggio and A. Tarlecki, editors, Recent Trends in Data Type Specifications, Volume 906 of Lecture Notes in Computer Science, pages 351-367. Springer-Verlag. 1995.

Macro Processing in Object-Oriented Languages

Shigeru Chiba
Institute of Information Science and Electronics, University of Tsukuba
and PRESTO, Japan Science and Technology Corporation
E-mail: chiba@is.tsukuba.ac.jp

Abstract

There are a number of programmable macro systems such as Lisp's. While they can handle complex program transformation, they still have difficulty in handling some kinds of transformation typical in object-oriented programming. This paper examines this problem and, to address it, presents an advanced macro system based on ideas borrowed from reflection. Unlike other macro systems, our macro system provides metaobjects as the data structure used for the macro processing instead of an abstract syntax tree. This feature makes it easy to implement a range of transformations of object-oriented programs.

1: Introduction

Macros are probably the oldest example of meta programming. They have been used for processing a source program at the meta level, that is, from a point of view other than the computation described in the program. Their *meta* view has been tokens or syntax trees; most macro systems, including the ANSI C preprocessor [1], deal with a source program as a sequence of tokens. Other systems, like Lisp's macro system, deal with it as a parse tree or an abstract syntax tree. These traditional macro systems have been satisfactory since the basic constructs of the target languages are procedures and functions, which are relatively simple.

However, the basic constructs of object-oriented languages are not procedures but objects, classes, and methods, which are semantically and syntactically rich concepts. This fact reveals the limitations of the traditional macro systems. Some kinds of source-level translation that are useful in object-oriented programming are extremely difficult with those macro systems. Such translation requires the ability to deal with a source program at a higher level than the level of tokens and syntax trees. For example, it may need the ability of adding a specific method to a given class if that method is not defined in the given class.

This paper presents our macro system called OpenC++, which addresses the problem above for the C++ language. This macro system was designed on the basis of some ideas borrowed from *reflection* [21, 17] and hence it allows programmers to deal with a source program from a logical viewpoint instead of a syntactic one. OpenC++ exposes the source program as a set of C++ objects representing the logical structure of the program. This logical representation makes it easy to implement macro processing typical in object-oriented programming. This fact is somewhat obvious but the contribution of this paper is that it reports that the logical representation that the reflection community has been studying is also workable for macro processing in object-oriented programming.

Some versions of OpenC++ have been available to the public since 1995 and they have been evolved according to the feedback from dozens of world-wide users (Several papers about research activities using OpenC++ are found in [7]). For example, one group is using OpenC++ to develop a C++ compiler to produce CORBA-compliant fault tolerant objects [12]. OpenC++ has been also used to implement a tool for analyzing a program and producing useful information such as an inheritance graph. The problem discussed in this paper has been articulated during the interaction with those users. This paper focuses on the recent improvement of OpenC++ for addressing that problem and presents details of its new programming interface. This is a new argument not included in the author's previous paper [3], which proposed the conceptual design of OpenC++ in the context of reflection.

This paper has six sections. In Section 2, we show an example of macro processing, which is typical in object-oriented programming but that current macro systems cannot easily handle. Section 3 presents details of OpenC++ and how it handles the example in Section 2. Section 4 shows other examples of the use of OpenC++. We discuss the comparison with related work in Section 5. Section 6 is conclusion.

2: Motivating Example

Programmable macro systems, such as Lisp macros, are powerful tools for meta programming. They enable programmers to implement various language facilities that the target language lacks, such as control statements, data abstractions, and even a simple object system. Macro systems are also useful for executing inline expansion of a simple function to improve runtime performance.

However, the current macro systems are not satisfactory for object-oriented programming. There are several examples that are typical in object-oriented programming but cannot be easily implemented by traditional macros. Since most of the macro systems can only transform function-call expressions, they are not practical if programmers want to transform statements or expressions that do not look like a function-call expression. This section shows one of those examples and mentions that another kind of macro system is needed in object-oriented languages.

"Design patterns" [8] show us a number of programming techniques called *patterns* to solve typical problems we frequently encounter in object-oriented programming. Although those patterns are well designed and tested, strictly following the patterns sometime causes the programmers to repeatedly write similar code. This tedious work should be automated by macros but traditional macro systems cannot handle this. A special preprocessor is needed for the automation.

We illustrate this problem with the visitor pattern. This pattern is used for visiting the elements of a given data structure such as a tree structure and performing different operations on every node. Suppose that we implement an abstract syntax tree for a compiler. The nodes of this tree structure are instances of different classes such as `AssignExpr` and `PrintExpr`. The visitor pattern implements operations on this abstract syntax tree, such as a type-checking operation.

A fundamental idea of the visitor pattern is to implement the type-checking operation separately from the implementation of the node classes. The program should include not only the node classes but also an abstract class `Visitor` and its subclass `TypeCheckVisitor`. These classes define the operations performed during the tree traversal. They have methods such as `VisitAssign-Expr()` and `VisitPrintExpr()`, each of which represents the operation executed when a node of the corresponding class is visited.

To execute the type checking, the method `Accept()` is called with an instance of `Type-CheckVisitor` on the root node of an abstract syntax tree. The visitor pattern requires that all the tree-node classes have this method. For example, `Accept()` of the class `AssignExpr` should be:

```
bool AssignExpr::Accept(Visitor* v) {
    return v->VisitAssignExpr(this);
}
```

This calls the method `VisitAssignExpr()` on a given `Visitor` object, which is an instance of `TypeCheckVisitor` in this case. The called method depends on the class; `Accept()` of the class `PrintExpr` calls `VisitPrintExpr()`. In either case, the invoked method recursively calls `Accept()` on the children of that node so that the child nodes are visited and the type checking is executed on this subtree.

A benefit of this design is that the programmer can define another subclass of `Visitor` and easily implement a tree traverse for a different operation. For example, the compiler would also need `CodeGenerationVisitor`. However, this benefit comes with a relatively complex class structure; all the tree-node classes must have a method `Accept()` and an abstract class `Visitor` needs to be defined. This extra work for taking advantage of the visitor pattern is not difficult, but is tedious and error-prone, since it is boring repetition of simple work, which is to add a method `Accept()` to all the tree-node classes and to define a class `Visitor` so that it has methods corresponding to every tree-node class.

A natural and simple idea for avoiding this problem is to use macros for automating this extra work for the visitor pattern. Ideally, only a simple annotation to the tree-node classes should invoke macro expansions so that the method `Accept()` is added and the abstract class `Visitor` is defined. Suppose that `visitorPattern` is an annotation. The following code:

```
visitorPattern class AssignExpr {
public:
    Expr *left, *right;
      :
};
visitorPattern class PrintExpr {
public:
    Expr* printed_value;
      :
};
```

should be processed by the macro system and translated into something like this:

```
class Visitor {              // abstract class
public:
    bool VisitAssignExpr(AssignExpr*) = 0;
    bool VisitPrintExpr(PrintExpr*) = 0;
};
class AssignExpr {
public:
    bool Accept(Visitor* v) { return v->VisitAssignExpr(this); }
    Expr *left, *right;
      :
};
class PrintExpr {
public:
    bool Accept(Visitor* v) { return v->VisitPrintExpr(this); }
    Expr* printed_value;
      :
};
```

The macro expansion shown above is, unfortunately, difficult to handle with traditional macro systems. Obviously, the standard C++ macro system cannot handle it since its macros are applied only to a symbol or a function-call expression. Even if the whole class declaration is given to a macro as an argument, the C++ macro system cannot expand the declaration to include the method `Accept()`. This is because the macro arguments are not divided into smaller pieces for performing complex substitution. For example, a macro m cannot expand `m(ABC)` into `ABxC` (the macro argument `ABC` cannot be divided into `AB` and `C`).

If a system like Lisp macros is used, macro arguments can be flexibly divided, transformed, and inspected. Lisp's macro system deals with macro arguments as a tree of symbols, which can be manipulated as other regular data structures. Such macro systems have been also developed for languages like C, which has a more complex grammar than Lisp [24, 13, 25, 16]. These macro systems are called programmable syntax macros since their macro arguments are not parse trees but abstract syntax trees (ASTs) so that it is easy to handle the complex grammar. Significant design issues for syntax macros are (1) how to specify places where a macro is expanded in a given AST, and (2) how to divide macro arguments into desirable subtrees. As for (1), A* [13] invokes a macro if a given AST matches a pattern written in BNF. This feature enables macro expansion without a macro name; for example, A* can transform all the `if` statements appearing in a program. As for (2), MS^2 [25] uses a special pattern-match language for parsing macro arguments. In this language, patterns are specified with tokens and the types of ASTs (that is, non-terminal symbols in the grammar).

These syntax macro systems are powerful and general-purpose systems, but they still require their programmers to write complicated patterns for describing a macro for the visitor pattern. Although adding a new method should be a simple operation in object-oriented languages, the syntax macro systems require writing a complex pattern or program to compute where an AST representing the added method is attached to the AST representing a class declaration. Writing a macro for defining an abstract class `Visitor` is also difficult. Although the macro needs to collect the names of all the tree-node classes, no direct supports are provided by the syntax macro systems. Again, the programmer has to write a complex pattern to retrieve the class names. XL [16] provides semantic information obtained by static program analysis in macro functions, but it is a functional language without object orientation. The semantic information provided by XL is limited to the static type of expressions and so on.

3: OpenC++

The first version of our C++ macro system called OpenC++ version 2.0 [3] had the same problem mentioned above. Since we noticed this in response to user requests on OpenC++, we have been examining a solution so that OpenC++ version 2.5 has a complete new interface meeting the users' demands. This section presents the new interface and how it addresses the problem.

3.1: Syntactic Structure vs. Logical Structure

Our observation is that a drawback of the current macro systems is that an abstract syntax tree (AST) is used for macro processing. This is good for languages such as Lisp and C, in which function calls are primary language constructs, but not for object-oriented languages such as C++. Because C++ has a complex grammar, the logical structure of programs is less aligned with the syntactic structure represented by ASTs than it is in procedural programs. C++ macros thus tend to be difficult to write. For example, it is not straightforward to remove a given method from the AST representing a class declaration in C++. To do this, the macro programmer is required to have detailed knowledge about the structure of that AST.

OpenC++ borrows ideas from reflection [21, 17] and thus, instead of ASTs, it provides *metaobjects* for macro processing. The metaobjects are regular C++ objects representing the *meta* view of the processed program in object orientation. As in other reflective systems like the CLOS MOP [11] and ObjVlisp [5], classes and methods (or members in the C++ terminology) appearing in a program are chosen as metaobjects. OpenC++ represents a program by a collection of those metaobjects, which corresponds to a logical structure of that program. Through these metaobjects, macro programs can access the semantic information of the program and even transform the program. For example, the class metaobjects provide methods to get a super class of the class, to get the list of methods of the class, and to add a new method to the class.

While ASTs represent the syntactic structure of a program, metaobjects represent its logical structure. In this logical representation, all the occurrences of language constructs related to each other but spread over a program are collected to form a single aggregate. For example, a class metaobject includes links to all the occurrences of language constructs involved with the class represented by that metaobject. Those language constructs are base classes (i.e. super classes), member functions, data members, expressions for calling a member function on an instance of that class, and so on. Macros can easily access and manipulate those constructs through the links of the metaobject. On the other hand, in the syntactic representation, the occurrences of those language constructs belong to different ASTs if they appear at different locations in the program. For example, an expression for calling a member function on an instance of a class does not belong to the AST representing the declaration of that class. It instead belongs to the AST representing a function body in which that expression appears. Therefore, it is significantly difficult to obtain an aggregate of language constructs involved with each other unless they are adjacently located in a program.

To provide the representation of a logical structure, the OpenC++ compiler first parses a source program into a parse tree and converts it to a collection of metaobjects. Then macros written by programmers, which are called *meta-level programs* in OpenC++, access and modify these metaobjects. The modifications applied to the metaobjects are finally reflected in the source program. The OpenC++ compiler re-converts the metaobjects to a source program according to the modifications and transfers the obtained source program to a regular C++ compiler such as GNU C++. This re-conversion is performed to enable the use of an off-the-shelf compiler for the back end.

3.2: Programming interface of OpenC++

OpenC++ provides two kinds of metaobjects: class metaobjects and member metaobjects (a member means a method or a field). The OpenC++ compiler reads a source program and makes a class metaobject for every class in the source program. The class metaobject contains member metaobjects, each of which represents a member of that class. We below illustrate how these metaobjects are used for macro processing.

3.2.1: Metaobjects

The class metaobjects provide an interface to access the definition of a class from the viewpoint of the logical structure. We below show some of the member functions defined on class metaobjects:

- `Ptree* Name()`
  This returns the name of the class. `Ptree` is the type representing parse trees or symbols.

- `Class* NthBaseClass(int n)`
  This returns the n-th base class of the class.

- `bool NthMember(int n, Member& m)`
  This returns `true` if the class has the n-th member. The member metaobject for the n-th member is returned in m.

- `void RemoveBaseClasses()`
  This removes all the base classes from the class.

- `void AppendBaseClass(Class* c, int spec = Public,`
  `                      bool is_virtual = false)`
  This appends a class c to the list of the base classes. The arguments `spec` and `is_virtual` specify attributes of the appended base class.

- `void ChangeMember(Member& m)`
  This changes the definition of the member m.

- `void RemoveMember(Member& m)`
  This removes the member m from the class.

- `void AppendMember(Member& m, int spec = Public)`
  This appends a new member m to the class.

The member metaobject returned by `NthMember()` provides an interface to access the definition of a member. The following are some of member functions defined on the member metaobject:

- `Ptree* Name()`
  This returns the name of the member.

- `Ptree* FunctionBody()`
  This returns the function body of the member.

- `void Signature(TypeInfo& t)`
  This returns the signature of the member in t. If the member is a data member, the type of that data member is returned.

- `IsPublic()`
  This returns `true` if the member is a public member.

- `void SetName(Ptree* new_name)`
  This changes the name of the member to new_name.

- `void SetFunctionBody(Ptree* new_body)`
  This changes the function body of the member to new_body. The new function body is given in the form of parse tree.

3.2.2: Macro definition

The class metaobjects are not only passive data structures processed by macros. OpenC++ macros are defined as member functions on class metaobjects. The OpenC++ compiler calls one of these member functions for translating every code fragment, such as a class declaration and an expression for reading a data member. The member function is invoked on a class metaobject representing a class involved with that code fragment. Recall that a class metaobject includes links to related code fragments. Programmers who want macro processing define a new metaclass, that is, a new class for class metaobjects, and override some of these functions.

This framework was originally proposed in OpenC++ version 2.0 [3] and inherited by the new version. However, the class metaobjects in version 2.0 deal with an AST for macro expansion and hence it causes the same problem as other AST-based macro systems. This problem has been addressed in the new version shown here so that the class metaobjects deal with metaobjects.

We below show the member functions for macro processing. All of them are defined on class metaobjects.

Initialization:

The OpenC++ compiler first calls a `static` member function `Initialize()` on every meta-class. It does not translate any code fragment but is used to register a new keyword to the parser so that the compiler accepts extended syntax.

Class declaration:

To expand a macro for a class declaration, `TranslateClass()` is called on every class metaobject. It is responsible for transforming the declaration of the class represented by the class metaobject called on.

Member function:

To expand a macro for the implementation of a member function, `TranslateMemberFunction()` is called on the class metaobject that the member function belongs to. `TranslateMemberFunction()` receives a member metaobject representing the implementation of a member function. It can transform a program through that metaobject.

Expression:

The OpenC++ compiler calls `TranslateMemberCall()` on a class metaobject if it encounters an expression calling a member function on an instance of that class. If the expression is `p->Move(3, 4)` and `p` is an instance of a `Point` class, then the compiler calls `TranslateMemberCall()` on the `Point` class metaobject. The result of this member function is substituted for the original expression `p->Move(3, 4)`. The compiler also calls different member functions if it encounters other kinds of expressions.

The member functions for translating expressions receive an AST and return another AST. This is the same protocol as AST-based macro systems; We chose this since the logical structures of expressions are well aligned with their syntactic structures. However, those member functions are called on a class metaobject and translate only expressions involved with a specific class. Other macro systems do not directly support this class-based macro expansion.

Finalization:

After all the expressions are processed, the OpenC++ compiler calls `FinalizeInstance()` on every class metaobject and `FinalizeClass()` on every metaclass. These member functions are used to append a code fragment at the end of a source program. Since the whole source program has been already processed, these member functions can access all the occurrences of related language constructs and append code fragments depending on them. A user-defined metaclass can override these member functions and append, for example, the declaration of a class inheriting from all the classes included in a source program. This kind of class declaration is extremely difficult to produce by traditional macro systems since only adjacent language constructs are accessible from macros.

3.3: The Macro for the Visitor Pattern

In the rest of this section, we illustrate how the macro for the visitor pattern is written in OpenC++. If using a macro written in OpenC++, programmers can write a program following the visitor pattern as below:

```
metaclass VpClass;

visitorPattern class AssignExpr { ... };
visitorPattern class PrintExpr { ... };
```

The `metaclass` declaration in the first lines informs the OpenC++ compiler that a macro set `VpClass` (visitor pattern class) is used. A keyword `visitorPattern` associates the following class with the metaclass `VpClass` and invokes the macro on that class.

The metaclass `VpClass` overrides three member functions inherited from the default metaclass `Class`:

```
class VpClass : public Class {
public:
    static bool Initialize();
    void TranslateClass(Environment*);
    static Ptree* FinalizeClass();
};
```

The first member function `Initialize()` is called by the OpenC++ compiler during initialization. It registers the keyword `visitorPattern`:

```
static bool VpClass::Initialize() {
    RegisterMetaclass("visitorPattern", "VpClass");
    return true;
}
```

The second member function `TranslateClass()` is a macro function for translating the declaration of a class associated with this metaclass. It adds `Accept()` to the associated class.

```
void VpClass::TranslateClass(Environment* e){
    Ptree* mf = Ptree::Make(
        "public: "
        "bool Accept(Visitor* v){"
        "   return v->Visit%p(this); }", Name());
    AppendMember(mf);
}
```

This member function first constructs a parse tree representing the member function `Accept()` and then appends it to the class. `Ptree::Make()` is a function to construct a parse tree from a character string. The occurrence of `%p` is replaced with the resulting value of `Name()`, which is the name of the class. `AppendMember()` appends to the class a member represented by either a member metaobject or a parse tree.

The last member function `FinalizeClass()` is called at the end of compilation. It produces the definition of an abstract class `Visitor`:

```
Ptree* VpClass::FinalizeClass(){
    ClassArray classes;
    int n = InstancesOf("VpClass", classes);
    // mems is the list of members
    Ptree* mems = nil;
```

```
for(int i = 0; i < n; ++i){
    Ptree* name = classes[i]->Name();
    Ptree* m = Ptree::Make("bool Visit%p(%p*) = 0;",
                            name, name);
    //  concatenate the constructed member to the rest
    mems = Ptree::Cons(m, mems);
}
ofstream* file = new ofstream("visitor.h");
file << Ptree::Make("class Visitor {"
                    "public: %p };", mems);
return nil;
}
```

This member function first calls `InstancesOf()` and collects all the classes associated with this metaclass. Then, it constructs a parse tree representing an abstract class `Visitor` and writes the constructed parse tree to a file `visitor.h`. Note that the implementation of `VpClass` assumes that all the tree-node classes are included in a single source file. This means that separate compilation is not possible if `VpClass` is used. To avoid this problem, the implementation of `VpClass` can be improved to record processed tree-node classes in a file and produce `Visitor` by referring to that file at the end of separate compilation. OpenC++ provides mechanisms supporting this improved implementation, but details of that are beyond the scope of this paper.

To perform the macro expansion by `VpClass`, the OpenC++ compiler first compiles the meta-level program describing the metaclass `VpClass` and then a source program including `Assign-Expr` and `PrintExpr`. If it encounters the `metaclass` declaration in the source program, it dynamically loads the compiled `VpClass` and performs the macro expansion according to the definition of `VpClass`. As we showed in Section 2, this macro processing produces the definition of an abstract class `Visitor` and appends a member function `Accept()` to all the tree-node classes.

4: Other examples

The power of OpenC++ for macro processing enables a number of useful class libraries and rapid implementation of extended C++ languages for distribution, transactions, persistence, and others. However, those realistic examples are complex and long. In this section, we instead present examples that are simple but useful to illustrate the functionality of OpenC++.

4.1: Wrapper

Making *wrappers* is a programming technique frequently used for adding extended functionality such as distribution and persistence to objects. It is also similar to the decorator pattern [8]. We below show how OpenC++ helps programmers make wrappers.

Although there are several variations of this technique, the basic idea is illustrated by the following source-code translation. Suppose that we have a class `Rectangle`:

```
class Rectangle {
public:
    void Stretch(int, int);
private:
    int ulx, uly, lrx, lry;
};
void Rectangle::Stretch(int dx, int dy){
    lrx += dx; lry += dy;
}
```

Making a wrapper means to rename `Stretch()` to `_Stretch()` and add another version of `Stretch()` to the class `Rectangle`:

```
class Rectangle {
public:
    void Stretch(int dx, int dy) { ++counter; _Stretch(dx, dy); }
    void _Stretch(int, int);
private:
    int ulx, uly, lrx, lry;
};
void Rectangle::_Stretch(int dx, int dy){
    lrx += dx; lry += dy;
}
```

The added member function `Stretch()` is a wrapper. It performs computation necessary for extended functionality (in the case above, to increment `counter` for counting the number of invocations of this function) and then calls the original function, which has been renamed to `_Stretch()`.

This translation, while conceptually simple, is complicated in an AST-based (abstract syntax tree based) macro system. The difficulties are due to the complexity of the grammar of C++. The first difficulty is to retrieve the name of a member function. Since the type system of C++ allows a member function to have a complex signature such as:

```
int (*Stretch(int, int))()
```

(This means that `Stretch()` returns a pointer to a function), it is not straightforward to write a general pattern that can retrieve the function name in all cases. Another difficulty is to retrieve the argument names, `dx` and `dy`. Since an argument name is optional in a declaration, it must be implicitly filled if it is not specified by the programmer. In the example above, since the original declaration of `Stretch()` does not include argument names, appropriate names must be chosen for constructing the declaration of new `Stretch()`.

The metaobjects of OpenC++ simplify these tedious tasks. The metaclass `WrapperClass` for performing the translation shown above is written as follows:

```
class WrapperClass : public Class {
public:
    void TranslateClass(Environment*);
    void TranslateMemberFunction(Environment*, Member&);
private:
    Ptree* Rename(Ptree* name);
    void MakeWrapper(Member& member, Ptree* org_name);
};
```

First, `TranslateClass()` performs renaming of member functions and adding wrapper functions:

```
void WrapperClass::TranslateClass(Environment* env)
{
    Member member;
    int i = 0;
    while(NthMember(i++, member))
        if(member.IsPublic() && member.IsFunction()){
            // execute the following code for every member function
            Member wrapper = member;
            // rename the original member
            Ptree* new_name = Rename(member.Name());
```

```
      member.SetName(new_name);
      ChangeMember(member);
      // add a wrapper function
      MakeWrapper(wrapper, new_name);
      AppendMember(wrapper, Class::Public);
   }
}
```

The function `Rename()` in the above code is also defined in `WrapperClass`. It returns a parse tree representing a new name such as `_Stretch()`. Note that the original member name is obtained by simply calling `member.Name()`.

The function `MakeWrapper()` makes a member metaobject for the wrapper from the metaobject for the original member function:

```
void WrapperClass::MakeWrapper(Member& member, Ptree* org_name)
    Ptree* body = Ptree::Make("{ ++counter; %p(%p); }",
                                org_name, member.Arguments());
      member.SetFunctionBody(body);
}
```

Note that the actual arguments for calling the original function is computed by `member.Arguments()`. This function inspects a member declaration and fills missing argument names if they are not specified. The programmer does not need to be concerned that formal argument names are optional in C++.

Finally, `WrapperClass` overrides the member function `TranslateMemberFunction()` to rename a member name appearing in the implementation of a member function:

```
void WrapperClass::TranslateMemberFunction(Environment* e,
                                            Member& mf)
{
    if(mf.IsPublic())
        mf.SetName(Rename(member.Name()));
}
```

This is called on the implementation of every member function. `mf` is a member metaobject representing that implementation. `SetName()` gives a new name to the member function specified by `mf` and the new name is reflected in the source program.

4.2: Simple Protocol Checker

OpenC++ can be used to produce a warning message specialized in a class library. Although class libraries often have a protocol that the programs using the class library must follow, regular C++ does not provide the ability to produce warning messages if the programs are not following the protocol. OpenC++ enables such warning messages. In fact, OpenC++ itself uses this ability for examining whether a meta-level program is correctly written.

Suppose that a class library includes a class `DialogBox` and its subclasses must not override a `virtual` function `move()` defined in `DialogBox`. To examine whether this protocol is followed by user's subclasses, the class library can include a metaclass `ProtocolCheckClass` associated with `DialogBox`. The metaclass `ProtocolCheckClass` overrides a member function `TranslateClass()` to include the following code:

```
Member m;
if(!Name()->Eq("DialogBox") && LookupMember("move", m)
                                        && m.IsVirtual())
```

```
WarningMessage("move() is not overridable.");
```

This code produces an warning message if a class except DialogBox defines a virtual function move(). Since subclasses of DialogBox inherit the metaclass, the code above is executed on all the subclasses and it examines whether they follow the protocol.

Also, suppose that the class DialogBox has provided a virtual function quit() but this member function is obsolete in a new version of the library. The metaclass ProtocolCheck-Class can be extended to produce a warning message if a subclass of DialogBox falsely overrides quit() of DialogBox, which does not exist any more. Regular C++ compilers cannot produce such a warning message because they recognize that quit() is not overridden but newly defined in the subclass.

5: Related Work

Although OpenC++ is a reflective system, its reflectiveness is for meta programming at compile time. Most of other reflective systems are for meta programming at runtime [23, 20, 19, 18, 22, 15, 6], and thus OpenC++ should be called a system based on compile-time reflection or, in other words, a macro system the programming interface of which is borrowed from reflection. As for runtime reflection, the usefulness of metaclasses for customizing a class structure has been studied by Classtalk [2, 14]. Although Classtalk is a variant of Smalltalk with runtime reflection but not a macro system, they also claimed that metaclasses were a good framework for implementing customization of a class, for example, adding a method, changing a super class, and so on. They also mentioned that the ability of such customization improved the design of class libraries.

OpenC++ version 1.0 and 2.0 were presented in different articles [4, 3]. Version 1.0 provided the ability of not compile-time reflection but runtime reflection. The difference between version 2.0 and version 2.5 presented in this paper is that the data structure used for macro processing in 2.0 is not a metaobject but an AST. Version 2.0 hence involves the same problem as other macro systems.

This problem is also found in other systems based on compile-time reflection [10, 9]. For example, MPC++ [10] executes macro processing with ASTs. Although MPC++ uses metaobjects, their metaobjects are the nodes of an AST but they do not enable logical accesses to a program. Hence MPC++ still involves a problem due to using ASTs although it provides programming supports for dealing with a complex AST.

6: Conclusion

This paper presented OpenC++, which is a C++ macro system based on a meta-level architecture borrowed from reflection. Unlike traditional macro systems, OpenC++ provides metaobjects as the data structure processed by macros. The OpenC++ macros, which are called meta-level programs, deal with those metaobjects to translate a source program. Since the metaobjects enable accesses to the logical structure of the program, they make it easier to implement typical macro processing in C++ than with other AST-based (abstract syntax tree based) macro systems. This is significant in object-oriented programming, in which the logical structure of programs are not directly reflected in the syntactic structure.

OpenC++ does not provide a general-purpose solution for complex macro processing. In some cases, other macro systems such as A* [13] and MS^2 [25] would be more appropriate. However, we believe that OpenC++ is effective for macro processing typical in object-oriented programming because the metaobjects enable logical accesses to a source program. As we showed in examples, this ability is what typical macro processing requires in object-oriented programming but A* or MS^2 do not provide since they use ASTs and a pattern-match language.

OpenC++ presented in this paper is freely available from the web site:

http://www.softlab.is.tsukuba.ac.jp/~chiba/openc++.html

The distribution package includes source files, documentation, and sample programs.

Acknowledgment

OpenC++ was initially developed when the author was staying at Xerox Palo Alto Research Center. I would like to thank Gregor Kiczales and John Lamping for their helpful comments. I would also thank all the OpenC++ users, who gave me code, bug reports, and valuable feedback.

References

[1] American National Standards Institute, Inc. *ANSI Standard on C*, 1990. ANSI X3.159-1989.

[2] Jean-Pierre Briot and Pierre Cointe. Programming with explicit metaclasses in smalltalk-80. In *Proc. of ACM Conf. on Object-Oriented Programming Systems, Languages, and Applications*, pages 419–431. ACM, October 1989.

[3] S. Chiba. A metaobject protocol for c++. In *Proc. of ACM Conf. on Object-Oriented Programming Systems, Languages, and Applications*, number 10 in SIGPLAN Notices vol. 30, pages 285–299. ACM, 1995.

[4] S. Chiba and T. Masuda. Designing an extensible distributed language with a meta-level architecture. In *Proc. of the 7th European Conference on Object-Oriented Programming*, LNCS 707, pages 482–501. Springer-Verlag, 1993.

[5] Pierre Cointe. Metaclasses are first class: The ObjVlisp model. In *Proc. of ACM Conf. on Object-Oriented Programming Systems, Languages, and Applications*, pages 156–167, 1987.

[6] J. C. Fabre and T. Pérennou. A metaobject architecture for fault tolerant distributed systems: The friends approach. *IEEE Transactions on Computers*, 47(1):78–95, 1998.

[7] Jean-Charles Fabre and Shigeru Chiba, editors. *Proc. of Workshop on Reflective Programming in C++ and Java*, UTCCP Report 98-4. Center for Computational Physics, University of Tsukuba, Japan, 1998. (held at ACM OOPSLA'98).

[8] E. Gamma, R. Helm, R. Johnson, and J. Vlissides. *Design Patterns*. Addison-Wesley, 1994.

[9] Yuuji Ichisugi and Yves Roudier. Extensible java preprocessor kit and tiny data-parallel java. In *Proc. of ISCOPE '97*, number 1343 in LNCS, 1997.

[10] Y. Ishikawa, A. Hori, M. Sato, M. Matsuda, J. Nolte, H. Tezuka, H. Konaka, M. Maeda, and K. Kubota. Design and implementation of metalevel architecture in c++ — MPC++ approach —. In *Proc. of Reflection 96*, pages 153–166, Apr. 1996.

[11] G. Kiczales, J. des Rivières, and D. G. Bobrow. *The Art of the Metaobject Protocol*. The MIT Press, 1991.

[12] M. O. Killijian, J. C. Fabre, J. C. Ruiz-Garcia, and S. Chiba. A metaobject protocol for fault-tolerant corba applications. In *Proc. of the 17th IEEE Symp. on Reliable Distributed Systems (SRDS '98)*, pages 127–134, 1998. (Also available as Research Report 98139, LAAS, France).

[13] D. A. Ladd and J. C. Ramming. A*: A language for implementing language processors. *IEEE Trans. on Software Engineering*, 21(11):894–901, 1995.

[14] Thomas Ledoux and Pierre Cointe. Explicit metaclass as a tool for improving the design of class libraries. In *Proc. of the 2nd Int'l Symp. on Object Technologies for Advanced Software (ISOTAS)*, LNCS 1049, pages 38–55. Springer, Mar. 1996.

[15] C. P. Lunau. A reflective architecture for process control applications. In *ECOOP'97 — Object-Oriented Programming*, volume 1241, pages 170–189. Spriner, 1997.

[16] William Maddox. Semantically-sensitive macroprocessing. Master's thesis (ucb/csd 89/545), University of California, Berkeley, 1989.

[17] P. Maes. Concepts and experiments in computational reflection. In *Proc. of ACM Conf. on Object-Oriented Programming Systems, Languages, and Applications*, pages 147–155, 1987.

[18] H. Masuhara, S. Matsuoka, T. Watanabe, and A. Yonezawa. Object-oriented concurrent reflective languages can be implemented efficiently. In *Proc. of ACM Conf. on Object-Oriented Programming Systems, Languages, and Applications*, pages 127–144, 1992.

[19] S. Matsuoka, T. Watanabe, and A. Yonezawa. Hybrid group reflective architecture for object-oriented concurrent reflective programming. In *Proc. of European Conf. on Object-Oriented Programming '91*, number 512 in LNCS, pages 231–250. Springer-Verlag, 1991.

[20] A. Paepcke. PCLOS: Stress testing CLOS Experiencing the metaobject protocol. In *Proc. of ACM Conf. on Object-Oriented Programming Systems, Languages, and Applications*, pages 194–211, 1990.

[21] B. C. Smith. Reflection and semantics in lisp. In *Proc. of ACM Symp. on Principles of Programming Languages*, pages 23–35, 1984.

[22] R. J. Stroud and Z. Wu. Using metaobject protocols to implement atomic data types. In *Proc. of the 9th European Conference on Object-Oriented Programming*, LNCS 952, pages 168–189. Springer-Verlag, 1995.

[23] T. Watanabe and A. Yonezawa. Reflection in an object-oriented concurrent language. In *Proc. of ACM Conf. on Object-Oriented Programming Systems, Languages, and Applications*, pages 306–315, 1988.

[24] B. Wegbreit. *Studies in Extensible Programming Languages*. Outstanding dissertations in the computer sciences. Garland Publishing, Inc., 1980. (based on the author's thesis, Harvard, 1970).

[25] Daniel Weise and Roger Crew. Programmable syntax macros. In *Proc. of Conf. on Programming Language Design and Implementation*, volume 28, no. 6, pages 156–165. ACM SIGPLAN Notices, 1993.

Forward vs. Reverse Traversal in Path Expression Query Processing

David Taniar
Monash University - GSCIT
Australia
David.Taniar@infotech.monash.edu.au

Abstract

Path traversals have been recognised as one of the strengths of object-oriented query processing, as information retrieval can be achieved through pointer navigation. There are two existing path traversal methods, namely "forward" and "reverse traversal". In this paper, we analyse and compare the two traversal methods. Our results show that forward traversal is suitable for path expression queries involving selection operations on the start of the path expression, as the selection operations provide a filtering mechanism. Furthermore, redundant accesses to the associated objects may also be avoided indirectly through filtering. In contrast, reverse traversal is suitable for path expression queries involving selection operations at the end of path expression, since the problem of redundant accesses to the associated objects may be avoided. From our analysis, we formulated two lemmas on path traversals. These lemmas are anticipated to be used as a foundation for future query optimization of general path expression queries involving an arbitrary number of classes connected in relationships.

1 Introduction

Objects are usually not independent, and they can be connected to each other through the *aggregation/association* relationships. This relationship forms complex objects that may include objects from many different classes. A typical object-oriented query is to retrieve objects that satisfy certain predicates. These predicates may appear at any classes connected through aggregation/association relationships. Queries on these hierarchies are known as *path expression queries* [6]. Processing these queries is usually done through path traversal.

Path traversals have been recognised as one of the strengths of object-oriented query processing, as information retrieval can be achieved through pointer navigation. For 2-class path expression queries, there are two types of path traversals: *forward* and *reverse* traversal. A *mixed* traversal between forward and reverse traversals can be applied to complex path expression queries involving more than two classes.

It is the aim of this paper to present a comparative analysis between forward traversal and reverse traversal in object-oriented query processing. The results of this comparison may be used as a guideline for optimising general path expression queries. General path expression queries normally consist of more than 2 classes connected through relationships. As these queries can be built upon multiple 2-class path expressions, the results of our analysis concerning forward and reverse traversals can be applied. The discussion on path expression query optimization is, however, out of scope of this paper.

The rest of this paper is organised as follows. Section 2 and 3 describe forward and reverse traversal techniques in path expression query processing. Section 4 presents a quantitative performance analysis of the two traversal methods. Section 5 presents the experimental results. Section 6 discusses related work. And finally, section 7 gives the conclusions and explains future work.

2 Forward Traversal Processing

Since path expression queries involve multiple classes along aggregation hierarchies, *forward traversal* exploits the associativity within complex objects. All associated objects connected to a root object assemble a complex object. This associative approach views a complex object as a cluster, and consequently processing these objects can be done together.

Figure 1 gives an example of class schema and its instantiations; and a forward traversal of the objects. In this paper, class *A* is referred to as a *root class*, whereas class *B* is called an *associated class*. Further, objects of a root class are *root objects*, and objects of an associated class are *associated objects*. The number of associated objects for a root object is known as the *fan-out* degree of that root object. In this example, the fan-out degree of a_1, a_2 and a_3 are equal to 2, 3 and 1, respectively. Lower case letters are used to indicate OIDs. We use a graph notation to represent class schemas and instantiations. Circles are classes, whereas quarter circles are objects. The lines represent the links/relationships among classes or object. A typical query from this schema is to select objects that satisfy some predicates of both class *A* and *B* [3, 6]. The following is the query which is expressed in OQL (Object Query Language) [4].

```
Select a
From a in A, b in a.rel
Where a.attr1 = constant AND b.attr1 = constant;
```

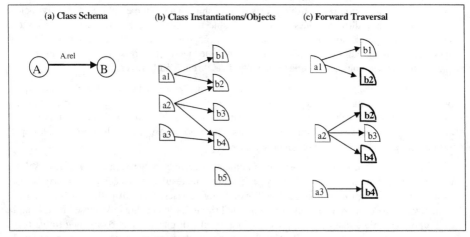

(a) Class Schema	(b) Class Instantiations/Objects	(c) Forward Traversal

Figure 1. Class Schema, Instantiations, and Forward Traversals

Using this associative approach, objects along the association path that are not reachable from the root object will not be processed (e.g. object *b5*). This method is very attractive mainly because of the filtering feature. In this case, objects that do not form a complex object described in the query predicate are discarded naturally.

A problem of forward traversal is that when the cardinality of the association is *many-many* or *many-one*, associated objects referred by more than one root object will need to be visited more than once. In the example, object b_2 and b_4 are visited twice, each.

3 Reverse Traversal Processing

Reverse traversal consists of two phases: *selection* phase and *consolidation* phase. Reverse traversal is influenced by the concept where the predicate of each class is invoked independently regardless of the associative relationship. The selection phase contains selection operations, whereas the consolidation phase gathers the results from the selection phase for final presentation. In the selection phase, all associated objects are evaluated against the selection predicate. The non-selected associated objects will make the links to this associated object destroyed from the working space. In the consolidation phase, all root objects are read, and checked whether or not the links to the associated class exist. If exist, the object is selected and is put in the query result. Otherwise, this root object is not selected, as the corresponding associated objects have been discarded in the selection phase.

Reverse traversal is influenced by the concept of object copying used in object-oriented query processing [10]. The process is basically as follows. Initially, both classes together with the links are copied to a temporarily working space. Each selection predicate selects or destroys objects as it scans and processes each object. If an object is selected, the object remains in the working space. The links, that this object has, are untouched. However, if the object is not selected, it is removed from the working space. Removing the object also implies that the directed links that the object has are also removed. But, the associated objects are not automatically deleted, as their life times are independent to other objects. At the end, only objects that have been selected by the selection predicate exist in the working space. The final query result is basically those selected root objects that exist in the working space and still maintain at least one link out to an associated object that also exists in the working space.

Reverse traversal does not filter unnecessary objects prior to processing. Non-associated objects will be processed, although these objects will not be part of the query results. The processing performance of a class will be down graded by $(1-\alpha)$ times 100% percent, where α is a probability of an object of having an association with objects from a different class. This problem will not exist if both classes have *total participation* in the association relationship ($\alpha =1$).

4 Quantitative Performance Evaluation

To compare performance of the two traversal methods, it is necessary, firstly, to describe the behaviour of each traversal method in terms of cost models, and secondly, to perform analytical performance comparison between the two methods. The cost models presented in this section are merely for relative performance comparison, not for estimating the query response time. Hence, common factors (such as processing unit cost) are left out. We measure the effectiveness of each model by counting the number of objects involved in the query processing. The notations used in the cost equations are given in Table 1. We assume that the data is already retrieved from the disk. This main memory based structure for high performance databases is increasingly common, especially in OODB, because query processing in OODB requires substantial pointer navigation, which can be easily accomplished when all objects present in the main memory [9, 11].

Variables	Descriptions
r_1	Number of root objects
r_2	Number of associated objects
r'_2	Number of accesses to the associated objects
λ_1	The average *fan-out* degree of the root class
σ_i	Selectivity which gives the probability (or proportion) that a given object of the ith class is selected.

Table 1. Notations used in the cost equations

4.1 Cost Models for Forward Traversal

The cost for forward traversal is the sum of the root class cost and the associated class cost. The root class cost is equal to the number of root objects r_1 multiply the processing unit cost tp.

$$r_1.tp$$

(1)

The processing unit cost tp is a cost for processing an object. There are two main components in the processing costs: *reading/loading time* and *predicate evaluation time*. The reading/loading time is influenced by the size of object, whereas the evaluation time is determined by the length of selection predicates in each class.

Processing associated objects can be accomplished by traversing each selected root object to all of its associated objects. The number of accesses to the associated objects is determined by r'_2, which is given by

$$r'_2 = r_1.\lambda_1$$

(2)

The symbol r'_2 is differentiated from r_2 (the original number of objects), since some associated objects are processed/visited more than once. Redundant accesses to the associated objects occur only in *many-many* and *many-one* relationships. The original degree of redundancy is determined by the degree of coupling between the root class and the associated class, partly shown by the fan-out degree of the root class λ_1. For example, if $r_1=100$, $r_2=200$, and $\lambda_1=5$, the number of accesses to the associated objects (r'_2) is equal to 500. It shows that the redundancy factor is more than double. Moreover, if the fluctuation of λ_1 is high, the redundancy factor will even be higher.

If the root class includes a selection operation, not all associated objects will need to be accessed. The selection factor is shown by σ_1, which is the probability of a root object to be selected by the selection operation. By incorporating equation (2) with the selectivity factor σ_1, the cost for processing an associated class becomes:

$$(\sigma_1.r'_2).tp$$

(3)

The sum of equations (1) and (3) gives the total processing cost for a 2-class path expression using a forward traversal technique.

$$[r_1 + (\sigma_1.r'_2)]tp$$

(4)

For path expression involving i classes ($i \geq 2$), the total cost using a forward traversal becomes:

$$r_1.tp + \sum_{i=2}^{m} \left(\sigma_{(i-1)}.r'_i \right) tp$$

(5)

4.2 Cost Models for Reverse Traversal

The cost for reverse traversal is determined by the selection cost and the consolidation cost. The processing cost for the selection phase depends on whether there is one or two-class selection in the query. If both classes contain a selection operation, the selection cost is:

$$(r_1+r_2).tp$$

(6)

The consolidation cost varies depending on whether the query involves a selection on the root class and where the target class is. When the root class does not include a selection operation, the consolidation cost is the cost for going through all root objects which is given by:

$$r_1.tp$$

(7)

However, when there is a selection operation in the root class, the consolidation cost will be influenced by the selectivity factor σ_1. Hence, the consolidation cost becomes:

$$\sigma_1.r_1.tp$$

(8)

If the associated class becomes the target class (i.e., projection operation on the associated class), the consolidation cost must be added to further retrieval cost of the associated objects for projection, which is given by:

$$\sigma_1.r'_2.tp$$

(9)

Because the selection phase and the consolidation phase shows an interdependency, in which the consolidation phase cannot start before the selection phase finishes, the total cost for reverse traversal is the sum of the selection cost and the consolidation cost.

4.3 Forward Traversal vs. Reverse Traversal

Forward traversal is not only simple but also attractive, and is particularly good when there are no redundant accesses to the associated classes. Reverse traversal, in contrast, is especially suitable for highly coupled association relationships. Since each class is processed independently, the selection process is free from any associativity independency.

It becomes essential to compare performance of forward traversal and reverse traversal. In a two-class path expression query, basically there are three different cases: 2 selections (selections on the root class and the associated class), 1 selection (a selection on the associated class), and 1 selection on the root class.

132

4.3.1 Case 1:

OQL:
```
Select a
From a in A, b in a.rel
Where a.attr = constant
And b.attr = constant
```

We shall determine the condition, under which the cost of forward traversal is lower than that of reverse traversal, i.e.,

Forward traversal cost < Reverse traversal cost

$$(10)$$

From equations (4), (6) and (8), condition (10) is equivalent to

$$r_1 + \sigma_1.r'_2 \quad < \quad r_1 + r_2 + \sigma_1.r_1$$

$$(11)$$

The processing cost tp has been factored out. And for $r'_2 = r_1.\lambda_1$, condition (11) becomes

$$\sigma_1.r'_1.\lambda_1 \quad < \quad r_2 + \sigma_1.r_1$$

Now as for $\sigma_1.r_1.\lambda_1 = x.r_2$; where x represents the replication factor, the above becomes

$$x.r_2 \quad < \quad r_2 + \sigma_1.r_1$$
$$\Rightarrow \quad x.r_2 \quad < \quad r_2 + (x.r_2)/\lambda_1$$
$$\Rightarrow \quad x \quad < \quad 1+\frac{x}{\lambda_1}.$$

$$(12)$$

In the case where the relationship between the root class and the associated class is *one-one*, the values of x and λ_1 are equal to 1. Therefore, condition (12) is trivially satisfied. If the relationship is *one-many*, where $x=1$ and $\lambda_1=m$, condition (12) is also satisfied since the left hand side is equal to 1 while the right hand side is greater than 1. If the relationship is *many-one* where $x=many$ and $\lambda_1=1$, condition (12) is true since the right hand side is always 1 more than the left hand side.

In the case of *many-many* relationships, the validity of condition (12) will be determined by the values of both x and λ_1. The replication factor x is very much influenced by the selectivity degree σ_1, which serves as a filter to the whole process. Hence, the value of x is expected to be small (can even be less than 1, if the total accesses to the associated objects are smaller than the original number of objects in the associated class). If the participation of the associated class to the relationship is *partial*, the replication factor x can be greatly reduced. In these cases, condition (12) can be expected to be satisfied.

4.3.2 Case 2:

OQL:
```
Select b
From a in A, b in a.rel
Where a.attr = constant
```

We shall determine that the cost of forward traversal is lower than that of reverse traversal, by showing that

Forward traversal cost < Reverse traversal cost

$$(13)$$

From equations (4), (6), (8) and (9), condition (13) is equivalent to

$$r_1 + \sigma_1.r'_2 \quad < \quad r_1 + \sigma_1.r_1 + \sigma_1.r'_2$$

$$(14)$$

Note that the selection phase consists of selection operation on the root class only. Now, condition (14) can be derived to

$$0 \quad < \quad \sigma_1 . r_1 .$$

In the case where the selection operation σ_1 obtains some objects r_1, the right hand side becomes positive, and condition (14) is satisfied. Consequently, condition (13) is also satisfied.

4.3.3 Case 3:

$$A \xrightarrow{\pi}_{\sigma} B$$

OQL: `Select a`
`From a in A, b in a.rel`
`Where b.attr = constant`

The cost of reverse traversal is *normally* lower than that of forward traversal, i.e.,

$$\textit{Forward traversal cost} \quad > \quad \textit{Reverse traversal cost}$$

$$(15)$$

From equations (4), (6) and (7), condition (15) is equivalent to

$$r_1 + r'_2 \quad > \quad r_2 + r_1$$

Note that here, there is no selection operation on the root class. Hence, the variable σ_1 in the forward traversal cost is eliminated. Also, the selection cost in the reverse traversal consists of the selection cost for the associated class only, whereas the consolidation cost is the cost to go through all root objects. Thus, the above becomes

$$r'_2 \quad > \quad r_2$$

And for $r'_2 = r_1 . \lambda_1$, we have

$$r_1 . \lambda_1 \quad > \quad r_2 ,$$

for $\lambda_1 \geq 1$, this implies

$$\lambda_1 \quad > \quad \frac{r_2}{r_1} .$$

$$(16)$$

If $r_2 \leq r_1$, condition (16) is satisfied.

If $r_2 > r_1$, and if as in case 1 $\lambda_1 = \dfrac{x . r_2}{\sigma_1 . r_1}$, we have

$$\lambda_1 \quad > \quad \frac{r_2}{r_1}$$

$$\Rightarrow \quad \frac{x . r_2}{\sigma_1 . r_1} \quad > \quad \frac{r_2}{r_1}$$

$$\Rightarrow \quad x \quad > \quad \sigma_1$$

Since $\sigma_1 = 1$, the condition becomes

$$x \quad > \quad 1$$

If the number of accesses to the associated class is larger than the original number of associated objects, the above condition is satisfied.

Based on the three cases discussed above, two lemmas about the forward traversal and the reverse traversal are given as follows.

LEMMA 1 (FORWARD TRAVERSAL).

Forward traversal is particularly good when there is a selection operation on the root class.

LEMMA 2 (REVERSE TRAVERSAL).

Reverse traversal is suitable for path expression queries especially when filtering is not possible and the number of accesses to the associated class through path traversal from the root class is greater than the original number of associated objects.

The first lemma is concerned with cases 1 and 2, while the second lemma relates to case 3 above.

5 Experimental Performance Evaluation

The experimental environment was a Dec Alpha 2100 model running under Digital Unix operating system. The size of main memory was 2Gb. The processors are based on the 64-bit RISC technology. The 64-bit technology breaks the 2-gigabytes limitations imposed by conventional 32-bit systems. Subsequently, the usage of very large memory is common to Digital Alpha servers. Very large memory systems significantly enhance the performance of very large database applications by caching key data into memory. The experimental program was written in C++. Two-class path expressions were created.

5.1 Validation of the Cost Models

5.1.1 Validation of the Forward Traversal Cost Models

A number of experimentations have been carried out to validate the forward traversal cost models. In the experimentations, the fan-out degree of the root class is varied from 1-10. A random number generator is used to generate the fan-out degree. The selectivity degree is 1%, 5%, 10%, and 20%. The values of the selection attributes are between 1-100. They are distributed randomly to all objects. Selectivity of 1% refers to an exact match of any one value of the selection attribute. Selectivity of 5% nominates any value within a range of 5 (e.g., selection attribute<=5). Using this principle, it can be approximated an arbitrary selection degree. The unit processing cost for an object is 5.9 μsec. This includes the cost for handling the relationship. The results of using each of this selectivity degree are presented in Figure 2.

A number of observations can be made based on the experimental results. First, performance modelling through analytical models has proven to be a difficult task. It is often impossible to achieve a zero percent error rate, due to unseen overheads, which deal with lower level architecture. To show whether an analytical model is reliable, a 10% tolerance is often set. Second, the error rate is within the tolerance of 10% for all cases. For the selectivity of 20%, the average error rate is below 5%. Third, filtering is not as good as predicted. This is most probably caused by a fixed overhead, which is not influenced by the degree of selectivity. Nevertheless, the accuracy of the model is still acceptable as shown by the minimum error rate.

The results from the experimentations validate the forward traversal models as shown by the minimum error rate. Since the basic forward traversal models are justified, the analytical models can be used to perform complex queries, which employ forward traversal as the basic building block.

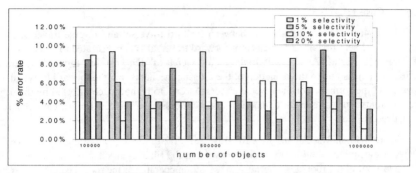

Figure 2. Validation of the Forward Traversal Cost Models

5.1.2 Validation of the Reverse Traversal Cost Models

In validating the reverse traversal cost models, a number of experimentations are carried out. In the experimentations, the associated class contains objects ranging from 50,000 to 100,000 objects. The selectivity degrees are 1%, 5%, and 10%. The fan-out degree of the root class is between 1-10, and is distributed randomly to all root objects. On average, the fan-out degree is around 4. The processing unit cost is equal to 7.6 μsec. It is higher than the processing unit cost for the forward traversal, since in the reverse traversal, the writing cost for the temporary results from the selection phase is incorporated. Figure 3 shows the experimental results.

A number of observations can be made. First, in a very few cases, the error rate is above the limit of 10%. In the majority, the error rate is well below 10%. The analytical models for the reverse traversal are shown to be quite reasonable. Second, the impact of the degree of selection on the elapsed time is not drastic, meaning that the processing cost is mainly for accessing all objects.

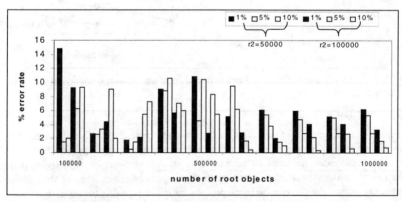

Figure 3. Validation of the Reverse Traversal Cost Models

5.2 Further Experimental Results

Further experimentations were carried out to validate the analytical comparative results of the three cases presented earlier.

5.2.1 Case 1:

Figure 4(a) shows a comparison between forward traversal and reverse traversal for query type 1 (i.e., 2 selections). Performance of forward traversal is demonstrated to be better than that of reverse traversal. As the selectivity factor increases, the cost for forward traversal also increases. This is due to the reduction of the filtering mechanism in the forward traversal. On the other hand, performance of the reverse traversal seems to be not much affected by the degree of the selectivity, since the major component of the processing is the cost for evaluating all root and associated objects.

Figure 4(b) shows that the forward traversal cost almost remains steady, until the fan-out degree is closing to a high degree. This shows that the filtering mechanism is not much affected by the fan-out of the root class, because the selection operator of the root class eliminates most of the associated objects. The trend of the reverse traversals is also similar to that of forward traversal. This is particularly because the cost is influenced by the size of the two classes. It is interesting to notice that the difference in performance between 10% replication and 20% replication of the reverse traversal is insignificant. This is due to the consolidation cost which focuses on the root class. The difference is reflected only by the selection cost of the associated class.

Overall, the results show a support for Lemma 1, where the influence of the selection operation in the root class plays an important role in bringing the forward traversal cost down.

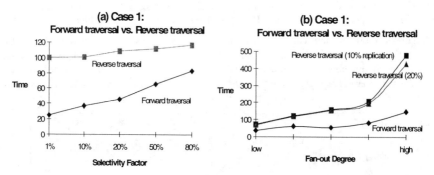

Figure 4. Case 1: Forward traversal vs. Reverse traversal

5.2.2 Case 2:

Figure 5(a) presents a comparative result for query type 2 (1 selection on the root class). Forward traversal still shows its superiority over the reverse traversal. As the selectivity factor of the root class increases, the costs for both traversal models also escalate. Moreover, performance of the reverse traversal becomes worse when the selectivity factor is more than 50%. This is because, the purpose of the consolidation process for query type 2 is to evaluate all selected root objects and their associated objects. The latter is needed, as the selected associated objects are to be projected and presented to users. This process is much influenced by the selectivity factor.

Figure 5(b) shows that the difference between the two traversal models is almost steady, regardless the fan-out degree of the root class. Performance of the two models relies heavily on the number of associated objects, which is partly shown by the fan-out degree of the root class.

It can also be concluded that for query type 2, performance of the forward traversal is better than that of reverse traversal, due to the filtering mechanism provided by the selection operator in the root class.

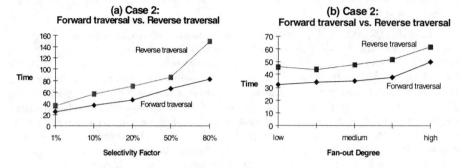

Figure 5. Case 2: Forward traversal vs. Reverse traversal

5.2.3 Case 3:

Figure 6(a) gives the results for query type 3 (1 selection on the associated class). As the selection operation is absent from the root class, the reverse traversal shows its superiority over the forward traversal, even when the size of the associated class is larger than the size of the root class. The number of accesses to the associated class significantly determines the performance of the forward traversal.

Figure 6(b) shows a comparison between the forward traversal and the reverse traversal according to the ratio between the size of the root class and the size of the associated class. The lower the associated class size, the better the performance of the reverse traversal. Performance of the reverse traversal degrades only when a lot of objects from the second class do not have any association with any root objects. This is when the associated class has a partial participation to the relationship between the root class and the associated class.

Both experimentation results shown in Figure 6 support Lemma 2, where it states, that in the absence of the filtering mechanism, forward path traversal will not enhance the performance. Therefore, the reverse traversal model is much more feasible for query type 3.

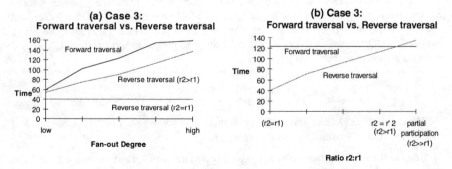

Figure 6. Case 3: Forward traversal vs. Reverse traversal

6   Related Work

Related work on path expression query processing can be divided into several categories, particularly *nested-loop* and *sort-domain* traversals, *path indices*, and *pointer-based joins*. They are described as follows.

The work by KimKC et al. [5] introduces four techniques for forward and reverse traversals, namely: *Nested-Loop Forward Traversal* (NLFT), *Sort-Domain Forward Traversal* (SDFT), *Nested-Loop Reverse Traversal* (NLRT), and *Sort-Domain Reverse Traversal* (SDRT). Extensive cost models of these four traversal techniques are reported in Bertino and Martino [2]. However, it lacks of conclusive comparison among these techniques. Our work reported in this paper has presented a comparative analysis of forward and reverse traversal, and has described two lemmas relating to the strengths of each of the traversal methods. Our aim is to bring forward rules that can be used by query optimization for optimizing complex path expression queries involving more than two classes. In optimizing such queries, the queries can be decomposed into a number of path expression sub-queries. For each sub-query, it will be determined which traversal technique is more efficient, taking the two lemmas formulated in this paper into consideration.

Path index is an index structure for path expression queries [1]. Path indices can be used to simulate reverse traversals. The reverse traversal process starts from the end class. By looking up the value of each entry of the indexed attribute, it can be determined the objects that have links to the end class. Path indices are particularly suitable for queries having a selection predicate on the indexed attribute of the end class. They were designed to simplify forward traversal technique, which is to start from a root class. If path indices are not available, traversal of such queries must start from the root object and follow the path that links to the end class. Ultimately, the selection predicate on the end class can be performed. With the availability of a path index based on the attribute of the selection predicate, there is no need for a traversal from the root class.

Path indices are designed with long path expression queries in mind. The application of such indices is also limited, since only queries having selection predicates on the indexed attribute of the end class can make use of path indices. The decision on which attribute to be indexed is known to be a classical secondary index selection problem. However, there is no doubt that when an index exists, the query that makes use of this index will be benefited.

Path expression queries are often processed by means of join, particularly *pointer-based join* [8]. The use of join in path expression queries, especially in reverse traversal, is influenced by the structure of the path expression queries expressed in OQL. Forward traversal can be easily expressed in OQL, since OQL provides a mechanism to phrase forward traversal. This is done through a dot notation. For example:

```
Select A
From A in ClassA, and B in A.rel
Where A.attr1 = constant AND B.attr1 = constant
```

The clause **B in A.rel** shows that the domain of relationship *rel* of A is pointed by B. This is a manifestation of forward traversal from A to B.

Reverse traversal mechanism is not explicitly declared in OQL. A reverse traversal can be expressed as a join. The above query can be re-written as follows.

```
Select A
From B in ClassB, A in ClassA
Where B in A.rel
AND A.attr1 = constant AND B.attr1 = constant
```

The query assumes that the relationship between *A-B* is where class *B* is at the *many* side (*one-many* or *many-many*) of the relationship. The clause **B in A.rel** checks whether each object of class *B* is a *member* of objects pointed by relationship *rel* of class *A*. If class *B* is at the *one* side, the clause **B in A.rel** can be written as **B = A.rel**. This checks whether each object of class *B* is *the same as* the object pointed by relationship *rel* of class *A*. The **B = A.rel** clause suggests that it is actually a join operation between class *A* and class *B*. The join is carried out between the OID pointed by relationship *rel* of class *A* and the OID of object of class *B*. Further investigation on reverse traversal in OQL can be very useful. This is reserved for future work.

7 Conclusions and Future Work

Simple path expression query processing is available in two forms: *forward traversal* and *reverse traversal*. An analysis and comparison between these traversal techniques have been described in this paper. Several points can be made which outline the feature of each traversal method.

Forward traversal is suitable for path expression queries involving a selection operation on the start of path traversal, as selection operation provides as a filtering mechanism. Redundant accesses to the associated objects may also be avoided indirectly through the filtering mechanism.

Reverse traversal is suitable for path expression queries involving a selection operation at the end of path traversal, since the problem of redundant accesses to the associated objects may be avoided through class independent processing. Because filtering is not performed, the forward traversal model is not a good choice for this particular query, and consequently, the reverse traversal model is the only option.

One main assumption used throughout this paper is that the path direction between the two classes in a path expression is *uni-directional*. A forward traversal is performed by following the path direction, that is starting from the root class and then following the path to the associated class. A reverse traversal is carried out by processing the associated class first and then the root class. The latter does not at all follow the path direction. In the case where the path is *bi-directional*, the forward traversal technique must choose where to start the pointer navigation. This matter is out of scope of this paper, and the issues regarding bi-directional paths have been discussed in our previous work (see [12]).

Understanding the strengths and weaknesses of each traversal technique is important for further work on optimization of general path expression queries involving arbitrary number of classes connected in relationships. In processing these complex queries, several steps may be involved. The *first step* is to decompose such complex queries into a number of sub-queries, in which each of the sub-queries forms a 2-class path expression. The query optimizer must formulate the decomposition process. The *second step* is to choose the most appropriate path traversal strategy for each of the sub-query. The two lemmas on path traversals established in this paper can be employed in deciding which path traversal technique to be used for each sub-query. Due to this important role of the lemmas in query optimization, it is very critical to understand the behaviour of each path traversal technique. This paper has not only described the two path traversal methods, but also analyzed and evaluated them. Hence, these lemmas are anticipated to become a foundation for optimization of general path expression queries.

References

[1] Bertino, E., "A Survey of Indexing Techniques for Object-Oriented Database Management Systems", *Query Processing for Advanced Database Systems*, J.C.Freytag, et al. (eds.), Morgan Kaufmann, pp. 384-418, 1994.

[2] Bertino, E. and Martino, L., *Object-Oriented Database Systems: Concepts and Architectures*, Addison-Wesley, 1993.

[3] Bertino, E., et al., "Object-Oriented Query Languages: The Notion and the Issues", *IEEE Transactions on Knowledge and Data Engineering*, vol. 4, no. 3, 1992.

[4] Cattell, R.G.G. (editor), *The Object Database Standard ODMG-93*, Release 1.1, Morgan Kaufmann Publishers, 1994.

[5] Kim, K.C., et al., "Acyclic Query Processing in Object-Oriented Databases", *MCC Technical Report*, No: ACA-ST-287-88, 1988.

[6] Kim, W., "A Model of Queries for Object-Oriented Databases", *Proceedings of the Fifteenth International Conference on Very Large Data Bases*, pp. 423-432, Amsterdam, 1989.

[7] Lanzelotte, R.S.G., et al., "Optimization of Nonrecursive Queries in OODBs", *Proceedings of the Second International Conference on Deductive and Object-Oriented Databases DOOD'91*, Munich, pp. 1-21, December 1991.

[8] Lieuwen, D.F., DeWitt, D.J. and Mehta, M., "Parallel Pointer-based Join Techniques for Object-Oriented Databases", *AT&T Technical Report*, 1993.

[9] Litwin, W. and Risch, T., "Main Memory Oriented Optimization of OO Queries Using Typed Datalog with Foreign Predicates", *IEEE Transactions on Knowledge and Data Engineering*, vol. 4, no. 6, pp. 517-528, December 1992.

[10] Meyer, B., *Object-Oriented Software Construction*, Prentice-Hall, 1988

[11] Moss, J.E.B., "Working with Persistent Objects: To Swizzle or Not to Swizzle", *IEEE Transactions on Software Engineering*, vol. 18, no. 8, pp. 657-673, August 1992.

[12] Taniar, D., and Rahayu, J.W., "Query Optimization Primitive for Path Expression Queries via Reversing Path Expression Direction", *Journal of Computing and Information*, 1998 (to appear).

From UML to IDL: A Case Study

Damien Watkins, Martin Dick and Dean Thompson
Faculty of Information Technology
Monash University, Australia
{damien,mdick,dean}@insect.sd.monash.edu.au

Abstract

Over the last two decades there has been an increase in the number of distributed object oriented systems being developed. To assist the development of these systems a number of object oriented modelling techniques have been developed. The Unified Modeling Language was principally designed to combine a number of methodologies into one. As this paper identifies, there are a number of limitations which exist between the mapping of UML designs into IDL. One solution has been to introduce additional keywords into IDLs to provide richer semantics. This paper demonstrates how semantics can be added to interfaces without extending interface definition languages and hence provide software developers with a mechanism to express the dynamic constraints of a distributed object oriented systems.

1: Introduction

Currently object oriented development techniques are being applied to the discipline of distributed heterogeneous systems development. Microsoft's Distributed Component Object Model (DCOM) and the Object Management Group's (OMG) Common Object Request Broker Architecture (CORBA) are two competing industry-standard architectures being developed for software engineers. Although both these architectures provide an infrastructure for the development of distributed systems, neither provides a complete or comprehensive analysis and design method.

The Unified Modeling Language (UML) is the amalgamation of three successful object oriented modeling techniques, the Booch Method [1], the Object Modeling Technique (OMT) [8] and Object Oriented Software Engineering (OOSE) [4]. Currently UML (and its constituent techniques) comprise the most widely adopted object oriented analysis and design methods.

This paper looks at how a distributed system specified in UML can be implemented in a distributed object oriented architecture. In the implementation process we see how many of the semantics and most of the richness of the analysis models are lost. To restore some of the semantics of the model, some extensions to the implementation are suggested.

```
int deposit(acct_no accountNumber, float amountToDeposit)
  semantics
  {
  balance(account) == @balance(account) + amountToDeposit,
  return == balance(account)
  };
```

Figure 1. Example of the Assertion Definition Language

1.1: Paper Structure

Section 2 reports on previous work which has been investigated to add richer semantics to IDLs and describes how some of these techniques have been applied to the case study. Section 3 describes the basic operation of a Radio Telescope Antenna, which is used as the case study in this paper. Section 4 shows a UML model of the Antenna system and contrasts the model and the IDL definition. This section highlights some of the problems in mapping the UML model into IDL. Section 5 and section 6 describe the effects of implementation on the architecture of the system. Finally, Section 7 draws some conclusions about the mapping of UML to IDL and the addition of semantic constructs to IDL.

2: Related Work: Extending Interface Definition Languages

The OMG's Interface Definition Language (IDL) is principally designed to provide developers with a means to be able to specify interfaces to objects independent of their implementation. Even though IDL has been successful in allowing developers to design distributed systems, as shown previously, it lacks the ability to be able to express various semantics. These semantics include the checking of pre and post conditions, the inability to specify real-time constraints on operations and not being able to specify the behavioral nature of objects.

In order to overcome this problem a number of authors have proposed extensions to IDLs. These extensions often take the form of additional keywords to support the advanced programming concepts.

2.1: Assertion Definition Language

As was identified in the PrimaVera research group at SUN Microsystems, OMG's IDL provides little support for the checking of post conditions on operations. The Assertion Definition Language (ADL) is a formal specification language principally designed to provide post condition checking. In order to achieve this the designers of ADL have provided support for encapsulation as well as defining types, objects, variables and operations [9].

In order for ADL to provide support for postcondition checking it is necessary to introduce some new keywords to the interface definition language [11]. These keywords include **semantics** which defines the semantics that an operation should follow and the symbol @ which is used to indicate where the post condition should be asserted.

As with most other IDLs, code fragments in ADL (shown in Figure 1) are written as separate units

```
type Shape
{
  model:
   boolean covers(Point p);
  interface:
   void move(Vector to);
  action specs:
   move(Vector to)
   {
     ...
   }
  invariants:
};
```

Figure 2. Example of an IDL++ definition

and hence do not embody the actual implementation code.

2.2: IDL++

IDL++ was developed by Desmond D'Souza and Alan Wills in 1996 [3]. The goal of IDL++ was to permit the developer to specify the behavioral aspects of an interface. To achieve this, IDL++ introduces a concept known as "traits".

A "trait" can best be described as being an individual specification which details the behavior of an interface or object. They normally consist of the signature of the function which is to have the behavior associated with it, along with the pre and post conditions, invariants and temporal constraints for the interface.

Traits are used as a method to formally specify the actual behavior of an operation within an interface. From IDL++ code it is possible for the software engineer to see what the actions of the interface are and hence remove any ambiguity associated with the interface name. The keywords used in IDL++ aim to enhance the actual interface definition. An example of an enhanced interface definition in IDL++ is shown in Figure 2.

Although the IDL++ code appears to be implementation code it is still a form of pseudo-code which assists the developer in understanding the semantics of the operation.

2.3: Real-time Interface Definition Language

As distributed systems develop, the need to specify quality of service (QoS) characteristics on each operation becomes important. In the original definition specified by the OMG [6] there was no provision for real-time information to be specified in the IDL. In order to address this issue, researchers at Washington University developed an interface definition language which provides the developer with the ability to specify real-time semantics for each operation [10].

Real-time Interface Definition Language (RIDL) is an interface definition language which allows the developer to specify the quality of service characteristics by making use of the RT_Operation interface and the data structure RT_Info. Once defined, these interface definitions are compiled

```
struct RT_Info
{
    Time_t worstcase_exec_time_;
    Time_t cached_exec_time_;
    Period_t period_;
    Importance importance_;
    sequence<RT_Info> dependencies_;
};
```

Figure 3. Example of a Real-Time structure in RIDL

and during compile time the associated priorities are assigned to the relevant sections of code.

An example of the RT_Info structure is shown in Figure 3 [10].

Although RIDL introduces no new keywords to the IDL it is important to note that the quality of service characteristics defined within the real-time structures are only factored in statically during compile time and cannot be dynamically expressed at run time.

2.4: Object Definition Language

The Object Definition Language (ODL) forms part of the TINA project which is the responsibility of the Telecommunications Information Networking Architecture Consortium [2]. ODL was principally designed as an extension to the OMG's IDL in an effort to address some issues that it did not cover.

These issues addressed by ODL include the ability to support multiple interface on objects[1], stream interfaces, quality of service descriptions as well as allowing the developer to specify the related behavior of an interface or object [7]. Specifically, TINA aims to address the issues of providing for application specification re-use, CASE tool development and providing the ability for type specification of application components needed at runtime.

Even though ODL is based upon OMG's IDL it does make some significant departures from the types of entities that can be defined. ODL provides support for the definition of groups, managers, objects, interfaces and data types through the introduction of new keywords. These keywords include: interface, object, group, components and supports.

An example of a definition defined by ODL is shown in Figure 4.

As mentioned above the keyword group is used to provide a level of encapsulation, the grouping together of components and objects. By encapsulating these components and objects it is necessary to provide global access points for components outside of the group to still interact with components within the group. These access points are achieved through the use of the contracts keyword which specify interfaces that components must conform to.

Additionally, within the grouped environment there also needs to be a component nominated for performing the instantiation and other initialization functions. This component is referred to as the *manager* and is specified through the use of the manager keyword.

To provide the quality of service aspects to an interface or operation the keyword with is used in conjunction with the keyword source for data which is flowing out of the component, similar to the

---

[1]This is very similar to DCOM where objects often implement numerous interfaces.

```
interface phoneJack
{
  // Specify flow types
  typedef ... VoiceFlowType;
  // Specify QoS type
  typedef ... VoiceQosType;

  source VoiceFlowType voiceDownStream
    with VoiceQosType voiceDownStreamQos;
  sink VoiceFlowtype voiceUpStream
    with VoiceQosType voiceUpStreamQos;
};
```

Figure 4. An interface definition represented in ODL

out keyword in OMG's IDL, or sink for data which is flowing into the component, similar to the in keyword for OMG's IDL.

The with keyword provides the quality of service arguments to the function being called. The type associated with the with keyword is of <type>QosType which has to be defined by the developer.

One final facility that ODL provides is the ability for the developer to specify the behavior of an object or interface. This is achieved through the use of the behavior, behaviorText and usage keywords. These keywords provide textual descriptions as to the behavior of the interface. These keywords are used more as documentation and are normally generated and interpreted with OMT packages associated with TINA.

2.5: Limitations of IDL extensions

One limitation with all of these techniques which have been mentioned above is that they require extra keywords to either COM and/or CORBA's IDL. The only exception to this is RIDL [10] which operates within the bounds of the current IDL syntax and keywords but makes use of a specialized IDL compiler which assigns priorities to the various operations to reflect the real-time nature of operations. It is important to note that RIDL only assigns these priorities at compile time and hence real-time characteristics are static in nature.

One consequence of adding keywords to IDL is that the language could grow to be all encompassing with a very verbose syntax, if every possible extension was included. The driving force behind the inclusion of all the commands into IDL, is to make the IDL files portable across all of the different systems. Hence the best solution to the problem would be to provide the extra functionality without having to extend the IDL.

Our research has proposed some concepts and facilities which can be added to IDL definitions without the need to add extra keywords but can be enforced in a running system. For a full description see [12, 13], but, in summary, this work has proposed adding:

- Path Expressions — a technique to allow the order of method invocations to be described, and
- Client Contract Objects — a technique where clients can dynamically express their requirements for method invocations.

These techniques have been implemented by:

- structured comments — where *aware* compilers can use the comments to embed semantics in the automatically generated proxy objects and *unaware* compilers merely ignore them, and
- contract objects — which are passed as ordinary parameters but which described the semantics requirements of the client. These can be Eva-luted by *aware* proxy objects or ignored by *unaware* proxy objects on distributed method invocation.

3: Radio Telescope Antenna

The system used in the case study throughout this paper is a simplified model based on the Australian Telescope Compact Array (ATCA) located at Culgoora, twenty-five kilometers west of Narrabri, New South Wales, Australia. The ATCA is operated by the Australian Telescope National Facility (ATNF) which is a division of the CSIRO. There are six radio telescope antenna at the site.

Five of these antenna are situated on a three kilometer rail track which allows the array to take on differing configurations. The sixth antenna is located to the west of the antenna array and is fixed to a separate sixty-one meter rail segment. The separation distance of the fifth and sixth antenna is three kilometers giving the array a total coverage of six kilometers. The simplified antenna simulation presented in this paper shows antenna that are capable of performing several operations, following is a brief explanation of these operations:

Activate — the antenna is turned-on, and performs self tests, effectively similar to booting a personal computer.

Calibrate — calibration of the antenna involves pointing the antenna to a *well-known* source in the sky known, as a *calibrator*, which emits a radio frequency. Based on the strength of the signal, the astronomers know when they are directly pointing at the signal.

Position — The position operation instructs the antenna to aim at a specified point in the sky. A point co-ordinate contains an elevation and azimuth for a location in the sky.

StartObservation – instructs the antenna to start reading radio waves. The signals from the antenna are sent to a correlator, to have any interference filtered from the readings, and then stored.

EndObservation — instructs the antenna to stop reading radio waves.

AdjustBandwidthTurret — adjusts a rotating turret located in the focal cabin which controls the frequencies that the signal processing unit is interested in sampling.

Stow — is responsible for placing the antenna into a safe position. This operation can take effect at any time as the antenna will automatically stow itself if the observation conditions get too dangerous for the antenna to continue. Additionally, the operator can call the stow operation when they are finished with the antenna.

The operations are only one part of the semantics of the Antenna interface. In addition to the operations there is an implied order in which the operations must be called, for example the `Activate` method must always be called first. Clients also have tight timing constraints when methods are invoked.

The radio telescope system located at Narrabri was selected as the case study for this paper due to it being a realistic example of a distributed system. The telescope array has to operate with very accurate timings so issues such as response times and the ordering of operations become very important in the day to day operations.

This paper aims to identify how the rich semantics which UML captures during the system analysis phase is lost when the system is designed in IDL. Additionally, this paper also introduces a concept where semantics such as dynamic behavior and ordering of functions can be preserved without the introduction of new keywords to an interface definition language.

4: UML to IDL Comparison

4.1: Class Diagram

A *Class Diagram* shows the classes within a model, their relationships and optionally the properties (state and behavior) of each class. The class diagram for the Antenna class is shown in Figure 5. In the current work, we are modeling in a naive way. Naturally in an implemented system, the antenna class would be broken down into several classes.

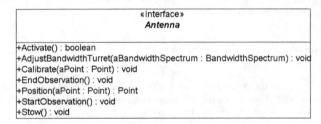

Figure 5. Antenna Class Diagram

Figure 5 and Figure 6 show the methods that can be called on the class, each method's parameter list and its type. The stereotype <<interface>> is used to designate that the Antenna interface can be implemented by many different classes.

The IDL file for the Antenna class is shown in Figure 6. As demonstrated in this figure, in general, the class diagram for an individual class maps consistently into a CORBA IDL definition. It allows the definition of the class and its methods. CORBA IDL does not permit attributes to be expressed, so attributes are not included in the mapping.[2]

A UML class diagram allows for the definition of relationships between class, such as *Aggregation, Association, Composition* and *Inheritance*. Of these only inheritance is directly supported by CORBA's IDL. Although not explicitly stated in the IDL file, the Antenna interface implicitly inherits from the superclass CORBA::Object. Other relationships are often implied by the use of other interface types as parameters, for example the use of Point as a parameter in some interface methods. Another indication of the relationship between difference interfaces is the use of module, which places related definitions into a single namespace.

---

[2] CORBA IDL does provide the keyword attribute to generate set and get methods for a logical state members, but these may or may not be actual members in the implementation class.

```
module RadioTelescope
{
  struct Point
  {
    float Elevation;
    float Azimuth;
  };
  interface Antenna
  {
    boolean Activate();
    void Calibrate(in Point aPoint);
    void StartObservation();
    void Stow();
  };
};
```

Figure 6. Interface Definition Language for Antenna

The IDL definition does allow software engineers to specify the exceptions that can be thrown on a method. In CORBA, a method without a user specified exception can still throw system exceptions, although this is not immediately obviously from the IDL file.

4.2: Dynamic Behavior

In a object oriented environment the dynamic behaviour of the system is equally as important as the structure of the system. UML, provides excellent support for describing the dynamic behaviour of the system as we will show IDL is deficient in this area.

4.2.1: State Diagram

The state diagram for the Antenna is shown in Figure 7. This diagram illustrates all of the states which exist within the Antenna class. The most salient aspect of this diagram is that the methods called on the Antenna must follow a clearly prescribed order. The concept of the ordering of methods in interfaces is not new. In fact the OMG's Object Management Architecture Guide [5] states that calling methods in an incorrect sequence may cause *Application Errors*. Although this diagram does show all of the states that exist in the antenna, there is no direct mapping from the state diagram to CORBA IDL. This is a significant lack in IDL given the importance of this requirement.

4.2.2: Sequence Diagram

The Antenna sequence diagram is shown in Figure 8. The sequence diagram highlights a significant aspect of the system, the time constraints on method calls. These are shown as guards on the transitions, such as [time < t1]. In any real-time system, time constraints are always important. Expressing these constraints early in the development process is important. Unfortunately the IDL definition offers no standardized facility to express these constraints.

It would be possible for the IDL file to include a parameter on each method to specify a completion time. But there would often be many different constraints required leading to a large number of

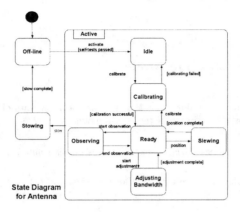

Figure 7. Antenna State Diagram

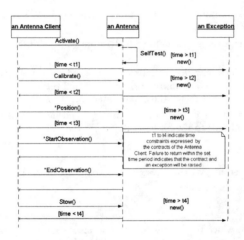

Figure 8. Antenna Sequence Diagram

ancillary parameters on each method call to allow developers to express their own requirements.

4.3: Evaluation

UML is a rich methodology as it needs to express the requirements of large systems. It therefore provides an array of techniques and models to allow software engineers to detail the semantics of systems in a language and platform independent manner. IDL however is much closer to the development phase as it must be *compiled* into executable code in a number of languages. It is this requirement that means that IDLs tend to be a minimum subset of the available programming languages, rather than a superset.

UML has generally been accepted by the object oriented community as the standard for the specification of Object Oriented systems. This paper aims to address the failings of IDL to address many of the semantics that are easily expressed in UML.

5: Logical Implementation Model

In this section we look at how adding semantics to IDLs affects the overall logical structure of the system. Following is a brief description of the logical model:

Client — a client object/process who invokes methods on distributed server objects through an interface.

Antenna Interface — is an interface definition for the Antenna, containing the methods and their parameters including a contract object and augmented with path expressions. This interface is implemented by numerous classes.

Antenna Object — is the actual server object that controls the Antenna. It implements the Server Interface.

Server Process — is the executable file that contains the server object and is launched by the ORB when a client requests a connection.

Exception — is a generic exception class in CORBA from which all user-defined exceptions must inherit.

Skeleton — is the server side proxy object that receives method invocations from clients, unmarshals parameters, invokes the method on the server object and returns the results from the server object to the client. It implements the Server Interface.

Stub — is the client side proxy object thats receives method invocations from clients, marshals and forwards method calls to the Skeleton object for the target server object. It implements the Server Interface.

All these classes would exist in any Orbix[3] system. The following classes are specific to our extended system:

Action — specifies what should happen if a Constraint is not satisfied. The Action is either to throw an exception, which terminates the method invocation or log the failure but continue with the call.

Condition — A Condition is a boolean expression that can be evaluated to either true for false. If a Condition evaluates to true, the Condition is deemed to be satisfied and no action is taken.

Contract — A Contract object has zero to many constraint objects.

Contract Failed — is a user defined exception which is thrown if a Condition fails and the Action indicates that the method invocation should be terminated.

Contract Validator — the client and sever proxy objects pass Contract objects to the validator to verify that the constraints are still valid. This relieves the proxies from the need to know or interpret any parts of the contract.

Constraint — A Constraint object is logically made up of three objects, a Condition, Location, and Action.

Invalid Operation Attempt — is a user defined exception which is thrown if an operation is invoked on an interface when that interface is not capable of performing that operation in its current state.

---

[3]Orbix is the CORBA compliant ORB used in this case study.

Location — Specifies where the Constraint should be check, either on the method call or on its return, and either at the client or server proxy object.

```
#include "contract.idl"

module RadioTelescope
{
  ... // Structure definitions removed to conserve space

  interface Antenna
  {
    // Initial state == off
    // state == off
    boolean Activate(in ContractData::Contract aContract)
      raises(ContractData::InvalidOperationAttempt,
        ContractData:: ContractFailed);
    // state == idle || state == off
    // state == idle
    void Calibrate(in Point aPoint,
                   in ContractData::Contract aContract)
      raises(ContractData::InvalidOperationAttempt,
        ContractData:: ContractFailed);
    // state == ready
    ... // Methods removed to conserve space
  };
};
```

Figure 9. Extended Interface Definition Language for Antenna

It is now possible for the software engineer to specify the logical sequence of method invocation and have the proxy objects ensure this sequence is followed. The use of a Contract object as a parameter in each method allows the client to dynamically express its requirements on each method invocation.

6: Implementation Model

The implementation model for the system is refined from the logical model and is shown in Figure 10. The major changes are that:

- the classes Condition, Location and Action reduce to enumerations,
- the class Constraint reduces to a structure,
- the class Contract reduces to a sequence of Constraint structures, and
- the Orbix infrastructure requires the generation of smart proxies and object filters to allow the *Contract Validator* to be called.

The reason that the classes Condition, Location and Action reduce to enumerations is that eventually they comprise only a single data member with access methods. The Constraint class also

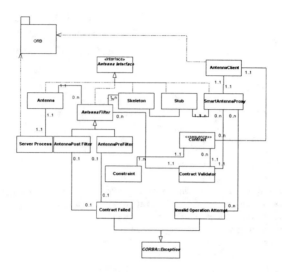

Figure 10. Class Diagram of the Implementation Model

reduces to a structure, again because it is comprised of only data members and access methods. The structure is augmented with an additional data member of type any. The data type any is a CORBA defined type that can assume the type and value of any other legally defined type. It is used to supply extra information, such as actual time values, when passing a Constraint structure.

The Contract class is implemented as a sequence. A sequence is a CORBA defined type, functionally similar to an array. As a Contract object reduces to a dynamic number of Constraint structures, the use of the sequence simplifies the result implementation code. All of these changes are minor and really a function of the programming language being used.

The major architectural changes in the implementation model are caused by the use of proxy and filter objects. These objects as a "level of indirection" between the clients/servers and the skeletons/stubs objects. Basically these objects perform two functions

- verify that each call in being made in a correct sequence, that is that the call is valid for the current state of the object, and

- they pass method invocations to the validator objects which verify that the client requirements that are expressed in the Contract object are satisfied.

7: Conclusions

Throughout this paper a number of problems have been identified with regard to the loss of semantics when systems have been specified in UML and are being mapped across to an IDL for implementation.

From the discussion which has taken place there is a clear correlation between mapping from individual classes in the class diagram to a CORBA IDL interface. A limitation which is apparent is that attributes of a class cannot be expressed.

The mapping of relationships between classes in the class diagram is poor. Only inheritance is naturally supported by IDL and in some cases this happens implicitly. Indications of the other relationships are suggested by the use of other types as parameters in method calls.

The mapping from the state diagram to CORBA's IDL is non-existent, despite the OMG identifying the problem of application errors being caused as a result of calling methods in an incorrect sequence. Additionally, the mapping for sequence diagrams and their associated guard conditions is also non-existent.

As has also been discussed there are two ways in which the addition of semantics to an interface definition language can be handled. Firstly numerous IDL extensions have been proposed to allow developers to express semantics. This idea has two limitations; the possibility of IDLs becoming verbose languages encompassing so many different requirements that they become unworkable and the possibly of IDL compilers supporting variations of IDL which will lead to incompatible IDL files.

The other method which has been discussed throughout this paper is a concept which requires no additional keywords being added to the IDL. This method solves the problems with the UML to IDL mapping and allows the IDL syntax to remain unchanged whilst at the same time maintaining compatibility with any standard IDL compiler.

References

[1] Grady Booch. *Object-Oriented Analysis and Design with Applications*. Benjamin Cummings, second edition, 1994.

[2] Martin Chapman and Stefano Montesi. *Overall Concepts and Principles of TINA*. Telecommunications Information Networking Architecture Consortium, 1.0 edition, Feb 1995.

[3] Desmond D'Souza and Alan Wills. OOA/D and CORBA/IDL: A Common Base. Technical report, ICON Computing, Inc., 1996.

[4] Ivar Jacobson. *Object Oriented Software Engineering : A Use Case Driven Approach*. Addison-Wesley, 1992.

[5] Object Management Group, Framingham Corporate Center 492 Old Connecticut Path Framingham, MA 01701 U.S.A. *The Common Object Request Broker: Architecture and Specification*, 2.0 edition, 1995.

[6] Object Management Group, Framingham Corporate Center 492 Old Connecticut Path Framingham, MA 01701 U.S.A. *The Common Object Request Broker: Architecture and Specification*, 2.2 edition, February 1998.

[7] A Parhar. *TINA Object Definition Language Manual*. Telecommunications Information Networking Architecture Consortium, Suite 110, 106 Apple Street, Tinton Falls, NJ 07724 U.S.A., 2.3 edition, July 1996. http://www.tinac.com/deliverable/deliverable.htm.

[8] James Rumbaugh, Michael Blaha, William Premerlani, Fredrick Eddy, and William Lorensen. *Object-Oriented Modeling and Design*. Prentice-Hall, 1991.

[9] Srirasm Sankar and Roger Hayes. ADL - An Interface Definition Language for Specifying and Testing Software. *ACM SIGPLAN Notices*, 29(8), August 1994.

[10] Douglas Schmidt, David Levine, and Sumedh Mungee. The Design of the TAO Real-Time Object Request Broker. *Computer Communications Journal*, 1997.

[11] X/Open SUN Microsystems. *ADL Language Reference Manaual*, 1.0 edition, 1996.

[12] Damien Watkins. Using Interface Definition Languages to Support Path Expressions and Programming by Contract. In *TOOLS 26*, volume 26 of *Technology of Object-Oriented Languages and Systems*, pages 308–317, 1998.

[13] Damien Watkins and Dean Thompson. Adding Semantics to Interface Definition Languages. In Douglas Grant, editor, *ASWEC '98*, Proceedings of Australian Software Engineering Conference '98, pages 66–78. IEEE Computer Society, 1998. ISBN: 0-8186-9187-5.

Session 3

Development
Environments, CASE

The Design of the Client User Interface for a Meta Object-Oriented CASE Tool

Chris Phillips, Steven Adams, David Page and Daniela Mehandjiska
Massey University
Palmerston North
New Zealand
email: {C.Phillips, D.Mehandjiska}@massey.ac.nz

Abstract

This paper describes the design of the client user interface for MOOT (Meta Object Oriented Tool). Both functional and non-functional requirements of the interface are defined, and design issues relating to the look and feel of the interface are discussed. Details of an instantiation for the Coad and Yourdon OOA/OOD methodology are presented and discussed. MOOT is an intelligent methodology independent customisable OO CASE tool. One of the major goals of MOOT is to provide flexible support for the description of the semantics and notations of arbitrary methodologies. This is provided through the employment of two distinct specification languages.

Introduction

A major weakness in today's CASE tools is the lack of support for multiple methodologies. Although various meta-CASE tools exist, their support for the description of the semantics of more than one methodology is limited [1]. A new CASE tool, MOOT (*Meta Object-Oriented Tool*) is being developed to address these and other identified deficiencies in CASE tool technology [2, 3, 4, 5, 6].

One of the major goals of MOOT is to provide flexible support for the description of the notation and semantics of arbitrary methodologies. Facilities are provided for methodology engineers to specify entirely new methodologies, or to adapt and extend existing ones. These specifications are in turn utilised by the tool to guide the manner in which software engineers interact with it. The aim is to provide a consistent look and feel across different methodologies, which should bring improvements in productivity.

Modern Computer Aided Software Engineering (CASE) tools are highly interactive graphics-intensive environments designed to support the development of computer based systems. Although the advantages of utilising CASE technology are well known, their adoption by industry has not been as widespread as might have been expected [7]. This situation is partly due to shortcomings in the usability and functionality of the CASE tools available today. These issues need to be addressed by the developers of CASE tools.

Research in the area of meta-CASE technology has focused largely on the underlying meta-models of such tools and the application of these meta-models to describing semantics of methodologies. Very little research has been conducted on the user interface requirements of meta-CASE tools. This is evidenced by poor results in the evaluation of their usability [8]. The design of the user interface is a much more difficult task than for a traditional piece of software, due to the high level of abstraction of meta-CASE tools.

The user interface of a meta-CASE tool is a shell that interprets definitions of the notations of the models supported by different software development methodologies. The

0-7695-0053-6/98 $10.00 © 1998 IEEE

user interface designer of a meta-CASE tool must therefore give consideration to all possible graphical notations, and is not free to make assumptions about the types of notations an end user may use. The flexibility provided by such a high level of abstraction presents additional challenges in terms of designing effective human-computer interaction mechanisms for the user interface.

This paper describes the design of the client user interface for MOOT. The architecture of MOOT is briefly described. Functional and non-functional requirements of the client interface are defined, and design issues are discussed. The issues are then focussed through the development and discussion of an instantiation of the client interface for the class diagram notation within Coad and Yourdon's OOA/OOD methodology.

Architecture of MOOT

The high level of customisation described above is provided through the use of two specification languages, SSL (Semantic Specification Language), and NDL (Notation Definition Language). These provide for the definition of the semantics and syntax of a methodology, respectively. It should be noted that the SSL description of a methodology might be associated with more than one graphical representation (NDL definition).

SSL is an object oriented language used to specify the semantics of the concepts and constraints of a particular methodology, and the various documents that are produced by application of the methodology [9]. SSL is a platform independent language with an associated virtual machine upon which it is executed [10].

NDL is a scripting language used to define the graphical notations of a methodology. NDL scripts describe how symbols and connections that appear in diagrams are rendered onto a computer display. An NDL description also provides facilities for logical distortion and binding actions to symbols and connections [11]. The logical and physical separation of the two languages is a fundamental design decision to promote reuse of semantic and syntactic methodology components.

The MOOT system consists of two logical sub-systems. The methodology development sub-system is an integrated tool-set allowing methodology engineers to specify, modify and test methodology descriptions. The CASE tool sub-system is the methodology CASE component of the MOOT environment. It is an integrated tool-set that allows a software engineer to develop software by applying methodologies described using the methodology development sub-system. Each software development project is an instance of the methodology the software engineers used to define it.

Both sub-systems make use of the MOOT Core, which insulates the underlying, shared, repository (Persistent Store). Software engineering projects and software development methodologies reside in the Persistent Store. Obviously both sub-systems have their own requirements in terms of human-computer interaction. It is the user interface requirements of the CASE tool sub-system (specifically the CASE tool client) that is the focus of attention for this paper. Figure 1 illustrates the MOOT architecture; the areas in dark grey are related to this paper.

CASE tool client

The CASE tool client provides the user interface of the CASE tool sub-system. The Case tool client is responsible for interpreting the NDL scripts that define graphical notations and managing the human-computer interaction with a software engineer. The Client propagates actions at the user interface that have an effect on the meaning of the model being derived (such as deleting or updating a symbol) to the MOOT core. Actions that do not effect the meaning of the model being drawn (such as dragging or resizing a symbol) are handled by the client.

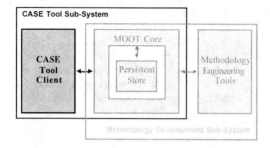

Figure 1: Architecture of the MOOT system

The client is parameterised by NDL descriptions of the notations associated with the current methodology in use. The architecture of the CASE tool client is shown in Figure 2. The Server Proxy isolates the client from the network communication protocol with the server. The Project Editor is used to maintain user projects. This includes opening and closing projects, creating and deleting models, and so on. A Model Editor is used to manage each model in a user project. Each Model Editor is responsible for maintaining the NDL description of the notations used in its diagrams. A Diagram Editor manages each diagram in a model. This includes the interaction with the user as they draw the diagram. The model and diagram editors use the NDL Interpreter to execute the NDL descriptions of the notations as the user builds diagrams.

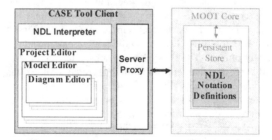

Figure 2: Architecture of the CASE tool client

The client has been implemented in Java [12] and as such can execute on any computer that has a Java interpreter.

CASE client user interface requirements

The client interface is based around a sketch-pad like working canvas. In this area the user builds graphical structures comprised of a limited number of pre-defined symbols. The structures are used to model the system under development. The symbols represent objects and the connections between them. For each OO methodology there are well defined rules concerning the appearance of each type of symbol, constraints on them, and the ways they can be linked together.

These requirements are incorporated into the CASE tool which supports the methodology. The goal in designing the client interface is to allow users to place, join and manipulate these elements quickly and easily. The tool must also support passive browsing, must fully support all aspects of the methodology, and must enforce the rules of the methodology, e.g. by not allowing illegal connections.

Both functional and non-functional requirements have been drawn up for the CASE client interface. These are described below.

Functional requirements

An analysis of the tasks involved in the construction and modification of diagrams representing OO models has been undertaken, and expressed as a set of use cases. The analysis produced the following set of broad functional requirements.

The user must be able to:

♦ *Create object symbols on the working canvas.* Once an object symbol has been selected, multiple placements must be possible. It must be possible to enter properties for the current object symbol, and to copy and paste object symbols from a repository.

♦ *Make changes to existing object symbols.* Object symbols must be selectable either singly or in groups. It must be possible to move, copy, paste and delete either individual object symbols or groups of object symbols. Trickle-down effects associated with deletion must be detected by the system, and the user prompted for further input if necessary. It must be possible to rename or resize an individual object symbol, alter its properties, and have its properties displayed on demand.

♦ *Create connections between object symbols on the working canvas.* These might describe relationships of generalisation, aggregation or association. The creation of complex or grouped connections between three or more artefacts, involving the user in linking object symbols via connector symbols must be supported.

♦ *Make changes to existing connections between object symbols.* It must be possible to rename or reshape a connection, to alter its properties (including its cardinality) and display the properties on demand. It must also be possible to delete connections. Any side effects associated with deletion must be detected by the system, and the user prompted for further input if necessary.

♦ *Edit diagrams.* It must be possible to re-arrange, annotate and partition diagrams. A range of general editing functions is also required, including UNDO and REDO.

♦ *Passively browse diagrams (selectively view and manipulate them at various levels of abstraction).* This includes moving, zooming, and rotating diagrams, in addition to hiding detail.

Non-functional requirements

It is not enough for the system merely to provide the above functions. The user must be able to carry them out efficiently, flexibly and easily, with particular reference to the following (note that 'graph objects' refer to any artefacts - object symbols or connections - which can exist on the working canvas):

♦ the ease of choosing and changing mode;
♦ the ease of initially placing graph objects on the canvas;
♦ the ease of selecting graph objects for manipulation;
♦ the ease of scaling (resizing) graph objects;
♦ the ease of relocating graph objects, both within a diagram boundary, and across diagrams (the tool must be capable of maintaining diagram integrity);

♦ the ease of manipulating graph object names (identifying strings), including the initial assignment of names, the scaling of names, renaming, and control over the location of a name on the canvas;
♦ the ease of viewing diagrams, and selecting viewing options, including the hiding of information, (e.g. message connections);
♦ the ease of scaling diagrams and portions of diagrams; and
♦ the ease of navigating (paged) diagrams.
More generally the system must support:
♦ the prevention of errors and ease of error recovery, including multi-level UNDO and REDO;
♦ flexibility of operation;
♦ consistency of operation across tasks; and
♦ efficiency and spareness of dialogue;
and provide:
♦ an effective help system;
♦ clear, well-structured and pleasing screens; and
♦ quality feedback at each stage.
Additionally, the system must show clearly at all times: the current mode, the current working position, potential artefacts for selection, the current artefacts being manipulated, and currently available options.

Design issues

The following critical design issues relating to the look and feel of the CASE client interface have been selected from the larger set uncovered by the above analysis, for exploration in an initial prototype. They are grouped to facilitate subsequent discussion:

Dealing with modality

♦ The need for the mouse cursor to carry information on the current mode, and to signal potentially illegal operations associated with that mode, for example illegal connections.
♦ The need to be able to select from a palette of graph objects (modes) during the construction of a diagram without shifting the mouse cursor from the canvas.

Manipulating object symbols

♦ The need for the initial placement of object symbols on the canvas, including multiple placements of the same type, to be simple and direct.
♦ The need for the selection of object symbols to be easy and direct, and for candidate symbols for selection to be clearly shown as the cursor is moved over them.
♦ The need for the moving of object symbols on the canvas to be simple and direct.
♦ Support of multi-level UNDO and REDO in connection with diagram construction.
♦ The need for the expansion and contraction of object symbols, to provide for data display at different levels of detail, to be simple and intuitive.

Manipulating names

♦ The need for the initial entry and subsequent manipulation of graph object names to be simple and direct, and for the automatic scaling of graph objects (to accommodate changes in name length) to be supported.

Making connections

♦ The need for the construction of complex or grouped connections, involving three or more object symbols, to be simple, intuitive and direct.

On a general level, there is a need to make the dialogue efficient and spare, with point-and-click or drag-and-drop for most operations, the use of dialogue boxes only where essential, and the availability of accelerators.

A class diagram interface for the Coad and Yourdon method

In order to explore these design issues, a client interface has been built to support the construction of class diagrams for the Coad and Yourdon method [13, 14]. The client shell interprets an NDL specification written for this method. The client interface is presented and reviewed under the headings in the previous section. The focus is on the Diagram Editor component (see Figure 2).

Basic interface modality

The interface is based around a sketch-pad like working canvas. In this area the user (software engineer) builds graphical structures comprised of a limited number of pre-defined symbols which are presented via a tool bar (Figure 3). Three broad classes of tool are presented: a general selection tool, object symbols, and connections. It should be noted that the toolbar buttons are not predefined in the shell interface, but are drawn at run-time directly from templates in the NDL specification.

Selection of a drawing tool places the interface in a particular drawing mode. In Figure 3 the selection tool is active, as denoted by the visual appearance of the button. The current drawing mode is also presented to the user via the mouse cursor (Figure 4) as a ghosted image of the graph object.

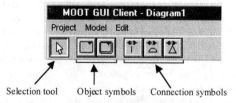

Selection tool   Object symbols   Connection symbols

Figure 3: Coad and Yourdon Toolbar

The mode may be changed by directly pointing and clicking on the toolbar buttons. However, this requires that attention is diverted from the drawing canvas and the cursor moved to the toolbar. Alternatively, using the free hand (assumed to be the left hand in the prototype), the user can use the TAB key to cycle through the drawing tools, while retaining the mouse cursor at the current point of working. In either case, changes in mode are reflected in both the toolbar buttons and the mouse cursor. A third option is also provided in the form of a pop-up menu which presents the toolbar options close to the point of working. This is brought up by clicking the right mouse button on an empty part of the canvas. The cursor is also used to signal potentially illegal operations associated with that mode, for example illegal operations during the construction of connections (see 'Making connections' below).

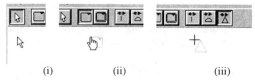

(i)   (ii)   (iii)

Figure 4: Conveyance of drawing modes via toolbar and mouse cursor for (i) selection, (ii) object symbol placement, and (iii) connection placement.

Manipulating object symbols

Object symbols are placed on the canvas by point-and-click. The ghosted image attached to the mouse cursor shows exactly where placement will occur. Following placement, the mode normally reverts to selection. Multiple placements of the same object symbol can be made by holding down the SHIFT key and repeatedly pointing and clicking on the canvas. Releasing the SHIFT key then causes reversion to selection.

The interface is based on the object-action model - an object must be selected before an action can be initiated. Object symbols are automatically selected when first placed on the canvas. In order to facilitate subsequent selection, candidate symbols are automatically highlighted as the mouse cursor is moved over them on the canvas, as shown in Figure 5.

**Figure 5: Auto-highlighting of candidate object symbol
as the mouse cursor moves over it**

Only symbols consistent with the current mode are highlighted. Once selected, object symbols can be moved by dragging them across the canvas in a simple and direct fashion. Movement of symbols causes attached connections to move with them.

In order to provide a flexible and forgiving environment, effectively unlimited UNDO and REDO operations are supported. A fully constructed diagram can be stepped back to a blank canvas, and then stepped forward to its last consistent state, provided no additional interactions are interspersed. Most object symbols defined in an NDL specification have one or more *active areas* associated with them. Active areas are areas which when selected trigger an action. Active areas are "activated" by double-clicking the mouse within the area on a selected symbol. This causes the action associated with the area to be initiated.

The NDL supports two types of active areas, one in connection with text updates (see next section) and one associated with symbol transitions (the expansion and contraction of object symbols). Symbol transitions for Coad and Yourdon class symbols are handled as shown in Figure 6. In this case, the presence (and current state) of the active area is denoted by the small arrow in the top right hand corner of the symbol.

Manipulating names

An active area associated with a text field initiates a request for text editing when it is activated. In general, a text field is activated through double-clicking on the area. In order to facilitate the entry and editing of text. It is possible to specify a *default text area* in NDL symbol template definitions. In this case, depressing any character key on the keyboard has the effect of activating the active area for that field. This means that following either the creation of a new object symbol or the selection of an existing object symbol, the user can immediately begin entering or editing the name from the keyboard without any other preliminary action.

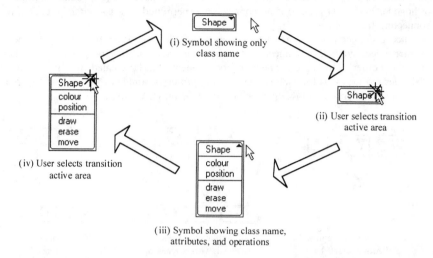

Figure 6: Symbol transitions for the class symbol

The visual cue as to the presence of the editor is a flashing cursor at the point of text insertion. As characters are typed (or deleted) the object symbol is automatically resized. The present implementation of the editor supports a number of features, including cursor movement, backspace, delete and cancel, all initiated via the keyboard. Figure 7 shows the appearance of the on-screen text editor (denoted by the text cursor) following the entry of the name 'Shape'. The entry of further characters would cause the class symbol to be automatically extended in size.

Figure 7: Text editing via on-screen editor

Making connections

Connections represent relationships that object symbols may have with themselves or each other. The aim has been to make the initial creation and subsequent manipulation of connections as intuitive and simple as possible. This has included attention both to the placement of connections on the canvas, and to the level of feedback provided at each stage. Figure 8 shows six stages in the construction of a grouped connection involving a connection symbol.

The connection modes supported by the notation are offered via the toolbar (see Figure 3). On selection of the required mode, the cursor appearance changes to reflect it. Figure 8(i) shows the appearance of the cursor with the Coad and Yourdon 'inheritance' mode selected. The object symbol originating the connection is selected via point-and-click. This 'hooks' a connector on to the object symbol. Moving the mouse away from the symbol creates a connecting line between the closest predefined 'docking area' on the symbol and the mouse cursor (see Figure 8(ii)), bowing to any constraints (e.g. being permitted only orthogonal lines). In general if no connection is permitted in a particular direction, then no connecting line is drawn.

Once a connecting line has been commenced, it can either be directly connected to another object symbol, or connected to a connection symbol (if appropriate), or anchored to create a "corner". Multiple connecting line segments can be created by clicking the mouse at the desired locations for each corner. As the prototype implements only orthogonal lines, successive segments are drawn perpendicular to the previous one.

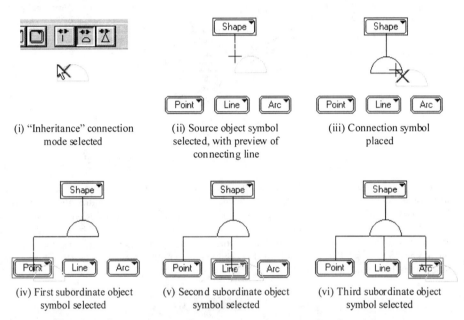

(i) "Inheritance" connection mode selected	(ii) Source object symbol selected, with preview of connecting line	(iii) Connection symbol placed

(iv) First subordinate object symbol selected	(v) Second subordinate object symbol selected	(vi) Third subordinate object symbol selected

Figure 8: Stages in creating a grouped connection involving the 'inheritance' connection symbol

Where the connection being constructed requires a connection symbol (as in the cases of 'inheritance' or 'composition' in the Coad and Yourdon notation), this must be placed on the canvas before the tool will permit the connection to be completed. Figure 8(iii) shows the placement of the inheritance connection symbol. Connection symbols are placed using a double mouse click. This attaches the symbol to the end of the last line drawn, correctly rotated as necessary.

To complete a connection, a connecting line segment must intersect an object symbol on an available docking area. When this situation occurs, the line "hooks on" to the destination object symbol, and is adjusted if necessary to fit with a connection terminator on that symbol. If the connection represents a binary relationship, the connection process is complete and the connection is added to the model. After a connection has been successfully completed, the tool returns to the selection mode.

If the connection supports grouped relationships (as in Figure 8), then multiple subordinate object symbols can be connected in two ways. With the SHIFT key held down, the user is required only to point and click on each subordinate object symbol in turn. The tool constructs the connecting lines, including an extendable link on the connector symbol (see Figures 8(iv) through 8(vi)). Alternatively the first link can be constructed in this manner, and subsequent links handled as independent connections between the connector symbol and the subordinate object symbol. This also supports the later addition of further subordinate object symbols.

Throughout the process of creating a connection, the user is made aware of potentially illegal actions through the appearance of the mouse cursor. If a particular canvas location is unselectable in the current context, then the mouse cursor is annotated with a (red) cross. Figure 8 shows two examples. In 8(i) prior to the selection of the originating symbol, the cross signifies that the cursor is not currently over an object symbol (connections must be attached to objects at both ends). In 8(iii) following placement of the connection symbol, the cross signifies that the next selection cannot be made inside the boundary of that symbol (the cross disappears once the mouse cursor is moved outside the connection symbol boundary). Other situations that are regarded as illegal include trying to make a connection to a symbol that is not an object (eg. a line segment), or trying to make a connection from or to a symbol that has no available docking area in that direction.

During the construction of a connection, it is possible to undo the placement of lines and connection symbols by pressing the BACKSPACE key (repeatedly if is desired to step back beyond the previous state). Each step back removes either the last anchor point of a connecting line or the connection symbol. Additionally, a partially-constructed connection can be deleted entirely by pressing the ESCAPE key. Connections can be edited in this way up to the point where they are completed, when they become subject to the normal UNDO and REDO facilities.

Connection symbols can be moved by point and drag, as for other objects. Attached connections move with them. Connecting lines may be dragged in a direction perpendicular to their orientation. Features yet to be implemented include the editing of connection terminator symbols, and text annotation of connections. Figure 9 shows a Coad and Yourdon class diagram constructed using the prototype, as it appears on the canvas.

Review

Key aspects of the client user interface to be supported by MOOT have been designed, and an instantiation for the construction of class diagrams within the Coad and Yourdon method has been produced. This has been achieved through the construction of a client shell, written in Java, which interprets an NDL specification for the Coad and Yourdon notation. Both functional and non-functional requirements of the client interface have been considered and specific design issues selected for exploration. As demonstrated in the above exposition, the current interface meets these design requirements and provides an efficient, flexible and supportive environment for the creation and modification of small-scale diagrams. Further development and extension of the prototype interface is needed, particularly in relation to constructing and viewing industry-sized models.

In regard to the tool as a whole, this interface is a pilot which has allowed ideas to be explored. Class diagrams are fundamental to OO CASE tools, and provide a good testbed for more generally applicable techniques. Work is proceeding on the design and prototyping of other aspects of the MOOT interface.

166

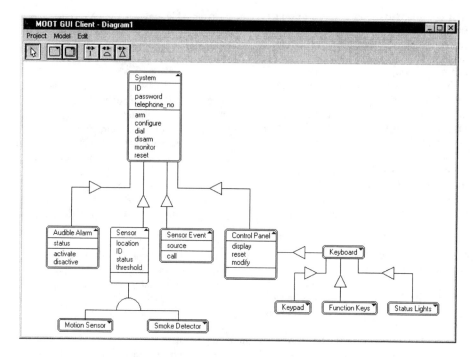

Figure 9: Completed Coad and Yourdon class diagram built using the prototype

References

[1]   Mehandjiska-Stavreva, D., Page, D. & Choi, M. (1996): Meta-modelling and Methodology Support in Object-Oriented CASE tools, proc. OOIS'96, pp 370-383.

[2]   Gobson, M. (1988): A Guide to Selecting CASE Tools, Datamation, July 1, pp 65-66.

[3]   Marttiin, P., Rossi, M., Tahvanainen, V. & Lyytinen, K. (1993): A Comparative Review of CASE Shells: A Preliminary Framework and Research Outcomes, Information and Management, Elsevier Science Publishers B.V.

[4]   Misra, S.K. (1990): Analysing CASE system characteristics: evaluative framework, Information & Software Technology, Butterworth-Heinemann Ltd, Vol. 32, No. 6, 415-422.

[5]   Nilsson, E. (1990): CASE Tools and Software Factories in Advanced Information Systems Engineering, CAiSE'90 Proc., Goos, G. & Hartmanis, J. (Eds), Springer-Verlag, Berlin.

[6]   Papahristos, S. & Gray, W. (1991): Federated CASE Environment in Advanced Information Systems Engineering, CAiSE'91, Goos, G. & Hartmanis, J. (Eds), Springer-Verlag, Berlin.

[7]   Sumner, M. (1992): The Impact of Computer-Assisted Software Engineering on Systems Development. IFIP Transactions - The Impact of Computer Supported Technologies on Information Systems Development, Kendall K.E, Lyytinen K, DeGross J I, (Eds), Elsevier Science Publishers, Amsterdam.

[8]   Phillips, C.H.E, Mehandjiska, D, Griffin, D, Choi, M.D. & Page, D (1998): The usability component of a framework for the evaluation of OO CASE tools, Proc of Software Engineering: Education and Practice (SE:E&P'98), Dunedin, January 1998, in print.

[9]   Mehandjiska, D., Page, D., Griffin, D. & Usherwood, L. (1997): The Methodology Representation Mechanism of an OO Meta-CASE Tool, proc. IASTED 1997, pp 243-247.

[10]   Page, D., Griffin, D., Usherwood, L & Mehandjiska, D. (1997): Implementation of a Semantic Specification Language Interpreter for a Methodology Independent OO CASE Tool, proc. IASTED, 1997, pp 239-242.

[11]   Page, D., Clark, P. & Mehandjiska, D. (1994): An abstract Definition of Graphical Notations for Object-Orientated Information Systems, in Proceedings OOIS'94, Springer-Verlag, London, pp 266-276.

[12]   Lewis J. & Loftus, W. (1998): *Java Software Solutions: Foundations of Program Design*, Addison-Wesley, 1998.

[13]   Coad, P. and Yourdon, E. (1991), *Object-Oriented Analysis*. Englewood Cliffs, New Jersey3: Yourdon Press.

[14]   Coad, P. and Yourdon, E. (1991), *Object-OrientedDesign*. Englewood Cliffs, New Jersey: Yourdon Press.

A Component-based Client/Server Application Development Environment using Java

Seungwoo Son   Injoong Yoon   Changkap Kim
Software Engineering Department
ETRI-Computer & Software Technology Laboratory
Yusong P.O. Box 106, Taejon, 305-600, Korea

email: {swson, dbs, changkap}@etri.re.kr

Abstract

Currently the most widely used client/server architecture is composed of client applica-tions that are based on graphical user interfaces and server applications that access data in commercial relational databases, usually in a remote server. To develop the applications, proprietary development environments such as PowerBuilder, Visual Basic, etc., are com-monly used for their ease of use and for supporting rapid application development. Tied closely to the popular client/server architecture for distributed computing, these development environments utilize particular proprietary or standard components that facilitate interac-tions among independent programs. However, the proprietary approach makes it difficult for the developers to maintain flexibility and choice. For examle, which DBMS is used with their applications and the generated applications are not easily scalable to an enter-prise level. To date Java, a very widely used object-oriented language, enables developers to develop applications that are platform-independent, and supports its component software, JavaBeans. In this paper, we propose a development environment based on the component platform, JavaBeans. The proposed environment enables developers to develop client/server applications that are easily scalable to the enterprise applications and to increase maintain-ability and ease of use.

1: Introduction

The term client/server was first used in the 1980s in reference to personal computers (PCs) on a network. The actual client/server model started gaining acceptance in the late 1980s. The client/server software architecture is a versatile, message-based and modular in-frastructure that is intended to improve usability, flexibility, interoperability, and scalability as compared to centralized, mainframe, time sharing computing [12]. A typical hardware and software configuration of two-tier client/server architecture, the most common model of modern client/server architectures, is shown in Figure 1.

Several stragejies are used to develop applications based on the client/server architecture shown in Figure 1, but most of them are based on Seeheim's model [11] shown in Figure 2. The feature of the Seeheim's model is that the applications are composed of user interface (UI) layer, application logic layer, and database logic layer. The UI layer is composed

0-7695-0053-6/98 $10.00 © 1998 IEEE

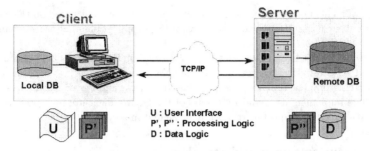

Figure 1. Two-tier client/server architecture

of presentations, dialog controls, and application interfaces. Viewed in the context of hardware configuration, the model is typically composed of PCs in the client side and workstations in the server side or workstations in the client side and mainframes in the server side. The client programs consist of window-based graphical user interface (GUI) and application logic including operations on input/output data. The server side programs have data management functions and access data from databases, mostly commercial relational DBMS (RDBMS).

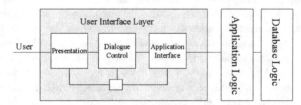

Figure 2. Seeheem's model

The pattern that is composed of GUI-based client programs and server programs that access commercial RDBMS, has emerged as 4th generation language (4GL)-based GUI builders such as PowerBuilder [1], Visual Basic [2]. However, the applications that reuse the supplied components in these tools are programmed under the constraint that they are dependent upon their proprietary components. To mitigate the shortcoming, most RAD tools support de facto component models such as DCOM and JavaBeans, to reap the reuse advantages that they offer. DCOM is language-independent but platform-dependent, whereas JavaBeans is language-dependent but platform-independent. DCOM's platform-dependency often makes it difficult for developers to maintain their legacy systems when heterogeneous and other database systems are introduced. This is particularly true when there are too many subsystems which are tightly coupled with others.

Java, widely used in developing internet/intranet applications, is an object-oriented programming language and is ideal for Internet applications [14, 7, 10]. Java is also a basis for component-based development. The addition of Remote Method Invocation (RMI) and the JavaBeans component architecture [9, 8, 4, 5] to Java facilitate the reuse of other people's software. Java components developed in this manner can have their interfaces examined, can communicate with one another over a network, and can be integrated with other components all without needing the source code. In this paper, we propose the basic architecture of a client/server application development environment based on the Java language, particularly using JDBC and JavaBeans, for the applications that access commercial databases.

The paper is organized as follows. In section 2 we explain the basic concept of component software and its strength and weakness of DCOM and JavaBeans. The design of the development environment that we'll propose based on Java and JavaBeans is presented in section 3. The implementation and its results of the environment are presented in section 4. Finally, the conclusion and future work is presented in section 5.

2: Component software and standards

Software components are reusable building blocks for constructing software systems [9, 15]. Components encapsulate semantically meaningful applications or technical services, such as rating insurance applicants or authorizing client access to service resources. Components differ from other types of reusable software modules in that they can be modified at design time as binary executables; in contrast, libraries and subroutines must be modified as source code.

Component-based software development (CBSD) focuses on building large software systems by integrating previously existing software components. By enhancing the flexibility and maintainability of systems, this approach can potentially be used to reduce software development costs, to assemble systems rapidly, and to reduce the spiraling maintenance burden associated with the support and upgrade of large systems. The foundation of this approach is the assumption that certain parts of large software systems reappear with sufficient regularity that common parts should be written once, rather than many times, and that common systems should be assembled through reuse rather than rewritten over and over. Component-based systems encompass both commercial-off-the-shelf (COTS) products and components acquired through other means, such as nondevelopmental items (NDIs). Development of component-based systems is becoming feasible due to the following: [9, 8, 4, 6]

- the increase in the quality and variety of COTS products
- economic pressures to reduce system development and maintenance costs
- the emergence of component integration technology
- the increasing amount of existing software in organizations that can be reused in new systems

Thus, component standards play a critical role in ensuring that developers achieve the anticipated benefits from reusable components - enhanced productivity, uniformity, ease of use, and faster time to market.

There are two main competitors in the de facto component software arena, DCOM and JavaBeans. Microsoft's component platform is based on DCOM, which consists of the Component Object Model (COM) binary standard, augmented with a runtime infrastructure to support component communication across distributed address spaces. Until recently, DCOM was restricted primarily to the Windows platform [8]. The platform dependent proprietary approaches are fine for a performance point of view, but are disadvantageous for users who wish to maintain flexibility and choose which DBMS is used with their applications. Maturing ports to Unix and MacOS reduce DCOM's platform dependency. Sun's

JavaBeans has emerged as the leading rival to DCOM, supplanting the OpenDoc standard from the now defunct Component Integration Laboratories. Component software is moving from its original focus on desktop-bound compound documents to enterprise applications that include distributed server components. JavaBeans has quickly gained market attention, emerging as the dominant competitor to DCOM. Whereas DCOM is language-neutral but platform-dependent, JavaBeans is platform-neutral but language-dependent.

3: Design of the C/S development environment

3.1: System configuration

The notion of a component is inseparable from the notion of component-based development environment or builder. The value of a CBSD depends heavily on the efficiency and usability of its integrated development environment (IDE). IDEs are rapidly moving from text-based programming toward the direct manipulation of visually rendered components. Commercial IDEs include Microsoft's Visual Basic [2], Sybase's PowerBuilder [1], IBM's VisualAge for Java, and Symantec's VisualCafé [3], supplemented with scripting languages such as VBScript, PowerScript and JavaScript. IDEs typically include or are evolving to include [6]

- one or more palettes for displaying available components (rendered as icons);
- a "canvas" container onto which components are placed and interconnected, typically through drag-and-drop operations and pop-up menus;
- property and script editors that let users customize components within their containers;
- Editors, browsers, interpreters, compilers, and source-level debuggers for developing new components and for testing and refining component applications.
- A component repository and associated design-time browser services to locate components by matching user search criteria and using inspectors to view component metadata; and
- Configuration management tools that structure and coordinate team-based development and release process - tools that are essential for large software projects.

Based on these principles, we designed a system that consists of Form Designer with palettes, Property Editor, Source Code Editor/Generator, Project Manager, Database Manager and Component Library. Form Designer is composed of component palettes and a form, interconnected through drag-and-drop operations. Through the Property Editor, application developers customize supplied bean components. A two-way programming technique is used to interconnect the Form Designer, Source Code Editor/Generator, and Property Editor through Java's Observable class and Observer inteface. This means the visual tools and Java source code always match. Reverse engineering source code to forms can be important for two reasons: better integration of manual programming, and importing Java projects. In addition, we added other functionality such as Project Manager, Source Code Generator, Database Manager etc. The detailed functionality of the each subsystem is described in Table 1.

Subsystems	Key Functionality
Project Manager	Add, delete, modify, view the application structure
Form Designer	Create and modify a form using supplied bean components – Align components – Call Source Code Editor – Add into Component Library – Call Property Editor
Source Code Editor	Supports automatic indentations, basic copy and paste operation.
Source Code Generator	Gererates the source code corresponding the designed form and supports two-way programming, and fully support JDK 1.1 event model
Event List Editor	Defines a new event handler block based on JDK 1.1 event model
Property Editor	Custmizes bean's property values
Database Manager	Create, modify and delete tables, indexes, views in connected databases
Component Library	Let users to register a newly created component and reuse the compoent already exists

Table 1. Detail functionality of each subsystem

To accomplish TWA programming, we interconnect the subsystems described in Table 1 through the mechanism shown in Figure 3. The Observer interface and Observable class provide infrastructure for implementing the object-oriented model-view paradigm in Java. We use the Observable class in the definition of a class of objects that may be observed. We simply derive the class for objects to be monitored, JCode say, from the class Observable. Any class that may need to be notified when a Jcode object has been changed must implement the Observer interface. In our system, Project Manager, Form Designer, Source Code Editor and Property Editor implement the Observer interface. When the JCode object changes, all the Observer objects are automatically notified a change has occurred, since they may well need to update what they display. Thus, any changes in Form Designer instantly applied to Source Code Editor and vice versa.

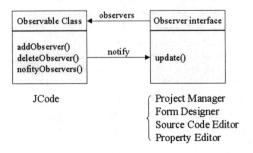

Figure 3. TWA mechanism

Developers can also customize existing bean components by setting property values and providing new handlers for their events through the combination of Form Designer, Property Editor and Event List Editor, as shown in Figure 4. Developers modify beans either explicitly, via IDE menus and editors, or implicitly, as side effects of visual manipulations such as dropping beans onto forms. Either way, the IDE must know how to access a bean's metadata to display and populate editors or handle drag-and-drop events.

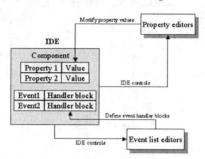

Figure 4. Customizing components in the IDE

Components that can be customized must know if they are executing in a runtime or design-time context. Components expose different interfaces and display different behaviors at these times. During design, the component collaborates with the IDE through its metadata to expose its property and event editors. At runtime, however, the component manifests the behaviors specified during design. For example, clicking on a button component during design generally opens an event editor; at runtime, the same mouse click signals the button's window container to perform some action, such as closing itself. The JavaBeans component APIs in the java.beans package are structured so that a bean's design-time code and run-time code can be encapsulated in separate classes.

3.2: Applications for JDBC

A typical configuration of applications that utilize JDBC is shown in Figure 5. As shown in Figure 5, JDBC features two API layers; the JDBC API that provides applications-to-JDBC manager connections, and the JDBC driver API that supports the JDBC manager-to-drive connection. It is the job of the database vendor to provide the JDBC driver interface; otherwise vendors may use a traditional ODBC connection. The drivers are really a group of Java classes (including Connection, Statement, PreparedStatement, CallableStatement, and ResultSet in the java.sql package). A developer who wants to access a database with JDBC uses these classes that can be linked to the database, sends a request, and processes the result set.

To handle data from database, a Java program generally follows the following steps. Figure 6 shows the general JDBC objects, the methods, and the sequence. First, the program calls the getConnection() method to get the Connection object. Then it creates the Statement object and prepares a SQL statement.

An SQL statement can be executed immediately (Statement object), can be a compiled statement (PreparedStatement object), or can be a call to a stored procedure (CallableStatement object). When the method executeQuery() is executed, a ResultSet object is returned.

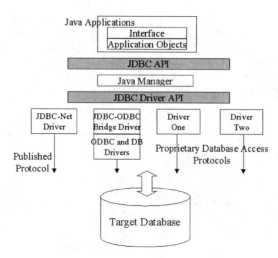

Figure 5. Features of JDBC applications

SQL statements such as update and delete will not return a ResultSet. For such statements, the executeUpdate() method is used. The executeUpdate() method returns an integer that denotes the number of rows affected by the SQL statement.

The ResultSet contains rows of data that is parsed using the next() method. In case of a transaction processing application, methods such as rollback() and commit() can be used either to undo the changes made by the SQL statements or to permanently affect the changes made by the SQL statements.

3.3: Choosing an appropriate JDBC driver

As previously mentioned, most of the client/server applications access data from databases. As a part of the Java Enterprise APIs, JavaSoft introduced JDBC specifications. JDBC provides a programming-level interface for communicating with databases in a uniform manner, similar to Microsoft's Open Database Connectivity (ODBC). Like ODBC, JDBC is based on the X/Open SQL Call-Level Interface. JavaSoft has taken the first step toward ensuring that JDBC implementations comply with the specification by defining a "JDBC-compliant" designation. To use this designation, a JDBC driver must support the ANSI SQL 2 Entry Level Standard and must also pass conformance tests provided by JavaSoft [14, 7, 9, 13].

There are currently more than 30 commercially available JDBC implementations. In implementing JDBC drivers, vendors have considerable freedom to distinguish themselves, in both the strategies for implementing the JDBC specification and in any extensions they provide. Still, current drivers fit into one of four categories defined by JavaSoft:

- JDBC/ODBC bridge (Type I).
- Native-API, partly Java driver (Type II).
- Network-protocol, all-Java driver (Type III).
- Native-protocol, all-Java driver (Type IV).

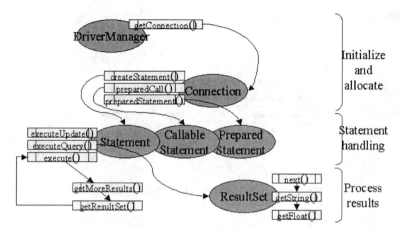

Figure 6. JDBC class hierarchy and a JDBC API flow

The Type I bridge provides JDBC access via most ODBC drivers. Note that some ODBC binary code and, in many cases, database client code must be loaded onto each client machine that uses this driver, so this kind of driver is most appropriate for a corporate network, or for application server code written in Java in a 3-tier architecture. The main advantage of this bridge is that applications can easily access databases from multiple vendors by choosing an appropriate ODBC driver. However, this type of database connectivity does involve considerable overhead and complexity, because calls must go from JDBC to the bridge to the ODBC driver, and finally from ODBC to the native client-API to the database [9, 13].

The Type II driver converts JDBC calls into calls on the client API for Oracle, Sybase, Informix, DB2, or other DBMS. Type II drivers, like the JDBC/ODBC Bridge, require that code (that is, the vendor library) be installed on each client. Thus, they have same software maintenance problems as Type I. However, Type II drivers are faster than Type I drivers because ODBC-to-JDBC translation layer is removed [9, 13].

The Type III driver translates JDBC calls into a DBMS-independent net protocol that is then translated to a DBMS protocol by a server. This net server middleware is able to connect all its Java clients to many different databases. The specific protocol used depends on the vendor. In general, this is the most flexible JDBC alternative. It is likely that all vendors of this solution will provide products suitable for Intranet use. In order for these products to support Internet access, they must handle the additional requirements for security, access through firewalls, etc that the Web imposes. Several vendors are adding JDBC drivers to their existing database middleware products [9, 13].

The Type IV driver directly converts JDBC calls into the network protocol used by DBMSs. This is a practical solution for Intranet access it and it allows a direct call from the client machine to the DBMS server. Since many of these protocols are proprietary the database vendors themselves will be the primary source for this style of driver. Because these drivers translate directly into the native protocol without use of ODBC or native APIs, they can provide for very high performance database access [9, 13].

In this project, we used the Type IV driver supplied by Oracle that is based on the two-tier architecture and the fastest of all the Type drivers. Figure 7 shows JDBC acces through a Type IV driver.

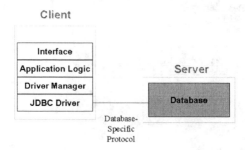

Figure 7. JDBC access via a Type IV driver

4: Implementation of the proposed system

4.1: Overview

The Overall architecture of the proposed environment is shown in Figure 8. We used Windows 95/NT as the client and Sun Solaris 2.6 as the server. Commercial RDBMS, Oracle7, was installed on both the remote server and the local client. Oracle7 JDBC thin driver is used for JDBC access.

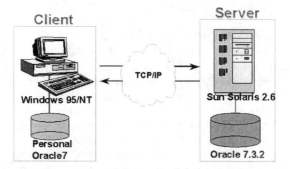

Figure 8. Overall architecture of proposed environment

4.2: Implementation of Beans

In the proposed environment, we supply four types of beans, which are described in Table 2. We supply standard JDK's AWT (Abstract Window Toolkit) and Swing components for developer's user screen objects or various report objects. The JDBC components that are modeled based on the JDBC class hierarchy in Figure 6 can be used for configuring JDBC connection arguments and for modeling ResultSet class. The ConnectionManager bean can manage several JDBC connections. The JdbcConnection bean is an invisible bean that extends its functionality from the java.sql.Connection class to configure connection arguments such as URLs, JDBC driver classes, user name and password, etc. The TableDefinition bean is also an invisible bean that is a logical view of database tables and views. Beans classified as DB category are the same GUI components as AWT or JFC components except for the data accessibility to database.

Type of beans	Contents	Purpose
Standard	Standard JDK's bean components such as Button, List, Label, etc	GUI design
JFC	Swing's bean coomponent such as JButton, JList, JLabel, JTable, etc. and have extended functionalilty over standard JDK beans	GUI design
JDBC	Invisible beans for connfiguring JDBC connections and table objects in database; ConnectioManager, JdbcConnection, TableDefinition	JDBC connection configuration
DB	Standard JDK bean component that can contain and view table or text data such as List, Grid, TextField, TextArea, etc.	GUI design that access data such as reports

Table 2. Four categories of supplied beans

4.3: Implementation and its results using the proposed IDE

We developed all parts of the proposed system purely in the Java language. We used the JDK 1.1.7 and JFC (Java Foundation Class) 1.1 (also known as Swing 1.0.3) for our GUI environment, JavaBeans for our basic component architecture and JDBC for accessing local and remote Oracle DBMS. The main screen of the proposed environment is shown in Figure 9. Figure 9 shows the main panel with palettes, Project Manager in the top-left position, ObjectInspector (Combination of Property Editor and Event List Editor) in the right position. The Form Designer in the middle and Source Code Editor on the bottem-left side are also shown. Developers can drag-and-drop the supplied components to design a form on the Form Designer in the middle. Then the Java source code corresponding to the designed form is automatically generated in the Source Code Editor. Developers also modify the property and event block of the component in the form using ObjectInspector without coding any lines of code. With the help of JDBC and DB beans, developers can easily compose a report form and the proposed environment generates all source code for JDBC applications. Figure 10 shows a sample JDBC application using the proposed environment. As the proposed environment generates Java source code, the designed applications are fully applicable to the Web applications as well as to current client/server applications.

4.4: Performance

Designed and implemented in pure Java, the performance of the proposed environment is a major consideration when deciding to use Java. We found that running the development environment on a 166-MHz Pentium with 128 MB of RAM under Windows NT significantly slowed down the performance. Running it on a 333-MHz Pentium II with same RAM and operating system is performs reasonably well. This is because Java does not utilize

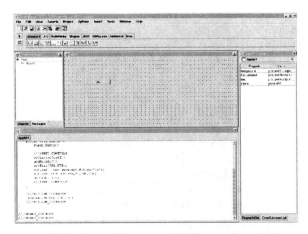

Figure 9. The main screen of the environment

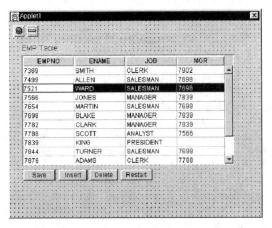

Figure 10. A sample JDBC application

a compiler, but an interpreter. Although we may expect the enhanced performance in JDK1.2, a static compiler is really needed at the present time.

5: Conclusion and Future work

In this paper, we proposed the component-based client/server application development environment that facilitates JavaBeans, a commonly used component architecture. By using Sun's JavaBeans, a de facto component standard, users exploit the benefits of component platform such as enhanced productivity, uniformity, ease of use, and faster time to market. Unlike DCOM, JavaBeans, the major competitor in recent component standards, comprises platform-independent applications. To extend the scalability to the enterprise-level applications, the adoption of a server platform solution like RMI and Directory services, Security services, Systems management services, and Transaction services should be included. In addition, to provide users with the easy-to-use Java language in the development environment designed to make users highly productive, it should include following features.

- Enhanced visual and form-based development
- Support for major database servers such as Sybase, Informix, etc.
- An advanced debugger that includes expression evaluations.

The proposed environment has not yet been completely implement; much work is remaining to produce a more complete system. Built in pure Java, the proposed environment shows considerable performance slowdown when executing. In order to enhance execution performance, a static compiler such as Symantec's win32 native compiler, can be used. By using the native compiler, however, the platform-independent merit may be excluded.

The proposed environment enables developers to easily develop internet/intranet applications using Java and to scale their systems to the enterprise systems by using Java's RMI and Java/CORBA interoperability.

References

[1] *PowerBuilder 5.0 User's Guide*. Sybase/Powersoft, 1996.

[2] *Visual Basic 5.0 User's Guide*. Microsoft, 1996.

[3] *Visual Café 2.0 dbDE User's Guide*. Symantec, 1997.

[4] Thomas A. A comparison of component models. *Distributed Object Computing*, pages 55–57, July 1997.

[5] Thomas A. Enterprise javabeans server component model for java. *http://java.sun.com/products/ejb/white_paper.html*, 1997.

[6] Richard M. Alder. Emerging standards for component software. *IEEE Computer*, 28(3):68–77, March 1995.

[7] M. A. Hamilton. java and the shift to net-centric computing. *IEEE Computer*, 29(8):31–39, August 1996.

[8] David Krieger and Richard M. Alder. The emergence of distributed component platforms. *IEEE Computer*, 31(3):43–53, March 1998.

[9] D. S. Linthicum. *David Lithicum's Guide to Client/Server and Intranet Development*. John Wiley & Sons, Inc., 1997.

[10] R. Orfali and D. Harkey. *Client/Server Programming with JAVA and CORBA*. John Wiley & Sons, Inc., 1997.

[11] Rosemary Rock-Evans. *Ovum Evaluation GUI Builders*. Ovum Limited, 1994.

[12] G. Schussel. Client/server past, present, and future. *http://www.dciexpo.com/goes*, 1995.

[13] M. Sood. Examing jdbc drivers. pages 82–87, January 1998.

[14] E. Yourdan. Java, the web, and software development. *IEEE Computer*, 29(8):25–30, August 1996.

[15] John C. Zubeck. Implementing reuse with rad tools. *IEEE Computer*, 30(10):60–65, October 1997.

RADIUS: Rapid Application Delivery, Installation and Upgrade System

Benchiao Jai
Computer Science Department
New York University
jai@cs.nyu.edu

Abstract

This paper describes an object-oriented application framework RADIUS, which facilitates automatic Application Delivery, Installation and Upgrade (ADIU). By extending the object-oriented programming paradigm to the document and file level, application files can be located and delivered through a mechanism similar to dynamic dispatch in most OOP languages and systems. RADIUS is designed to be document-centric. All necessary information is stored with the documents and assigned at the application developers' end and thus requires no user intervention of any kind in locating, installing and upgrading applications. RADIUS is light-weight and requires no extensions to the programming languages and operating systems, and therefore is easy to integrate with other object or component systems.

Motivation

Today's computing environment is globally connected, distributed, shared, dynamic and changing rapidly. New techniques such as component-based reuse, and new Rapid Application Development (RAD) tools such as Delphi or Visual Café, are making it much easier to write programs. The Internet is making it easier and faster to publish programs. Anyone can write software or publish data. Software and data can be stored anywhere and can change anytime. Data can in fact be software. We are witnessing the era of "personal computer" being replaced by the era of "the network is the computer". We can foresee that like cable television catering to small groups of audiences, software will be rapidly developed for small groups of users. These developments are bringing new pressure on a growing bottleneck in software activity: Application Delivery, Installation and Upgrade (ADIU).

ADIU has always been an annoying detail for software developers and users. It has to be done, but it has very little direct contribution to our productivity. Indeed, a vast amount of time and money has been spent on 1) creating installation and upgrade packages (on the developers' end) and 2) setting up and maintaining software configurations (on the users' end). The demand on 1) can be observed in the immense success of InstallShield™, which transforms a major part of the process of creating an installation package into a checklist with fill-in blanks. The size of 2) can be recognized by the number of employees in the technical support departments in large companies. Consider the following situations, and one can imagine how much time and effort can be saved if applications can be installed and upgraded automatically:

1. A scientist receives a file containing the animation data of an exciting new discovery. The file is in format XYZ. After contacting OPQ, the originator of the data, the proprietary software D** developed by OPQ for format XYZ is sent over. The local installation of D** complains about missing files, so another request is sent to OPQ. This

0-7695-0053-6/98 $10.00 © 1998 IEEE

process is repeated five times and the presentation is finally seen after a month.

2. A manager gets Word Processor Version 7.0 installed on her workstation. Now many people in the company can't read her memos because they only have Version 6.8. The technical support department has to schedule each employee to vacate his/her workstation for half an hour and spend 1000 staff-hours on upgrading everyone.

As the new technologies and tools make the task of creating applications easier, it is becoming cost-effective to write single-use software. For example, an experimental computer scientist can build small animated presentations to demonstrate a new algorithm to a special interest group; or an economist can use special software to show a newly found niche market to the investment bankers. For this kind of "disposable" application, the ADIU overhead has to be reduced to near zero for them to be practical. Not only do we need a system that is light-weight on the users' side, we also need it to be light on the programmers' side because these programmers are not professional software engineers.

In this paper we describe a system RADIUS (Rapid ADIU System) dealing with the ADIU problem. It is an object-oriented software architecture that makes ADIU totally transparent to both the developers and the users.

Overview

In the OOP concept a class is a collection of declarations of data (a.k.a. members) and procedures (a.k.a. methods) and an object is an instance of a class. From an abstract point of view, an object can be thought of as a piece of data with some indications of what operations can be performed on the data. In most OOP language designs, these indications are pointers to methods. In our system, we extend the idea to include "pointers" to applications. An object in RADIUS contains a tag to indicate which application should be used to handle the object.

As in any object-oriented system, the basic entities in RADIUS are objects. A document is the persistent representation of an object in the form of a file. An application is a program file containing the code of one or more classes. A RADIUS object has a tag containing two data members, namely the class identifier and the class code locator. The former is used to identify the class to the object factory [5], the latter is used to find the application file and the application server hosting it. The actual implementation of these two data members could be of arbitrary type, but for practical reasons we choose to implement them as a strings. The class identifier can be an arbitrary string while the class code locator is a URL (Uniform Resource Locator). For simplicity they can be short descriptive names, however, for real world applications they should be made unique to avoid conflict with other people's applications. Our suggestion is to use the string representation of an OSF DCE style 128-bit UUID (Universal Unique Identifier) [9] plus a readable name. For example:

```
A46AB944-A4A7-A6E6-A4D1-A455ACB0A4BD-Text
http://RADIUS.org/A46AB944-A4A7-A6E6-A4D1-A455ACB0A4BD-Text.dll
```

All major operating systems nowadays support long filenames, so this should not pose any difficulty on implementing the system.

The command shell for RADIUS is the object browser, in which the documents can be opened for viewing and editing. The actual viewing and editing functions are implemented in the class code which RADIUS does not control directly, so the programmers are free to use any programming models and tools as they see fit.

Operation model

Under our architecture, a software developer designs a class by extending the base RADIUS class and adding new functionality, implements the application and puts it on the application server, then distributes the sample documents or just posts them on a Web site. The application can be implemented using any development tool the programmer likes. The only requirement is that the classes of the document objects implement the RADIUS programming interface. In the C++ version the developers would include the header file of the RADIUS base class in the application code, and link the import library of the RADIUS object browser into the application in order to use the functions in the object browser. In the Java version the developers simply import the RADIUS base class file.

To start using RADIUS applications, the only thing that the users need is a copy of the RADIUS object browser, which can be run as a standalone program or a Web browser add-in. When a user opens a document (either the original sample document or a modified document from another user) in the object browser, the object browser loads the application from the application server and installs (and later upgrades) it onto the local machine. This process is better illustrated in Figure 1.

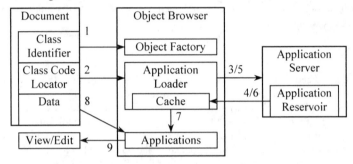

Figure 1: RADIUS Operation Model

1. The user asks the object browser to open a document. The object factory reads the class identifier in the document and tries to create an object of the specified class. If the object factory recognizes the class identifier, the application is already in memory, go to step 8.
2. The application loader reads the class code locator from the document and looks for the application in the local cache. If the application is in the cache, go to step 5.
3. The application loader sends a "request for application" to the application server.
4. The application server returns the application file and the application loader installs it into the cache. Go to step 7.
5. A "request for upgrade" is sent to the application server while the process proceeds with step 7.
6. If the application server eventually returns an upgrade of the application, the upgrade is installed when appropriate.
7. The application loader loads the application into memory.
8. The data portion of the document is read by the application and the object creation is finished.
9. A viewer/editor window of the document is created by the application.

If an object contains other objects (making up a compound object), this process is applied recursively. An application is unloaded from memory when all objects handled by the application have been destroyed.

The application loader is somewhat similar to the class loader [8, 15] in Java. In fact, the Java version of RADIUS can be implemented by extending the Java class loader and adding the caching mechanism. The applet class loaders used in Web browsers are doing some of the jobs already.

The application loader can also be configured to look for the applications in different places:

- From the CD-ROM or other removable storage media, for applications distributed in the conventional way.
- From a LAN file server for centralized configuration control.
- From proxy servers to reduce network traffic.
- From a list of mirror sites when the specified application server is not available.

Furthermore, even the cache can be set to a network path to make diskless workstations ("Network Computers") possible.

The decision to store the applications in a cache also solves another common problem: application un-installation. When disk space is needed, application files that have not been used for a long time are removed to make room. This can reduce the bloating phenomenon observed in many recent commercial software packages, and encourage "trying out" new applications since the users don't need to worry about wasting space on their installation.

Implementation approach

In the past few decades, a large portion of research efforts in object-oriented systems were devoted to designing new object-oriented programming languages or new operating systems. Some high-caliber object systems such as COM [14] or CORBA [11] offer very powerful reuse mechanisms, but the overhead involved in starting to use them cannot be justified considering the throw-away nature of our target applications. For simple applications, these tools seem too complicated for programmers to overcome the initial learning curve. Powerful object-oriented programming tools are often not popular because the dominance of the market has very little to do with technical merit, but very much to do with compatibility. The users tend to pick the ones that are easy to learn and use, readily available and well-supported. A tool can not gain wide acceptance quickly if it requires massive extensions to the operating system or the programming language.

Java [7] has been successful so far, but the language design is not the major reason for its acceptance. It is popular because of the close resemblance to C++, cross-platform virtual machine, abstract windows toolkit and the class delivery mechanism [4]. We claim that in order for an object-oriented tool to be practically useful, it is not necessary to create new languages or operating systems. Novel ways of utilizing existing technologies will be appreciated far more by the real-world users. We choose to implement RADIUS with existing mature technology with no extension to either the programming languages or the operating systems.

We intend to implement two versions of RADIUS, one for C++ on Windows 95/NT platform and one for Java. Documents will be binary-compatible so that data can be exchanged between the two versions, while giving the programmers the freedom of choosing the tool to implement their applications. The C++ version applications will be implemented as dynamically linked library (DLL) files and the Java version will use Java class files. Note that the class code locator does not need to be changed between the two versions because the object browser can decide which file name extension (.dll or .class) to append before making the request to the application servers.

Our approach is orthogonal to other object systems, such as CORBA or COM, and is easy to integrate with them without conflict. For example, we can add the standard CORBA core functionality and Internet Inter-ORB Protocol (IIOP) [12] to our system to make it inter-operable with other CORBA-compliant object systems over the Internet; or add an ActiveX [6] wrapper to our object browser to make it function from within the Microsoft Internet Explorer. On the other hand, the functionality of RADIUS can be modeled as an interface (COM,

CORBA and Java all use the same term) of other object systems and added to them as an enhancement.

Current status and future work

We currently have skeletal implementations of both a C++ version and a Java version. Each consists of the application developer's kit, the object browser and a few sample applications. The application server is just a simple HTTP server configured to deliver DLL and Java class files. From this part of work we learned that it is very easy to develop RADIUS applications and the applications are extremely light-weight. The C++ version of RADIUS developer's kit includes header files totaling less than 200 lines of code, and a 25 KB library file. The Java version of RADIUS developer's kit contains only 6 KB of class binary. Programmers can use their favorite development environment to create the application deliverables.

From this experience we also see a few issues and possibilities for future development. They are described in the following sections.

Object persistence and serialization

Unlike Java [4, 7], C++ does not provide a language mechanism for specifying the persistency of variables. RADIUS application developers have to code the persistence routines manually (unless the tool they use has an extension for it). In the Java version, this burden can be unloaded from the developers, thanks to the Java object serialization mechanism.

Distributed computing

The application returned by the application server could actually be a stub module for performing remote procedure calls over the Internet. This way not only are the objects distributed, the application is also distributed. RADIUS is again orthogonal to this issue. The application developers are free to use any tool to generate distributed code. They just have to define the client portion as a RADIUS application to make it deliverable through RADIUS.

Scripting

We also see that, with little work, we can add scripts to the objects to make them programmable. After the viewer/editor window is created, graphical user interface (GUI) events start to get passed to the application. The application may handle the events itself or pass them further to the scripts in the object. We plan to construct interfaces which can be used to connect to ActiveScript-compliant [3] scripting engines such as VBScript or JavaScript. The possibility of integrating Tcl/Tk is being studied. We also plan to create a light weight native scripting engine that can be used to manipulate RADIUS objects in a simple way. With the addition of scripts, each application is essentially a programming environment by itself. The purpose of this work is not only making developing programs easy, but also making developing programming environments easy!

Security and Licensing

Our current design does not have any security measures, which makes it insufficient for use in developing commodity software. Some authentication and sandbox technologies should be employed in future versions to make it safer for the users. Nevertheless, it is good enough for intranet software as is.

Software licensing is another issue that should be addressed. The requests sent by the object browser provides a basic mechanism for license control. The application server can challenge the object browser for digital licenses, or simply look up a database for registered users. Since the object browser also asks for upgrades, this may even enable developers to catch software piracy. Of course the user can always disconnect the computer from the Internet to avoid being detected, but then the application may be useless anyway if it was designed to rely on the Internet (e.g. Mail, Chat, Internet Game).

Related work

The conventional way of using an application is to install it first, then start creating, viewing and editing its documents. The object-oriented programming (OOP) paradigm suggests that it should be done the other way: the data should lead you to the code. However, almost all the software we see in the real world still does it the old-fashioned way. While the software uses OOP at the program level, the operating system it runs on does not have the necessary mechanisms to support OOP at the file level.

Microsoft Windows and some Unix shells use part of a file's name to look for its application, thus allowing only a many-to-one mapping while limiting the freedom to name files.

The Macintosh operating system stores a piece of application information with each file entry in the directory structure, but it does not go down to the object level and does not perform the mapping recursively. The OpenDoc [1] architecture works at the object level recursively, but does not install nor upgrade the applications for the user. Its dependence on a centralized database for component-application relationship is also limiting the freedom of usage.

Microsoft's COM/OLE [2] mechanism also relies on a centralized database (the Windows Registry) to find library files for objects. This is again many-to-one, and does not work before the application is installed.

Netscape's Plug-In Finder points users to an information page but leaves the downloading and installation tasks to the users. Netscape's SmartUpdate [10] enables applications to be installed and upgraded over the Internet. However, it is still an application-centric paradigm instead of a document-centric paradigm. It does not locate and launch applications from documents. Also, the initial installation must be initiated by the users manually.

Pal [13] described an application delivery and upgrade mechanism for Java applications. It extends the Java class loading mechanism to enable Java applications to be loaded in a manner similar to Java applets, yet caching the application files to avoid the performance penalty associated with reloading. It is different from our approach in several aspects:

- It works with Java applications only. Our approach works with any object-oriented programming language that produces dynamically-linked program modules.
- It needs a special purpose server (one per application) and associated programs to encode the upgrade information. Our approach uses a simple HTTP server.
- It requires a customized bootstrap program for each application, or the user has to input a server designator for each application. Our approach uses a unified object browser for all applications and the application information is encoded in the documents so the users don't need to remember them.

The Java class loader [8, 15] mechanism allows class files to be loaded in ways prescribed by developers. By default it does not cache the loaded class files and does not "install" them in any way, let alone upgrade them. Two most commonly seen class loaders are:

1. The Primordial Class Loader in Java Virtual Machines. Given a class name, it finds the class file in a set of reservoirs specified in the CLASSPATH environment variable. The

search is limited to the storage accessible through the local file system.
2. The Network Class Loader in Web browsers. Given a URL, it finds over the Internet the applet class file and the class files used by the applet. The loaded classes are subject to all kinds of security restrictions.

Our work is a document-centric application framework which, in addition to other functions, generalizes case 1 to find and load the class files over the Internet, but does not impose the security restrictions in case 2.

Conclusion

This paper proposes and implements a new object-oriented application framework to facilitate the delivery, installation, upgrade and un-installation of software. In addition to its intended purposes, RADIUS can be seen playing several different roles:

- An information distribution system that distributes programs as well as data. This is very useful for the "Network Computer" paradigm.
- A distributed object oriented programming environment builder. It provides a framework for easily building programmable objects.

One important attribute of RADIUS is that it achieves these objectives without requiring any new technology. No extensions to either the programming languages or the operating systems are created. We believe that this characteristic should enhance the potential usage of this system.

BIBLIOGRAPHY

1. Apple Computer, Inc. *OpenDoc.* http://opendoc.apple.com.
2. Box, Don. *Essential COM.* Addison Wesley, Reading, Massachusetts, 1998.
3. Box, Don. *Say Goodbye to Macro Envy with Active Scripting.* Microsoft Interactive Developer (February 1998), Microsoft Press. Also available at http://www.microsoft.com/mind/0297/activescripting.htm.
4. Flanagan, David. *Java in a Nutshell.* O'Reilly, Sebastopol, California, 1997.
5. Gamma, Erich, et al. *Design Patterns: Elements of Reusable Object-Oriented Software, Chapter 3.* Addison-Wesley, Reading, Massachusetts, 1994.
6. Grimes, Richard, et al. *Beginning ATL COM Programming.* Wrox Press, Birmingham, UK, 1998.
7. Gosling, James, et al. *The Java Language Specification.* Addison-Wesley, Reading, Massachusetts, 1996.
8. Liang, Sheng, and Gilad Bracha. *Dynamic Class Loading in the Java™ Virtual Machine.* Proceedings of the OOPSLA '98, 1998 (Vancouver, BC, Canada, October 18-22, 1998) ACM, New York, 1998 pp. 36-44.
9. Lockhart, Harold W. *OSF DCE.* McGraw-Hill, New York, New York, 1994.
10. Netscape Communications Corporation. *SmartUpdate for Content Developers.* http://developer.netscape.com/docs/manuals/communicator/jarforcd/index.htm.
11. OMG. *The Common Object Request Broker: Architecture and Specification, V2.2.* ftp://ftp.omg.org/pub/docs/formal/98-02-01.pdf.
12. OMG. *CORBAservices: Common Object Services Specification.* ftp://ftp.omg.org/pub/docs/formal/corbaservice-97-12-02.pdf.
13. Pal, Partha Pratim. *A Flexible, Applet-like Software Distribution Mechanism for Java Applications.* Software Engineering Notes vol 23 no 4, July 1998, pp. 56-60.
14. Sessions, R. *COM and DCOM: Microsoft's Vision for Distributed Objects.* John Wiley & Sons, New York, New York, 1997.
15. Venners, Bill. *Inside the Java Virtual Machine.* McGraw-Hill, New York, New York, 1998.

Design and Development of *Melbourne IT Creator*™ – a System for Authoring and Management of Online Education

Steve B. Goschnick
Department of Computer Science
The University of Melbourne
Parkville, Victoria 3052, Australia
July, 1998
gosh@solidsoftware.com.au.

Abstract

This paper presents a Case Study in the symbiotic use of new internet based technologies and an SQL server, to develop a software tool in a new category of generic software: a system for authoring and delivery of web-centric learning. In the design and implementation of the system, the developers drew upon the latest available languages and platforms, aiming for a high benchmark in this new software genre: Java for cross platform authoring tools; JavaScript and HTML V4 for scripting and markup; applets, video and other media types as object components; IIS (Microsoft's Internet Information Server technology) to deliver dynamically constructed HTML markup. Behind the interfaces and business rules is robust SQL server technology, which is taking on an expanded role in proliferating web-based information systems. In the latter half of the paper, problems and solutions are discussed, including the use of metadata and XML (the eXtensible Markup Language) as part of the solutions.

1: Introduction

This paper partially documents the experience in specifying and developing an ambitious product in the rapidly moving fields of *Internet web technology* and *distributed multimedia learning objects*. It takes an innovative company with a committed focus on education, research and intellect property, to undertake such a project in these uncertain technological times - an era when major software tool vendors are more often in court than not, attempting to prove the others intent at monopolizing markets and breaking *open standards*.

The development of *Melbourne IT Creator*™ - the underlying subject of this paper - is one companies attempt to genuinely advance the tools available to online educationalists (whilst not trying to derail any of our perceived competitors), so that teachers may get on with online endeavours useful to the students of mankind, in fields beyond market dominance, corporate law and dry economics.

Towards the end of this paper, a serious effort is made to flag any technologies and standards that were used during this project development, which do appear to be consolidating as *certainties* in the near future of software development.

2: Knowing the users, the users and the users

The requirements gathering phase for this *online education, authoring and delivery* system, included evaluating, interviewing and then designing for three quite different groups of users:

1. Teachers / Authors.
2. Students / Participants.
3. Administrators (System, Course and Subject Administration).

Full advantage was taken of the different requirements and profiles of these distinct user groups, to gain maximum leverage from appropriate technology, on applicable platforms i.e. three different software delivery strategies were used, taking into consideration the needs, average computing power and the relative size of each distinct group:

1. The authoring tools are written in 100-percent Java V1.1 in order to reach the maximum number of desktops of *academic* and other content *authors*, be they users of MS Windows, Apple Mac or Unix platforms.

2. Content delivery to *students* is done via markup in HTML V4 [1] and scripting in JavaScript. Subsets of those languages were used in order to be compliant with both the perceived dominant web browsers in the marketplace, extrapolated into the timeframe of delivery of the final product i.e. Netscape Navigator V4 and Microsoft Internet Explorer V4.

3. Those same language technologies used to give client student access, were used to deliver *administrative functionality*, however the default minimum hardware standards were raised: the recommended minimum screen resolution for Creator *administrators* is 800x600 pixels, while the default minimum for *student* client screens is 640x480 pixels. The administrative tasks tend to be more form-based user-interface screens.

The whole system is founded upon robust SQL server technology in the form of Microsoft SQL Server V6.5. Standard SQL stored procedures are used, keeping the logic of business-rules out of SQL, to minimize porting the backend to any other SQL server, as required.

The relative number of users across these groups also affected the choice of minimum hardware configurations and recommendations. For example, 1600 students may do a subject that is developed and authored by as few as 2 or 3 teachers. The hardware that teachers have on their desktops usually has more memory and processor power than the hardware in computer labs or at the student end of a modem connection.

3: Technical goals

The most significant technical goals for the system development set at the outset, were:

- Delivery of content to a diverse client window base - the education market representing probably the most diverse hardware market in a single market segment.

- Base it upon server-side, robust, scalable SQL servers supplemented with transaction monitoring technology as necessary, or exchange SQL engines if required by customers.

- The middleware - between the server and the client window - needs to be cutting-edge technology, in both *object component* building and the *scripting languages* used to glue the components together, all within an Internet delivery context.

- Embrace emerging Internet standards as early as possible.

- With regard to versions of standards one does embrace, always aim high (e.g. HTML V4). There are two reasons: it takes time to develop a significant software project, during which time the customer base moves on; secondly, you only get the chance once to aim high - at the first version of your product. After releasing your own software at Version 1, you then have direct responsibility to your own client base for backwards compatibility, i.e. to all the standards you ever embraced.

There is a delicate tradeoff between the third and fourth goals, with significant risk involved in trying to pick a standard early. Prototyping with an open mind to technologies and tool vendors is most important in the pre-standard phase of an evolving area of Computer Science - scripting languages in proprietary web browser technologies, being the main example during the course of this project.

The selection of SQL amongst the setting of goals, was a more multifaceted decision than is usual, and therefore worth expanding on:

- It offered robust proven technology, refined over two decades, based on sound theory, which hedged against some risks associated with employing evolving technologies client-side.

- Whether you transmit programmed-objects directly, or data-imprints of objects via data records and then instantiate the objects at the client end, leans heavily in favour of the data-imprints, *whenever the object types are known in advance.* The short-hand data imprints (lists of regular data fields) have several benefits: they fit well into relational database systems; they are much more efficient to transmit; don't have nearly as many security concerns as transmitting a programmed-object such as an ActiveX component. (Note: Melbourne IT Creator™ does also allow for external object types if the user client machines are capable of displaying them. E.g. objects such as: ActiveX components; Shockwave; JavaBeans and Java Applets, are all allowable in the system.)

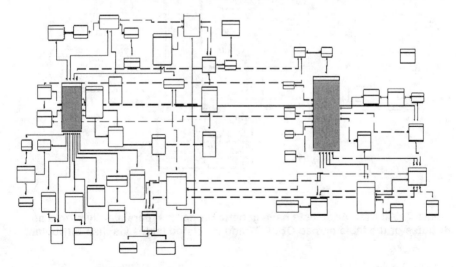

Figure 1. Birds-eye view of *Melbourne IT Creator™V1* database schema

- The Java interface to SQL via JDBC (Java DataBase Connection) was a mandatory option in selecting SQL server technology.

4: System Analysis and Design.

From the requirements of the various users outlined above, I did a system *analysis and design*, which included an extensive database schema, in January '97. A proof-of-concept was rapidly developed in the two following months, dubbed the Version 0.5. It had several purposes: *to gauge the technical chances of a successful product; to get some early usability feedback for a generic product for which no obvious predecessor existed in the marketplace; to attract internal and external support for what was an ambitious project; to rationalize and refine the initial design.*

With some tradeoffs to reduce complexity, the schema was narrowed down to 56 entity tables, which hold both media content and administrative data [3,4]. A cursory glance of the birds-eye view in Fig. 1 above, reveals a convergence of relationships about two tables in particular (marked as black rectangles): one is the generic *Object* entity, centre-left in the figure and the second is the *Person* entity, centre-right. Generally, the tables that are clustered around the Object entity are *content specific*, while those clustering around the Person entity are *administrative specific*. Naturally there are tables with relationships to both these sub-areas of the Creator schema, e.g. *Object_Author*, see Figure 2 below.

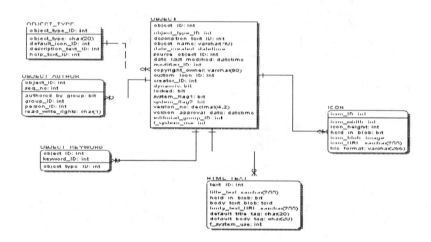

Figure 2. All Creator objects have generic properties, persistently stored as attributes of the table named OBJECT and in related tables via their attributes.

4.1: Object components

Although MS SQL Server V6.5 is a relatively standard relational database system, the Creator design built upon it, is really an Object-Relational system, enacted via custom-coded Java classes which use the JDBC interface to SQL Server tables. There are 15 internal Creator object types that are fully catered for within the Creator system, as follows:

1	ICON
2	IMAGE
3	HTML_TEXT
4	HTML_TABLE
5	PAGE
6	QUESTION
7	RESOURCE_PALETTE
8	REFERENCE_WORK
9	LEARNING_ACTIVITY
10	VIDEO
11	AUDIO
12	ANIMATION
13	DOCUMENT
14	KEYWORD_LIST
15	EXTERNAL OBJECT (Applet, ActiveX, Shockwave, etc)

The 15th type, *External Object*, includes support for many other objects types such as: Java Applets; Shockwave Applets; ActiveX controls; etc – basically anything that can be displayed in a bounding rectangle, within an HTML V4 browser window, during the page authoring process. Such external object types may take numerous parameter types such as: *environment*, *input*, and *output* parameter types, and then any number of actual parameters. It is then up to the customers of Creator to enable all their relevant client machines to support the various external object types that they have decided to allow within their courseware (i.e. they'll need to install the appropriate browser or browser plug-ins).

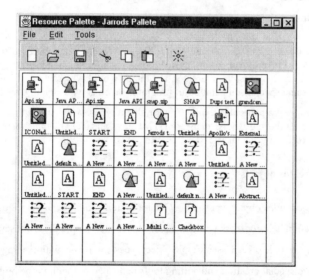

Figure 3. All Creator object types can be accessed via the *Resource Palette*.

All objects share the common base of properties represented in Figure 2. Whenever a particular object is re-instantiated, the base information is read from SQL by a Java coded super-class, from which all other object types are derived. Then, the extra persistent properties for a specific object type, are correctly read from appropriate associated tables.

At a certain basic level, all objects are equal within the Creator system. Figure 3 represents a screen-shot of the *Resource Palette*, which is one of the tools within the *Creator Authoring Tools* package [5], written in Java V1.1. The different icons represent different object types, while specific individual objects have individual names. Though the view seen here is a *grid-layout view*, the user may flip to a *table view* of resources, in which each object occupies one whole line of the display, allowing the user to inspect more detailed object information. In addition, a *property-sheet* window may be popped-up via the right-mouse button for any object within the current Resource Palette, to inspect the full property details of an object - including recursive references to embedded sub-objects (e.g. an *Image* within a *Page* within a *Reference-work*).

A consequence of all content being represented by objects, is that common functionality such as *keywords*, can be used to reference all types of content, e.g. videos and applets. Hence, by using keywords, the same search strategies and interfaces can be used to find any sort of content, even if different indexing methodologies are used to assign those keywords.

[Note: The menus, toolbars and layouts of the GUIs featured in Figures 3, 4, 5 and 6 are largely courtesy of JavaSoft's recent JDK/Swing UI interface classes. The earlier beta version of the Creator Authoring Tools where based on in-house developed GUI components, by necessity. However, because the Java V1.1 event-model was programmed to, from the beginning, the conversion to JFC/Swing components took less than one week].

4.2:   Simple creator objects

Most of the 15 object types are termed *simple* Creator object types, because they are self-contained e.g. Icon, Image, Animation, even Video, are self-contained object types. Most of these objects are created outside of Creator, i.e. Image would typically be a .GIF or a JPEG file, created in some specialised paint or art program. Video is typically a QuickTime file.

However, there are two particular *simple* Creator object types, which are authored within the built-in Creator Authoring Tools, namely: HTML-text and HTML-table objects, both of which are catered for by special WYSIWYG (What-You-See-Is-What-You-Get) editors.

4.3:   Complex creator objects

There are some *complex* object types in the Creator system, complex in the following ways:

• the information held for them while in a persistent state, is spread across several tables;

• they usually include other lesser/simple object types e.g. Image within a Page;

• they all have special creation and editing tools dedicated to them, in the built-in Creator *Authoring Tools* (discussed more fully further down).

Complex Creator object types include: *Reference-work*; *Learning-activity*; *Page*; *Question*; *Resource-Palette*. I'll expand a little on *Reference-work* and *Learning-activity*:

4.3.1: Hypermedia reference works

A Creator *Reference-work* is a hierarchical arrangement of pages. A Creator *Page* object is equivalent to an HTML page, from the browsers point of view. However, unknown to the browser, such pages are dynamically constructed behind the scenes from other objects, both simple and complex ones. So a hypermedia online book or even an encyclopedia with images, sounds, animations, applets and videos, placed throughout the text, can be constructed within Creator as a single *Reference-work*. Figure 4 below, is a screen-shot of the deceptively simple opening screen of *The Outliner*, the built-in authoring tool used to create and edit a *Reference-work*. Each node on the Outliner tree represents a *Page* object, equivalent to a *HTML page* - the basic building block of the Web.

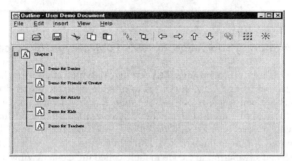

Figure 4. Opening UI screen of *The Outliner*

Apart from the hierarchical contents-page-like opening interface of the Outliner, normal HTML hyperlinks can be inserted within any page in a Reference-work, linking them to other internal pages or external URLs, in a networked hypertext manner.

4.3.2: Generic learning activities

The complex object type *Learning-activity* is a generic model that caters for the online rendering of numerous learning activities, with conventional names like:

> *Lecture; Tutorial; Lab Session; Prac Session; Case Study; Exercise; Exam; Test; Assessment unit; Period; etc.*

The term *Learning-activity* is a generic name used within Creator, for any type of activity that has associated with it, a set of *milestones* or *goals*. The other main difference between Creators *Learning-activities* and Reference-works, is that Learning-activities have a network of inter-relationships, graphically created during the authoring process, based on conditions. See Fig. 5 further down, which represents a screen-shot of the *Page Linker* (also sometimes called *the Networker*), the Creator Authoring Tool used to create Learning-activities.

5: The Authoring Tools

The Creator Authoring Tools custom-coded in Java V1.1 and the JDK/Swing, are largely for the creation and editing of the complex object types: *Reference-work*, *Learning-activity*, *Page* and *Question*. See Table 1 below, for an overview of which Authoring Tool is used to edit what complex object type.

Tool Name	Creator object-type	Screen-shot
The Outliner (tree structure)	*Reference-work*	*Figure 4.*
Page Linker (network struct.)	*Learning-activity*	*Figure 5.*
Page Designer	*Page*	*Figure 6.*
Question Editor	*Question*	
Resource Palette	*can hold any/all object types*	*Figure 3.*

Table 1. Authoring Tool name, by edited object-type, by screen-shot.

The *Page Linker* is used to create and edit Learning Activities of all sorts, by constructing a network of paths and using *Question objects* to provide alternative user-driven hyperlinks. Question objects are constructed with the *Question Editor* - a sub-component of the Page Linker. Currently it can be used to create and edit several question types that transparently allow the browser user to interact with *out-of-line* links, i.e. multi-choice links, much like the newly proposed Xpointer links in XML [6]. In Creator they are activated via standard HTML V4, CSS and JavaScript, in a code module called the Content Viewer [7].

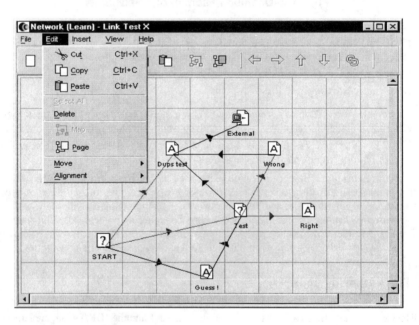

Figure 5. The *Page Linker,* used to build networks of paths between pages.

Creator's *Learning-activities* and *Reference-works* can be thought of as two styles of *online interactive documents*, each made up of numerous related pages. The *Page* object has special significance within Creator, in that it is outwardly equivalent to an HTML browser page. Fig. 6 below, is a screen-shot of Creator's WYSIWYG HTML V4 editor, the *Page Designer*. It allows the user to drag-and-drop all object types which can have a rectangular representation on-screen, i.e. *HTML-text* boxes, *HTML-table*, *Image*, *Video* and *External-Object* types including: *Java Applets*, *JavaBeans*, *Shockwave* and *ActiveX* controls.

Figure 6. Page Designer, a WYSIWYG editor used to glue together various Creator objects using underlying HTML V4 markup.

6: Characteristics of the resulting system.

Some interesting characteristics and observations drawn from the resulting system include:

- By using cascading style-sheets (CSS) to place a component at a specific (x,y) location, the HTML V4 language renders the browser window a *universal application window*, rather than just a universal *presentation* window. All component object types that can be bounded by a rectangle on the screen, appear at specific locations within the browser window, as directed by the content-developer in the WYSIWYG authoring tools. That is: the scripting language JavaScript and the presentation language HTML V4, together exhibit a symbiotic relationship with component objects - themselves written in all sorts of languages - empowering non-programming users to form complex and feature rich applications. This near-universal window to client platforms is limited only by memory and bandwidth, rather than by operating systems and vendors.

- In the absence of significant cooperation between the two main browser makers (Netscape Inc. and Microsoft Inc.), Java V1.1 and JFC/Swing has enabled cross-platform, Internet aware applications, to reach heights that the general browser user can still only imagine.

- The Creator system via the Object-Relational design adopted, can be thought of as an *object factory* that:
  1. Instantiates complex objects from persistent data held in a standard SQL server.
  2. Holds *Learning Activity* repositories.
  3. Holds *Reference Work* repositories.
  4. Instantiates a user profile via the Administration System.
  5. Provides an online Examination system, also based on the dynamic multi-pathed Learning Activity model.
  6. Has sophisticated WYSIWYG authoring tools for creating and editing objects.

7: Problems encountered and their solutions

Obviously a project of this size, scope and mixture of evolving technologies and standards, came with considerable problems, both in technical and management terms:

7.1: Staff recruiting and rival technologies

As the newly appointed Project Manager in May'97 for version V1, my first task was to build up the necessary team. I started with just one software engineer who had been involved in the proof-of-concept (POC) which had been contracted to a related company (Clearview Pty Ltd, a Melbourne IT incubator company [8]). The POC included some browser interfaces to about one-quarter of the tables in the first design, using Microsoft IIS [2] and .ASP files (HTML with embedded JavaScript, which IIS uses to build HTML on the fly, via calls to SQL). Some content object types were enabled in the POC, but it wasn't possible for non-programming users to author them.

I took the project down two distinct technology paths to cater for the different user groups outlined in section 2 above, which meant building up two teams with different skills. It took until December '97 to get the two teams to full strength with six software engineers apiece:

Team 1 skills: SQL Server, IIS, HTML and JavaScript for dynamic web coding;

Team 2 skills: Java for the WYSIWYG Authoring Tools.

Melbourne IT P/L, as a commercial entity owned by the University of Melbourne, has several advantages in developing new technology, one of which is recruitment, via its proximity to the Department of Computer Science (one floor away). I hired five recent graduates most of them with double degrees, high final grades and good recommendations. Several of them had dabbled in Java in their course related project work – projects done for industry clients. I put some of them through industry based Java training courses. I hired two team leaders with 3 and 5 years of commercial hardened experience, who'd previously worked for Microsoft Solution Providers, to provide each team with complementary skills: open-mindedness to new technology and multiple vendors; and team leadering. More than anything else, this skill mix has enabled the Creator Team to deliver an ambitious, complex project, using cutting-edge technology at the forefront of a new application software genre.

A benefit of the difficult technological mix was that a constructive, friendly, rivalry developed between the Java team and the IIS/Dynamic Web team. Though they worked in different technologies, there were two common elements of the technology that affected both: the SQL backend and the client window front-ends. The embracing of both Java and IIS technologies removed more technical problems than it created. The technical synergy between system programming languages and scripting languages experienced during this project, is getting timely recognition in software engineering literature [9].

The complexities and problems went from technical ones to management ones: e.g. double the coordination and versioning of code modules. To maintain Creator team cohesion and keep in check the cross-team rivalry, off-site one-day team building events were held during the course of the project, to reinforce a sense of *One Team, One Goal*. With competitive vendors openly warring in the public arena on a constant basis, such team events are not just useful but have become necessary when using multi-vendor tools and platforms.

7.2: Early adopters beware

A management decision was taken to release alpha versions to a few early customers (at their own risk) and then attempt to cater for their needs during development of the generic product. Since a lot of the raw material for an online course consists of components: images, HTML-text, videos, animations, other simple-objects - a lot of material is not necessarily wasted, if a version of the generic system changes substantially. Therefore, several willing early adopters were found. The intention was to give the product an early commercial focus and to add pressure and focus to the young team, but the consequences were too often:

- distraction from the main goal;
- significant attempts at compromising the design for expediency, rather than refining it;
- untimely and unnecessary nitpicking regarding user-interfaces, icon designs and usability, long before functionality had even been addressed properly, which in turn adversely affected some senior management views of the underlying technology;
- unnecessary extra pressure on a young team, already used to significant pressure via exams, projects and other activities associated in obtaining recent high qualifications.

7.3: Design oversights

There were two significant positive aspects arising from the intake of early customers that helped to counter the associated problems. Firstly, a few design oversights were uncovered earlier than would otherwise have been the case. Secondly, it forced the early bedding-down of the database schema design, while application coding continued and functionality grew. Note: The database schema was really a second generation version, as significant refinement of the design came out of the POC version.

7.3.1: Externally authored pages

While one goal was to develop a WYSIWYG HTML authoring tool, in the first release it was never intended to be a complete drag-and-drop, fully-featured HTML V4 editor. Instead, a subset of tags representing a solid core of HTML V4 tags were supported, with particular emphasis on cascading style sheets (CSS), to place the rectangular representation of objects within the browser window, at (x,y) locations chosen by the user at design-time, using drag'and'drop. A perceived marketing strength of the Authoring Tools was that they would run across all major platforms (Windows, MAC and Unix), rather than do everything, on just one platform. The plan was then to cover all HTML V4 tags in a follow-up version of the Page Designer.

A problem that grew from this partial treatment of HTML, picked up by the early adopters, was the requirement to import some individual pages into a Creator Reference Work or Learning Activity, that had been authored in third party HTML authoring tools.

The Creator *Page* entity and the *On_page_object* entity had enough design flexibility to handle this new requirement for *externally authored HTML pages* with minimal change, due to the Data Normalization techniques used in the original Data Analysis, and to the use of Booch methodology for the interfacing Java classes. It simply required an import mechanism to place the externally authored pages at appropriate pre-determined URLs on a Creator Server, where the IIS/.ASP code could expect to find them. It was a one week fix.

7.4: Extended problems and their solutions, in the pipeline

Reference-works and Learning-activities authored in Creator are persistently stored across many database tables. While the authoring tools and the browser interface can readily access them, page-by-page in a client window, the transfer of such a document type, from one installation (database), to another, represents a significant import/export programming task. Ideally it requires an ASCII encoded go-between format, one that preferably retains the data structures, while in the transient state between databases.

A second consequence of the database backend, is that all content can be and usually is, put behind a username+password access screen. This is good for controlling access to commercially sold instructional material developed in Creator, but it prevents search engines from finding and indexing Creator-held content, thereby impeding potential discovery by new courseware customers. Both these problems are being addressed by drawing upon the XML language, for neat and clean solutions, involving metadata.

7.4.1: XML in a nutshell

The widely embraced XML (eXtensible Markup Language) - enables software developers and content publishers alike, to structure data in an ASCII file format. XML is being seriously considered as the foundation technology to transform the Internet from a globally distributed *information system* to a globally distributed *knowledge system [10]*. There is a strong parallel between an *SQL database schema* and an *XML DTD* (Data Type Definition) file. An XML DTD can be thought of and used as, an ASCII rendered database schema. Similarly, the actual data records in an XML file conforming to a specific XML DTD, are essentially ASCII database records, i.e. a lightweight database system with no vendor DBMS such as ORACLE or MS SQL Server, necessary – hence, one of the attractions of XML to current web publishers, including online educational content developers.

7.4.2: Importing and exporting content via XML

Given the SQL backend and the componentized nature of the data, getting content and other data between Creator database installations (e.g. between home and office PCs), or between Creator and other systems, requires an import and an export operation. A proprietary XML DTD, which represents all the complexities of the current Creator SQL schema, is currently being developed at Melbourne IT, to specifically streamline import and export of complex object content.

7.4.3: EML, the Educational Metadata Language

Melbourne IT is in the process of developing a metadata language, dubbed *Educational Metadata Language* or *EML,* to facilitate metadata output from Creator. The main purpose of EML metadata is to present information in publicly accessible XML and HTML file/s, that adequately advertises to human web-surfers and web search engines alike, the details of instructional content held within any given Creator Server site [11,12]. The metaphor used is that of the Department Handbook, with course and subject information outlined uniformly.

7.5: Complexity in using SQL server technology

The Creator V1 database schema consists of 56 inter-related tables, making it a complex database system. This is partly due to the ambitious nature of the project (almost a Virtual University, plus Authoring Tools) and partly due to the design not being a simple relational database schema, but one that uses SQL Server to serve as a persistent store of objects - both simple and complex ones.

From a users point of view the complexity is hidden behind friendly GUI interfaces and WYSIWYG authoring tools. However, it is still worth identifying and differentiating the *types of data* held in SQL tables, in a quest to see where XML might be gainfully employed to simplify things when XML browser technology becomes mainstream:

- Student data: *conventional relational database (DB) usage.*

- Subject data: *conventional relational DB usage.*

- Keyword and Thesaurus: *conventional relational DB usage.*

- Simple Creator Object data. e.g. Images; Video: *using DB as a persistent store.*

- Complex Creator Object data including: tree-structures; link-lists; networks-webs: *Object-Relational DB usage.*

It is in the latter area of the complex object types that XML may help in the future, if large percentages of browser users end up using XML+ HTML parsing browsers. For example, tree-structures such as those used by outliners, are very well suited to XML.

8: Conclusions

In developing Creator, the use of old technology in the form of SQL and new technology in the form of Java, HTML V4 and JavaScript, has proven a successful strategy to deliver an innovative product, in a new genre of software: *authoring and delivery tools for online education.* Drawing from the experience, what follows are several wide ranging personal insights and conclusions, about the future of some of the main technologies used:

8.1: Java is ready for prime time

With the release of Java V1.1, the distributed Java event model came of age. With the recent release of the JFC/Swing GUI component package, as demonstrated by the Creator

Authoring Tools interfaces, Java has gained a professional UI toolset. *Performance* improvements remain as the most significant aspect of Java that requires timely attention from JavaSoft Inc. There are positive signs that this is happening: while performance benchmarks between C/C++ and Java are *not* in Java's favour, comparisons between Java and the more populist language Visual BASIC, definitely *are* in Java's favour.

I view the performance arguments for programming in either C/C++ vs. Java, as analogous to the old performance arguments between character-based interfaces and GUIs: the non-performance gains by using Java over C/C++ are of that same order of magnitude of using GUIs over character-based UIs. Some performance hit will be more and more tolerated by developers, as the language settles down and the standard hardware platform gets faster and has more memory.

The biggest strength of Java I've seen in context of the Creator project was in the productivity that recent graduates can achieve in Java, without the *go-slows* via pointer errors and other difficult bugs, that a project manager usually sees with the same cohort of programmers using C/C++ tools.

8.2: SQL is holding its own

The relational theory behind SQL servers formed a very solid foundation for information systems. While OOP languages such as C++ and Java are a quantum advance over procedural languages, many made the mistake of assuming OODBMS's would leapfrog Relational DBMS - not so. As discussed earlier, the extra life gained by SQL Servers is largely to do with the *best time and place* to instantiate an object: sometimes it is client-side, other times it is server-side. So we've seen some SQL server vendors adding Object-Relational APIs to their wares, and there are numerous application developers adding their own Object-Relational API's to SQL servers, as is the case with Melbourne IT Creator™.

8.3: Application areas where SQL server technology has ongoing advantage

Here are the most compelling ongoing reasons for storing certain information types within tables in an SQL server, now and for some considerable time to come:

- Volatile data: allows for rapid adhoc access to large amounts of centralized data.

- Secure data: an added level of security and encryption of content.

- SQL engines represent 20 years of performance enhancing development, suitable for large amounts of data, that can be accessed very quickly. Significant performance gains via TP Monitors promise new life to SQL servers in distributed systems.

- To simplify micro-tracking of discrete elements of content e.g. for novel web-based e-commerce charging/tariff models.

- Continual collaborative online publishing is possible (i.e. continuous multi-user editing).

8.4: XML today and tomorrow

XML has immediate and significant uses in importing and exporting complex data between applications, and in metadata definitions and rendering. Whether these applications use open standard or propriety XML DTD definitions, doesn't affect the viability of XML as a major standard language for defining other languages and definitions – it is already safely *home* in this regard.

Looking forward a little, if the mainstream browsers do become standard XML parsers (for information structure), as well as HTML/CSS/XSL parsers (for information presentation), as seems probable, then XML will take on a wider role including many of the areas where Relational DBMS are currently employed in web-based distributed systems, and in new areas such as data storage on handheld devices.

References:

1. Lagoze, C., Lynch C.A. and Daniel R., Editors (1998). *HTML V4.0 Specification.* W3C Recommendation, April 1998, URL http://www.w3.org/TR/REC-html40/

2. IIS White Paper. *Internet Information Server.* Follow URL http://www.microsoft.com/iis/

3. Goschnick, S., Smart, T., Bruno, A. and McMaster, T. (1998). *Creator V1.0 Database Design Document.* Melbourne IT Internal Report.

4. Ahmed E.U. and Smart, T. (1998). *Creator V1.0 Detailed Design - Functional Security System*, Melbourne IT Internal Report.

5. Goschnick, S.B., McMaster, T., Valentine and D., Bakal (1998). *Creator V1.0 Detailed Design - Authoring Tools*, Melbourne IT Internal Report.

6. Bray T., Paoli J. and Sperberg-McQueen, C. M., Editors (1998). *Extensible Markup Language (XML) 1.0*, W3C Recommendation. URL http://w3c.org/TR/1998/REC-xml-19980210/

7. Saengpetch, S. (1998). *Creator V1.0 Detailed Design - Content Viewer System*, Melbourne IT Internal Report.

8. Melbourne IT Incubator Companies. Home page of Melbourne IT P/L, URL http://www.MelbourneIT.com.au

9. Ousterhout, J.K. (1998). *Scripting: Higher-Level Programming for the 21st Century.* Computer, March'98 issue, pp23-30.

10. Cassin, A. (1998). *Survey of XML Technology.* URL http://www.cs.mu.oz.au/agentlab/publications.html. University of Melbourne.

11. Cassin, A. (1998). *Survey of Metadata Technology.* URL http://www.cs.mu.oz.au/agentlab/publications.html.

12. Cassin, A. and Goschnick, S.B. (1998). *System Requirement Specification for Melbourne IT Creator Metadata Agent.* Internal Report, pp.23, July'98.

Some Melbourne IT Creator™ Web-sites:

a) Home Page of Melbourne IT Creator. URL http://www.creator.com.au/

b) An Introductory AI course is being developed and delivered using Melbourne IT Creator V1. Currently under-construction at: URL http://www.solidsoftware.com.au/courses/ai/

Steve Goschnick B.E. has 19 years experience as a software developer, software publisher and IT manager. He has written numerous conference, magazine and newspaper articles on software related issues. He wrote a weekly column called *Cutting Code* for the computer section of *The Age* Melbourne daily newspaper throughout 1993. He did the analysis and design for Melbourne IT Creator in January 1997. After the proof-of-concept proved successful, he signed on for one year with Melbourne IT P/L as Project Manager to build a team and develop Creator V1.0 - which was delivered in early March 1998, for testing and usability refinement. In June 1998, he began a deferred Masters by Research degree within the Computer Science Department at the University of Melbourne. He is the recipient of an Australian Research Council/DEETYA SPIRT research award, sponsored by industry partner Ericsson Australia Pty. Ltd., based on the merit of his research topic.

Session 4

Simulation and Testing

Support for Object-Oriented Testing

Michael Kölling
School of Computer Science &
Software Engineering
Monash University
Australia

John Rosenberg
Faculty of
Information Technology
Monash University
Australia

michael.kolling@csse.monash.edu.au

johnr@fcit.monash.edu.au

Abstract

Object-orientation has rapidly become accepted as the preferred paradigm for large scale system design. There is considerable literature describing approaches to object-oriented design and implementation. However discussion of testing in an object-oriented environment has been conspicuous by its absence. At first sight it appears that decomposition of a system into a potentially large number of information-hiding classes greatly increases the cost of testing. However, in this paper we show that by taking an object-oriented approach to testing, and the inclusion of appropriate tools in the development environment, testing time can be greatly reduced and special purpose test code can be virtually eliminated.

1 Introduction

Object-orientation has rapidly become accepted as the preferred paradigm for large scale system design. The reasons for this are well known and understood. First, classes provide an excellent structuring mechanism. They allow a system to be divided into well defined units which may then be implemented separately. Second, classes support information-hiding. A class can export a purely procedural interface and the internal structure of data may be hidden. This allows the structure to be changed without affecting users of the class, thus simplifying maintenance.

Third, object-orientation encourages and supports software reuse. This may be achieved either through the simple reuse of a class in a library, or via inheritance, whereby a new class may be created as an extension of an existing one. In both cases the result is a reduction in the amount of software which must be written and, as a result, an improvement in the reliability of the resultant system since previously tested classes may be utilised.

If we are to capitalise on the potential advantages of object-orientation then it is important that the object-oriented approach is adopted and supported throughout the software development process. The design phase is now reasonably well understood (although notoriously difficult) and there are various tools to assist with the process. Similarly there are tools to support the implementation phase. Library browsers may be used to assist with locating existing classes which may be reused in the project and tools provide support for editing, compilation, etc.

However, testing is often ignored by the designers of software tools and the programmer is left to his/her own resources. Some may argue that testing should not be difficult (or even necessary at all) if a proper design and implementation process has taken place. We all know this not to be true and we must subject new software to rigorous testing before it can be used in a production environment.

Unfortunately the very advantages of object-orientation cited above become potential disadvantages when we consider testing. The structuring of the system as a set of independent classes requires that each of these must be tested and there may be a large number of them. In addition, information-hiding, which encourages designers of classes to have purely procedural interfaces, makes it difficult to determine whether the class is working correctly, since the state of internal data may not be accessible via the interface.

The result is that the programmer must effectively develop a test program for each class. Each such test program must create an instance of the class being tested and include calls to each of the methods supported by the class. The test program will need to prompt the user for the parameters for these method calls so that various combinations can be exercised. The test program must also display the results of each method call. The result is that the test program may well be more complex and larger than the class being tested.

Once we have written such a test program, we still may not be able to ascertain whether the internal data of the class being tested is correct because of the inability to access all of the internal data via the procedural interface.

There are at least two solutions to this problem. First, " debug" print statements could be added into the class code to print out relevant internal data when methods are called. This has several associated problems. The insertion of new test code could well introduce errors in itself and these can detract from the original testing process. In addition if there are several classes, the volume of output can become difficult to interpret.

The second solution is to use a symbolic debugger to insert breakpoints and examine the data. This adds further complexity to the process. In addition, the symbolic debugger may not be able to adequately display complex linked structures.

Clearly what is required is tools specifically designed to assist with testing object-oriented applications. In particular we would like to reduce the amount of code which must be written in order to test classes. Ideally no special testing code should have to be written. These tools should be an integrated component of a complete object-oriented development environment.

This paper describes an environment which supports this ideal by allowing the interactive creation of instances of classes and interactively invocation of their methods. This, coupled with the ability to examine the internal state variables of objects, allows the programmer to interactively test their classes without writing a single line of test code.

The tools described have been developed as a part of a larger project known as Blue [3]. Blue is both an object-oriented programming language [4, 6] and a program development environment [5] and has been specifically designed for teaching programming to first year students. The system has been in use for nearly two years. The authors are currently working on a new version of the environment designed for Java developers.

The tools described in this paper are only those used for testing. There is still a need for specialised debugging tools which in the Blue system include breakpoints, single-stepping, display of variable values, etc. It must be emphasized that we see a clear distinction between testing, which is required for every program, and debugging, which is only required if testing finds a failure.

In this paper we first discuss a general approach to testing object-oriented programs. We then show how this technique has been included in an object-oriented program development environment. This is followed by a brief description of the technology employed to implement this environment.

2 Object-oriented testing

The key advantage of the object-oriented paradigm is that it provides a uniform structure for all components in the form of a procedural interface. Although as indicated above, this appears to complicate the testing process, it may be exploited to support an object-oriented approach to testing.

In order to test a class the programmer must be able undertake the following activities:

(a) create an instance of the class, i.e. an object, passing the appropriate parameters to the constructor

(b) call the methods of the object passing parameters and receiving results

(c) examine the internal data of the object

As discussed above, this can be achieved by writing a test program for each class and the inclusion of debug statements. However, it could also be achieved by the inclusion of appropriate mechanisms in the program development environment itself. This would eliminate the need for both test programs and the modification of the class being tested.

The mechanisms would work in the following manner. First, the environment provides the user with the ability to interactively create an object of any class. The class is selected and the system prompts for the constructor parameters. Once the object has been constructed, any of its methods may be interactively invoked; again the user is prompted for parameters. Results (return parameters) are displayed in a dialogue box.

Second, the environment provides an inspection facility which allows the internal data of an object to be examined. The data is displayed in a dialogue box along with the types of each field.

The mechanisms described so far are sufficient to test classes with scalars as parameters. However, it is of course common to pass other objects as parameters. The system can support this by allowing an arbitrary number of objects of arbitrary classes to be constructed. These may then be composed, i.e. one such object can be passed as a parameter to another.

A further problem is that results of method calls may include objects, as may the internal data of a class. How should such objects be displayed? Our approach is to initially display these as a typed object reference. The user may then choose to display the contents of the object referred to by such a reference. The contents may contain further object references and these may be accessed in the same manner. This facility allows arbitrary data structures to be examined and traversed.

We call this an object-oriented approach to testing because it exploits the uniform nature of classes and objects to provide a generic testing facility. The major advantage of the approach is that it virtually eliminates the need to write special purpose testing code.

Note that Smalltalk environments [2] traditionally come close to meeting some of these goals. Especially an " instance centred" variation of Smalltalk, named " Portia" supports similar techniques [1]. Smalltalk, however, has disadvantages in other areas, many of which result from the fact that it is a dynamically typed language. More recent environments for statically typed languages seem to have neglected this area.

3 Testing in the Blue environment

The Blue environment is an integrated graphical environment which supports the techniques described in the previous section. Its main window presents a graphical overview of the application structure. Each class in the application is represented by an icon, and relationships between class are displayed (figure 1).

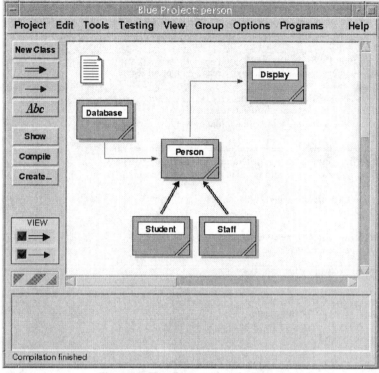

Figure 1: The Blue main window

Double-clicking a class icon opens an editor displaying the class' s source code. Each class or the whole application can be compiled with a click on a " compile" button. (For a more detailed description of the Blue environment, see [5]).

The empty area at the bottom of the main window is the *object bench*. We discuss below how it is used to interact with objects.

Once a class within a project has been compiled, objects of that class may be created. Interactive creation of objects is achieved by selecting the class and clicking the " Create" button. (Clicking the right mouse button on a class provides a shortcut to the same function.)

This operation is similar to interactively sending a " new" message to a class in a Smalltalk environment. An instance is interactively created and available for operation. No equivalent of this operation is available in common environments for more recently developed, statically typed programming languages.

Invoking the creation operation on a class results in a normal object creation, including the execution of the creation routine (the " constructor" in C++/Java terminology). As an example, we will use a class " Person" which stores some information about a person and provides interface routines to change and access that information. This class is not meant to be complete or really useful in any sense – it is used here only as an example to demonstrate the Blue object interaction facilities. The interface of the class is shown in figure 2.[1]

---

[1] This example uses the Blue language. The language itself is not important here, and a similar environment can be constructed for other languages.

```
class interface Person is
=====================================================
== Author:     M. Kölling
== Version:    1.0
== Date: 8 June 1998
== Short:      Person class for university management project
==
== The class Person implements object representing a person
== in a university management project. It contains
== information common to all persons in the university...
==
=====================================================
  creation (firstName : String, lastName : String, age : Integer)
     == Create a new person with given name and age.
     pre
       lastName <> nil and age <> nil

routines
  changeNames (firstName : String, lastName : String)
     == Change the names for this person
     pre
       lastName <> nil

  changeAge (newAge : Integer)
     == Set a new age for this person
     pre
       newAge <> nil

  getNames -> (firstName : String, lastName : String)
     == Return both names of this person

  getAge -> (age : Integer)
     == Return age of this person

end class
```

Figure 2: Interface of class " Person"

When the create operation is invoked a dialogue is displayed to let the user enter routine parameters (figure 3). At the top of this dialogue, the interface of the creation routine is displayed. The interface includes the routine header and the routine comment. Further down is a text field for entering parameter values. Under the parameters is another field to provide a name for the object to be created. A default name is provided and is often adequate. The name will be displayed on the object after it has been created. The large area in the middle of the dialogue is a (currently empty) list of previously used parameter lists. It is provided for convenience during testing of a class: previously made calls can be easily repeated by selecting a parameter combination from the list.

```
                    Create Object

  creation (firstName : String, lastName : String, age : Integer)

  == Create a new person with given name and age.




                        Enter parameter(s):

  create Person (  "John", "Smith", 75                     )

  Name of instance:  Person_1


    OK              Cancel              Help
```

Figure 3: Object creation dialogue

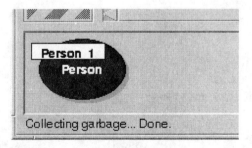

Figure 4: An object on the object bench

Once the dialogue is filled in and the OK button is clicked, the object is created and displayed on the object bench (figure 4). The object is then available to the user for direct interaction. Many different objects of the same or different classes may be created and stored on the object bench at the same time.

Clicking on the object with the right mouse button displays a menu that includes all interface routines of that object (figure 5). Also included in the menu are two special operations available for all objects: *inspect* and *remove*. The remove operation removes the object from the bench when it is no longer needed. The inspect operation is discussed below.

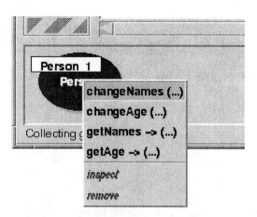

Figure 5: Calling a routine on an object

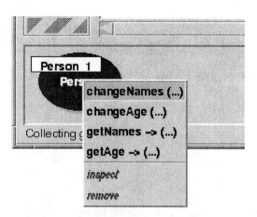

Figure 6: Routine call dialogue for " changeNames"

Symbols in the routine menu indicate whether a routine has parameters or return values. When a routine is selected from the menu, a call to that routine is executed. If the routine has parameters, a parameter dialogue similar to the one seen at the creation of the object is displayed (figure 6). On the click of the OK button the routine is executed and, if the routine returns results, the result values are displayed in another dialogue. Figure 7 shows a function result dialogue for a call to the routine " getNames"[2].Again, at the top of the dialogue window the interface of the called routine is displayed. Below, the actual call is shown in standard Blue syntax (the name of

---

[2] In Blue, a function can return more than one value. Return values are named, similar to parameters in a parameter list.

the called object, the routine name and – if present – actual parameters). This is followed by a list of the result values of the function. For each result its name, type and value are displayed.

The result of the facilities described so far (interactive creation of objects, interactive routine calls and result display) is that a project can be incrementally developed. There is no need to complete all classes in a project before the first tests can be performed. Instead, each class can be tested as soon as some of its routines have been completed without the need to write special purpose test code. This possibility dramatically changes the style of work available to the developer.

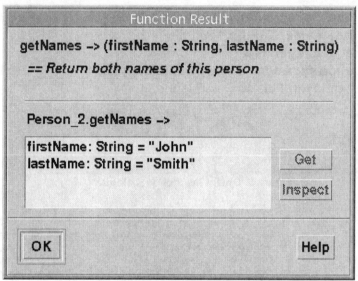

Figure 7: Result dialogue for function " getNames"

4   Composition

During the interactive testing of the system, objects accessible on the object bench may be composed, i.e. one object may be passed as a parameter to the routine of another object. If, for instance, a project includes a database class and a person class with the intention of creating a database of persons, then objects of these classes may be combined. Several person objects could be created. Then a database object is created and its " addPerson" routine is invoked. When the routine call dialogue is visible on the screen, a click on one of the person objects on the object bench will enter its name into the parameter field of the routine call dialogue. The object will be passed as a parameter. This can be done repeatedly to add all the persons from the object bench to the database.

5   Inspection of objects

As mentioned above, a mechanism is needed to examine instance data of objects for cases where an object does not provide accessor functions for that data. This functionality is provided by the *inspect* operation. Using the inspect operation (by selecting it from the object menu or, as a shortcut, double-clicking the object) opens the object and reveals its internals. Figure 8 shows the dialogue displayed as a result of inspecting a person object.

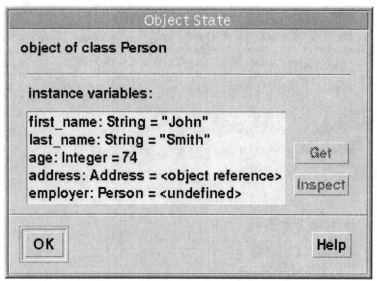

Figure 8: Object inspection dialogue

For this example, we have modified the above definition of the class " Person" to include *address* and *employer* variables, so that we can show how more complex objects can be inspected. The *address* variable holds a reference to another user-defined object of class " Address" ; the *employer* variable refers to another person.

The names, types and values of all instance variables of this object are shown. For manifest objects, which have a simple textual representation, values are shown as literals. For variables holding more complex objects only the state of the variable is displayed (whether it is undefined, contains *nil* or an object reference). Those variables may then in turn be inspected by double-clicking on the variable or selecting the variable and then clicking the " Inspect" button. Another window will be opened displaying the internals of that object. An example is shown in figure 9 for the inspection of the address object.

Note that we are able to examine any object reachable from an object available on the object bench. Sometimes it can become clumsy to repeatedly navigate through object references to reach an object we wish to examine. The " Get" button on the inspection dialogue (figure 8) allows a reference to any existing object to be placed on the object bench so that it can be re-examined at a later time. This also allows the user to interactively call interface routines of objects that were created internally.

Overall, inspection of objects assists users in thoroughly testing objects of any class by allowing users to observe the effect of routine executions on internal data.

Finally, there is a record facility in Blue which will textually record all interactive object creations, method invocations, return values, text input and text output. This may be used to document the testing that was carried out.

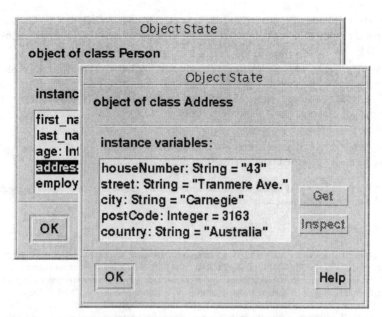

Figure 9: Inspection of " Address" object

6 Pedagogical benefits

The Blue environment was initially developed as a teaching environment for first year students. While the testing facilities described here are generally applicable to all forms of object-oriented software development (educational as well as professional) and thus a teaching environment is only one example of possible applications of these techniques, it is worthwhile summarising the educational benefits which Blue gained from these tools.

- *Incremental development.* Projects can be incrementally developed and tested. There is no need to even syntactically complete a whole application. As soon as one class (or even one routine) is completed it can be compiled and objects can be created, executed and tested. This leads to greater motivation (results are visible more quickly) and a better ability to cope with errors (since early errors can be found and removed before more errors are made, avoiding the harder to find cases of multiple interacting errors). This is clearly also an advantage professional software development situations.

- *Class/object distinction.* Students often have difficulties understanding the relationship between classes and objects. Allowing the direct creation of and interaction with objects greatly facilitates the understanding of these fundamental issues. The pure act of creating a number of objects from a class demonstrates in a powerful way the respective roles of the concepts. If a student has, for example, a class " Person" and creates three different people with different names, the role of the class and the role of each object becomes much more directly understandable.

- *Programming without I/O.* Since input/output operations are often difficult to understand initially (because they often do not conform to language rules or force the use of advanced concepts), it might lead to a clearer understanding of the abstraction concepts if routine calls are taught before language exceptions (like I/O operations) are shown [7].

- *Interface/implementation distinction.* The distinction between the interface and the implementation of an object – itself an important concept – is clarified. Since only the interface operations are visible to a human user when directly interacting with an object the concept that this is the only part of an object visible to other objects seems a logical conclusion.

- *Testing support.* As was our initial goal, good testing, essential to all serious software development, is supported much better than in conventional systems.

Overall, the interaction and inspection facility provided by the object bench not only meets our initial goal, but offers additional benefits beyond the area of testing.

7   Implementation

To execute an interactive call, the Blue environment uses linguistic reflection. A class is constructed internally that includes the interactive call as its only statement in its creation routine. This class is then passed to the compiler to be translated. An object of the resulting class is instantiated which, as part of the creation, executes its creation routine and with it the interactive call. Result values are stored in this internal object and can then be extracted for display in the result dialogue. To illustrate this technique let us consider an interactive call to the following routine:

```
extract (line: String, o: Object) -> (word: String, valid: Boolean)
```

In Blue, return values are written in a list after a " – >" symbol. Thus, the routine shown has two parameters and two return values. The actual call we want to execute is

```
parser.extract ("input line", obj1)
```

We assume that parser and obj1 are the names of objects on the object bench. To execute this call, the Blue system internally creates the source for another class, usually referred to as the *shell class*. The source code created for our example call would look like this:

```
class __SHELL__ is
  == shell class for interactive call
  uses Parser, Object
  internal var word: String
              valid: Boolean
  interface
    creation (parser: Parser, obj1: Object) is
        == execute interactive call
      do
        word, valid :=
              parser.extract ("input line", obj1)
      end creation
end class
```

The interactive call is then executed by creating an object of the shell class. Creation of the shell object automatically includes the execution of the interactive call as part of its creation routine execution.

The shell class is constructed to have one instance variable for every return value of the interactive call. The return values are stored in those variables and can, after the call, be retrieved from the created object to be displayed to the user. The display of the return values is, in fact, nothing else than an inspection of the shell object.

Several advantages are associated with this technique. Firstly, the parameter list does not need to be parsed and evaluated by the project management part of the system. The compiler is used for this purpose, thus avoiding duplication of equivalent code. The project manager sets up only the parameter list for the shell creation routine, which contains only object references. Secondly, error messages for mistakes found in the parameter list are produced by the compiler and are thus guaranteed to be the same messages that would be produced for the same error in a non-interactive call. This increases consistency in the environment. Thirdly, the only call ever to be initiated by the object bench (the call to the shell creation routine) has a simple and known interface. Most importantly, it has only object parameters, no literals. This greatly simplifies the implementation. The interactive call, having an arbitrary parameter list, is turned into an internal call completely handled by the runtime system.

8   Conclusion

The object-oriented paradigm has brought obvious advantages to the software development process. However, these advantages have not been exploited in the testing phase. In this paper we have shown how testing itself can be achieved in an object-oriented manner. We have described generic tools which support this process and virtually eliminate the need to write special purpose test code. This approach fully supports incremental software development, allows testing to take place earlier in the project and results in a considerable reduction in overall testing time.

The system described has been implemented for a teaching language known as Blue. The authors are currently constructing a similar environment for Java. A limited version of the environment is currently being tested and should be available for general use by the end of 1998.

References

[1] E. Gold and M. B. Rosson, *Portia: An Instance-Centered Environment for Smalltalk*, in OOPSLA 91 Conference Proceedings, ACM, 62-74, 1991.

[2] A. Goldberg, *Smalltalk-80: The Interactive Programming Environment*, Addison-Wesley, 1984.

[3] M. Kölling, B. Koch and J. Rosenberg, *Requirements for a First Year Object-Oriented Teaching Language*, in ACM SIGCSE Bulletin, ACM, Nashville, 173-177, March 1995.

[4] M. Kölling and J. Rosenberg, *Blue - A Language for Teaching Object-Oriented Programming*, in Proceedings of 27th SIGCSE Technical Symposium on Computer Science Education, ACM, Philadelphia, Pennsylvania, 190-194, March 1996.

[5] M. Kölling and J. Rosenberg, *An Object-Oriented Program Development Environment for the First Programming Course*, in Proceedings of 27th SIGCSE Technical Symposium on Computer Science Education, ACM, Philadelphia, Pennsylvania, 83-87, March 1996.

[6] M. Kölling and J. Rosenberg, *Blue - Language Specification, Version 1.0*, School of Computer Science and Software Engineering, Monash University, Technical Report TR97-13, November 1997.

[7] J. Rosenberg and M. Kölling, *I/O Considered Harmful (At least for the first few weeks)*, in Proceedings of the Second Australasian Conference on Computer Science Education, ACM, Melbourne, 216-223, July 1997.

CDFA: A Testing System for C++

Chi Keen Low [*]
Department of Computer Science
The University of Melbourne
Melbourne
Victoria 3052
Australia
clow@cs.mu.oz.au

Tsong Yueh Chen [†]
Department of Computer Science
The University of Melbourne
Melbourne
Victoria 3052
Australia
tyc@cs.mu.oz.au

Abstract

CDFA is a dynamic data flow analysis system for testing C++ programs. It instruments C++ programs with code that reports actions on data. The instrumented program is executed and monitored for anomalies. To effectively test C++ programs, CDFA incorporates extended actions, extended state transition diagrams, implicit state variables, functional instrumentation and object-based instrumentation.

Keywords: testing C++ program, dynamic data flow analysis, implicit state variables, functional instrumentation, object-based instrumentation.

1: Introduction

C++ is a popular programming language for object-oriented [1, 14] software development. Many tools and integrated developments environments have made C++ software development even easier. However, these tools and environments mainly concentrate on the design, implementation and debugging phases of software engineering [10]. *Testing* [8] is an important phase in software engineering but it does not receive enough focus.

We present a testing system for C++ called CDFA. We explain the underlying theoretical concepts behind CDFA and demonstrate how CDFA tests a system. CDFA uses *dynamic data flow analysis* to detect *anomalies* in a program. Our dynamic data flow analysis methodology has a few innovative concepts which allows it to detect anomalies in C++ more effectively.

In the next section, we discuss the background of CDFA. We start by providing an overview of *classes* in C++. Then we discuss data flow analysis and how it is used in testing software. Section 3 presents the important ideas in our dynamic data flow analysis methodology. Section 4 discusses the evaluation of our methodology in CDFA and we conclude with Section 5.

Direct all correspondence to Chi Keen Low, Department of Computer Science, The University of Melbourne, Melbourne, Victoria 3052, Australia. Tel: 61-3-9344-9101 Fax: 61-3-9348-1184 Email: clow@cs.mu.oz.au

†This research is supported in part by grants of the Hong Kong Research Grants Council.

2: Background

C++ is a object-oriented programming language designed for flexible and efficient software development. We provide a simple overview of *classes* in C++. For more information on the C++ programming language, readers should refer to the many reference materials [3, 15] available for C++.

The key concept in C++ is *class*. It allows the creation of *objects* that are meant to represent real-world items and concepts. A class has two kinds of class members, *data members* and *member functions*. *Data members* are attributes of classes while *member functions* provide methods to manipulate and interface classes. Class members have three access levels, namely *private, protected* and *public*. Private class members are only accessible by member functions of the same class or *friend* classes. The *protected* access level is designed for *inheritance*, another concept in the object-oriented paradigm. Protected class members are accessible by member functions of the same class, derived classes or *friend* classes. Public class members are accessible by any class and any global functions.

Data flow analysis was initially used in compilers during the optimisation phase. It analyses variables for *liveliness* and *availability* so that instructions can be reordered for optimal execution. Since then, data flow analysis has been applied in many different fields. It has been used in test case generation [4, 6, 13], static testing [9] and dynamic testing [2, 7]. We will discuss how data flow analysis has evolved through different uses and how we will use it in our dynamic data flow analysis methodology.

Data flow analysis is used in static testing by analysing the actions on data. Actions are applied on data through identifiers in a program. These identifiers include variable names, constants, function names, etc.. In general, we use the term data and variables interchangeably unless otherwise specified. Initially, the following are the three actions proposed [9].

- define action (d)
- reference action (r)
- undefine action (u)

The *define* action occurs on data when it is assigned a value. The *reference* action occurs on data when the value of the data is used. The *undefine* action occurs on data when it is initially declared in the a function or program and when the function exits or program terminates. In some programming languages such as Fortran, a loop control variable has an *undefine* action when the loop is terminated. In C++, a variable can be declared in any part of the program and thus the *undefine* action can occur at any time besides the start and end of a function or program.

These actions are analysed and detected for *anomalies*. *Anomalies* are not necessarily errors, they indicate improper use of data. The analysis is interested in consecutive actions on data. Certain sequences of actions are anomalies because they indicate improper use of data which can lead to errors. For example, the anomalies detected by static analysis are as follows.

- ur anomaly
- dd anomaly
- du anomaly

The *ur* anomaly indicates that a variable is declared (*u* action) but not initialised with a value, and then it is referenced (*r* action) in a statement. In programs which automatically initialise all declared variables to a certain value, this may not be a problem as long as the initialised value is the value expected by the programmer. However, most programming languages do not enforce the initialisation of declared variables. This means that the referenced variable can contain any value. This can cause errors. It is also bad programming practice to use variables without initialising them.

The *dd* anomaly indicates that a variable is assigned with a value and then assigned with another value without using the first value. At first, this may not seem like a problem. However, this means that the first assignment is redundant. Or is it? Perhaps the variable name has been misspelt and the wrong variable has been assigned with a value. This is an error. Data should not have two consecutive *d* actions because of performance reasons (redundancy) or use of incorrect variable (misspelling).

The *du* anomaly is similar to the *dd* anomaly. The *du* anomaly indicates that a variable has been assigned a value and is then discarded. Since it is not referenced, it should not be assigned in the first place. It could also be caused by misspelling and using the incorrect variable.

Static analysis is useful and effective in detecting anomalies. However, it has some drawbacks. It cannot effectively detect anomalies related to arrays, dynamically allocated memory, structures and classes. For example, the following is a simple swap between array elements.

```
temp = a[i];
a[i] = a[j];
a[j] = temp;
```

Static analysis considers the array a as a variable and thus immediately detects a *dd* anomaly in the second and third line. However, it is not an anomaly as long as i is not equal to j. The analysis then reports this as a false alarm and in a non-trivial program, false alarms are not desired. It can be a hindrance to software development. This is where dynamic data flow analysis is useful.

Dynamic testing executes the program and during the execution, the values of i and j are known. This means that a[i] and a[j] are considered as two different variables as long as i is not equal to j. This does not report any false alarms.

It must be mentioned that neither of these methods is better than the other. Static analysis can analyse most paths through the program, while dynamic analysis can only analyse the path that it executes dynamically. These two methods are considered complimentary.

The detection of anomalies is usually implemented with a state transition diagram. Data is associated with a *state variable*, usually its identifier. Data is then initialised with a state and state transitions occur with actions performed on the data. The states are as follows.

- D: defined
- R: referenced
- U: undefined
- A: anomalous

The state transition diagram is shown in Figure 1.

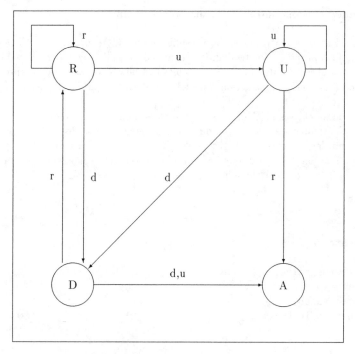

Figure 1. State transition diagram

3: Dynamic data flow analysis

Our dynamic data flow analysis methodology is designed to detect anomalies in C++. The methodology has a few important concepts which allows it to effectively test C++ programs.

- extended actions and state transition diagram
- implicit state variable
- functional instrumentation
- object-based instrumentation

Although the initial classifications of actions and state transition diagram for static testing were defined without explicit reference to any particular language, Fortran was the implicitly referred language [5]. The characteristics of data types, data structures and operations on data must be taken into consideration in defining the actions, states and state transition diagrams for better anomaly detection and location.

In the following subsections, we describe the important concepts of our methodology. We will describe it by first describing a problem and how the concept overcomes the problem.

3.1: Extended actions and state transition diagram

The actions used in static testing are insufficient for C++ programs. When data flow analysis was first proposed for testing, it was aimed at analysing *atomic* variables representing only one piece of data. In C++, variables can be objects which can represent many variables and functions. Thus, actions on such variables are quite different from the initial proposal.

Let us examine classes in C++. Its private class members can be only be accessed by members of the same class, its protected class members can be accessed by members of the same class and derived class, and, the public members can be accessed by anyone. This means that an action is either allowed or not allowed on a class member, depending on the class of the action. Consider the following example.

```cpp
class Base
{
private:
  int private_value;
protected:
  int protected_value;
public:
  int public_value;
  void function_in_base();
};

class Derived : public Base
{
public:
  void function_in_derived();
};

void global_function()
{
  ...
}
```

In global_function(), an action on public_value is allowed and the usual state transitions occur. However, an action on either private_value or protected_value will cause a transition into the anomalous state.

In function_in_derived(), actions on both protected_value and public_value are allowed. Only actions on private_value will lead to an anomaly. In function_in_base(), all actions on the three variables private_value, protected_value and public_value cause the usual state transitions.

Most compilers will detect such errors. However, a change in the program can cause the program to be compiled safely but still cause the above problems.

```cpp
class Base
{
private:
```

```
    int private_value;
protected:
    int protected_value;
public:
    int public_value;
    void function_in_base();
    int& get_private_value();
};
```

By adding a function `int& get_private_value()` into the base class which returns a reference to the private class member `private_value`, actions from any class or function is allowed! Though it is standard practice to write `get()` accessors and `set()` modifiers, this function `int& get_private_value()` allows the private value to be modified! The compiler cannot detect such errors. The following is an example.

```
Base b;
int& x = b.get_private_value();

// The following two lines change private_value!!
x = 4;
b.get_private_value() = 5;
```

We extend our actions to incorporate class information so that only allowed actions can be applied on class members. In addition to the information on the operations to be applied, information about the class from which the action is initiated is essential to determine whether a sequence of actions is proper. Each action has two attributes, the action and the class in which the action originates from, that is, Action (*type*, *class*). Similarly, the states in the state transition diagram is extended to include class information, that is, State (*value*, *class*).

For members of data in class '*', the states are defined as follows:

- State (D, *): defined
- State (R, *): referenced
- State (U, *): undefined
- State (A, *): anomalous

The symbol '**' is used to denote any class that is allowed to access a member of the class '*' and the symbol '$$' is used to denote the remaining classes. From the above discussion, different members of the same class, may have different '**' and '$$'. The actions are defined as follows:

- Action (d, **) or Action (d, $$): define action on a variable
- Action (r, **) or Action (r, $$): reference action on a variable
- Action (u, **) or Action (u, $$): undefine action on a variable

Figure 2 shows the state transition diagram for objects. In the figure, the action denoted as (all,$$) denotes all of (d,$$), (r,$$) and (u,$$). In many implementations of data flow analysis, once the anomalous state is entered, it remains in that state. We will discuss this aspect later.

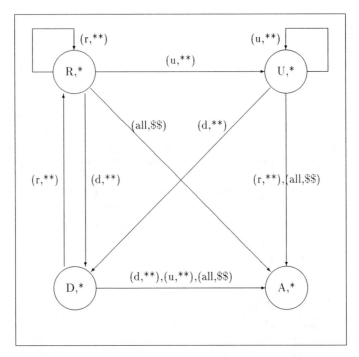

Figure 2. State transition diagram with class information

3.2: Implicit state variable

In the previous example, a private class member is illegally accessed via a reference returned by a function. The anomaly is not detected by simply analysing the *explicit state variable*. It uses the *implicit state variable* [11, 12].

The *explicit state variable* is the state variable associated with the identifier of the variable. The *implicit state variable* of a variable is the memory location of the variable, identified by its starting address and the size of the variable. For example, the variable m has the *explicit state variable* of state_m, and, the *implicit state variable* of (&m, sizeof(m)). This allows dynamic data flow analysis to detect anomalies on variables such as the example shown above. The name of the private variable (private_value) is *aliased* to another name (returned by get_private_value()) and illegal access is attempted on the private value by other classes and functions. This cannot be detected by the compiler and the execution of the program does not report any errors. However, accessing a private value is not allowed, and dynamic data flow analysis will detect it through *implicit state variable*. In the example above, any variable not belonging to the class of private_value that attempts to refer to the private value will cause Action (r, $$) because the memory locations of the variable are the same as the memory locations of the private value. This leads to the anomalous state.

3.3: Functional instrumentation

The *short cut evaluation* in C++ poses an interesting problem. In a conditional predicate, not every boolean expression has to be evaluated. Consider the following example.

```
if ((i > j) || (m++ > n--))
{
    ...
}
else
{
    ...
}
```

The conditional predicate has two boolean expressions joined by a disjunction. The first predicate is a simple relation while the second predicate compares and modifies the values of m and n. The modification of the values is only carried out if the first predicate is false. If the first predicate is true, the second predicate is never evaluated and hence the values of m and n do not change. This can lead to confusion, not to mention the complication during data flow analysis.

The solution is to use *functional instrumentation* [11, 12]. Each variable is instrumented with a function which returns a reference to the variable. An action on a variable is only reported when the function is executed. In *short cut evaluations*, if some predicates are not evaluated, their actions are not reported.

As an example, the integer variable m is instrumented as follows.

```
((int) dfa(m, "rd", &m, sizeof(m), __FILE__, __LINE__))
```

The dfa() function expects the following parameters.

- Variable. The variable that the action is being applied on.
- Actions. A string of actions being applied on the variable.
- Implicit state variable. The pair of starting address and size of variable, representing the implicit state variable.
- File name. The source file of the statement. This is used in debugging. In C++, the macro __FILE__ indicates the current file.
- Line number. The line number of the statement. This is used in debugging. In C++, the macro __LINE__ indicates the current line.

Since dfa() returns a reference to the variable, if can be incremented in the program. The example is instrumented as follows.

```
if ( \
  ( \
  ((int) dfa(i, "r", &i, sizeof(i), __FILE__, __LINE__)) > \
  ((int) dfa(j, "r", &j, sizeof(j), __FILE__, __LINE__)) \
  ) || ( \
  ((int) dfa(m, "rd", &m, sizeof(m), __FILE__, __LINE__))++ > \
  ((int) dfa(n, "rd", &n, sizeof(n), __FILE__, __LINE__))-- \
```

```
      ) \
      )
{
   ...
}
else
{
   ...
}
```

3.4: Object-based instrumentation

Functional instrumentation is useful but can become complicated and confusing as in the above example. To simplify the syntax, our methodology also uses *object-based instrumentation*. *Object-based instrumentation* converts all basic data types such as integer, float and character into classes. All operators are defined for the basic types to report the appropriate action which is to be checked for anomalies. For example, the following is a fragment of the class for integers.

```
class BasicInteger
{
protected:
   int value;
public:
   operator int();
};
```

The BasicInteger class replaces any int declaration of a variable so that whenever the variable is referenced as an integer, the overloaded member function int() is called. This function reports the appropriate action and checks for anomalies. This is an object-oriented approach for data flow analysis. It encapsulates the analysis within classes. With *object-based instrumentation*, only variable declarations are modified. Program statements can remain unchanged. As an example, the following are fragments of a program without instrumentation.

```
...
int main()
{
   int m, n;
   ...
   if (m > n)
   {
      ...
   }
}
```

After the instrumentation, the program is as follows.

```
#include "dfa.h"
```

```
...
int main()
{
  BasicInteger m, n;
  ...
  if (m > n)
  {
    ...
  }
}
```

Object-based instrumentation cannot be easily implemented on all data types especially complicated user-defined types and classes. Most user-defined classes are defined with its own operators and can conflict with the operators which we define for *object-based instrumentation*. We use *functional instrumentation* for user-defined types and classes but data members of basic types can be *object-based instrumented*.

The program in Appendix A is a complete working program demonstrating how a class is declared for an integer type.

4: Evaluation

4.1: Implementation issues

Our methodology is being tested in a prototype dynamic data flow analysis system called CDFA. CDFA is written in C++ and implements the concepts described in this paper. CDFA instruments C++ programs and then compiles and links the programs. The programs are executed and CDFA dynamically detects data flow anomalies. There are a few implementation issues to consider.

Firstly, an instrumented program increases in size, and from our observations and as well as observations of other researchers, instrumentation increases the size of programs by approximately four times. Testing C++ programs with CDFA in limited space may pose a problem.

Secondly, the timing and speed of an instrumented program is different to the original program. This is a problem when testing real-time systems. Debugging real-time systems with instrumentation can be very difficult. Executing the systems with and without instrumentation can produce different results.

Thirdly, many implementations of data flow analysis by other researchers cease state transitions on a variable when the anomalous state is reached. The state of the analysis remains in the anomalous state until the termination of the program. This only reports one anomaly, i.e. when the anomalous state is first entered. Details about any other anomalies on that variable after that point is not shown. Our implementation continues the analysis after an anomaly but marks the variable as anomalous. This means that we can detect many anomalies for a given variable in one execution.

Fourthly, some variables in a program do not belong to any particular class. CDFA has a default class `cdfa__global` for any variable which does not belong to a class, for example global and local variables.

4.2: Prototype

CDFA instruments a program which can then be compiled and executed. The actions on data are sent to a graphical user interface which displays the actions in real-time. The actions is also be saved to a file for further analysis and debugging purposes. The graphical user interface of CDFA is shown in Figure 3. The cell grid represents the data in a program. In Figure 3, at the time that the screen was captured, seven variables were registered with CDFA. The letters that appear in the cells are the states of the data. A small "A" in the bottom right corner of a cell indicates that a cell had previously entered the anomalous state. To show the details of the variable associated with the cell, select the cell and the information is displayed in the text area at the bottom of the screen. The information displayed is as follows.

- Anomaly detected.
- Variable name.
- Start of memory locations.
- Size of variable.
- Line number of source file.
- Name of source file.
- Class of variable.

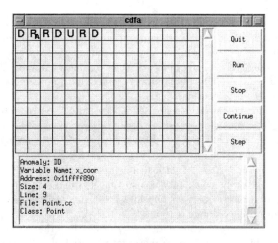

Figure 3. Screen of CDFA detecting data flow anomalies

As shown in the figure, CDFA has buttons to control program execution but it is not a complete debugger. It only has limited control over program execution. It can run, stop, continue and step a program. The program execution control is implemented in the instrumentation. The program and the graphical user interface of CDFA use bidirectional communication to exchange instructions and information.

5: Conclusion

We have presented our dynamic data flow analysis methodology and implemented it in CDFA. CDFA tests C++ program by instrumenting the program, executing the program and detecting anomalies in the program. It uses extended actions and states to capture anomalies related to the object-oriented characteristics of C++. The analysis is based on implicit state variables which are state variables associated with the memory locations of data, instead of explicit state variables, which are state variables associated with the identifier name. By using functional instrumentation and object-based instrumentation, the actions on data are properly captured and analysed. CDFA also includes a graphical user interface that captures and analyses data flow information in real-time.

Future work on CDFA includes expanding the debugging features of CDFA to better locate errors. Another option is to integrate it into integrated development environments such as ObjectCenter, Rational, Borland C++ and Microsoft Visual C++. These environments already support a complete debugger.

Data flow analysis has been found to be effective in detecting anomalies in C++ programs and it is hoped that the underlying methodology of CDFA can be applied on other object-oriented programming languages.

References

[1] G. Booch, *Object-oriented Design with Applications*. Benjamin / Cummings, second ed., 1994.

[2] T. Y. Chen and C. K. Low, "Error detection in C++ through dynamic data flow analysis," *Software—Concepts and Tools*, vol. 18, no. 1, pp. 1–13, 1997.

[3] H. M. Deitel and P. J. Deitel, *C++ How To Program*. Prentice Hall, second ed., 1994.

[4] R.-K. Doong and P. G. Frankl, "The ASTOOT approach to testing object-oriented programs," *ACM Transactions on Software Engineering and Methodology*, vol. 3, no. 2, pp. 101–130, 1994.

[5] L. D. Fosdick and L. J. Osterweil, "Data flow analysis in software reliability," *Computing Surveys*, vol. 8, pp. 305–330, Sept. 1976.

[6] P. G. Frankl and E. J. Weyuker, "An applicable family of data flow testing criteria," *IEEE Transactions on Software Engineering*, vol. 14, pp. 1483–1498, Oct. 1988.

[7] J. C. Huang, "Detection of data flow anomaly through program instrumentation," *IEEE Transactions on Software Engineering*, vol. 5, pp. 226–236, May 1979.

[8] G. Myers, *The Art of Software Testing*. John Wiley and Sons, 1979.

[9] L. J. Osterweil and L. D. Fosdick, "DAVE—a validation error detection and documentation system for Fortran programs," *Software—Practice and Experience*, vol. 6, pp. 473–486, 1976.

[10] R. S. Pressman, *Software Engineering: A Practitioner's Approach*. McGraw-Hill Book Co., fourth ed., Aug. 1996.

[11] D. A. Price, "Program instrumentation for the detection of software anomalies." M. Sc. thesis, Department of Computer Science, University of Melbourne, 1985.

[12] D. A. Price and P. C. Poole, "Dynamic data flow analysis — a tool for reliability," in *Proceedings of the 1st Australian Software Engineering Conference*, pp. 97–100, May 1986.

[13] S. Rapps and E. J. Weyuker, "Selecting software test data using data flow information," *IEEE Transactions on Software Engineering*, vol. 11, pp. 367–375, Apr. 1985.

[14] J. Rumbaugh, M. Blaha, W. Premerlani, F. Eddy, and W. Lorensen, *Object-oriented Modeling and Design*. Prentice Hall, 1991.

[15] B. Stroustrup, *The C++ Programming Language*. Addison-Wesley, third ed., 1997.

A: Class for basic integer

```cpp
#include <iostream.h>

class BasicInteger
{
protected:
    int value;
public:
    operator int ()
    {
        cout << "r\n";
        return (value);
    }
    int& operator=(int i)
    {
        cout << "d\n";
        value = i;
        return (value);
    }
    int& operator++(int)
    {
        cout << "rd\n";
        value++;
        return (value);
    }
    int& operator--(int)
    {
        cout << "rd\n";
        value--;
        return (value);
    }
};

int main()
{
    BasicInteger m, n;  // Use BasicInteger instead of int m, n.

    m = 4;
    n = 5;
    if (m-- > n++)
        cout << "m > n\n";
    else
        cout << "m <= n\n";
    cout << m << n << endl;
    return (0);
}
```

Testing Inheritance Hierarchies in the ClassBench Framework

Jason McDonald and Paul Strooper
Software Verification Research Centre
Department of Computer Science and Electrical Engineering
The University of Queensland, 4072, Australia
email: {jasonm, pstroop}@csee.uq.edu.au

Abstract

Inheritance is a feature of the object-oriented paradigm that permits substantial reuse of code. For us to have confidence in reused code, it must be adequately tested. Whilst object-oriented analysis, design and implementation techniques have received much attention in recent literature, object-oriented testing has been given comparatively little consideration. This paper presents an adaptation of the ClassBench methodology to the testing of inheritance hierarchies in C++. A small case study which applies the strategy to an inheritance hierarchy of a commercial class library is presented.

1 Introduction

With object-oriented methods, productivity and reliability can be vastly improved, primarily through reuse. Because reliability depends on testing, this improvement cannot be realized without effective class testing. The tests for class C must be repeated often: for the initial version of C, after each modification to C, and when C is reused in a new environment, such as a new operating system or compiler. This requirement for repeatability suggests that test execution should be automated. Automation of test development is less important because it is performed less often.

With the ClassBench methodology and framework [11, 12], the test programmer performs three tasks:

1. *Develop the testgraph.* The testgraph nodes and arcs correspond to the states and transitions of the Class Under Test (CUT). However, the testgraph is vastly smaller than the CUT state/transition graph.

2. *Develop the **Oracle** class.* The main purpose of the **Oracle** is to check the behaviour of the CUT during testing. **Oracle** provides essentially the same operations as the CUT, but supports only the testgraph states and transitions.

3. *Develop the **Driver** class.* At test run-time, the testgraph is automatically traversed. Each time an arc a is traversed, **Driver::Arc** is invoked, which should produce the CUT transition associated with a. Each time a node n is reached, **Driver::Node** is invoked, which should check that the CUT behaviour is correct for the state corresponding to node n.

The focus of our testing is *collection classes*—those providing sets, queues, trees, etc.—rather than graphical user interface classes. We also focus on programmatic testing, with little human interaction; the input generation and output checking are under program control.

Inheritance is a feature of the object-oriented paradigm that provides great potential for reuse, but it introduces special testing concerns. Perry and Kaiser [17] have shown that functions inherited from a base class may need retesting in the context of a derived class. Harrold et al. [7] extend this work by considering what member functions must be retested, guided by how the class is derived from the base class. Hoffman and Strooper [10] propose a method for testing derived classes by focusing on reducing the cost of test generation by reusing base class tests and test code. In this paper, we show how the ideas from [7] can be applied in the context of the ClassBench methodology, to determine how the testing for a base class might be

```
class Bag : public Collection {
public:
        Bag(int);
        void add(int):
        void detach(int);
        int getItemsInContainer() const;
        int hasMember(int) const;
private:
        ...
}
```

Figure 1. Bag declaration

modified to produce an adequate test for a derived class. To experiment with the method, a small inheritance hierarchy from the Borland Container Class Library [1] was tested.

In Section 2, we summarize the related work. Section 3 introduces the ClassBench methodology and framework using a simple example. In Section 4, we explain the method for testing a derived class based on the testing of the base class, and the case study is discussed in Section 5.

2   Related work

Class testing has much in common with module testing. Early work by Panzl [16] on the regression testing of Fortran subroutines addresses some of the issues. Chow [3] conducted early work on the generation of test sequences from state machine specifications of protocols. The DAISTS [6], PGMGEN [8] and Protest [9] systems all automate the testing of modules using test cases based on sequences of calls.

In object-oriented testing, Frankl et al. [4] have developed a scheme for class testing using algebraic specifications. A testing methodology for object-oriented systems is proposed in [15]. Within this framework, the ACE tool, an enhancement of PGMGEN [8], was developed to support the testing of C++ and Eiffel classes. Turner and Robson [19] propose a state-based approach to class testing, in which, just as for testgraphs, test cases are based on the possible states of an object.

Little work has been published on the testing of inheritance hierarchies. Perry and Kaiser [17] show that code inherited from a base class may need to be retested in the context of a derived class. Harrold et al. [7] extend this work by considering what member functions must be retested, based on how a class is derived from its base class. Smith and Robson [18] use regression analysis to determine which member functions should be tested and then perform the tests guided by how the base class was tested. Inherited routines that are not affected by the derived class are not retested. Both Fiedler [5] and Cheatham and Mellinger [2] discuss subclass testing, but neither approach tries to reuse the base class's test suite.

3   ClassBench basics

We illustrate the ClassBench methodology with a simplified version of the **Bag** class from the Borland Container Class Library [1].

3.1   Bag class

Bag provides access to a bag of integers. Its C++ declaration is shown in Figure 1. The constructor **Bag(n)** creates an empty bag; the parameter n represents the maximum size of the bag. Assuming that **cut** is an object of type **Bag**, **cut.add(x)** adds x to **cut**; **cut.add(x)** does not change **cut** if **cut** is full. If x is in **cut**, **cut.detach(x)** removes one copy of x from **cut**; otherwise, there is no change. **cut.getItemsInContainer** returns the number of elements in **cut**, and **cut.hasMember(x)** returns **true** or **false** according to whether x is in **cut**.

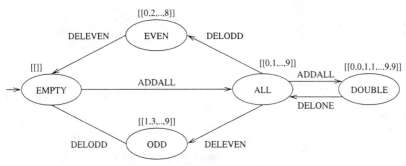

Figure 2. Testgraph for Bag

3.2 Testgraph for Bag

A *testgraph* is a directed graph in which the nodes have unique identifiers and there is a designated start node; the arcs of a testgraph are labeled (arc labels need not be unique). Figure 2 shows a testgraph for **Bag**. We use an arc with no source node to indicate the start node **EMPTY**.

For testing purposes, a testgraph is a partial model of the CUT state-transition graph. Each testgraph node corresponds to a CUT state and the start node to the initial state; each arc corresponds to a sequence of one or more CUT state transitions. While the CUT state space is normally very large, the testgraph state space is vastly smaller. The CUT state space contains all states that *can* be reached; the testgraph state space contains those states that *will* be reached by the test suite.

To add flexibility to the testgraph scheme, we associate a *test suite parameter* with each test suite. By supplying a value for this parameter, the tester selects a particular mapping from testgraph nodes to CUT states. Typically, a handful of parameter values are chosen and the suite is run once for each value selected. For the **Bag** testgraph, the test suite parameter N is the size of the CUT state corresponding to the testgraph node **ALL**. In Figure 2, we have used $N = 10$.

We generate test cases by repeatedly traversing the testgraph beginning at the start node; test cases are derived from the paths that are followed. We are interested in paths that, in some sense, cover the testgraph. We consider three types of coverage: *node coverage*, *arc coverage*, and *path coverage*—analogous to statement, branch, and path coverage in structural testing [13]. As in structural testing, arc coverage subsumes node coverage and path coverage subsumes arc coverage but path coverage is difficult to achieve—impossible if the testgraph is cyclic. Currently we use a traversal algorithm that achieves arc coverage and for the testgraph shown in Figure 2, this algorithm generates the following two paths.

⟨ EMPTY, ALL, DOUBLE, ALL, ODD, EMPTY ⟩
⟨ EMPTY, ALL, EVEN, EMPTY ⟩

3.3 Test oracle for Bag

Automated testing produces many test cases, making manual checking of test results infeasible. We introduce an **Oracle** class to assist with the automated checking of test results. The **Oracle** class is similar to the CUT, except that its states and transitions are restricted to those in the testgraph. **Oracle**'s state variables represent the current testgraph state; its member functions invoke the testgraph state transitions and reflect the current testgraph state.

A partial class declaration for the **Bag** oracle is shown in Figure 3. The state variables are **node**, the current testgraph node identifier, and **max**, the test suite parameter. Thus, a (**node,max**) pair represents the bag containing integers between 0 and **max**−1 inclusive that match the "pattern" indicated by **node**. For example, (**DOUBLE**,3) represents ⟦0, 0, 1, 1, 2, 2⟧ and (**ODD**,3) represents ⟦1⟧.

The test suite parameter is passed as the argument to the class constructor **Oracle**. The current node can be changed to n by a call to **setNode**(n), where we represent nodes using integer identifiers. The call **getNode**

```
class Oracle {
public:
    Oracle(int);
    void setNode(int);
    int getNode();
    int getItemsInContainer() const;
    int hasMember(int) const;
private:
    int node;
    int max;
}
```

Figure 3. Partial Bag oracle declaration

```
class Driver {
public:
    Driver(int);
    void reset();
    void arc(int);
    void node();
private:
    Bag cut;
    Oracle orc;
    int max;
}
```

Figure 4. Partial Bag driver declaration

returns the current node. The other two **Oracle** member functions, **getItemsInContainer** and **hasMember**, imitate those of **Bag**, returning the correct values for the current (**node, max**) pair.

3.4 Test driver for Bag

The testgraph traversal algorithm generates calls to the member functions of the class **Driver**, which must be supplied by the tester. A partial class declaration for the **Bag** driver, **Driver**, is shown in Figure 4. All driver declarations are generally the same. The constructor takes the value of the test suite parameter as its argument. The member function **reset** is called each time a new path is started. **arc**(l) is called when the arc with label l is traversed, and changes the state of the CUT and the oracle. The function **node** is called each time a testgraph node is reached, and compares the behaviour of the CUT with the oracle. The private variables **cut**, **orc**, and **max** store the CUT, the test oracle, and the value of the test suite parameter.

In **Driver**, **arc**(l) is implemented as a case statement, with one case per arc label l in the graph. For example, **arc(ADDALL)** makes calls to **cut.add**(x) to add the appropriate integer values x to the CUT and a call to **orc.setNode(ADDALL)** to change the state of the oracle. The **node**() function compares the return values of **cut.hasMember**(i) and **orc.hasMember**(i) for $i \in \{0, 1, \ldots, \textbf{max} - 1\}$. It also compares the return values of **cut.getItemsInContainer** and **orc.getItemsInContainer**.

3.5 The ClassBench framework

With the ClassBench methodology, the test programmer performs three tasks: design the testgraph, develop the **Oracle** class, and develop the **Driver** class. To assist the tester with these tasks, the ClassBench framework provides:

- *A graph editor*: The testgraph editor provides the facilities commonly available in today's graph editors. Testgraphs can be accessed from disk; nodes and arcs can be added and deleted.

```
procedure TestInheritanceHierarchy( Hierarchy );
begin
        fully test root class of Hierarchy;
        for each subclass in Hierarchy do
        begin
                inherit the base class test suite;
                classify the member functions of the subclass;
                modify the test suite based on the member function types;
        end;
end;
```

Figure 5. Strategy for testing inheritance hierarchies

- *Graph traversal algorithms*: The algorithms automatically traverse a stored testgraph, calling the appropriate **Driver** member functions.

- *Support for debugging and regression testing*: During regression testing, we typically run all of the available test cases, frequently numbering in the thousands. The framework allows us to run regression tests with no output except for failure messages. The framework supports debugging by allowing the tester to select small groups of tests and to generate detailed messages for those test cases.

- *Code skeletons and demonstration test suites*: Skeleton files are provided for **Oracle** and **Driver**, and for test documentation. A modest collection class library (CCL) has been developed, including sophisticated test suites. This library is used heavily by the ClassBench software itself; the test suites have played an important role during development.

The ClassBench methodology and framework are described in detail in [12].

4 Testing inheritance hierarchies

Earlier attempts at testing inheritance hierarchies in ClassBench have been informal in nature [10]. This section outlines a systematic strategy for the testing of inheritance hierarchies using ClassBench.

4.1 Strategy

Inheritance allows significant reduction in the cost of software development via the reuse of code. When deriving one class from another, we need only write new code when the inherited code is not adequate to meet the specification of the derived class. Similarly, significant reduction in the cost of testing inheritance hierarchies can be achieved via the inheritance and reuse of testing information. Then we need only make changes to the inherited test suite where it is not adequate to meet our testing requirements.

The types of modifications to be applied to the test suite are naturally dependent upon the modifications that have been applied to the parent class in deriving the subclass. To simplify the task of modifying the test suite, we take a divide and conquer approach. The member functions of the subclass are partitioned into nine categories, each of which has a specific testing strategy associated with it.

The "high-level" strategy is shown in Figure 5. The complete strategy appears in the Appendix. In our strategy, we attempt to cover the most common cases. In the extreme case, a parent class may be modified by inheritance to such an extent that it is better to build an entirely new test suite rather than trying to derive one from the parent class's test suite. Testers must exercise judgement in determining whether this is the case.

4.2 Member function types

There are two criteria used in classifying each member function of a derived class as belonging to one of the nine member function types. Constructors, destructors and operators involving multiple objects are not included in the classification scheme.

```
class Set : public Bag {
public:
        Set(int);
        void add(int);
        int isEmpty() const;
private:
        ...
}
```

Figure 6. Set definition

The first criteria is the manner in which the inheritance relation applies to the member function, i.e. how is it derived from the base class. We have adopted a refinement of the classification scheme used by Harrold et al. [7]. The first criteria for classification will mark each member function F of the subclass as one of:

New: Member function F is defined in the subclass but does not occur in the parent class.

Unchanged: Member function F is defined in the parent class but not in the subclass.

Redefined: Member function F is defined in the parent class and also in the subclass.

The second criteria is the manner in which the member function interacts with the class state. In presenting ClassBench, Hoffman and Strooper [10] distinguish three varieties of member functions: *set* functions modify aspects of the state of the class, *get* functions retrieve aspects of the state, and *set+get* functions both modify and retrieve aspects of the state. This distinction is important in the context of ClassBench. For example, the normal case of a *set* member function is typically exercised in the transitions associated with testgraph arcs, while the normal case of a *get* member function is typically exercised in the checking associated with each testgraph node. Thus, distinguishing between these types will assist us in determining how best to modify an inherited test suite.

4.3   Example: testing a subclass

To illustrate the use of the strategy, we present a simple inheritance hierarchy consisting of the base class **Bag**, described earlier, and the derived class **Set**, shown in Figure 6.

The **Set** class redefines the member function **add** and introduces the member function **isEmpty**. The **add** member function is redefined so that an element is only added if it is not already contained in the set, thus ensuring that the set does not contain any duplicate elements. The **isEmpty** member function returns **true** if the set contains no elements and **false** if the set contains one or more elements.

4.4   Testing the root class

The first step in testing any inheritance hierarchy is to test the root class of the hierarchy. The test suite of the root class will form the basis of the test suites of its subclasses. For our example hierarchy the root class, **Bag**, is tested using the test suite described earlier.

4.5   Modifying the inherited test suite

The procedure presented in the Appendix shows the strategies for handling each of the nine member function types identified above. Justifications for each of these strategies are given in [14]. This section provides an example of handling the two member function types found in our sample **Set** class.

The **add** member function appears in the **Bag** class and modifies the state, so it is categorised as (*redefined, set*). The **isEmpty** member function does not appear in the **Bag** class and examines the state, so it is categorised as (*new, get*). The other member functions of Bag (**detach**, **getItemsInContainer** and **hasMember**) are inherited unchanged in Set and are therefore categorised with the *unchanged* inheritance type and keep their behaviour types of *set*, *get* and *get* respectively.

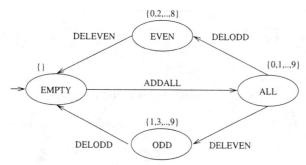

Figure 7. Testgraph for Set

4.5.1 The add member function

Since **add** constrains the set to contain only one copy of each element, the state space of **Set** is different from that of **Bag**. The consequence for the test suite is that the state labelled **DOUBLE** in the testgraph for **Bag** does not fall within the valid state space of **Set**. Therefore, the node **DOUBLE** and its attendant arcs must be removed from the testgraph.

The present test suite (with **DOUBLE** removed) is not adequate to test the **add** member function. It does not provide a test involving the addition of an element that is already in the set. The addition of a node check that attempts to add to the set all of its current elements is sufficient to adequately test this behaviour. The resulting testgraph for **Set** is shown in Figure 7.

The next step is to determine which of the other member functions are affected by the redefinition. This process involves an analysis of the data flows between member functions via the state of the class. The affected member functions in the **Set** class are **detach**, **getItemsInContainer**, and **hasMember**. Having identified the affected member functions, we must make sure that the test suite is modified in a way that adequately tests these member functions. In this case the remaining portion of the testgraph is adequate, so no more changes to the testgraph are required.

The necessary additions and removals of arcs and nodes require corresponding changes to the implementations of **Oracle::getItemsInContainer**, **Oracle::hasMember**, and **Driver::arc**. The extent of these modifications is small.

4.5.2 The isEmpty member function

Since **isEmpty** is a (*new,get*) function we must add suitable testing for it to the checking performed at each testgraph node. We do this by adding an **isEmpty** member function to the oracle and adding a comparison between the return values of **orc.isEmpty** and **cut.isEmpty** in **Driver::node**.

4.6 Comparison with previous work

In this section, we contrast our strategy with that of Harrold et al. [7] who also propose a strategy for reuse of base class testing information in testing derived classes. Apart from the fact that our method uses ClassBench and Harrold's method does not, there are several significant differences between the two approaches.

First, the Harrold method determines which inherited test cases should be rerun when testing the subclass. The nature of ClassBench is that all tests are run when a test suite is executed. Since test execution in ClassBench is automated, this is not a significant disadvantage.

The Harrold method uses a *classgraph* to show the data flows between the member functions of a class. So far we have used manual examination of the source code for this, in both the subclass testing strategy and ClassBench in general.

One curious feature of Harrold's method is that the virtual and non-virtual attribute types are separated but both are then treated in the same way, making the distinction unnecessary.

Class	Oracle				Driver			
	Total	Added	Changed	Deleted	Total	Added	Changed	Deleted
Bag	213	N/A	N/A	N/A	197	N/A	N/A	N/A
Set	212	4	9	5	191	8	14	14
Dictionary	234	22	4	0	239	52	12	4

Table 1. Summary of test suite changes

The Harrold method does not generate or execute any test cases — it simply states *where* the test suite must be changed and which test cases must be rerun. By contrast, our strategy indicates *how* the test suite should be changed and provides a framework for the execution of the test cases and the checking of their results.

5 Case study

This section outlines a small case study that was undertaken during the development of the strategy discussed above. The case study is described in greater detail in [14]. The case study applied the strategy to the **Bag** — **Set** — **Dictionary** branch of the Borland Container Class Library supplied with version 3.0 of the Turbo C++ compiler package. The Borland Container Class Library provides a set of general purpose container classes. Detailed documentation for the library is available in [1]. The documentation was used as the basis for the design of the test suites.

The **Bag** and **Set** classes are substantially expanded versions of the **Bag** and **Set** classes presented earlier. As the root class of the tested hierarchy, the **Bag** class required the development of a complete test suite. The test suite of the **Bag** class was then modified for the testing of the **Set** class, and the test suite of the **Set** class was then modified for the testing of the **Dictionary** class.

5.1 Test Results

The testing process revealed a memory management problem in the underlying implementations of the classes. This error causes intermittent corruption of the class's data structures.

The documentation for the Borland Container Class Library consists of informal English descriptions. The testing process revealed a number of deficiencies in the documentation and inconsistencies between the documentation and the observable behaviour of the classes. Most of these problems relate to either (1) confusion between objects with the same identity (i.e. two references to the same object) and objects with the same value (possibly two different objects), (2) references to "first element" and "last element" where the **Bag**, **Set**, and **Dictionary** classes store unordered collections of elements, or (3) lack of distinction between single and multiple occurrences of element values in the **Bag** class.

5.2 Evaluation

This case study, though modest in scale, has shown that a high level of reuse of testing information is possible with ClassBench. The effort involved in developing the test suites for the **Set** and **Dictionary** classes was significantly less than the effort that would have been required to develop entirely new test suites. Table 1 shows the number of lines of code that were added to, changed and removed from each test suite.

6 Conclusions

Despite the lack of attention given to object-oriented testing in the literature, it is a crucial area; reuse depends on reliability, which in turn requires thorough, automated testing. In this paper, we have shown how the ClassBench methodology can be used to ensure that classes which reuse code via inheritance can be adequately tested without the need to develop an entirely new test suite.

In testing the base class of an inheritance hierarchy, the tester performs three tasks; design the testgraph, develop the oracle, and develop the driver. For each subclass the tester inherits the base test suite, classifies the member functions of the subclass, and modifies the inherited test suite accordingly. This approach gives a substantial reduction in testing costs via the reuse of existing testing information. This is achieved without compromising the thoroughness or adequacy of the testing applied to a class.

In the future we hope to perform a much larger case study than that outlined here. Such a study would be aimed at identifying and overcoming any scaling-up problems.

At present a separate test suite is maintained for each CUT. We are currently working to eliminate this maintenance problem by using inheritance in the test code rather than the present method of copying and modifying the test suite.

Acknowledgements

The authors would like to acknowledge the assistance of Dr. David Carrington, Dr. Daniel Hoffman, Ian MacColl and the anonymous referees in the preparation of this paper. We would also like to thank Shelina Bhanji for her helpful comments and suggestions on drafts of the honours thesis [14] on which much of this paper is based.

References

[1] Borland International. *The Container Class Libraries*. Borland International. 1992. Online manual.

[2] T.J. Cheatham and L. Mellinger. Testing object-oriented software systems. In *Proc. 1990 Computer Science Conference*, pages 161–165, 1990.

[3] T.S. Chow. Testing software design modeled by finite-state machines. *IEEE Trans. Soft. Eng.*, SE-4(3):178–187, May 1978.

[4] R. Doong and P.G. Frankl. The ASTOOT approach to testing object-oriented programs. *ACM Trans. on SW Eng. and Methodology*, 3(2):101—130, 1994.

[5] S.P. Fiedler. Object-oriented unit testing. *Hewlett-Packard Journal*, pages 69–74, April 1989.

[6] J. Gannon, P. McMullin, and R. Hamlet. Data-abstraction implementation, specification and testing. *ACM Trans. Program Lang. Syst.*, 3(3):211–223, July 1981.

[7] M.J. Harrold, J.D. McGregor, and K.J. Fitzpatrick. Incremental testing of object-oriented class structures. In *Proc. 14th Int. Conf. on Software Engineering*, pages 68–80, 1992.

[8] D.M. Hoffman. A CASE study in module testing. In *Proc. Conf. Software Maintenance*, pages 100–105. IEEE Computer Society, October 1989.

[9] D.M. Hoffman and P.A. Strooper. Automated module testing in Prolog. *IEEE Trans. Soft. Eng.*, 17(9):933–942, September 1991.

[10] D.M. Hoffman and P.A. Strooper. Graph-based class testing. *The Australian Computer Journal*, 26(4):158–163, 1994.

[11] D.M. Hoffman and P.A. Strooper. The testgraphs methodology — automated testing of collection classes. *Journal of Object-Oriented Programming*, pages 35–41, November-December 1995.

[12] D.M. Hoffman and P.A. Strooper. Classbench: A methodology and framework for automated class testing. Technical Report 96–03, Software Verification Research Centre, The Univ. of Queensland, April 1996. Submitted to *Software Practice and Experience*.

[13] W.E. Howden. Reliability of the path analysis testing strategy. *IEEE Trans. Soft. Eng.*, SE-2(3):208–215, September 1976.

[14] J. McDonald. Inheritance and genericity in object-oriented testing. Honours thesis, Department of Computer Science, University of Queensland, November 1995.

[15] G.C. Murphy, P. Townsend, and P.S. Wong. Experiences with cluster and class testing. *Commun. ACM*, 37(9):39–47, 1994.

[16] D.J. Panzl. A language for specifying software tests. In *Proc. AFIPS Natl. Comp. Conf.*, pages 609–619. AFIPS, 1978.

[17] D.E. Perry and G.K. Kaiser. Adequate testing and object-oriented programming. *Journal of Object-Oriented Programming*, 2:13–19, January 1990.

[18] M.D. Smith and D.J. Robson. A framework for testing object-oriented programs. *Journal of Object-Oriented Programming*, 4(6):45–53, June 1992.

[19] C.D. Turner and D.J. Robson. A state-based approach to the testing of class-based programs. *Software Concepts and Tools*, 16(3):106–112, 1995.

Appendix

This appendix presents the complete strategy for the treatment of an inheritance hierarchy in the Class-Bench framework.

procedure TestInheritanceHierarchy(Hierarchy);

type
      TMemberFunction = (new, get), (new, set), ... ;

function MemberFunctionType(F, P, S) : TMemberFunction;
      { Returns the type of member function F based on the definition of the parent class P and the subclass S. }
...

procedure TestNewGet(F);
begin
        while current set of testgraph states is not adequate **do**
        begin
            add new state to testgraph;
            add new state to oracle member functions;
            add new arcs to testgraph to produce the new state;
            add new arcs to Driver::arc;
        end;
        add node checks for F to Driver::node;
        add a member function corresponding to F to the oracle;
end;

procedure TestNewSet(F);
begin
        repeat   { must add at least one arc }
            add arc to testgraph to exercise F;
            add arc to Driver::arc;
        until testing is adequate for normal cases of F;
        for each exception that can be thrown by F **do**
        begin
            if no existing state can be used to cause the exception **then**
            begin
                add a new testgraph state from which the exception can be thrown;
                add the new state to the oracle functions;
                add arcs to the testgraph to establish the new state;
                add the new arcs to Driver::arc;
            end;
            add node checks to Driver::node to cause the exception to be thrown;
        end;
end;

procedure TestNewSet+Get(F);
begin
      TestNewSet(F);
      TestNewGet(F);
end;

procedure TestUnchangedGet(F);

```
begin
      if F is affected by new or redefined member functions then
      begin
            for each testgraph state S that is unreachable in R do
            begin
                  remove S from the testgraph;
                  remove S from the oracle member functions;
                  remove checks at S from Driver::node;
                  remove arcs connected to S from testgraph;
                  remove arcs connected to S from Driver::arc;
            end;
            remove any unnecessary node checks for F from Driver::node;
            while current set of testgraph states is not adequate for F do
            begin
                  add new state to testgraph;
                  add new state to oracle member functions;
                  add new arcs to testgraph to produce the new state;
                  add new arcs to Driver::arc;
            end;
            if additional node checks are required then
            begin
                  add the new node checks for F to Driver::node;
                  modify the oracle member function corresponding to F if necessary;
            end;
      end;
end;

procedure TestUnchangedSet(F);
begin
      if F is affected by new or redefined member functions then
      begin
            while current set of testgraph states is not adequate for exceptional cases of F do
            begin
                  add new state to testgraph;
                  add new state to oracle member functions;
                  add new arcs to testgraph to produce the new state;
                  add new arcs to Driver::arc;
            end;
            if node checks Not adequate for exceptional cases of F then
                  modify the node checks for F in Driver::node;
            while testing is not adequate for normal cases of F do
            begin
                  add arc to testgraph to exercise F;
                  add arc to Driver::arc;
            end;
      end;
end;

procedure TestUnchangedSet+Get(F);
begin
      TestUnchangedSet(F);
      TestUnchangedGet(F);
end;
```

```
procedure TestRedefinedGet(F);
begin
        remove node checks for old F;
        TestNewGet(F);
end;

procedure TestRedefinedSet(F);
begin
        remove arcs with calls to old version of F;
        remove node checks for exceptional cases of old F;
        TestNewSet(F);
end;

procedure TestRedefinedSet+Get(F);
begin
        TestRedefinedSet(F);
        TestRedefinedGet(F);
end;

begin        { TestInheritanceHierarchy }
        fully test root class of Hierarchy;
        for each subclass S in Hierarchy do
        begin
                inherit test suite of Parent(S);
                for each member function F of the subclass S do
                begin
                        case MemberFunctionType(F, Parent(S), S) of
                                (new, get) : TestNewGet(F);
                                (new, set) : TestNewSet(F);
                                (new, set+get) : TestNewSet+Get(F);
                                (unchanged, get) : TestUnchangedGet(F);
                                (unchanged, set) : TestUnchangedSet(F);
                                (unchanged, set+get) : TestUnchangedSet+Get(F);
                                (redefined, get) : TestRedefinedGet(F);
                                (redefined, set) : TestRedefinedSet(F);
                                (redefined, set+get) : TestRedefinedSet+Get(F);
                        end;
                end;
        end;
end; { TestInheritanceHierarchy }
```

Session 5

Distributed Systems

A Case for Meta-Interworking:
Projecting CORBA Meta-data into COM

Glenn Smith, John Gough and Clemens Szyperski

E-mail: smith@dstc.qut.edu.au, {j.gough, c.szyperski}@qut.edu.au

Phone: +61 7 3864 5120   Fax: +61 7 3864 1282

Faculty of Information Technology

Queensland University of Technology

Brisbane Qld 4000

Australia

Abstract

The pressure to reduce the time and effort required to produce and update software components, together with the existence of multiple competing component worlds, has forced the introduction of interworking standards. Unfortunately the interworking standards fail to suitably address the need for access to meta information. In the light of meta-data being increasingly important for component environments this inaccessibility of meta-data can lead to components being unusable by their intended clients. What exasperates the situation is that if access to meta-data repositories is provided using an implementation of the interworking standard, the information retrieved is incorrect. This paper describes these difficulties. To exemplify the solution, the construction of an adapter is described. This adapter provides access to the Common Object Request Broker Architectures' (CORBA) Interface Repository via the interfaces of the Component Object Model's (COM) Type Library. This solution provides access to meta-data which is essential if the full benefit of interworking is to be realised.

1: Introduction

The rapid expansion of the Internet has provided new opportunities for software vendors to deliver products and services to their clients. This coupled with the emergence of a variety of component environments, has provided clients with a range of options for accessing services. The pressure to be competitive in this software market is high. Service providers must support their products in the same range of environments as their clients use. This added requirement of supporting multiple versions of the same product reduces the benefits gained from using component environments. The construction of interworking solutions between the major component environments hopes to realise their full benefit.

Service providers which produce their products using traditional software engineering practices are becoming less competitive. The production of large monolithic software systems is too slow and inflexible to meet clients' needs, this has lead to the increasing use of component software systems. A component is a self contained piece of executable code which can be coupled together with other components to produce a larger system [15]. The time required to produce a component is much less than that for an entire system, thus updates to component systems can be provided in less time. A range of components can more easily be provided allowing the client to choose those which best suit their needs, hence tailoring the system more closely to the customers' requirements.

If there were only one component environment, service providers would only need to support components for that environment. However, in reality there exists several component environments, these include the Object Management Group's (OMG) Common Object Request Broker Architecture (CORBA) [8], Microsoft's Component Object Model (COM) [10], and Sun Microsystem's JavaBeans [4]. The existence of multiple competing component environments forces service providers to produce versions of their products for each of these environments in order to capture the widest possible market. A viable solution which overcomes the burden of producing these multiple versions is to provide interworking solutions between component worlds.

Interworking solutions provide local access to foreign components, hiding the issues of communication between the component environments. Local access is provided by what appears to be a component native to the client's environment. This local access component, or view, uses an interworking bridge to access a foreign component on the client's behalf. Thus using a foreign component is no different to using a native component.

The benefits which interworking provides has prompted much activity, both in the production of standards and subsequent implementation of these standards. Recently an interworking standard between Microsoft's COM and the OMG's CORBA has been produced by the OMG as part of the greater CORBA standard [8]. There are many implementations of this interworking standard, called interworking bridges, and these currently include OrbixCOMet from Iona Technologies, Object Bridge from Visual Edge Software, CORBAplus from Expersoft, and NEO Connectivity from Sun Microsystems.

Within component environments descriptions of component interfaces are provided using Interface Definition Languages (IDLs). Interface descriptions provide essential information to clients for interacting with the described components. Both COM and CORBA provide a meta-data repository which stores the interface descriptions in a form which is accessible to clients at run time. In CORBA this facility is provided by Interface Repositories, in COM it is provided by Type Libraries.

Interworking implementations must provide access to the meta-data describing the views provided; the interface to the view is no different from the interface to any other component. The term meta-interworking has been coined here to describe this access to meta-data. If meta-interworking is not done, many clients will not be able to make use of the views. The COM/CORBA interworking standard does not specify how access to this meta-data should be provided more than to say that it should be provided, and indicating the interface by which it may be provided [8].

Access to meta-data has been implemented by interworking bridges, in the case of OrbixCOMet this is done by copying all meta-data into a cache storing it in an environment neutral binary format [6]. From this cache Type Libraries and IDL files can be constructed. This relies on the monotonic properties of the meta-data, that is, once it has been created it is immutable. This produces a management problem requiring the cache to be rebuilt when it becomes inconsistent with the meta-data repositories. When new meta-data is provided in the repositories, the cache will fail on the first access to this information, requiring the cache to be updated. The user creates Type Libraries using this cache.

Caching meta-data will always work, however it is a rather heavy weight solution if the meta-data required is used infrequently, or accesses to the available meta-data are sparse. This is the case when browsing meta-data for instance, or possibly when sampling a range of components. In these cases it would be far more appropriate to access the meta-data repositories directly from the foreign component environment. As meta-data repositories are also components, it may be assumed that access to these repositories could be provided by the use of an interworking bridge as for any other component. However the information obtained in this manner would be incorrect as it would describe the foreign component, not the local view.

This paper presents a mechanism for providing intuitive, and more importantly, correct access to foreign meta-data repositories. This mode of access is not addressed in the OMG interworking standard, although the mechanism described builds upon interworking standard implementations. This paper illustrates how CORBA meta-data can be presented to COM clients via Type Library interfaces. To do this a generic adapter is used. A naive implementation of an adapter will fail as there are subtle problems which must be overcome to provide clients with correct meta-data, these problems are described and solutions to them presented. This paper focuses on the particular example of the adaptation of Type Libraries and Interface Repositories, however the underlying mechanisms used are generally applicable to many service adaptation scenarios which arise due to the introduction of interworking technologies.

The following section provides an overview of related work. Section 3 describes the structure of the interworking bridge. Section 4 briefly describes the Type Library. Section 6 describes the Interface Repository. Section 7 proposes an interworking solution for the Type Library and Interface Repository. The concluding section provides a discussion of the work presented in this paper.

2: Related Work

The use of Adapters [5] to increase the reusability of software, particularly object-oriented software, has generated much interest. There are many different approaches to aiding the production of Adapters [1, 9, 12, 16]. In general these approaches create a specification language with which to specify the behaviour of adapters, or attempt to automate the construction of an adapter using some additional specification of the behaviour of the components involved. These approaches are all aimed at method level interoperability. Work on object level interoperability has also been conducted [7]. The work presented in this paper uses adapters as a mechanism for achieving the goal of providing a service via a well known interface. It will become apparent from the problems faced in creating this adapter that existing adaptation mechanisms would struggle to provide a satisfactory solution.

The OMG interworking standard only indicates via which interfaces access to meta-data may be provided, it does not specify how this should be done. As mentioned in the Introduction, interworking bridges provide mechanisms to access meta-data. These mechanisms have been developed out of necessity, not through guidance of the interworking standard. Implementations which use a central cache of meta-data can easily co-exist with the direct access mechanism proposed in this paper. In fact it would seem that each solution is optimal for different usage patterns, although both will work in all cases.

3: Interworking Bridge Structure

A full implementation of the interworking standard can map components between both the COM and CORBA worlds. There are many different levels of capability provided by interworking solutions, we will assume the existence of a fully compliant, bi-directional, COM/CORBA interworking bridge. In this paper only the mapping of components from CORBA to COM will be considered. This is not to say the problem of mapping information in the reverse direction does not exist, only that it is outside the scope of this paper. The interworking standard also specifies a parallel mapping between OLE Automation and CORBA. This is effectively a subset of the COM/CORBA mapping as the set of types which can be passed via the bridge is very restricted. There are some differences in the way the mapping occurs, these will be discussed where necessary, otherwise OLE Automation/CORBA interworking will not be considered as the solutions presented for COM/CORBA interworking are generally applicable.

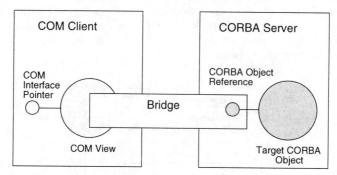

Figure 1. Interworking bridge structure

The COM/CORBA interworking standard specifies how to project a View of a component from one world to the other. A View is an object in the local world that presents the identity and interface(s) of an object in a foreign world using local object structure. this is shown in Figure 1. An implementation of the interworking standard forms a bridge between the two worlds. Clients can make calls of the views' methods projected by this bridge as if they were native objects.

The interworking specification defines how everything from basic data types to interface relationships are mapped between component worlds. These mappings are deterministic, and are defined by a simple set of rules. For instance, when mapping a CORBA interface that multiply inherits other interfaces, the mapping simply breaks this inheritance relationship, and a COM interface which inherits only from *IUnknown* (as all COM interfaces must do) is presented. It should be noted that the OLE Automation/CORBA mapping in this particular case is slightly different. Using the rules defined in the interworking standard, an interface is always mapped to the same kind of view. This is very important as users of interworking bridges can rely on the same kind of view to be presented for any given foreign component.

The interworking specification also defines a set of interworking interfaces which support a view. These supporting interface implementations provide access to information and operations which exist in the foreign world, this includes creation of persistent object references, creation of objects, retrieving object references, and establishing object identity. This set of supporting interfaces do not address the need for meta-data. The following two sections will briefly describe the meta-data repositories of interest; Type Libraries and Interface Repositories.

4: COM Type Library

A COM Type Library has five basic interfaces, *ICreateTypeLib*, *ITypeLib*, *ICreateType-Info*, *ITypeInfo*, and *ITypeComp*. As with all COM interfaces these derive from *IUnknown*. The *ICreate** interfaces are used for adding meta-data, while the remaining interfaces are used to access meta-data. There are usually many Type Libraries per COM environment. A TypeLib object is the top level object of a type library, it implements the *ITypeLib* interface. TypeLib objects contain TypeInfo objects and other attribute information. A TypeInfo object implements the *ITypeInfo* interface and can describe an interface, a Dynamic Linked Library module, a user defined type, or a class. If it describes a class it contains other Type Information objects to describe the constituent elements of that class. This containment structure is shown in Figure 2.

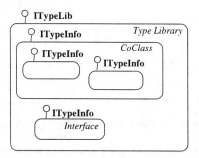

Figure 2. Type Libraries contain TypeInfo objects

The *ITypeComp* interface is used for quick access to the type information by compilers, this interface will not be considered further in this example as its use is out of the scope of this paper. The remaining two interfaces, *ICreateTypeLib* and *ICreateTypeInfo* interfaces, are used in construction of type information, this paper assumes the pre-existence of this information and will not consider these interfaces further.

5: CORBA Interface Repository

Each Object Request Broker (ORB) may have more than one Interface Repository, although this is unusual, and for the purposes of discussion we will assume there is only one per ORB. The Interface Repository consists of many nested objects. The containment hierarchy is shown in Figure 3, as specified in the CORBA/IIOP v2.1 [8]. Each Interface Repository contains a single root object appropriately named *Repository*. All objects contained within this root object are reachable from it. The containment hierarchy for an

Interface Repository is more complex than the Type Library containment hierarchy. This highlights the distinct structure of the two repositories.

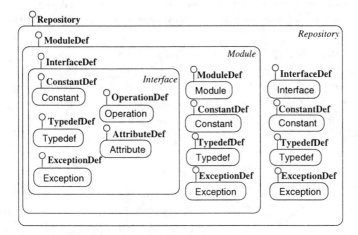

Figure 3. The containment hierarchy for Interface Repository classes

In the Interface Repository there is no separation of classes based on the way the objects interact with the meta-data, that is, an instance of a class can potentially add, as well as access, the meta-data. This is in contrast to the Type Library which provides separate classes for creating meta-data and for accessing meta-data. This means that all classes must be considered in the mapping to the Type Library access classes.

6: Mapping the Interface Repository to the Type Library

To allow COM clients and programmers to access meta-data within CORBA Interface Repositories in a natural way meta-data must be provided using Type Library interfaces. This concept is supported by the interworking specification as it suggests that meta-data can be provided via COM's *IProvideClassInfo* interface which has only a single method which returns a pointer to a Type Library interface. The specification does not however suggest how this should be implemented. The goal of the work presented in this paper is to provide direct access to the meta-data within the Interface Repository, via the Type Library interfaces. To enable this an interworking bridge is used to provide a local view of the Interface Repository within the COM environment.

The production of a view applies a set of mapping rules to the interfaces and all types involved. This mapping unfortunately cannot be configured to define the form of the resulting interface. This is an important point as the mapping of the Interface Repository interfaces cannot be configured to produce Type Library interfaces, hence after the mapping an adapter, or wrapper, needs to be applied to the mapped Interface Repository interfaces. As an example of how the interworking bridge maps the interface structure, consider the inheritance mappings specified by the interworking standard. Note that CORBA objects can only have a single interface and support multiple inheritance of class interfaces, whereas COM objects can have multiple interfaces but do not support inheritance of classes. When a COM view of a CORBA object is created, the inheritance structure must be flattened in some way to align with COM's interface structure which uses the methods of the *IUnknown* interface to navigate between multiple interfaces. The rules defined in the interworking standard [8] for mapping the inheritance structure are listed here and illustrated in Figure 4:

- Each CORBA interface that does not have a parent is mapped to a COM interface deriving from *IUnknown*.
- Each CORBA interface that inherits from a single parent interface is mapped to a COM interface that derives from the mapping for the parent interface.
- Each CORBA interface that inherits from multiple parent interfaces is mapped to a COM interface deriving from *IUnknown*.

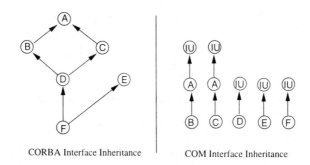

CORBA Interface Inheritance COM Interface Inheritance

Figure 4. CORBA to COM interface inheritance mapping

At this point it would seem that the construction of an appropriate adapter to match the interfaces would provide a suitable solution. However there is a more subtle problem in presenting the Interface Repository information. Even if all interfaces have been appropriately mapped to allow COM clients to use the Interface Repository through Type Library interfaces, the information provided to the client will not describe the current form of the COM views of the CORBA objects. The interworking bridge mutates the CORBA types to present them as COM types. The information in the Interface Repository describes the objects before they have been mapped by the interworking bridge. This situation is illustrated in Figure 5.

To provide accurate descriptions of the COM views created from CORBA objects, the same mapping process which is applied to the CORBA objects to produce the COM views needs to be applied to the meta-data describing the CORBA objects. Considering the example of interface inheritance, if the Interface Repository returns a description of an interface which inherits from more than one other interface, this description must be altered to describe the interface as if it inherits from *IUnknown*. This will be the structure of the COM view for that interface.

There are two distinct issues involved in the adaptation of Interface Repositories to provide Type Library interfaces. The most obvious issue is the mapping of the interfaces, the less obvious issue is the mapping of the contained meta-data. The mapping which needs to be applied to the meta-data can be derived from the Interworking specification, however the mapping is not explicitly defined there. Interworking implementations which

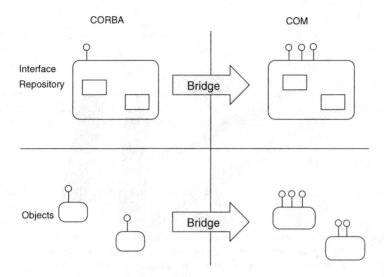

Figure 5. COM view of the CORBA Interface Repository

cache the meta-data information in an intermediate form apply this mapping to the meta-data by translating an entire interface description. Although in the case of direct access to the Interface Repository discussed here, this mapping needs to be applied in much smaller pieces. That is, for each method invocation which retrieves meta-data from the Interface Repository this fragment of information needs to be mapped also. As this mapping is pre-determined it will not be discussed further in this paper.

The other part of the adaptation process is the mapping of the required interfaces. In this case the functionality of a Type Library must be provided using an instance of the Interface Repository. The functionality is well defined for both the required interfaces, that is the Type Library, and the provided interfaces, that is the Interface Repository. Achieving the required functionality utilising the provided functionality with a minimal amount of adapter code is a difficult task. Before attempting this the relationships between the required and provided interfaces must be well understood.

7: How the repositories match

Type Libraries and Interface Repositories have been developed independently under different component paradigms, however they both provide similar functionality which is essential for adaptation. Potentially the most obvious distinction between these two repositories is the structure of their interfaces. Given the distinct structure of the two services, there seems to be a large gap to overcome. This gap is made smaller by considering how the adapter would be used. The client which uses such an adapter would do so as if it were a Type Library. Thus only the functionality provided by the Type Library needs to be coerced from the Interface Repository. Any additional functionality which is provided by the Interface Repository need not be considered. Only the meta-data access interfaces of the Type Library are of interest in this paper, these are the *ITypeLib* and *ITypeInfo* interfaces.

Where Type Libraries provide information which is not present in Interface Repositories, such as help documentation, either an appropriate error message is returned or some sensible default value. Recall the intended use of a Type Library adapter which directly accesses the Interface Repository, it will be used to browse the Interface Repository or when components are infrequently or sparsely accessed. If the usage pattern is other than this a Type Library for the required component can be constructed using the interworking bridge and additional information added. The adaptation of the *ITypeLib* and *ITypeInfo* interfaces are discussed individually in the following subsections.

7.1: Matching the ITypeLib Interface

The TypeLib object can be thought of as a container for TypeInfo objects. This compares well with the functionality of the Interface Repository's *ModuleDef* class. The main function of *ModuleDef* is containment of the Interface Repository's constituent objects. The methods of the *ITypeLib* interface provide the ability to navigate meta-data held within the Type Library. A *ModuleDef* object provides methods for navigation of the Interface Repository. In fact the *Container* class provides most of the navigation methods. *ModuleDef* derives from this class.

The *ITypeLib* interface defines index values which are used to identify contained objects. this index identification scheme is not used by the Interface Repository. The index values therefore must be created and maintained by the adapter. When an adapter object is created it is effectively attached to part of the Interface Repository, hence at creation time the adapter initialises an index table which corresponds to the sets of Interface Repository view objects it represents. This is an example of where the adapter must provide extra functionality to fill the gap between the required and provided interfaces.

When creating an adapter object care must be taken not to recreate an existing contained adapter. Thus the *ITypeLib* adapter must maintain a table of active adapters. These are identified by the type which the adapter provides and the set of Interface Repository view objects used. This is supported by the use of interworking facilities which provide the foreign object reference associated with each view object. Figure 6 outlines the implementation of the *ITypeLib FindName* method.

7.2: Matching the ITypeInfo Interface

A TypeInfo object can describe an interface. a DLL module, a user defined type, or a class. This covers a wide variety of information, thus the correspondence between Interface Repository classes is not as simple as that for *ITypeLib*. The adapter class which implements the *ITypeInfo* interface must be capable of adapting all of the Interface Repository classes except for the Repository and *ModuleDef* class, although in most cases only one object needs to be adapted per adapter instance. The adapter must be able to dynamically modify its functionality based on the type it is to represent and the set of Interface Repository view objects which it must adapt. To support this the adapter constructed is guided by specification. These specifications determine which method implementations, provided in Dynamic Link Libraries (DLLs), will be loaded and used. The use of these guiding specifications makes the underlying adapter architecture more flexible and reusable in a

ITypeLib Method	Description	Adapter Implementation
FindName	Finds occurrences of a type description in a type library. This may be used to quickly verify that a name exists in a type library.	Invoke the lookup_name method of the adapted *ModuleDef* view object. This returns a sequence of Interface Repository objects which must be converted to an array of TypeInfo objects. Each TypeInfo pointer must adapt one of the object references in the sequence returned by lookup_name. An array of the indexes to these adapters must be created in consultation with the active adapter table. FindName has an in-out parameter which indicates the maximum number of values which can be returned. This should be read and only up to that number of values entered into the return array. The value is set to the actual number of values returned if this is less than the maximum specified.

Figure 6. Implementing ITypeLib

variety of situations. Figure 7 outlines the implementation of some methods of the *ITypeInfo* interface.

The TypeLib and TypeInfo adapters presented here are the subject of a prototype implementation. This prototype will provide COM Type Library clients with direct access to the CORBA Interface Repository. The issues of mapping the Interface Repository meta-data can then be fully investigated using this prototype. Further details of this work can be found in [13]. The completed prototype system will form a critical component of the overall interworking between COM and CORBA.

8: Discussion

The usefulness of interworking bridges between COM and CORBA is currently limited by the inflexible support for accessing meta-data which describes the components. In this paper we have highlighted the issues involved in providing direct access to this meta-data using the COM Type Libraries and the CORBA Interface Repositories. The use of the interworking bridge to map the Interface Repository into the COM world only achieves part of the goal. For COM clients a mapping between the Interface Repository interfaces to the Type Library interfaces is required. This is achieved using adapters. The meta-data in the Interface Repository must also be mapped to reflect the changes the interworking bridge imposes on CORBA objects when providing the COM views.

The adaptation problem is complex, as illustrated by the example in this paper. The development of a generic architecture and infrastructure which supports the construction of adapters described in this paper is well advanced. A supporting run-time infrastructure for these adapters is also under development, further detail can be found in [14]. The example provided in this paper is motivating in itself, however the adapted components are

ITypeInfo Methods	Description	Adapter Implementation
CreateInstance	Creates a new instance of a type that describes a component object class (coclass).	Call CoCreateInstance with the appropriate values for the class described by this *ITypeInfo*. This requires that a view of the described class is available via the interworking bridge.
GetFuncDesc	Retrieves the FUNCDESC structure that contains information about a specified function.	This function returns a structure providing all information which describes a function. The adapter must retrieve description information from the adapted OperationDef view object and pack this into the structure to be returned.
GetTypeAttr	Retrieves a TYPEATTR structure that contains the attributes of the type description.	This method returns a structure to describe a type. Much of this information can be retrieved from the adapted AttributeDef and TypedefDef objects. Other values can be set to some sensible default.

Figure 7. Implementing ITypeInfo

significant only in the service which they provide. Thus the adaptation process is applicable to any other pair of components from different worlds which overlap in functionality. Providing an architecture which supports generic adaptation would significantly reduce the effort required to access such services.

This paper highlights the need for interworking solutions to provide flexible access to meta-data in a way which is natural for both client components and programmers. If this flexibility is not provided then the benefit of using interworking bridges may be severely diminished. Providing access to meta-data is not a simple case of applying the interworking bridge to the meta-data repositories, this would provide access to meta-data in an unnatural form, and more importantly it provides meta-data which is incorrect for the client. This paper addresses both of these problems and describes the construction of adapters which solve these problems. The proposed adapters are a promising solution, without which the full benefit of interworking between component worlds will not be realised.

9: Acknowledgements

The work reported in this paper has been funded in part by the Cooperative Research Centres Program through the Department of the Prime Minister and Cabinet of the Commonwealth Government of Australia. It was also partially supported by an Australian Government Postgraduate Scholarship (APA).

References

[1] B. W. Beach. "Connecting software components with declarative glue". *Proceedings of the 14th Inter-*

national Conference on Software Engineering, 120–136. 1992.

[2] K. Brockschmidt. "Inside OLE. 2nd Edition". *Microsoft Press*, Washington, 1995.

[3] W. Brookes, A. Berry, A. Bond, J. Indulska and K. Raymond. "A type model supporting interoperability". *Proceedings of the First International Conference on Telecommunications Information Networking Architecture, TINA '95"*, 1995

[4] D. Flanagan "Java in a Nutshell. 2nd Edition". *O'Reilly and Associates*, 1997.

[5] E. Gamma, R. Helm, R. Johnson and J. Vlissides. "Design Patterns: Elements of Reusable Object-Oriented Software. *Addison-Wesley*, Massachusetts, 1995.

[6] IONA Technologies PLC. "OrbixCOMet Desktop Programmer's Guide". *Ireland*, 1998.

[7] D. Konstantas. "Object oriented interoperability". *ECOOP'93 Object-Oriented Programming, Lecture Notes in Computer Science*, 707:80–102, 1993.

[8] Object Management Group (OMG). "The Common Object Request Broker: Architecture and Specification". *version 2.1, Rev. August*, 1997.

[9] J. M. Purtilo and J. M. Atlee. "Module reuse by interface adaptation". *Software Practice and Experience*, 21(6):539–556, June 1991.

[10] D. Rogerson. "Inside COM". *Microsoft Press*, Washington, 1997.

[11] Sun Microsystems. "JavaBeans". *http://java.sun.com/beans*, 1.01, July 1997.

[12] S. R. Thatte. "Automated synthesis of interface adaptors for reusable classes". *ACM SIGPLAN-SIGACT POPL'94*, ACM Press. New York. 1994.

[13] G. Smith. "Conciliation in the COM environment". *Technical Report FIT-TR-98-01. School of Computer Science, Queensland University of Technology.* 1998.

[14] G. Smith, G. Gough, and C. Szyperski. "Conciliation: The Adaptation of Independently Developed Components. *Series on Parallel and Distributed Computing and Networks*, IASTED, 1998.

[15] C. Szyperski. "Component Software: Beyond Object-Oriented Programming". *ACM Press*, New York, 1998.

[16] D. M. Yellin and R. E. Strom. "Protocol specifications and component adaptors". *ACM Transactions on Programming Languages and Systems*, 292–333, 1997.

Dynamic Deployable Distributed System

Takanobu Ando
Object Technology Center, Toshiba Corporation
3-22, Katamachi, Fuchu-shi, Tokyo, 183 Japan
E-mail : ando@sitc.toshiba.co.jp

Abstract

This paper describes one flexible distributed system that we are proposing. In general, distributed system is needed for using the computer network efficiently. Recent computer network becomes larger and changes the structure frequently with the progress of the hardware technology. The distributed system needs flexibility to be adapted to such a network dynamically. Our distributed system, which is applied to client server application, can deploy and move the server process to an arbitrary all network nodes that is selected at run time. Such dynamic deployment of server process is useful for some purposes. For example, total throughput improvement or load balancing. We implemented the system in Java and created some simple applications based on it. This paper also shows one of these examples and the effects of our system.

1. Introduction

Flexible distributed system is needed for recent computer network composed of various machines. Technologies of hardware for computer network progress so fast that the computer network is growing more complex. Distributed systems are required to use such network effectively. However traditional static distributed systems are not enough to use such dynamically changing network effectively. We think that the dynamic flexibility is needed for the recent distributed systems.

The dynamic deployment of the server process is one of the expected functions for the flexible distributed system used for the client server application. So we propose one flexible distributed system which can deploy and move server processes at the execution time. All networked machines, which include client machines, are possible to be selected as the execution place for the server process.

In our system, networked machines are categorized into three types according to their roles. They are Component Server Node, Sub-server Node, and Client Node. Furthermore the server process, which is called Server Component, may be composed of three kinds of blocks. They are Main Processing Block, Client-side Resource Access Block, and Server-side Resource Access Block.

We implemented our system in Java[1]. Each block of Server Component is composed of some parts, which correspond to Java class mostly. So a Server Component is consists of many Java classes. To simplify the Server Component development, we also provide development tool for Server Component. The tool generates skeleton source code for Java classes from the Server Component information, which include the interface definition like CORBA object.

In this paper, we state the basic concept of our system in section 2 Then, we describe the detail of our system implemented in Java in section 3 One sample application is shown in next section and we checked the effect of our system through this example. Finally, we conclude and state feature plan of our system.

2. Basic concept

In this chapter, we describe the concept for our suggested distributed system.

First, we state some current technologies for the distributed system and point out the required features which the distributed system expects but the current technologies do not provide. Then we describe the concept and merit of our system.

2.1. Current technology

Computer network is composed of various machines. Distributed systems based on such network are needed to use these connected machines effectively. Client server system is one of traditional distributed system. In recently, hardware and network technologies are progressing day by day. As such progress, the distributed system becomes more complex than simple client server system. So, the new distributed system including development, execution, and management technology is required for such recent network environment.

Nowadays, one of popular distributed system is web-based system using Java applet or something like that. Mobile agent system[2,3] also attracts many attentions. Furthermore the cluster system[4,5] is usually used for load balancing and fault tolerance. In the rest of this section, we describe these technologies briefly.

Web-based system is the most popular way to develop distributed system. It has some merits. For example, many platform can connect to it because it bases on standard technologies (e.g. HTTP, IIOP, and so on). In addition, application programs, such as Java applets, and CGI, are available on the web-based system. However, in case of using Java applets, the client machine needs enough resources(e.g. CPU power, memory, and so on), otherwise if CGI programs are used, performance problems might be happened when many clients connect to the server. Besides them, in general, web-based system needs high speed network.

Mobile agent is new technology of distributed systems. Mobile agent is a kind of process, and it roams around the network. This technology is good for collecting ubiquitous information, or observing specific machines on the network. But the service provided by the mobile agent is restricted. In addition, the mobile agent is basically disconnected from client when it works, so it is not good for thick connected client server system.

Cluster is the distributed system for multi-server environment. This technology is mainly used for load balancing and fault tolerance. This is good for relatively large system or high reliable system. But the cluster system needs high speed network to mediate among all servers. In addition, the server process generally doesn't run on client machine, because the server machine is obviously distinguished from the client machine. Furthermore, the server processes should be installed in all server machines.

2.2. Required flexibility for recent distributed system

According to the progress of hardware and network technologies, the computer network grows dynamically and rapidly. In other words, the network structure changes frequently. For example, one old machine might be replaced with a number of new machines. So distributed systems are expected to be flexible enough to be adapted to such environment.

Most distributed systems using current technologies are basically supposed to have static structure and the structure is designed before the installation time. That is, the execution places of the server process and the client process are fixed statically. So the structure can't be configured or changed easily to be adapted to the network changing frequently.

To solve this problem and others stated above, flexibility of the system structure is needed for the recent distributed systems. In this case, flexibility mainly means that the execution place of the server process should be decided at run time and all connected machines including client machine should be proposed for the server process execution. Moreover, it should be able to change the execution place while the server process is running.

2.3. Our concept

We suggest one distributed system which can be adapted to dynamically changing network flexibly. In the concrete, the system structure can be changed dynamically to be adapted to the network at that time, or the execution place of server process can be changed flexibly. An outline of our system is shown in Fig 2-1.

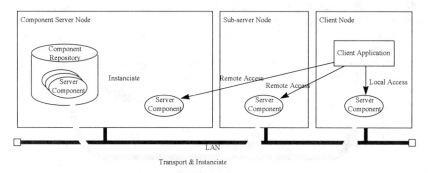

Fig 2-1 Basic Concept for Whole Our System

Basically, applications working on our system are constructed as client server structure. So they consist of server part and client part. Server part, which is called Server Component, implements server logic. Server part can be executed on all machines relating to the system. Client part, which is called Client Application, accesses the Server Component which is placed anywhere in this system. The Server Component is stored and managed in database, which is called Component Repository, transported to appropriate place and executed (instantiated).

From the Server Component management and execution point of view, the networked machines of this system are classified into three nodes. They are Component Server Node, Sub-server Node, and Client Node. Component Server Node has Component Repository and can run the Server Component. Sub-server Node only can run the Server Component. Client node has Client Application and can run the Server Component. Their details implemented in Java are denoted in section 3.1

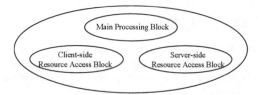

Fig 2-2 Server Component Basic Structure

Server Component itself may be also divided into three blocks according to its role. They are Main Processing Block, Client-side Resource Access Block, and Server-side Resource Access Block. Main Processing Block implements server process logic. Client-side Resource Access Block and Server-side Resource Access Block are placed on specific node and they can access the specific resource on the node. Server Component can access the specific resource on the specific machine through these Resource Access Blocks wherever the main logic is executed. For example, Server Component can have GUI anytime displayed on client machine by the Client-side Resource Access Block, or can access database on another machine through Server-side Resource Access Block. These are obviously different feature from general mobile agent. The details of these blocks implemented in Java are explained in section 3.2

2.4. Advantage of our distributed system and the application

Our distributed system enables developer to build flexible client server system that server processes can be deployed dynamically. According to this feature, the system based on our distributed system can be fit for the unsettled structured network. For instance, the system can deploy the heavy server process from higher loaded machine to lower one which did not exist when the system was developed or installed.

Our distributed system might be applied for many purpose. For example, it would be good for the CPU load balancing and network traffic reduction. Or it might be applied to other new systems. One case is component selling system, which publishes Server Component running only on the server for trial use and deploys the Server Component to client machine when the user decide to buy it and pay for it.

3.Suggested system

We implemented our concept described in chapter 2. We chose Java as implementation language because Java can be used on multi-platform and is suitable for implementing distributed systems.

In this chapter, we describe our distributed system written in Java. The system is divided into two parts: One is the Server Component and the other is the based system that manages the Server Component. The latter is called the Base System. In this chapter, the architecture of Base System is described first. Secondly, we describe the Server Component framework. Thirdly, we show one sample case to make clear how our system works. Then lastly, we present the way to develop the Server Component and show our development tool.

3.1. Suggested Base System architecture

The network nodes of our system are classified into three kind of node which are Component Server Node, Sub-server Node, and Client Node. Our Base System are composed of three parts corresponding to these node types. The architecture of our Base System is shown in Fig 3-1. The lower layer of our system is formed by OS and Java Virtual Machine(JVM) because this our system is implemented in Java. So the OS needs to be able to execute JVM. We adopted Java RMI[6] as distributed object communication technology. Main parts of the Base System are corresponding to the gray parts of Fig 3-1. In this section, we describe the role of each gray part at every node type.

258

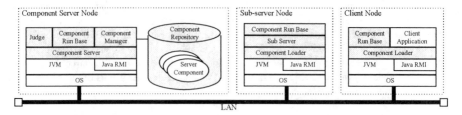

Fig 3-1 Base System Architecture

Component Server Node consists of five parts. They are Component Server, Judge, Component Run Base, Component Manager, and Component Repository. Component Server is main part of this node. It receives client's request for a Server Component, and then it asks to Judge part where the requested Server Component should be executed. The Component Server part works in agreement with the judgment made by Judge part. For example, the Component Server may get the necessary parts of the Server Component from Component Repository, then transfer each part to appropriate place, and if necessary, instantiate some of them at the Component Run Base in this node. The Judge part decides the execution place of the requested Server Component. The result of judgment is one of the connected machine that is a kind of three node types described above. Various criteria are considered to make judgment. One criterion might be the constraint on the execution place which is decided by component developer or system manager in advance. One of the other criterion might be aimed to reduce the specific CPU or network load average. Besides, the Judge part can instruct to re-deploy the working Server Component. The Judge part manages the list of current working Server Component to realize re-deployment. The Component Run Base part executes some parts of the Server Component. More precisely, Component Run Base creates instances of the component parts handed from Component Server and initializes them. The Component Manager part and the Component Repository part manage the registered Server Components.

Sub-server Node consists of three parts. They are Component Loader, Sub-server and Component Run Base. The Component Loader part receives some Server Component parts from Component Server through the network and passes them to its Sub-server part. The Sub-server part receives these Server Component parts from its Component Loader part and passes them to its Component Run Base part. The Sub-server part can also cache the Server Component parts for the purpose of performance improvement. Furthermore the Sub-server part controls whole of the node(e.g., initialization of the node). The Component Run Base part works in the same manner as that of Component Server Node.

Client node consists of three parts. They are Component Loader, Component Run Base and Client Application. The Component Loader part works in the same manner as that of the Sub-server Node. The Component Run Base part also works in the same manner as that of the Component Server Node. Client Application on our distributed system is provided by application developer. It uses the Component Loader part to load some parts of the Server Component from the Component Server Node. It also uses the Component Run Base part to execute them.

The Base system described above was implemented in Java. So the Java classes constructing the base system are provided as one kind of class library or executive.

3.2. Server Component framework

The Server component consists of three blocks, Main Processing Block, Client-side Resource Access Block, and Server-side Resource Access Block. The Client-side Resource Access Block and the Server-side Resource Access Block are optional. Fig 3-2 shows the Server Component framework. The gray parts in Fig 3-2 are significance parts. These parts carry out the server logic implemented by Server Component developer. We state about Server Component development in section 3.4 In this section, we describe each blocks of Server Component.

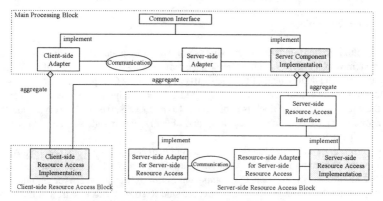

Fig 3-2 Server Component Architecture

The Main Processing Block is essential block of Server Component. This block provide basic services of this Server Component. This block consists of five parts. They are Common Interface, Server Component Implementation, Client-side Adapter, Server-side Adapter, and Communication Part. The Common Interface part defines the methods of the Server Component and their signatures. The Client application can access the Server Component through the defined way in the Common Interface part. The Server Component Implementation part is the main part which implements the server logic. This part must implement the Common Interface part. The Client-side Adapter part and the Server-side Adapter part simply relay the method call from client application to the Server Component Implementation part. They are used only if the Server Component run on another node differ from the Client Node. The Client-side Adapter part must implement the Common Interface to receive the client request. The Communication part is structured with general distributed communication mechanism. We use Java RMI to implement this part. Because of using Java RMI, the Server-side Adapter part implements a interface that extends *java.rmi.Remote* interface.

The Client-side Resource Access Block can access resources on the Client Node. For example, it can display GUI panel or check client machine configuration. This block have only one part, which is Client-side Resource Access Implementation. The part implements a interface that extends *java.rmi.Remote* interface because of using Java RMI.

The Server-side Resource Access Block can access resources on the specific node which is differ from the Client Node. For example, it can access a database or a file existing on specific node statically. This block consists of five parts. They are Server-side Resource Access Interface, Server-side Resource Access Implementation, Server-side Adapter for Server-side Resource Access, Resource-side Adapter for Server-side Resource Access, and Communication part. The Server-side Resource Access Interface part defines the methods of the Server-side Resource Access Block and their signatures. The Server Component Implementation part can access the Server-side Resource Access Block through the defined way in this interface. The Server-side Resource Access Implementation part implements the logic of this block. This part must implement the Server-side Resource Access Interface. The Server-side Adapter part and The Resource-side Adapter part of this block simply relay the method call from the Main Processing Block to the Server-side Resource Access Implementation part. They are used only if the Main Processing Block and the Server-side Resource Access Block run on different node each other. The Server-side Adapter part must

260

implements the Server-side Resource Access Interface part. We also use Java RMI for the Communication part. Because of using Java RMI, the Resource-side Adapter part implements the interface that extends *java.rmi.Remote* interface.

3.3. Execution Examples

In this section, to help understanding our system, we show a sample case which demonstrates how the system works internally. This sample case representing the cooperation of each parts of the Base System and the deployment of the each parts of the Server Component.

In this example, we suppose that the requested Server Component has both resource access blocks, the Main Processing Block is deployed at Component Server node, Server-side Resource Access Block is deployed at Sub-server Node, and of course Client-side Resource Access Block is deployed at Client Node.

Fig 3-3 shows this example. After the Server Component is requested from the Client Application, the Component Server part decides execution place for each block of the requested component through the Judge part. In this case, the Component Server retrieves the Server Component Implementation part, the Server-side Adapter for Server-side Resource Access part and the Server-side Adapter part from the Component Repository and instantiates them by its Component Run Base. The Component Server part retrieves the Server-side Resource Access Implementation part and the Resource-side Adapter for Server-side Resource Access part from the Component Repository and transmits them to the Sub-server Node. In the Sub-server Node, these parts are instantiated by its Component Run Base. The Component Server part also retrieves the Client-side Resource Access Implementation part and the Client-side Adapter part from the Component Repository and transmits them to the Client Node. In the Client Node, these parts are instantiated by its Component Run Base. After transmission and instantiation, they connect between each corresponding parts.

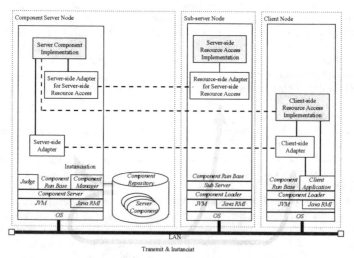

Fig 3-3 Working Example 1

3.4. Server Component Development

As shown in section 3.2, the Server Component consists of many parts, so it seems more troublesome to develop the Server Components than the usual server processes. But most parts of the Server Component are simple interfaces or classes which merely relay the method call. Only few parts needs complex implementation for each server logic. Those are the Server Component Implementation part, the Client-side Resource Access Implementation part, and the Server-side Resource Access Implementation part.

We provide the Server Component development tool to reduce development cost. This tool creates three skeleton Java source files for the Server Component Implementation part, the Client-side Resource Access Implementation part, and the Server-side Resource Access Implementation part(gray parts in Fig 3-2) , and also creates some complete Java source files for the interfaces and method relay classes(white parts in Fig 3-2). The Server Component development flow using this tool is shown in Fig 3-4.

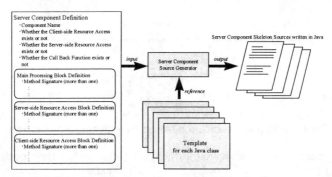

Fig 3-4 Creating Skeleton Sources of Server Component

To create the Server Component using this tool, the Server Component developer have to specify following information:
- Server Component Name
- Whether the Client-side Resource Access Block exists or not
- Whether the Server-side Resource Access Block exists or not
- Whether the Call Back Function exists or not
- Main Processing Block Definition(signatures of all method)
- Client-side Resource Access Block Definition(signatures of all method, optional)
- Server-side Resource Access Block Definition(signatures of all method, optional)

The block definitions are list of method's signatures including the method name, the number of arguments and their type, and return value types.

The Template files are provided by us with this development tool. They describe general information to create class or interface file in Java.

Most output Java source files are complete. Only the three skeleton source files stated above need to be implemented the server logic by the Server Component developer.

4.Suggested System Prototype

We implement a prototype of our distributed system and made some application on the system. For example, database access application, simple calculator application, and so on. In this chapter, we show an image processing application as one example of these application. Through this example, we indicate the effects of our system.

4.1.Sample: Image Processing System.

In this section, we show distributed image processing application. This application execute some image processing functions. For example, smoothing and mono-color filtering. Each image processing is implemented as a Server Component individually. The Client Application displays a target image, requests Server Components to the Component Server, and executes image processing through the Server Component. Here, we show the difference in processing times, depending on the deployment of the Server Component, in the case of using the Smoothing Server Component.

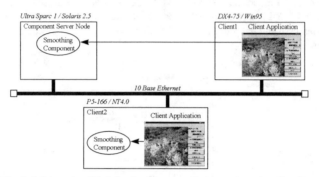

Fig 4-1 Sample: Distributed Image Processing Application

This image processing system is implemented and executed as Fig 4-1. There are three machine, Solaris 2.5 on Ultra Sparc 1 as a Component Server Node, Windows95 on PC(which has DX4-75 CPU) as a Client Node(called Client1), and WindowsNT4.0 on PC(which has Pentium-166 CPU) as another Client Node(called Client2). They are connected through 10 Base Ethernet. Fig 4-1 shows one case of execution that the Client1 uses the smoothing component running on the Component Server Node and the Client2 uses it running on the Client2 itself. Off course, the other cases are possible.

We measured processing time for all pair of client machines and Server Component place. The target image data is 640x480 pixels and 32bit per pixel. The mask size of smoothing process is 3x3. The result of this experiment is shown in Table 4-1.

Client Machine	Server Component Place	Processing Time(sec)
Client1	Client1	60.6
Client1	Component Server	44.2
Client2	Client2	34.1
Client2	Component Server	41.0

Table 4-1 Experimental Result

In the case of the Client1, the processing time is better while the Server Component was deployed at the Component Server Node. That is because the Client1 has lower power CPU and smoothing image needs high performance CPU, so it is more desirable to transfer the image data to the node which has higher power CPU and process it there. In opposition to this case, the processing time is better while the Server Component was deployed at Client2. That is because the Client2 has higher power CPU and the image data size is large, so it is more desirable to process smoothing at Client2 than to transfer the image data to another node to process it at there.

According to these results, desirable places of the Server Component are differ due to the client feature. In this case, slower client should use the Server Component at another faster machine, and faster client should use it on its machine.

5.Conclusion and future enhancements

We provide one new flexible distributed system which can deploy the server process, called the Server Component, to arbitrary networked machine at runtime. Through some sample application prototype based on our system, we can find some effectiveness of our system. From sample of image processing, the throughput was improved by deployment the Server Component to appropriate place.

In addition, our system might be able to apply for load balancing or fault tolerance. Furthermore the management cost for the Server Component may be low because the Server Component are only installed and managed on only a few Component Server Node, in other words, the Server Component do not have to be installed all server machine.

We now consider some future extensions of our distributed system. For example, using CORBA[7] as distributed object technology is desired because Java RMI is used in only Java environment. The security of the Server Component and certification of the user are important for such system too. For the performance or load balancing, automated Server Component deployment is need for the Judge part.

References

[1] James Gosling, Bill Joy, and Guy Steele. The Java Language Specification. ADDISON-WESLEY. 1996.

[2] S. Covaci, Z. Tianning, and I. Busse. Java-based intelligent mobile agents for open system management., In 19th IEEE International Conference on Tools with Artificial Intelligence. 1997.

[3] D. B. Lange, M. Oshima, G. Karjoth, and K. Kosaka. Aglets: programming mobile agents in Java. In WWCA'97. 1997.

[4] D. Andersen, Tao Yang, V. Holmedahl, and O.H. Ibarra. SWEB: towards a scalable World Wide Web server on multicomputers. In IPPS '96. 1996.

[5] B. Narendran, S. Rangarajan, and S. Yajnik. Data distribution algorithms for load balanced fault-tolerant Web access. In the 16th Symposium on Reliable Distributed Systems. 1997.

[6] Java Remote Method Invocation Specification. Sun Microsystems, Inc. 1997.

[7] OMG. The Common Object Request Broker. Architecture and Specification   revision 2.0 Technical report. Object management Group. 1995.

[8] E.Gamma, R.Helm, R.Johnson, and J.Vlissides. Design Patterns: Elements of Reusable Object-Oriented Software. Addison-Wesley. 1995.

[9] Grady Booch. Object-oriented analysis and design with applications, second edition. The Benjamin/Cummings Publishing Company Inc. 1994.

[10] Ivar Jacobson, Magnus Christerson, Patrik Jonsson, and Gunnar Overgaard. Object-Oriented Software Engineering - A Use Case Driven Approach. Addison-Wesley Publishing Company and ACM Press. 1992.

[11] UML Semantics -ver.1.0. Rational Software Corp. 1995.

[12] Noureddine BELKHATIR. An Object Oriented Framework for Distributed, Interoperable Process Engineering Environments. In TOOLS23. 1997.

[13] D.C.Schmidt. Using Design Patterns to Develop Reusable Object-Oriented Communication Software. Communication of ACM, Vol.38, No.10. 1995.

[14] S.Sparks, K.Benner, C.Faris. Managing Object-Oriented Framework Reuse. IEEE Computer, Vol.29, No.9. 1996.

Inter-Server Transport Performance of Java Bytecode in a Metacomputing Environment

J.A.Mathew, A.J.Silis and K.A.Hawick

Advanced Computational Systems Cooperative Research Centre,

Department of Computer Science, University of Adelaide, SA 5005, Australia

Tel +61 08 8303 4728, Fax +61 08 8303 4366,

Email {jm,din,khawick}@cs.adelaide.edu.au

Abstract

In a distributed metacomputing environment, facilities for the movement of code from one server node to another are highly desirable. Often movement of code to data is preferable to the movement of data to code, particularly where the data is large. In this paper we describe our 'Code Server' or database of Java byte code which is searchable on code attributes. We discuss design and implementation issues and results of performance benchmarking. We focus on a practical image processing example. We also discuss how our implementation addresses issues such as namespaces, client-server communication and distribution. Our results show that code serving appears viable, but more work remains to identify a suitable general database schema for describing code attributes.

1 Introduction

DISCWorld [6] is a metacomputing environment which allows collaborating users to share resources through the provision of well defined and high granularity services. DISCWorld is implemented as a software daemon executed on each participating host, offering services to users and other systems. In this paper we describe our efforts to provide a mechanism for dealing with the movement of code between DISCWorld nodes.

There are a number of reasons why the transport of code is desirable. One reason is that often the data required for an operation, or group of operations, is much greater in size than the code to perform the operations. Hence, code movement can help to reduce total data transfer required for an operation. We provide a framework which enables code to be moved to execute on systems with the most appropriate computational resources. Another reason is that a metacomputing framework such as DISCWorld requires some way of moving code for bootstrapping services since each node may not necessarily have code for all operations when it is initially started. This enables new services to be added more easily.

Due to it's inherent portability the code that we are concerned with is mainly Java [4] bytecode. However it should be possible to extend our framework to support the storage of native code, which may provide substantial performance improvements in the execution of some services. We may also support the storage of data such as images or serialised Java objects which will allow us to persistently maintain the state of each node, allowing nodes that fail to be restarted in a consistent state and hence improving the robustness and reliability of the system.

We use the Code Server in preference to applets that are downloaded from a web server. An applet approach would impose access limitations on the services. It is also more difficult to provide searchability and the ability to dynamically choose the components to be downloaded. Our performance measurements also show that in most cases Code Server performance is superior to using a web server.

We facilitate the movement of code in the DISCWorld using a 'Code Server' - a database of code. Associated with the bytecode, we store contextual information (metadata), to provide for searching the Code Server according to some criteria. This approach differs from that of having autonomous mobile agents [13], as in our system the code is moved in response to a request from a remote client, rather than the object autonomously deciding to move. It also differs from the approach of having a node offer the executes the code as a remote method, as this requires the subject data to be transferred to the node.

The integrity of the code is also of concern, since we want to be able to authenticate the sender and ensure the code has not been tampered with. The problem of securely transmitting and storing portable code objects is an important one for scalable, wide-area distributed computing environments. We have previously described how authentication might be incorporated into the Code Server framework [5]. The Code Server supports distribution transparently in that each user need only to know about one DISCWorld (and hence Code Server) node. If the user makes a request that can't be fulfilled by the node, the node itself will forward the request to other nodes, obtain the result and return it to the user. We discuss distribution issues in more detail in section 2.3.

We have tested our Code Server with some benchmarks and some practical image manipulation operations. A number of simple image operators are implemented in Java bytecodes and are available as portable code objects in the distributed DISCWorld database. Images processing operations are a good example of class of operations in which the code is likely to be much smaller than data, particularly for satellite imagery.

2 Architecture

The Code Server that we have implemented is based on a client-server architecture. The system stores code as well as 'metadata' or 'auxiliary data' which is contextual data describing the code. We have chosen to store the metadata in a relational database, while the actual Java bytecode is stored on a conventional file system. We discuss the reasoning behind this design in section 2.1.

The client and server are implemented in Java and are portable across platforms. The server communicates with a database using the Java Database Connectivity (JDBC) package, and makes use of pure Java database drivers. The client and server communicate using Java Remote Method Invocation (RMI). We have also implemented a version of the Code Server that uses sockets instead of RMI in order to compare the performance of the two approaches. The design we have adopted allows both the client and server to be installed on new platforms quite easily. We have successfully tested the Code Server on a number of platforms including Digital Unix, Linux (i386), Windows NT, Solaris (SPARC) and Solaris (i386). Databases that we have successfully tested with the Code Server include PostgreSQL [12] under Solaris (SPARC), Digital Unix and Linux as well as Informix [8] Dynamic Server under Solaris.

Applications seeking code for specific services will interact with a particular instance of the Code Server. Our current model has a single database for each Code Server, with Code Servers having the ability to communicate with each other. This approach was chosen as we intend to have a DISCWorld daemon running on each participating node and controlling all the resources and services for that node. However, the database does not necessarily have to reside on the same host as the server, and only trivial modifications to the existing system are required to allow a single Code Server to deal with multiple databases.

If a server receives a request that it can not satisfy, it can forward the request on to other servers, obtain the relevant code fragment, and send it back to the requesting application. This distribution is implemented transparently, so that the users or applications that want to use the code servers only need to deal with a single host, and if the host is unable to satisfy the request it will forward it to other servers, obtain the result and send it back to the requesting application or user.

2.1 Metadata

A problem that needs to be addressed in developing our Code Server is how to identify the code fragment of interest based on some sort of request from a client. We achieve this by providing search functionality for the metadata. A relational database provides a convenient means of searching through the data and locating items of interest. We have previously discussed querying auxiliary data in the DISCWorld environment in [10]. Our initial list of metadata attributes is provided in table 1. When code is entered into the system, the metadata must be provided along with the bytecode. The class name is mandatory, while the other fields are optional.

Metadata Item	Description
Unique ID	A unique key value generated by Java
Group ID	A unique key value to group a set of related classes as chosen by the developer
Class name	The fully qualified class name (including package)
Code Description	A free text description of the code
Category	Each code fragment is assigned to one of a set of predefined categories (domains)
Keywords	One or more keywords or phrases describing the code functionality
Input Parameters	Input Parameters of the code and their types represented as strings
Return Type	Return type of the code and it's type
Dependencies	Other code modules required to execute this code
URL	Pointer to the developers of the code
Address	Address of developers
Citation	Any published material describing the code
Vendor, Product, Version, Development Platform	Since the various Java implementations have subtle differences, it may be important to have some knowledge of development platform and software
Platform	If the code includes native methods, this specifies what platform(s) it can execute on
JDK version	Version of the Java Development Kit used to compile the code

Table 1. Bytecode Metadata used in the Code Server Prototype

The attributes described in the table are a trial set of attributes we have chosen. In the future we will intend to transform our metadata to conform to standards such as Dublin Core [3]. From our experiences in actually using the system, we will use feedback from developers to further refine the metadata list. We are also intending to introduce extra metadata to store feedback on the performance of the code on various platforms and usage patterns.

Our Code Server implementation uses a class 'ClassMetaData' to describe Java classes stored in the system. All of the fields described are represented by Java Strings. The role of this class for querying is described in section 2.2.

As previously mentioned, the Code Server daemons communicate with the databases using the JDBC package. This provides significant advantages over using a proprietary solution, the most important of which is portability. The particular database product and version used by each site is unimportant as long as an appropriate JDBC driver is available. Substituting one database for another can be achieved by simply creating the appropriate tables using an SQL script, and referring the server to the appropriate JDBC driver and host.

A design decision that arises is whether the database should hold Java byte code as well as the metadata, or whether it is better to store the bytecode on the file system. In our initial implementation, we chose the later alternative since our preliminary tests have shown that there is a significant performance overhead associated with storing large binary objects in a database, and hence no real advantage in doing so. In the future the relative advantages and disadvantages of storing the byte code within the database will be investigated more thoroughly. Each class is assigned a unique ID when entered into the system, and this ID is used for the filename to store the bytecode on the file system. Java has a mechanism to generate unique IDs as part of the distributed garbage collector class. We use this VMID() method of java.rmi.dgc to generate the unique IDs. The ID generated is based on the IP address and current time and is unique assuming the IP address is fixed.

2.2 Querying

The Code Server can handle two basic forms of query. The first case is where the class name is known and the corresponding bytecode is required. The second is where the class name is unknown and the appropriate code needs to be identified based on a query. In the later case, the query method is called with a ClassMetaData class as its input parameter. The class is populated with data to be used for matching. In addition, the user specifies a weight to be assigned to each attribute in order to determine how 'good' a match is. The classes are returned sorted in order of how good the match is. An example is provided below in table 2.

Attribute	Code Attribute	Query Attribute	Query Weight
Filename	CloudCover.class	Cloud*	10
Category	Image	Image	20
Keywords	GMS5	GMS5	15
Total	-	-	45

Table 2. Query Matching in Prototype Code Server

One of the metadata attributes that we have defined is a group. The group is a mechanism for identifying related files and serves two purposes. Firstly, if classes are known to refer to each other, it may be preferable for the client to download all such classes at once, instead of downloading them one at a time. This is particularly useful in the case of small files, where the latency for each RMI call can be a very significant overhead, and the extra overhead of downloading code that may not be required is minimal. This is similar to the approach of using Java 'jar' [9] file archives, except that we are not using any compression. Compression may be incorporated into the system at a later time. The performance advantages of this approach are investigated in detail in section 3.

The groups also allow for more effective management of the class name space. The class name that is stored in the system is the fully qualified class name including package name. We can deal with name clashes by storing the classes in different groups. When a request is made for a particular filename a group must also be specified if the filename is not unique. A group can contain one or more packages and a package can be spread across groups.

When code is entered into the system, a group can be assigned by the developer. If a group is not specified a new group is created, with the code being entered as the only member of the new group.

In our current implementation, each class can only belong to one group, and the groups are not hierarchical. In the future, there may be advantages in supporting this, since this could provide finer grained control over which classes are loaded and allow for performance to be optimised.

A number of querying functions have been provided. Some methods return a single class, others return the metadata for classes that match a query while others return a group of byte classes. In all the methods that accept the filename as an input parameter, the group must be specified if the filename is not unique.

Since both client and server are implemented in Java, RMI provides a convenient communications mechanism. An alternative to RMI is CORBA [11], [1], however in our experience CORBA is more difficult to work with, since it is a more 'heavy weight' interface and implementations of CORBA are not as portable, robust and inter-operable as Java RMI. CORBA has two main advantages over RMI, which are the ability to incorporate non Java objects and the extra functionality it provides such as traders [2]. These are of no benefit to us since our system is pure Java and the DISCWorld daemon itself provides much of the extra functionality that CORBA offers over RMI.

We have also implemented a sockets based version of the Code Server and comparisons between the performance of the RMI and sockets based version can be found in section 3. The sockets based version is a simplified version, and the server listens on a defined port. This was developed only for a performance comparison with the RMI implementation, and only supports a subset of the full Code Server functionality. When a connection is made the server attempts to read the filename of the class being requested, searches the database to find the appropriate ID, loads the file and writes it to the socket.

2.3 Distribution

Our Code Server was designed so as to provide support for distribution transparent to the user. We have implemented distribution by making each Code Server a client of the others. When a server is initialised it binds to other Code Servers that it knows about in it's database. This database needs to be bootstrapped by the system administrator of the DISCWorld node. When a request is made for code that is unavailable, a server can request the code from other code servers, and return the result to the client. Thus each client need only know about and interact with one server. Our initial implementation allows interaction across two servers, but this can be easily extended to further servers. If each request to another server is spawned off as a separate thread, the extra latency introduced will be largely independent of the number of servers. We have to be careful not to generate cycles for requests that cannot be fulfilled. This is avoided by tagging each request with a unique ID, and if a server receives the same request ID more than once, it will not generate further requests to other Servers for the code.

The approach of each Code Server knowing about all other Code Servers is obviously unscalable. In the DISCWorld framework, we introduce the concept of 'gossip' between hosts, where each Server knows about some number of servers which in turn know about other servers. Since this framework is not hierarchical it is likely to be more scalable and there is no possibility of a single point of failure. Work into how many hosts each host needs to know about in order to maintain connectivity between hosts and what patterns of connectivity are necessary is still ongoing

Another potential mechanism for efficient distribution in a large system is to propagate the metadata between servers. Hence each server will know what code exists on other servers, and can hence can request code from a server that is known to store it, instead of requesting code from all servers that it knows about. If this approach is combined with the gossip idea, it is likely that the code can be transported efficiently and effectively.

2.4 Client and Class Loader

The client operates by making use of a network class loader. This first attempts to find the class locally by searching the class path. If this fails, it makes an RMI method call to obtain a byte array with the class data and then makes use of Classloader methods defineClass() & resolveClass() to actually instantiate the class. Each class is stored in a hashtable when downloaded so that the class does not have to be downloaded again if it is reused. The client can make use of Java Reflection to determine what constructors, method names and class variables are available for a particular class. The client can either download a single class at a time, or choose to download an entire group at a time in order to minimise the number of RMI calls. We have also implemented a client that saves the bytecode to the local file system and then loads it like a 'normal' class in order to determine whether there is any overhead introduced by the network class loader. By default Java will attempt to verify the integrity of any code loaded via a network class loader, but not code loaded directly from the file system. Our performance measurements attempt to measure both approaches. We have previously investigated the throughput of the Code Server with authentication enabled [5]. In the DISCWorld framework, we assume that other DISCWorld nodes are trustworthy and our security framework only needs to verify that that the code does originate from where it is claimed to. Hence, digitally signing the code is a good way of achieving this, and in this case it is quite reasonable to disable verification of code by the Java Virtual Machine (JVM).

3 Performance

We have performed extensive testing of our Code Server to investigate the performance of the system. Our tests were intended to investigate a number of major issues. These include the portability of server and client across platforms, and influence of the JVM (version and platform) on performance. We also investigated the overhead introduced by RMI both in terms of initial binding and latency for each method call. Other issues include the influence of network factors, such as latency and bandwidth and the choice of database product on performance. We were not attempting to benchmark the performance of databases for complex queries, so all test queries simply involved searching by filename.

Our initial experiments made use of different versions of the JDK, and we found that most implementations of RMI prior to JDK 1.1.6 are defective. These early versions had memory leaks and problems with distributed garbage collection that cause them to crash after a period of time. We have not observed this behaviour when using JDK 1.1.6.

The measurements presented here are based on three series of tests. The first set of tests was devised to investigate the performance as a function of code size. The second set involves measuring the performance of a set of chained classes (classes that call each other). A set of ten classes was constructed, each of which had a method that simply instantiated the next class, and called the appropriate method on the this class. These tests were designed to allow us to investigate the latency of loading each class, and the trade offs associated with loading a group at a time. The final test compares the performance of an image processing example in the cases where we move the code to the data (using the Code Server) and the alternative of moving data to code. All tests were performed on relatively unloaded networks and hosts and for at least twenty iterations. Any results that we believed to be anomalous were repeated to confirm their accuracy. Measurements were performed by calling the System.currentTimeMillis() method of Java.

3.1 RMI Binding Overhead

Measured binding times for various client and server combinations are provided in table 3.1. Cairngorm and Turquoise are Digital Alpha Stations 255/300 located in Adelaide, Bremerer is an SUN Ultra-1 located in Adelaide, while dhpc01 and dhpc02 are Digital Alpha Stations 500/266 MHz located in Canberra. It is important to note that the Canberra Alphas are significantly faster than those at Adelaide. Canberra is approximately 1100 km from Adelaide, so the light speed limited latency for a round trip is about 7.5 ms. Using the Unix 'ping' command, the measured latency is about 16 ms. The measured binding times are about two orders of magnitude greater than this, and so the network latency appears to be a relatively minor component in the binding time. Issues such as the the hardware configuration of the machine and Java Virtual Machine type appear to be more important. From these figures we can conclude that the binding process, where an RMI client obtains a reference to a remote server object, is extremely inefficient. For the sockets based implementation, the initialisation time is of the order of a few hundred milliseconds: an order of magnitude less than for RMI. In the subsequent results, we do not include the binding times, and measure the time to obtain code from the Code Server assuming a remote reference already exists.

Client	Server	Time (s)
Alpha 255/300 (Adelaide)	Same as client	2.6
Alpha 255/300 (Adelaide)	Another Alpha 255/300 (Adelaide)	3.3
Ultra-1 (Adelaide)	Same as client (Adelaide)	4.0
Alpha 255/300 (Adelaide)	Alpha 500/266 (Canberra)	2.7
Alpha 255/300 (Canberra)	Same as client	1.2
Alpha 500/266 (Canberra)	Another Alpha 500/266 (Canberra)	1.7
Alpha 500/266 (Canberra)	Alpha 255/300 (Adelaide)	1.5

Table 3. RMI binding times

3.2 Influence of Class Size

For this test a set of classes of varying size were created. Each class had a filler method, which had a variable number of 'println' statements to pad the size. The classes also had a generic 'Hello World' method, which was the method actually called by the test client. For each client/server/database combination the following tests were performed. The results with the key 'verification' had verification by the Java interpreter enabled. Those labelled 'no verification' had the JVM verifier disabled. Those marked 'group' were performed by loading an entire group at a time with verification disabled. The 'socket' results used the version of the Code Server that used sockets instead of RMI, and also had verification disabled. Finally, the results labelled 'file' were those for which the code was saved to the file system and then loaded as 'normal' classes. These tests where also performed with verification disabled. Classes with sizes of between 1 kB and 200 kB were used in the tests. We found that the verifier could not verify classes with sizes greater than 50 kB on all platforms and JDK versions that we tested. We believe this to be a bug in the Java interpreter.

Timing measurements were made of both the time to bind to the RMI registry and get a reference to the remote object, and to obtain a class having previously obtained the reference. Measurements were made for Digital Alpha hosts located in Adelaide and Canberra. The hosts at Adelaide were Alpha Station 255/300s while those at Canberra were Alpha Station 500/266s. All hosts were equipped with 128 MB RAM and JDK 1.1.6 revision 2. Hosts at Adelaide were connected via a 10 Mb/s LAN while those at Canberra were connected by OC-3 ATM rated at 155 Mb/s. The link between Adelaide and Canberra was using AARNET with typical available bandwidth of about 4 Mb/s.

First we consider the case where client and server reside on the same host. These results can be seen in figure 1. In this case there is obviously no effect attributable to network issues. A number of conclusions can be drawn from these results. Firstly, it is obvious that verification of the bytecode is an expensive process. We believe that use of digital signatures is a better security mechanism in our system. It is also apparent that as class size increases the overhead associated with saving the bytecode to the file system and reloading it becomes quite significant. Thus there are no unexpected overheads associated with instantiating a class from bytecode in memory.

The performance of the sockets based version is very similar to the RMI version. This is somewhat surprising as given the large overheads of RMI for binding we might expect that there will also be significant overheads for each method call.We also see that the overall performance of the Canberra Alphas is superior due to their faster processors. An interesting point to note is that although the loading of the entire group (containing all of the test classes) is obviously a bad idea in this case, the overhead is surprisingly low. For example the overhead in the case of code size of 1 kB is a factor of four, despite loading 288 kB of code when only 1 kB was required. This is due to the large invocation overhead associated with making an RMI method call.

Now we consider performance across a LAN. These results are presented in figure 2. It is apparent that performance for small code sizes is quite variable. This is believed to be a TCP effect due to to Nagle's algorithm [14]. Nagle's algorithm restricts the number of outstanding small segments that have not been acknowledged to one for each TCP connection. Hence additional small segments will collected into a larger segment and sent when an acknowledgement for the outstanding segment is received. This algorithm is designed to reduce congestion in networks due to excessive numbers of small packets, but can also but can also increase the latency for sending a small message. The Digital Alphas computers used in our tests used a segment size 1500 bytes.

We believe that in JDK 1.1 it is not possible to alter the TCP settings used by RMI, and hence Nagle's algorithm can not be disabled. The upcoming JDK 1.2 release will have facilities for tuning the TCP settings used by RMI. The results for the Canberra LAN show that performance is virtually identical to the case where client and server were located on the same host. This shows that there is virtually no overhead introduced by using the network in this case, due to the presence of the 155 Mb/s ATM. In the case of the Adelaide LAN, where the network was 10 Mb/s Ethernet, some overhead was introduced when using the network. We again see that verification introduces significant overhead. Performance for both RMI and sockets based versions is quite similar. As expected in the case where a group was loaded at a time was roughly constant. Due to the faster network in Canberra, the case where files are saved to the file system is more expensive, on a relative basis, than at Adelaide. We also see that the trends are the same as for the case where client and server were on the same host, although actual measured values are higher.

Results of performance measurements between Adelaide and Canberra are presented in figure 3. These results are remarkably similar to the LAN measurements, given the much greater network latency and reduced bandwidth. The reduced bandwidth results in the performance of loading an entire group to be worse, although the worst case overhead is a factor of six. As discussed in section 3.1, client initialisation is significantly quicker for the sockets based version. It may be be better to have both versions running simultaneously and allow each client to determine which alternative is better in a particular case.

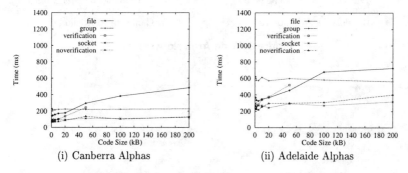

(i) Canberra Alphas   (ii) Adelaide Alphas

Figure 1. Client and Server on the same host

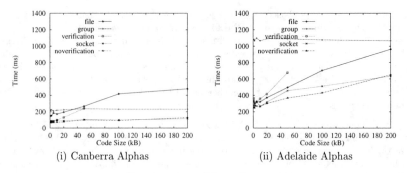

(i) Canberra Alphas   (ii) Adelaide Alphas

Figure 2. Local Area Network

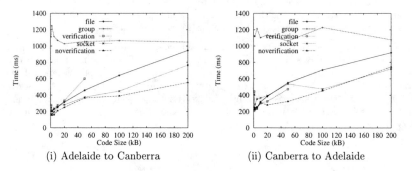

(i) Adelaide to Canberra   (ii) Canberra to Adelaide

Figure 3. Wide Area Network

3.3   Class Chaining

This test measures the performance of a set of classes that reference each other. The results are presented in figure 4. Results ending with '(single)' are for loading a single class at a time, those ending with '(group)' are for loading an entire group at a time, while those ending with '(direct)' are for tests where the client loaded the code directly from the local file system and did not make use of the Code Server. These last set of results are included to provide a baseline for the comparisons. As might be expected, in the case where classes are loaded one at a time, the time taken increases linearly with the number of classes that need to be loaded. In the case where a group is loaded at once, the execution time is roughly constant. For the Adelaide Ethernet based LAN the point at which it becomes more efficient to load a group at a time is between 2 and 3 classes, while the corresponding trade off point is between 4 and 5 classes for the ATM LAN in Canberra. The difference is most likely due to the fact that the machines in Adelaide are "slower", so that the overhead for each call to the server is higher. For the Wide Area tests between Adelaide and Canberra, the results show that the trade off point at which is is quicker to load a group at a time is between 1 and 2 classes for a client in Canberra connecting to a server in Adelaide, and between 4 and 5 classes for an Adelaide client connecting to a Canberra server. The results indicate that the biggest influence on performance is the "speed" of the server machine, not the network interconnect or latency.

For a particular application the trade off points will vary with class sizes and the number of classes in each group, but the above figures give an indication that effective use of grouping can substantially improve performance. It is important to note that the results presented here represent a worst case scenario as each class does nothing other than call the next one. In a more realistic situation some processing will be performed so the overhead compared to the direct case will be less. An interesting point to note is that in general, better performance is obtained by an Adelaide client obtaining a group of classes from Canberra than locally. This is another example of how network issues are less important than Java performance which is determined by the CPU of the host and JVM type.

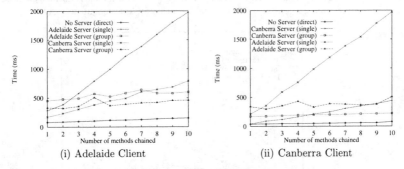

(i) Adelaide Client   (ii) Canberra Client

Figure 4. Class chaining

3.4   Other Performance Tests

The performance of the Code Server, working in distributed mode was also investigated. In these tests, a client at Adelaide first attempted to obtain code from a Code Server at Adelaide. The code was not available locally, so the Code Server forwards the request to a Code Server located in Canberra. We present results for these test in figure 5. Results are presented for loading a single class at time without verification, and loading groups at a time, for the case where the code is available locally and the case where it is not. For small code sizes, the overhead introduced by the distribution is minimal, and it increases with code size. This shows that the bandwidth is the limiting factor, not the latency.

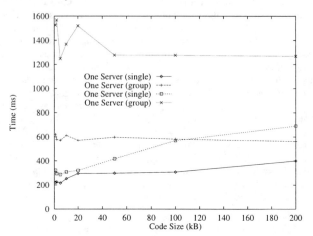

Figure 5. Distributed Code Server Performance

We also performed some tests to compare the influence of database type on performance. The results are presented for client and server on an UltraSparc-1 host with Informix and PostgreSQL databases in figure 6. It is evident that Informix offers superior performance, particularly in the case where classes are loading one at a time, resulting in many database accesses. This could be due to the PostgreSQL database driver creating a new connection for each database access while Informix creates a connection on initialisation and uses this for subsequent accesses.

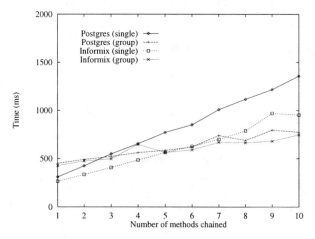

Figure 6. UltraSPARC Host:Comparing Informix and PostgreSQL

We also performed the tests using a RMI classloader to download the classes from a HTTP server in order to compare the performance of the Code Server with that of the more widely used approach of applets downloading byte code from a Web server. The results showed that there each call to the

RMIClassloader always incurs a significant fixed time cost of approximately 3 seconds, as compared with a once off similar cost for the Code Server as outlined in 3.1.

In the initial prototype system that we are building we are using imaging functions to investigate the Code Server performance for real world applications. We currently archive images from the GMS5 satellite, and we consider the particular example of calculation of percentage cloud cover for these images [7]. Every hour, we obtain four 8 bit raster images (1 visual & 3 infrared) each of which is 2291 by 2291 pixels in size. Uncompressed, each of these images is over 5.2 MB in size, and even when compressed the images are still quite large. (The exact size varies significantly with time of day). Finding cloud involves looking for 'cold & bright' areas, and requires analysis of a visual image and one of the infra red bands. The final result required is a scalar percentage value. The Java bytecode to perform the analysis is under 10 kB in size, while the data required over 10 MB uncompressed (for two images), and on average 4-5 MB when compressed using unix compress or gzip.

We performed tests with the client (the host with the image) data at Adelaide and server at Canberra and vice versa. The two cases we considered were firstly where the Code Server was used to download the code to the client site, and in the second case the file was transferred to the server using the Unix 'rcp' (remote copy) command and then the code was directly executed locally. As we expected, the results show that use of the Code Server provides a substantial improvement in performance. This improvement would be magnified in an environment with lower network bandwidth availability. The results of the tests are provided in table 4 below. In this case the overhead introduced by the Code Server is minimal compared to the overhead of moving the data required by the operation.

Client	Server	Remote Copy time (s)	Execution time without Code Server (s)	Total time without Code Server (s)	Execution time with Code Server (s)
Alpha 255/300 (Adelaide)	Alpha 500/266 (Canberra)	21	4.0	25.0	5.4
Alpha 500/266 (Canberra)	Alpha 255/300 (Adelaide)	21	3.6	24.6	4.0

Table 4. Percentage Cloud Cover Calculations

4   Conclusions and Future Work

We have described our Code Server and discussed how we addressed the various issues that arose during it's design and implementation. The performance results show the Code Server is a viable means of facilitating the dynamic movement of code.

The results show that in a typical scenario where an operation requires a number of small class files, the Code Server introduces an overhead of a few hundred milliseconds for a typical system. We see that the overhead is mainly due to latency that can be attributed to the Java virtual machine and RMI and that network latency has a relatively minor effect in typical cases. This may change in the future as the efficiency of the available JVMs improves. Our results show that verification of the Java bytecode by the JVM is expensive, and we suggest that digital signatures are a better alternative. They also reveal that appropriate use of groups in our system can provide a substantial boost in performance, as well as helping to deal with naming conflicts. In the Code Server system, we have found that although RMI introduces significant initialisation overheads compared to sockets, once a remote object reference is obtained the time to obtain each class or group of classes is comparable in both cases.

Future work on the system that we are planning include investigating issues that arise through extending the distribution framework, such as suitable protocols for finding a server with the appropriate code and for the sharing of information about code between servers and also suitable policy for determining what metadata and codes should be stored locally by each server. An enhancement that could improve the performance for large byte classes under some circumstances is to compress the bytecode being transmitted, and we would also like to investigate the performance tradeoffs associated with this approach.

5 Acknowledgements

This was work was carried out under the Distributed High Performance Computing Infrastructure (DHPC-I) project and the Online Data Archives (OLDA) program of the Advanced Computational Systems (ACSys) Cooperative Research Centre (CRC). This work was funded by the Research Data Networks (RDN) CRC. ACSys and RDN are funded under the Australian Commonwealth Government's CRC program.

References

[1] "CORBA/IIOP 2.0 Specification", http://www.omg.org/corba, July 1998.

[2] "Federating Traders: an ODP Adventure", Corba Services 2.0 Specification, Chapter 16. http://www.omg.org/corba, July 1998.

[3] "Dublin Core Metadata Element Set: Resource Page", see WWW address http://purl.oclc.org/metadata/dublin_core/, July 1998

[4] "Java Language Specification", James Gosling, Bill Joy and Guy Steele", Pub. Addison Wesley, 1996.

[5] "Authenticated Transmission of Discoverable Portable Code Objects in a Distributed Computing Environment", D.A. Grove, A.J. Silis, J.A. Mathew and K.A.Hawick, To appear Proc. Int. Conf. Parallel and Distributed Processing Techniques and Applications (PDPTA) 1998. Also available as DHPC Technical Report DHPC-027, April 1998. http://www.dhpc.adelaide.edu.au/reports/

[6] "DISCWorld: An Environment for Service-Based Metacomputing", K.A. Hawick, P.D. Coddington, D.A. Grove, J.F. Hercus, H.A. James, K.E. Kerry, J.A. Mathew, C.J. Patten, Andrew Silis, F.A. Vaughan, invited paper for a special issue of the Journal of Future Generation Systems, to be published. Also available as DHPC Technical Report DHPC-042, April 1998. http://www.dhpc.adelaide.edu.au/reports/

[7] "A Web-based Interface for On-Demand Processing of Satellite Imagery Archives", H.A. James and K.A. Hawick, Proc ACSC'98 Perth, Februray 1998. Also available as DHPC Technical Report DHPC-018, April 1998. http://www.dhpc.adelaide.edu.au/reports/

[8] "Informix WWW Site", http://www.informix.com, July 1998

[9] "JAR Guide", http://www.javasoft.com/products/jdk/1.1/docs/guide/jar/jarGuide.html, 1998

[10] "Querying and Auxiliary Data in the DISCWorld" J.A.Mathew, K.A.Hawick, Proc 5th IDEA Workshop, Freemantle, February 1998. Also available as DHPC Technical Report DHPC-030, January 1998. http://www.dhpc.adelaide.edu.au/reports/

[11] "The Essential CORBA: Systems Integration Using Distributed Object", Thomas J. Mowbray & Ron Zahavi, John Wiley & Sons, Inc., 1995.

[12] "PostgresSQL WWW Site", http://www.postgres.org, July 1998

[13] "The Artificial Life Route to Artificial Intelligence", Luc Steels, Rodney Brooks (Editors), Pub Lawrence Erlbaum Associates, 1995

[14] "TCP/IP Illustrated Volume 1", W. Richard Stevens, Addison-Wesley 1994.

Session 6

Software Architecture

A Simple Architecture Description Model

Andry Rakotonirainy and Andy Bond
{andry,andy}@dstc.edu.au
CRC for Distributed Systems Technology
Level 7, General Purpose South,
University of Queensland 4072 - Australia

Abstract

This paper presents a simple composable architecture description model. Components are core modeling concepts. Components describe their relationship with other components by means of interface provision and requirement descriptions. These interfaces define the connectors that structure and compose components together.

1: Introduction

Distributed object technology and middleware products have shown their ability to ease the design of a system. Although those concepts are very useful for creating "connectivity" between objects; they fail to meet the composition and re-use features that were promised with the advent of distributed object computing. This is not a technology failing but rather a symptom of the unbalanced relationship between interacting components.

Future software needs a framework to build applications from the composition of components rather than building separate applications which interact to form a software system. The difference here is a recognition of the composition itself as a separate building block in the construction of interacting components. Unfortunately the only abstraction features that current Object Oriented (OO) technology offers is the class which is not good enough to build and compose different components.

The composition feature is crucial to the next generation of software because software needs to evolve and adapt to new requirements over its lifetime. The composition framework can provide this adaption without needing to change existing objects. A range of Architecture Description Language (ADL) have been developed by software engineers in an attempt to meet this compositional challenge.

ADLs are high level descriptions that aim to model distributed enterprise systems in terms of components and interconnections between components. They are reference models that every component must follow to inter-operate. They feature a conceptual framework and a language for component composition. ADL is meant to ease the plug-and-play of heterogenous components to build new software.

Despite their interesting features, most ADLs are either too abstract (formal) or do not exhibit features that allow description of specific domain requirements such as security and QoS specification [6, 4, 10, 3, 5].

0-7695-0053-6/98 $10.00 © 1998 IEEE

This paper proposes a model that has the following advantages compared to existing ADLs. Our model

- captures the natural way we see components interacting by means of a network of components where a subset of components require another subset to provide a given service,
- maps (refines) easily to existing programming languages so that component instantiation and interaction is straightforward and doesn't require complex refinement,
- explicitly describes the distribution of components,
- facilitates the composition of components (adaptability),
- supports QoS specification, and
- will be implemented easily on the top of existing distributed object environments such as CORBA

The remainder of this paper is organised as follows. The next Section presents an architecture description model. Section 3.1 shows how we specify composition of components, QoS and adaptability. Section 4 gives a tentative syntax for our architecture model as well as outlining some engineering consoderations. Section 5 describes a scenario. The conclusion and future work is given in section 6 and section 7.

2: Component Architecture

It is necessary to distinguish actions that a component can provide from the events it awaits. The interaction relationship in the client/server (and thus the remote method invocation in distributed object systems) is unbalanced. The server publishes the provision of its service through an interface definition but the client using the service makes no such external publication of its requirements. Our model advances beyond the client/server paradigm to treat objects as peers with a set of interface requirements and provisions. The relationship between interfaces used and provided by a component may be conditional on the fulfilment or some quality characteristics on other interfaces.

2.1: Assumptions

Before introducing our ADL, we describe our assumptions :

- All objects can be encapsulated and accessed within an ORB environment. We use OMG IDL [8] to describe interfaces provided by and used by an object. This significantly simplifies the complexity of the composition feature of our ADL.
- An object guarantees interface provision once the interface requirements have been fulfilled. This simplifies reasoning about Quality of Service.

The above assumptions hve been put forward from observations of IT trends where the OMG is starting to be a de facto standard and on maturing QoS work in ODP [7].

2.2: Components

Components are a software abstraction. In OO terminology, a component is a set of interacting objects (or even a single object). An object has states which are visible to the environment and some which are not. Visible states are represented through interfaces. Interfaces describe event (operation, signal, stream) interaction behaviour between the object and its environment.

The interfaces of components are classified into *Require*, *Provide* and *Management* interfaces. The *Require* interfaces describe what a component requires from its environment. *Provide* interfaces describe what it can provide to its environment. By assuming that an object will behave provided that the environment does, such an approach eases the reasoning about Quality of Service. The *Management* interface allows the update of *Require* and *Provide* interfaces in terms of removing or adding object behaviour.

Concretely, a component has three types of interfaces. They are:

- Provide: describes a set of interfaces that an object can provide. The description is given as a set of CORBA interface references.

- Require: a set of interfaces describing the dependencies of this object to its environment. The environment comprises other components. The description references CORBA interfaces which this object depends upon.

- Management: *(i)* contains a high level description of the behavioural interaction of *Require* and *Provide* interfaces. *(ii)* provides a means to add or remove interfaces belonging to *Require* and *Provide* interfaces. *(iii)* provides means to change the above behaviour.

The Management interface allows us to enrich a component dynamically. For example a component could initially have only the Management interface with which *Provide* and *Require* interfaces are added and modified. Modifying a *Require* or *Provide* interface implies the change of the whole system since the system is a network of components glued with *Require* and *Provide* interface descriptions.

Figure 1 shows that our architecture has two levels. The upper level is the component architecture description (grey boxes). A component is a first class object that exhibits the structure or the relationship between distributed components. Arrows between components represent the relations that have been fulfilled in terms of Require and Provide. The lower level is the IDL (CORBA) description of objects. Note that the mapping between component and object can be one-to-many and does not necessarily need complex refinement.

3: Expressiveness of our Model

Most known ADL have the notion of "connector" to glue components together. Our model does not explicitly have such a concept. However the tuple $< Require, Provide >$ can be considered the equivalent of a connector. The rest of this section shows the expressiveness of our model by using the core model in the context of composition, QoS and adaptability.

3.1: Composition

Composition is the process of building a component by connecting a set of other components. Our model support hierarchical composition. Meaning that a set of components can be abstracted away into a single component that *Provide* and *Require* a set of services based on what the set of composed components may provide and require.

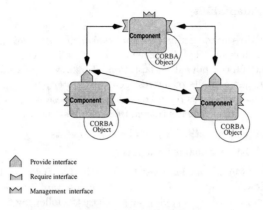

Provide interface

Require interface

Management interface

Figure 1. Component Architecture

An application is represented as a set of components that have fulfilled the required connections between *Provide* and *Require* interfaces. The rest of this section shows the rules that govern the composition of *Provide* and *Require* interfaces.

Two interfaces can be connected if they are complementary:

$$\overline{Provide} = Require$$

The complementary property can be as trivial as matching names (Trader) or more complex such as a subtype relationship. The Provide statement can fulfill the Require statement if they are compatible. A call to an event in *Require* becomes a call in the *Provide* statement.

During the composition one might use the Management interface of an object in order to check the consistency of the composition. Checking the compatibility between require and provide clauses will implicitly generate a checking of all require/provide clauses of all components that each involved component depends upon. This paper does not address consistency checking issues.

3.2: QoS and Component Configuration

QoS specification pertains to the non-functional properties of a service. It is a set of quality requirements on the collective behaviour of one or more objects [7].

QoS specification should assert that the system performs properly if the environment does; it should not assert that the environment performs properly [1]. Thus in order to build distributed systems with QoS requirements, we need to specify two statements. A statement describing the advertised QoS (using connection constraints from the Provide clause) and a statement describing the environmental constraints associated with the advertised QoS (Require statement).

An overall system satisfies its QoS specification if all its individual components satisfy their specification. Thus the *Require* statement of each individual component is the necessary post condition for the fulfilment of the overall composed QoS.

Our component model was designed with support of QoS in mind. It's one of the major reason why we included the *Require* and *Provide* statements in the core component model.

3.3: Supporting Adaptability

Adaptability features allow components to evolve and dynamically change their behaviour during their lifetime. The Management interface is in charge of all static and dynamic configuration of a component. Adaptation, also known as dynamic re-configuration, consists of watching some events of interest generated internally or from the environment and taking appropriate action, as required, to adjust to these new environment conditions. There are two separate requirements that must be addressed:

- Watching/Emitting quantifiable and observable events.
- Taking action that reconfigures components.

The ability to perform adaptation must be advertised at the same time as the interface of a component. However, instead of advertising the adaptability rules entirely, which are basically Event/Condition/Action tuples, we publicise the following functions as interfaces.

- The ability of a component to consume and emit events.
- Management functions that allow the addition/removal the *Require/Provide* interface and associated behaviour.

Such externalisation is useful for composition where the management flow of significant events within the environment must be handled carefully by components designer [1].

All components are bound together via their *Require* and *Provide* statements; a change in one of the statements (links) will change the topology of the network of components. Thus the whole set of components will adapt themselves to meet the new requirement. One might limit the propagation of adaptability to avoid the domino effect by specifying *profiles*. Profiles are policies that allow the user to customise the adaptation rules.

4: Description of Components

One way to specify a component is to add three keywords (Require, Provide, Management) in the CORBA IDL. However our aim is not to develop a new compiler to support our framework. Therefore we've chosen a simpler approach which consists of using the current IDL compiler and specify component in Python on top of it as suggested in Figure 1. In this section we will presents the basic syntax through an example but first we must consider some engineering issues.

4.1: Engineering Considerations

The component framework has been prototyped in Python and the DSTC Object Request Broker called Fnorb [2]. We use these tools to illustrate our architecture throughout this section.

The implementation of the components were in Python. The reflection power of python allows us to access the object namespaces and do runtime evaluation. Object implementations and thus interface provision can be added or removed dynamically in Fnorb and Python.

---

[1]Note that we do not introduce a special notation to specify event management for the sake of simplicity.

The binding between the *require* statement and fulfilling *provide* statement is completed with a trader. Interfaces are advertised in the trader. The trader together with a factory object will instantiate a component that matches the required interface of another component.

The requirements of the object that the trader has chosen must also be fulfilled. All requirements of each component have to be fulfilled and instantiated before going further.

4.2: Simple Description Example

We will go through an example to show how a component is described. IDLs are merely imported. By importing IDL we actually import the automatically generated skeleton and the stub of the interface. IDL's are included either in the *Require* or *Provide* statements. In the following example, interfaces *foo.groucho* and *foo.harpo* are used in the Require statement. Interfaces *bar.mickey*, *foo.chico*, and *bar.minnie* are what the component provides.

The management interface inherit from a generic Management interface where methods to add, remove, and view the behaviour are defined. Thus our Management specification inherits from the *_GenericManagement* class, it allows us to add/remove *Require* and *Provide* interfaces and their associated behaviour. A Behaviour is merely a piece of code (Python in our case) providing the semantics referred to in *Require* and *Provide*. In the following example Behaviour specifies that a call from the method *foo.harpo.baz* must precede that of *bar.mickey.boodle*.

```
#
# A component that uses foo and bar modules
#

#import the skeleton and stubs of modules
import foo.idl, bar.idl

component  A_SimpleComponent:
   Require:          # required interfaces
     foo.groucho, foo.harpo
   Provide:          # provided interfaces
     bar.mickey, foo.chico, bar.minnie
   Management(_GenericManagement):
      ...
     # method foo.harpo.baz must be executed before bar.mickey.boodle
     Behaviour =    ''foo.harpo.baz; bar.mickey.boodle''
      ...
end component
```

Currently we do not restrict the behaviour syntax for the sake of simplicity. The use of Python to describe the behaviour gives us the possibility to have complex synchronisation such as $if - then - else$ or guards between interfaces.

The dynamic addition of a *Provide* statement can be achieved in two ways:

- by adding the reference (IOR) of an interface instance, or

- by sending the IDL together with the implementation. In this case the skeleton will be generated on the fly from the IDL and the new interface will be registered.

We assume that if an interface is removed then all information related to the removed interface (including behaviour) must also be removed to have a consistent specification. It means that an addition or remove of an interface can be refused or might be the subject of negotiation.

5: Scenario

The following example demonstrates how we perform adaptability and support QoS.

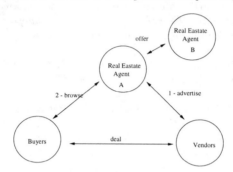

Figure 2. Component Architecture

Let's assume we model three parties involved in a real estate purchase. The three components are Buyer, Agent A , and Vendor. During runtime the Agent includes offers from others, say Agent B described in figure 2. Although the interaction between these components might be complicated we give a simplified version.

1. Vendors advertise their merchandise to the agent.
2. A Buyer browses the agent catalogue with more than 100 entries.
3. A Buyer contacts the vendor through the agent and makes a deal.
4. Another real estate agent collaborates with the current agent to enrich its offers.

```
#  Real Eastate Agent initialisation
import Buyer, Vendor, Watch
....
Require = Vendor.offer , Watch.offer
Provide =  Buyer.browse > 100 entries
# Behaviour , offers must precede  list, browse and buy
behaviour = ''Vendors.offer;Buyer.browse;Buyer.buy''
#create a component
comp  = component(Behaviour,Require,Provide)
Watch(subscribe(''newAgent''), do_this)
...
```

Agent A is dynamically notified by the event notification service that Agent B has made an offer. The *do_this* function described below is executed and the Behaviour is changed, the provided QoS is increased and the new Agent is added to the *Require* clause in order to guarantee the newly arranged QoS.

```
def do_this(newAgent):
    ...
    #Dynamic modification of component
    # add the newagent offer in the behaviour
    Behaviour = ''newAgent.offer;'' + Behaviour
    # offers from newAgents are now required.
    Require =  Require + newAgent.offer
    # The QoS is better provided that Require is fullfilled
    Provide = Buyer.browse > 10.000 entries
    management.add(Behaviour,Require,Provide)
    ...
```

6: Related work

A good Architecture Description Language should provide three separate mechanisms. They are *Components*, *Connectors* and *Configuration*. Most ADLs, including our framework, include these characteristics in different ways.

Unfortunately, there is no common method to achieve the refinement of such specification into implementation. There is still a gap between the ADL specification and the middleware. We believe that a mixture of an OO language, CORBA and a scripting language is the natural way to tackle the software architecture refinement.

Although OO in general has been widely proved to be good software engineering practice, they somehow lack the notion of *Connectors* which is usually hidden behind interfaces.

CORBA, JavaBeans, design patterns, and VisualAge products provide helpful mechanisms and tools to achieve introspection (publish operation), properties (control over layout of component), customisation (control over changes that each component requires), high level abstraction to describe a system and the possibility of coupling the abstractions to some underlying implementation. Though useful, each tackles a specific domain and fails to provide a graceful way to describe connectors or the overall architecture style.

7: Conclusion

Our approach avoids having a global view of the distributed interconnection between components as we see in many ADL [4, 7, 10, 5]. Such ADLs are hard to implement and manage in a distributed system.

Our model can be considered a partial description of interaction between ODP [7, 9] roles but we feel the requirement propagation fills many of the requirements from the ODP binding world. From such a partial description we can always build the entire ODP binding from a connection of components.

This paper has described a simple architecture model easy to implement on top of OMG CORBA architecture. Our architecture allows us to describe the distributed structure of the system from a local view of a component. It also allows us to build a system with QoS requirements. The major contribution of this paper is its simple refinement from the component architecture description level to the existing CORBA architecture.

Acknowledgments

The work reported in this paper has been funded in part by the Cooperative Research Centres Program through the department of the Prime Minister and Cabinet of the Commonwealth Government of Australia.

References

[1] M. Abadi, L. Lamport "Composing Specifications " *DEC Technical report 66, October 1990*

[2] M.Chilvers " An Object Request Broker in Python" *http://www.dstc.edu.au/Fnorb/*

[3] P. Clements , L. Northrop, "Software Architecture: An Executive Overview" *Technical Report CMU/SEI-96-TR-003 - http://www.sei.cmu.edu/publications/documents/96.reports/96.tr.003.html*

[4] D. Luckam, J.Kenney, L. Augustin, J.Vera, D.Bryan, W. Mann "Specification and analysis of system architecture using Rapide." *IEEE Transactions on Software Engineering, 21(4): April 1995*

[5] J. Magee, N. Dulay, S. Eisenbach and J. Kramer "Specifying Distributed Software Architectures" *In Proceedings of 5th European Software Engineering Conference (ESEC 95), Sitges, Spain, September 1995*

[6] N. Medvidovic, R Taylor "A Framework for Classifying and Comparing Architecture Description Language " *Proc Software engineering Notes, ESEC/FSE'96 - LNCS Vol 22 numer 6 - November 1997*

[7] ISO/IEC 10746-1 10746-2 10746-3. " Basic Reference for Open Distributed Processing." *http://www.iso.ch:8000/RM-ODP*

[8] The Object Management Group. " Architecture and Specification Rev 2 " *http://www.omg.org/*

[9] A.Rakotonirainy, A.Berry, S.Crawley, Z.Milosevic " Describing Open Distributed Systems: A foundation". *The computer Journal Vol 40, No 8, 1997*

[10] M. Shaw and D. Garlan "Software Architecture: Perspectives on an Emerging Discipline". *Prentice Hall, 1996.*

Manifolds:
Cellular Component Organizations

Charles Herring and Simon Kaplan
{herring,kaplan}@dstc.edu.au

Department of Computer Science and Electrical Engineering
CRC for Distributed Systems Technology
The University of Queensland
Brisbane, Queensland QLD 4072

Abstract

This extended abstract reports on initial investigation into a software architecture for component systems. Described is a geometrically-based, cellular framework for the organization of component computation and communication. These structures are called Cellular Component Manifolds. The starting point for this work is the observation that the concept of address space is a pervasive abstraction across all computing and communicating systems. Accordingly, a generalized model of an idealized address space is proposed. A particular geometry with a suitable algebraic structure is chosen to provide addressing within this model. This results in an n-dimensional, hierarchical, cellular-aggregate address space that is also a vector space with "nice" properties. The address space, when populated with suitable components, becomes a Cellular Component Manifold. A component system architecture is given. This software architecture consists of three major layers: component framework framework, component frameworks, and components. In addition to providing a basis for component system organization this structure natively supports a range of scientific and engineering applications. As an example, the architecture is applied to the problem of handoff management in wireless overlay networks.

1: Introduction

The component-oriented approach to software construction and deployment within economically viable component market places apparently represents the next stage in the evolution of software practice. However, there are few examples of component systems, i.e., component frameworks and component system architectures. Thus far developers have concentrated primarily on individual, isolated components and today there are only basic component interoperation facilities. If components are to achieve the impact that many are hoping for, discovery of organizing principles enabling design and development of component system architectures is required. The search for such organizing principles on which to base component system architectures motivates the work described in this paper.

The component architecture presented here came about by examining a wide range of computing and communications system with the goal of identifying key abstractions that are present in all systems. This search revealed the concepts of **address, addressing and address spaces** to be fundamental abstractions across all systems. This is true as all entities in computing and communications systems must be referenced by numeric labels - addresses. Human-friendly character strings, such as file names and URL's, are always mapped to numbers at some lower level in the system.

Now, systems evolve over time and the global communications and computer networks have been built up, subsystem by subsystem, layer by layer, over the last hundred or so years. However, systems are rarely designed to operate over more than one address space. Addressing within the various layers and subsystems are ad hoc, determined by preexisting conditions, or forced by hardware. As systems mature and more complex interconnections become desirable and feasible, these systems are required to communicate across subsystem boundaries. Usually some sort of address translation or mapping can be arranged.

The focus on the concept of address space as central to future component systems is driven, in part, by the fact that computing and communications technologies are rapidly coming together to form a global, integrated, information infrastructure. Major trends driving this merger are:

- Integration of telephony, television, and computer networks
- Integration of wireline and wireless networks
- High bandwidth, low latency communications
- Ubiquitous computing
- Smart buildings and smart appliances.

These developments are prompting a rethinking of the fundamental structure of basic support systems such as operating systems and network protocols. In order to realize the potential of greater functionality, recognition and promotion of new levels of abstraction in software architectures is required. Research projects driven by these forces include next-generation distributed operating systems such as Sun's Jini [1], and Microsoft's Millennium [2]; and integration of heterogeneous wireless networks as in the Wireless Overlay Network effort at UC Berkeley [3]. The position taken here is that addressing is at the heart of many critical architectural issues, e.g. scalability and seamlessness, that motivate these and other projects.

The rest of the paper is organized as follows. Section 2 explores the concept of address space in some detail to bring out the essential features that must be present in any general model. Based on this analysis, an initial generalized address space model is outlined in Section 3. This model includes the basic notions of centers, boundaries, boundary crossing, and hierarchy. The next step is incorporation of an addressing scheme within the model. The search for an appropriate addressing system resulted in choosing a particular geometric structure. This geometric system, the Generalized Balanced Ternary, is briefly described in Section 4. The result of combining this geometric addressing scheme with the general model results in a hierarchical, n-dimensional cellular-aggregate address space that is also a vector space with "nice" properties. This structure, when populated with components, is a called a Cellular Component Manifold. Instances of these are the "containers" for software components. How a component system architecture based on this structure might be organized is the subject of Section 5. An example is developed in Section 6 to illustrate the proposed use and benefits of the component organization. The example concentrates on one critical aspect of wireless systems: the handoff of a mobile host between stations.

2: The Address Space Concept

In every area of computing and communications addresses, in some form, exists. Perhaps the most familiar address spaces are in the context of operating systems where memory management is a major concern. There, several types of address spaces are recognized and their structures are described in detail. In networking, e.g. IPv6 addressing, great care is taken to provide a suitable addressing scheme for routing and other network management needs. However, it appears not to have been necessary to develop a general model or theory about this central abstraction. (In conducting a literature review one title did give hope: "A Grand Unified Theory of Address Space" [4]. Alas, it only covered operating systems.) The task of this section is to identify the key aspects of addressing and address space common to all systems on which a model can be based.

Looking down from outer space on the global information infrastructure the first structures we see are the various satellite communications systems. Zooming in closer we see microwave transmission towers, telephone poles, etc. If we could see through the skin of the Earth we would see coax cables, fiber and power lines. Continuing in this manner we see WANs, MANs, and LANs. Soon we are inside a computer "looking" at its hardware and software internals. At each step in our zooming we are crossing levels of the system. Large software systems, such as operating systems and network protocols, are (at least conceptually) made up of layers that encapsulate and shield implementation details from higher layers. Within each level, the subsystems that make up that level are defined by their boundaries with neighboring subsystems. These boundaries are usually different address spaces. Thus complex systems are composed of layers or hierarchies of subsystems. Subsystems are identified by boundaries between address spaces.

The concept of an address space takes many forms and is known by many names. Some examples will illustrate. The most familiar use of the concept is in relation to operating system processes. The address space of a process is that portion of memory allocated to it by the operating system. Internally it is divided into regions such as the stack, heap, etc. where threads belonging to the process manipulate code and data. Another example is the Internet Protocol that relies on the use of a 32-bit address containing the network and host identifiers for packet routing. There are several layers of addressing in IP such as the Address Resolution Protocol that maps IP addresses to 48-bit Ethernet addresses. The concept of Name Space is also related and provides a human readable mapping to underlying numerical address space notations as in DNS. A cell in a GSM telephone system is another example. There are several possible address spaces of interest in this complex system. The physical extent of the cell is one. Each subscriber within the cell is located at a physical address expressible in some real world coordinate system. The number and range of frequencies available for control, transmission and reception might be another.

An address space is a *homogeneous* region from the standpoint of higher level systems. The operating system allocates a range of memory to a process and turns it over to the application. It is the lower subsystem, e.g. user application, that organizes that memory allotment into regions, (e.g. stack, heap, invocation frames, data.) To the operating system it is a chunk of memory that is now someone elses responsibility – almost. The operating system manages the life cycle of that piece of memory. It must also handle exceptional events related to the process. That is, events generated by the subsystem may be passed up to the operating system. A classic event in this case is an unresolved pointer reference. In a virtual memory operating system, a number of possible actions may take place based on this event. These range from swapping memory from disk to termination of the process – all operating system decisions. In the case of the cellular telephone system, a basic event is the "handoff" when a subscriber passes out of range of its current base station and is passed off to another station.

To summarize, the above examples show several important aspects of multi-level systems and their subsystems. Large systems organize themselves hierarchically a means of managing complexity and achieving scalability. At each level there are subsystems that interact with other subsystems at the same level and may interact with subsystems at both higher and lower levels. Systems are defined by boundaries. Address spaces are homogeneous regions, defined by boundaries, whose life-cycle and exception handling is the responsibility of systems higher in the hierarchy. Various subsystems may collaborate to utilize the address space. Interaction requires that information pass across boundaries. Information passes between these subsystems as boundary crossing events that may trigger the interest of higher system levels. The work of the next section is to specify a model that captures the above features.

3: The Generalized Address Space Model

A simple conceptual model of an idealized address space is *outlined* in this section. The characteristics of address spaces identified in the previous section are restated as the minimum requirements for this general model:

- Supports hierarchical, layered, and/or nested configurations of component subsystems
- Boundaries can be identified and defined
- Supports an addressing or indexing scheme
- Is n-dimensional in general.

An address space does not exist for its own sake. It provides a structure to support components (objects, entities) and permit operations such as communications between components. The goal of the general model is to capture the basic "patterns" of component interaction within an address space. The following components are chosen to accomplish this:

Address Space Manager (ASM): The ASM manages and services the components residing within its assigned address space. It knows the types and locations (addresses) of all components. It knows the range of its addresses and can read from and write values to those addresses. It knows the addresses of its nearest neighboring ASM's and the address of the ASM at the next level in the system. If it is asked to access an address outside of its range it will do one of two things. First, it can determine if the requested address lies within the range of addresses managed by one of its neighbors. In this case it will ask the neighboring, "horizontal", ASM to perform the read or write on its behalf. Otherwise, the address is not within the range of a neighbor and it will ask the ASM at the next higher level, "vertically", to provide the needed service (read or write a value).

Boundary Manager (BM): The BM handle boundary crossing events as directed by the ASM. Bound crossing events include reading and writing to addresses in other address spaces. An address space may have boundaries with different types of address spaces necessitating different types of BM. Also, there may be more than one type of boundary crossing for a given boundary. When called upon by the ASM, the BM establishes contact with a BM in the neighboring address space to provide the requested action, i.e. fetch a value. Use of components in lower layers in the hierarchy may be required.

Services Manager (SM): It is convenient for now to identify the role of a SM to provide anticipated functions such as persistence, transactions, translation, query, etc.

Fixed User (FU): In this simple model the only behavior of the FU is to read and write values to addresses. It has a fixed immutable address within the address space. Addresses for reading and writing are not constrained to be within the FU's address space.

Mobile User (MU): The MU is a FU that can "move" between address spaces and still be written to (receive) values at its "home address". This implies support for a scheme like Mobile IP in that the MU will be assigned a new address as it moves into a new address space, leave a "forwarding address" as it moves around, etc.

Again, the goal of this model is to capture the fundamental patterns of component interaction in an address space. An example will help. When an FU tries to read the value of a foreign address space, the ASM invokes a BM to handle fetching the value from the neighboring address space. The BM contacts the BM in the foreign address space. A number of operations (marshaling, translation, etc) results in the FU ultimately getting the value across the address space boundary. This is the essential pattern found in systems such as virtual memory and distributed programming (DCOM, CORBA). The notion of "vertical" as well as "horizontal" coordination among the hierarchy of ASM's will be important later. The next step in the development of the model is to give it a proper addressing mechanism.

4: A Geometric Foundation

A geometric construct is chosen as the basis for addressing in the hierarchical, n-dimensional address space model. In searching for a sound basis for the address space model, a structure called the *Generalized Balanced Ternary (GBT)* was uncovered. This section gives the briefest possible overview of GBT, some background and a more detailed description is on line at [5] and [6].

GBT is a hierarchical, uniformly adjacent, addressing system defined on Euclidean n-space. It was developed by Lucas [7] and applied by him and others to support a range of scientific and engineering applications. (Vince offers a thorough treatment of addressing in self-replicating structures including GBT [8] and is highly recommended.) Lucas discovered an algebraic system permitting the construction of vector spaces in n-dimensions that support vector addition and multiplication. GBT is an algebra defined on a lattice of cells. This lattice is the hexagonal tiling in 2-dimensions. The addresses of cells are a generalization of the Knuth's *Balanced Ternary* [9] to 2-dimensions and is a base 7 system. The labeling of cells is geometrically arranged such that powers of two are maximally distant and uniform. This is done to simplify mathematical operations. A first level aggregate is shown in Figure 1. Note that 7 is used as the address of the overall aggregate.

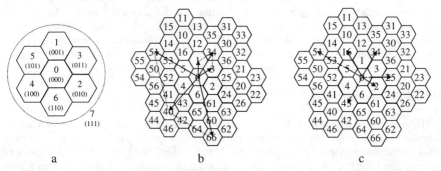

a   b   c

Figure 1. Level-1 aggregate (a), Level-2 aggregate showing addition (b) and multiplication (c).

At each hierarchical level cells are defined as aggregates of lower level cells. A second level aggregate is also shown in Figure 1 and is composed of a central cell and six surrounding cells. Now we look at how addition and multiplication are performed based on this system of addressing. From the level-1 aggregate we see that 1+2 = 3, 1+ 4 = 5, and so on. However, 1+3 lies outside the level-1 aggregate. As shown in Figure 1, the sum of 1 and 3 being 34. Also shown is the sum 51+66 = 40. Using the level-2 aggregate a table of "carries" and

292

"remainders" for addition is easily constructed. Examples of multiplication are also shown in Figure 1. There, 34 multiplied by the unit-length vector 2 to yield 16. Note the effect of multiplication by the unit vector results in a 60^0 rotation. The second example is 43 * 25 = 51. A "remainders" table for multiplication can be constructed and is equivalent to multiplication in the complex plane.

It is seen from the above examples that a GBT address is a sequence of integers that specify a "path" to a particular cell. The addresses are written left to right with the most significant digit on the left. The most significant digit represents the highest level aggregate, the next digit the next level aggregate and so on. An address of the form 67, for example, represents the aggregate containing all lower cells whose first digit is 6, i.e. 60 - 66.

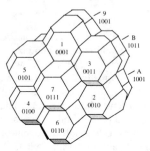

Figure 2. 3-Dimensional level-1 aggregate.

The GBT cells in 3-dimensions are truncated octahedra that pack 15 around 1. Thus a first level aggregate will consist of 16 cells as shown in Figure 2. The cells are labeled 0... E with 0 being the central cell and F referring to the overall aggregate (just as 7 is used in the 2-dimensional case). From the 2-dimensional examples of addressing, addition and multiplication it can be seen how similar operations can be developed for three and higher dimensions. Space does not permit further exposition of the GBT addressing system. The important concepts to take away from this section are that this structure is a hierarchical, uniformly adjacent, addressing system in n-dimensions that endows Euclidean space with a algebra that provides a vector space with "nice" properties such as addition and multiplication. This type of structure is required by engineering and scientific applications such as computer vision, image analysis and recognition, multi-variate data analysis, and many others.

5: Cellular Component Manifolds

The hope of this section is to show how components might be organized into computing and communicating systems based on the generalized address space model. First, some necessary terms and definitions are given. Szyperski [10] identifies three major tiers of component systems. The three tiers are defined below and their relationships are shown in Figure 3. Note the layered structure within a tier.

- A *component system architecture* consists of a set of platform decisions; a set of component frameworks; and an interoperation design for the component frameworks.
- A *component framework* is a dedicated and focused architecture, usually around a few key mechanisms, and a fixed set of policies for mechanisms at the component level.
- Software *components* are binary units of independent production, acquisition and deployment.

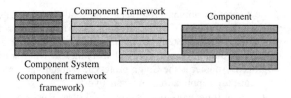

Figure 3. Component system architecture

The multi-tiered component system architecture of is Figure 3 redrawn in Figure 4 to show how components interoperate with each other directly and via frameworks. These are *instances* of runtime components and the dashed lines indicate direct and framework mediated communication. Component frameworks may appear as components within some contexts. That is, a component framework may offer an interface for use by components or by frameworks. The distinction is arbitrary in many cases.

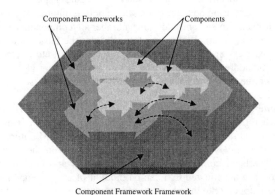

Figure 4. Component instance interoperations

Given the above, a **Cellular Component Manifold** is defined as:

*The "crystalline" structure formed by a distribution of components within a component framework whose organization is based on the generalized address space model where **all** addressing is in GBT.*

With these concepts established, a software architecture is now described. The three tiers are associated with specific system functionality as follows:

Component Framework Framework:	Virtual Machine
Component Framework:	Cellular Component Manifold
Component:	Component

The first tier, the component framework framework, is a Virtual Machine (VM). The VM is a virtual platform that encapsulates underlying, possibly heterogeneous, operating systems, networks and other resources. It is similar to the Java or Smalltalk VM's. This layer provides services to instances of Cellular Component Manifold (CM). Most importantly it permits CM's to be instantiated and activated. Other services include life-cycle management such as creation and allocation of resources (e.g. memory, cpu) to the components in the manifold and garbage collection. The VM has the ability to distribute the components across processors and networks.

Several research projects are developing prototypes whose advanced capabilities point the way toward the type of VM desired here. Two in particular are part of Microsoft's Millennium next-generation distributed operation system effort. The Borg prototype is a Java VM that automatically distributes computation over clusters of machines in what is called the single system image (SSI) approach. Another is the Coign prototype that automatically partitions and distributes COM component-based applications over a network.

The next tier, the component framework tier, is composed of instances of CM. Instances of CM are realizations of the generalized address space model. They are hierarchical, n-dimensional, structures based on the geometrical-algebraic GBT system. CM provide for the organization of components into computing-communicating wholes by acting as containers for components and providing for component and framework interoperation. A minimal CM is instantiated in the VM with the following parameters:

- N : number of dimensions
- R_{1-n} : the range of addresses in each dimension
- S : a specification for populating the address space with components.

Thus an instance of a CM is an address space with a define number of dimensions, definite range of addresses in each dimension, and some number of components located at specific addresses. The CM have an internal structure derived from the basic pattern of components discussed earlier (the Address Space Manager, Boundary Manager, etc.). On instantiation of a CM, the VM returns the address of the new CM. These addresses are globally unique and are used by other parts of the system to access the CM's interfaces. Also, the VM is used to resolve (external) addresses requested by a CM.

The VM plus a number of CM instances combine to produce a global virtual machine. This is a conceptual design for the generalized address space model. Implicit in this hierarchical model is the *interoperation design* that specifies how the various CM component frameworks interoperate within the overall system architecture – by reliance on the global address space model. The various levels of components within the system are a set of nested "plug-in" component manifolds. The instantiated CM can be thought of as a "component tilings" of the address space that are mapped onto the physical infrastructure resources by the VM. The basic pattern of address space components (the Address Space Manager, Boundary Manager, etc.) will become specific components suited to the particular task. These ideas are illustrated in Figure 5 where the rectangles are VM's and the ovals are CM's. As was mentioned earlier, it is somewhat arbitrary to distinguish between component manifolds and components. In the design presented here the Virtual machines could be instances of Component Manifolds.

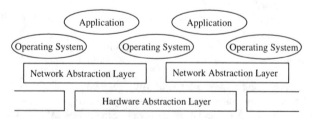

Figure 5. Hierarchy of VMs and CMs

A major goal of this approach is to have a global addressing scheme wherein the addresses (and the underlying mechanisms) perform useful services beyond current addressing schemes. For example, Microsoft 's COM system relies on the use of Globally Unique Identifiers (GUID), Interface Identifiers (IID), Class Identifiers (CLSID) and Category Identifiers (CATID). These are 128-bit numbers whose only feature is that they can be generated on separate machines and are guaranteed to be unique. The GBT-based addressing system could be used to generate such identifiers with some added benefits. The GBT addresses are indexes into and n-dimensional data structure that can store information about the indexed item. The address space of GUID's for a component architecture could be organized to store and access information on component versions, vendors, licensing, security, or any other information that is useful in enhancing the functionality of the system. Another addressing scheme that could possibly benefit from such an approach is Internet Protocol addressing now under revision.

6: Example Application

An example is developed to make concrete the ideas presented in the preceding sections. The intent is to illustrate how the Cellular Component Manifolds organization might be used in a real world application. The specific problem of handoff management of mobile users in *heterogeneous wireless networks* is chosen for this purpose. This section relies on considerable work done by the Bay Area Research Wireless Access Network (BARWAN) project [3].

The BARWAN project takes as its main task development of protocols for use in wireless overlay networks. Wireless overlay networks are hierarchical, physically overlapping networks composed from different types of wireless systems. For example, in-room IR and in-building RF. These various systems are developed by different vendors, use different protocol and antenna/modems. The BARWAN effort has prototyped an "Overlay IP" protocol that permits mobile hosts to roam seamlessly though this hierarchical, heterogeneous wireless network. A major part of their work focuses on how to make low-latency handoffs between the different networks. A simplified version of their testbed is described next for purposes of this example.

Assume a campus setting with a number of buildings. There is a campus-area packet relay network that covers the entire campus with a bandwidth of 64 kbps and latency (between mobile host and wireline) on the order of 100 ms. The cell size is 500 m. Each level within a building has a spread spectrum RF network with 1 Mbps bandwidth, 10ms latency, and 100 m cell size. Each room has an IR network that can support 5 users with near wireline performance. Further assume a typical campus-wide wireline network gatewayed to the wireless networks. Students are supplied PDAs with modems capable of communicating on and switching between the two RF nets and IR net. The students are set in motion.

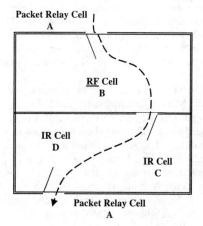

Figure 6. Typical building

A typical building fitted with RF and IR networks is shown in Figure 6. The building is in campus packet relay network cell A. There is one in-building RF network, cell B, and two in-building IR network cells D and C. The path of a student with a PDA (mobile host) requiring continuous service is also shown. Given this setting and scenario, the conceptual design for a software system to manage handoffs between the different networks is developed.

The goal of the design is to minimize handoff latency. This latency is bounded by *discovery time*: the time it takes a mobile host (MH) to realize it has changed cells. Typical (homogeneous) wireless systems rely on signal strength to manage handoff. This introduces unacceptable discovery times in wireless overlay systems. The design here relies on knowledge of the environment to anticipate cell changes and initiate handoffs. The system consists of instances of Cellar Component Manifolds (CM) that implement a model of the physical address space of the wireless networks. These are called Handoff Controllers (HC) and they are one of the modules comprising the overall network management system.

The basic design for a HC is as follows. It is a CM based directly on the "pattern" of the components in the general address space model presented in Section 3. The components are specialized for this purpose:

Address Space Manager (ASM): Implements a model of the physical address space. Its internal GBT addressing is scaled to the specified resolution of the actual geographic and geometric system being modeled. Important environmental entities are represented as components within this model's address space. These component models will be buildings, rooms, furnishings, equipment and mobile hosts.

Boundary Manager (BM): Handles boundary crossing events. The BMs are tailored to the types of wireless cell boundaries that exist in the system. They operate under control of the ASM.

There are three types of HCs for this system corresponding to the three types of wireless networks. The campus Packet Relay HC (PR-HC), the in-building RF HC (RF-HC) and the in-building IR HC (IR-HC). For purposes of this example they are instantiated as 2-dimensional address spaces with ranges in each dimension appropriate to the geometry of their cells. The components that populate them correspond to physical entities important to modeling the handoff. In the case of the PR-HC, a basic hexagonal cell of 500 m diameter is modeled at 10 m resolution. Included are location and geometry of buildings. Information about the boundaries of other wireless systems within this cell is also needed. The RF-HC and IR-HC are also 2-dimensional and model the interior of the building at 1 m resolution along with any specifics concerning furnishings, etc. Also, information on wireless boundaries is included. Further, the location of mobile hosts is known at all times and dynamically updated in their current HC.

The operation of these HCs, based on the path of the roaming student shown in Figure 6, is now discussed. The path of the MH causes a number of handoffs:

Packet Relay Cell A → RF Cell B: The PR-HC for cell A is servicing the MH. It is also tracking the position and speed of the MH. Based on this information the PR-HC anticipates that the MH may enter the building. The ASM (of the PR-HC) instructs the BM that manages the packet relay to RF boundary to take interest in the MH. The BM contacts the BM of the RF-HC of cell B and informs it that a handoff may take place. This results in the formation of a multicast group containing cells A and B. Thus packets for the MH are delivered simultaneously to both cells. If the MH enters the building, the handoff is accomplished. The BM of RF-HC registers the new MH with the ASM. The packets are already buffered in cell B and MH switches its modem to RF. This is a *downward vertical* handoff.

RF Cell B → IR Cell C: The MH is a member of the RF network of cell B and is moving toward the door. The ASM (of RF-HC) informs the BM and a sequence of events similar to those described above result in a *downward vertical* handoff to IR cell C.

IR Cell C → IR Cell D: Here the MH moves between two IR cells in a large room. The actions are similar to those above except that signal strength is also monitored to effect the handoff. This is a conventional *horizontal* handoff.

IR Cell D → Packet Relay Cell A: The IR-HC for cell D notices the MH is headed toward the door leading outside the building. The BM responsible for that boundary event is informed. The BM contacts the BM for the packet radio cell A and multicast group is formed in anticipation of the MH joining cell A. An *upward vertical* handoff takes place as the MH leaves the building.

The example illustrates a number of points about the component architecture. The handoff controllers are instances of Cellular Component Manifolds tailored to model the environment of a hierarchical, heterogeneous, wireless network. The basic pattern of the underlying generalized address space model and its components seem to map well on to this particular task. The handoff controllers combine to form a hierarchical system of nested controllers. In a complete system based on this approach *all* addressing could be made consistent. That is all "addressable" entities would be components within some Cellular Component Manifold. Also, not brought out above is the geometric modeling inherent in the controllers. The address space of the handoff controller is a vector space. This permits complete geometric modeling of the environment. A 2-dimensional system was used in the example for simplicity. In a real implementation it could easily be 4 or more dimensions, e.g. 3 dimensions for space and one for time.

7: Conclusion

Little is known about how to build component systems. This paper presents first thoughts on how the concept of address space can be generalized to serve as a basis for a component system architecture. The motivation for proposing what may appear to be a rather complex software architecture is the goal of supporting both advanced component systems as well as a wide range of applications in a single, consistent, general-purpose component framework. The algebraic/geometric basis of the architecture provides, at a fundamental level, support for applications such as: image analysis [11], target recognition [12], geographic information systems and multi-variate data analysis in general [13], and fluid dynamics [14] to name a few. In addition to providing a convenient modeling environment for application developers, many of these "applications" will be necessary to achieve advanced *systems* functionality. In particular the need to manage an increasingly complex information infrastructure will require the use of many of these types of applications. In short, all of these engineering approaches will be needed to permit the development of executable models of the system itself. The example of Section 6 is an illustration.

8: Acknowledgements

Supported in part by the United States Defence Advanced Research Projects Agency and by a Co-operative Research Centre Program through the Department of the Prime Minister and Cabinet of Australia. The views and conclusions contained in this document are those of the authors and should not be interpreted as representing the official policies, expressed or implied, of the Defence Advanced Projects Research Agency or the U.S. Government.

References

[1]   Jini, *JavaSoft*. http://www.javasoft.com/products/jini/, 1998.

[2]   Millennium, *Microsoft*. http://www.research.microsoft.com/sn/Millennium/, 1998.

[3]   Katz, R. and E. Brewer. *The Case for Wireless Overlay Networks*. in *Proceedings 1996 SPIE Conference on Multimedia and Networking, MMCM '96*. 1996. San Jose, CA.

[4]   Lindstrom, A., J. Rosenberg, and A. Dearle. *Grand unified theory of address spaces*. in *Proceedings of the Workshop on Hot Topics in Operating Systems, HOTOS*. 1995. Orcas Island, WA, USA: IEEE.

[5]   Herring, C., *Geometrical Backgroud: The Premutahedron*. http://www.dstc.edu.au/TU/staff/herring/Appendix-A.pdf, 1998.

[6]   Herring, C., *The Generalized Balanced Ternary Addressing System*. http://www.dstc.edu.au/TU/staff/herring/Appendix-B.pdf, 1998.

[7]   Lucas, D., *A multiplication in N-space*. Proceedings of the American Mathematical Society, 1979. **74**(1): p. 1-8.

[8]   Vince, A., *Replicating Tessellations*. SAIM Journal of Discrete Mathematics, 1993. **6**(3): p. 501-521.

[9]   Knuth, D.E., *The art of computer programming*. Vol. 2, Seminumerical algorithms. 1969, Reading, MA: Addison-Wesley.

[10] Szyperski, C., *Component Software*. 1998, New York: Addison-Wesley.

[11] Gibson, L. and D. Lucas, *Vectorization of Raster Images Using Hierarchical Methods*. Computer Graphics and Image Processing, 1982. **20**: p. 82-89.

[12] Gibson, L. and D. Lucas. *Pyramid Algorithms for Automatic Target Recognition*. in *Proceedings of the IEEE NAECON*. 1986. Dayton, OH.

[13] Gibson, L. and D. Lucas. *Spatial Data Processing Using Generalized Balanced Ternary*. in *Proceedings of the IEEE Conference on Pattern Recognition and Image Analysis*. 1982.

[14] Hasslacher, B., *Discrete Fluids*. Los Alamos Science, 1987. **15**.

Tool Integration, Collaboration and User Interaction Issues in Component-based Software Architectures

John Grundy[+], Rick Mugridge[++], John Hosking[++] and Mark Apperley[+]

[+]Department of Computer Science
University of Waikato
Private Bag 3105
Hamilton, New Zealand

[++]Department of Computer Science
University of Auckland
Private Bag 92019
Auckland, New Zealand

{jgrundy, M.Apperley}@cs.waikato.ac.nz

{john, rick}@cs.auckland.ac.nz

Abstract

Component-based software architectures are becoming increasingly popular solutions for use in a wide range of software applications. Particular areas in which these architectures may provide improved software development support include tool integration, distribution and collaborative work support, and human interaction and end-user configuration. However, a number of open research issues exist to do with the deployment of component-based solutions in these areas. We review our recent research experiences in deploying component-based solutions in these problem domains, and overview potential research directions.

1. Introduction

In recent years there has been an increasing interest in the use of component-based software architectures (also known as "componentware"). These architectures use the notion of a software component object, which advertises its methods, properties and events for use by other components, and use large-scale component composition to build up software applications. This contrasts with traditional software construction using libraries and frameworks, which results in "monolithic" software applications that are difficult to build and dynamically reconfigure. Component-based systems often allow end-users to reconfigure the components that make up their applications, and "plug and play" third-party components.

Various software architectures have been developed using components, including JavaBeans [16], COM/DCOM [18], and OpenDoc [1]. Tools allowing such architectures to be used to specify components and component-based applications include JBuilder [4], Visual Javascript [21] and Visual Age [15]. Component-based solutions offer great potential for reusing components that support tool integration, collaborative work and object distribution, and end-user interaction and configuration of applications. Component-based solutions contrast to more traditional approaches such as federation [5], toolkits and frameworks [17], and UIMS [20] used to implement these aspects of software applications. However, careful design is required to make reuse of these aspects straightforward.

We describe our recent research into component-based software architectures. This focuses on support for component-based architectures, component-based tool integration and collaborative work support, and issues of end-user interaction with and reconfiguration of component-based software systems. Examples of systems we have developed using component-based solutions are discussed, with particular emphasis on difficult and unsolved research issues. Our research has led to the formulation of a design and implementation approach we call "aspect-oriented" component-based system development. We briefly discuss this approach and illustrate tool support for it, which characterises aspects of components concerned with human-interfaces, end-user configuration, distribution and collaboration.

This paper begins with an example component-based software application, a process modelling and enactment environment. The following sections overview the use of components in supporting tool integration, collaborative work, human interaction and configuration in this environment and its software architecture. The use of aspects to characterise parts of components supporting these facilities is examined, and our research compared and contrasted to related architectures and systems. We conclude with a summary of our experiences with component-based software architectures and our future research plans.

2. Problem domain

Figure 1 shows a screen dump from Serendipity-II, a component-based workflow management system [12]. The top two windows show parts of a work process model (in this case, a simple process for modifying a software system). The dialogues show information about process enactment (i.e. work history), and a to-do list for each user of the system. This application allows users to design models of their work processes, enact (run) these process models and use them to guide their work, and to track actual work performed using the processes [12] [10].

Software components are used throughout the implementation of Serendipity-II. Figure 2 illustrates the software architecture of part of Serendipity-II. Icons and editing tools used for the graphical views are all reusable components that we have deployed in other applications. These are linked to application-specific "process stage" and "process model view" components, used to represent process model information. The Collaboration menu is the interface to a "collaborative editing" component, also reused elsewhere. The enactment history dialogue is the interface to a generic "change history" component that is used throughout our component-based applications to store and display events for users.

Users can add components on-the-fly, which we call event filters and actions, to provide useful additional functionality, modify how existing facilities of Serendipity-II work, or provide interfaces to third-party systems [12]. Event propagation is used extensively to keep process models consistent, record change histories, support collaborative editing, and drive process enactment. The shaded lines in Figure 2 indicate propagation of "change event" objects between components in Serendipity-II.

Serendipity-II illustrates several uses of component-based software architecture solutions:

- *Tool integration.* We have integrated Serendipity-II with several other tools, including communications software, a file sharing server, CASE tools, programming environments, and office automation tools. These third party tools were integrated with Serendipity-II process models by using filters and actions to "wrap up" the functionality of the tools, and thus provide component-based interfaces to them.

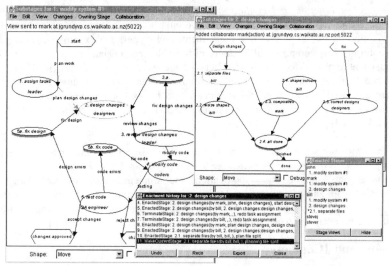

Figure 1. Serendipity-II: example of a component-based software system.

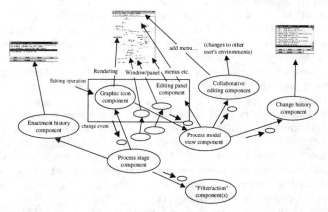

Figure 2. The component-based architecture of Serendipity-II.

- *Distribution and collaborative work.* Serendipity-II environments support multiple users, and thus process models and enactment information needs to be both distributed and collaboratively accessed and edited. Components comprising the architecture must support distribution and appropriate collaborative editing facilities must be provided to users. Our component-based software architecture provides basic component object distribution and event propagation mechanisms, which are leveraged by components in Serendipity-II to provide versioning, configuration management and collaborative editing.

- *End-user interaction and configuration.* Users of Serendipity-II need to be able to interact with the components that make the environment in appropriate and consistent ways, and be able to plug in new components and reconfigure existing components. As Serendipity-II is comprised of a variety of reusable components, these should provide a consistent look-and-feel to users. Users of the environment are provided with both simple configuration "wizards" to add new components and reconfigure components, and with advanced, visual interfaces to carry out complex component configuration. This allows users to extend their environment's functionality and to integrate other tools with Serendipity-II process support facilities.

In the following section we describe our component-based software architecture and its support tools with which environments like Serendipity-II are built. We discuss and illustrate how these tools support the specification and implementation of tool integration, collaborative work and user interaction facilities in our environments. We then overview our recent work in identifying and codifying these and other "aspects" of component-based systems, and compare our work with other research in this area.

3. JViews and JComposer

We have been developing component-based software architectures for the construction of design environments for several years [13] [11]. Our latest architecture, implemented using the JavaBeans component-based API, is JViews [14]. Figure 3 shows the basic characteristics of JViews-based systems: components (rectangular icons), component relationships (oval icons), inter-component links, and the propagation of events (which we call "change descriptions"), along links and relationships. These abstractions provide structural foundations for representing application data, interconnectivity and inter-component dependency and constraints. Additionally, event filter and action components provide reusable event-handling behaviour. Component interconnection can be both statically and dynamically specified.

JViews provides a richer range of event detection and propagation mechanisms than do other component-based approaches like JavaBeans, COM and CORBA. This includes the facility for components to listen for change descriptions generated both before and after component state has been modified, and to handle change descriptions sent to other components both before and after a third component's state has changed. Change descriptions can be stored, used to support undo/redo and versioning, and propagated to other users' environments to support collaborative editing [11].

For example, in Figure 3 a repository process stage component is linked to: a view relationship, linked to view components representing some aspect of the process stage (e.g. graphical view icons and textual view descriptions); other process stage components, via an event flow relationship; and an event filter component. When the state of the process stage is modified, e.g. its name property changed, JViews change descriptions are sent to the linked components. Relationship components typically handle the event and update other linked components appropriately, while directly linked components respond to the event themselves e.g. updating their own state, redisplaying their icon/text, enforcing a constraint etc.

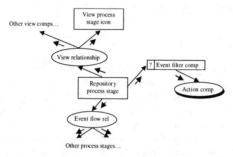

Figure 3. The JViews component-based software architecture.

JViews is implemented as a set of framework classes in Java, extending the JavaBeans componentware API. Developing applications with the JViews framework classes directly is tedious, time-consuming and error-prone. We developed a CASE tool, using JViews, to assist developers to build component-based environments. Called JComposer [14], the tool provides visual languages for specifying components, relationship components, links, filters and actions, and a range of interdependency links between these components. JComposer generates JViews class specialisations, implementing the specified environment as a set of JViews components. A set of reverse engineering tools allows developers to construct JComposer specifications from JViews classes, or to reverse engineer JViews specifications which "wrap" JavaBeans classes. JComposer specifications can be saved to persistent store and can be collaboratively edited using the same facilities as in Serendipity.

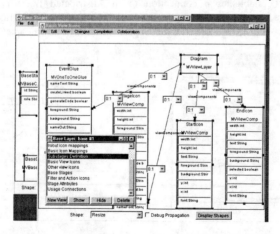

Figure 4. An example of JComposer being used to specify Serendipity-II.

Figure 4 shows JComposer being used to specify Serendipity-II. A number of views of Serendipity are used, each providing specification of different aspects of Serendipity such as graphical specifications of components, filters and actions, or Java code implementing specialised JViews methods for detailed processing.

4. Tool integration

In order to effectively use component-based environments like Serendipity-II, appropriate integration of third party tools and components must be supported. Serendipity-II 's filter/action event handling language, based on that of JComposer, allows users to plug in components representing third-party tools and link them to Serendipity artefacts and other reusable filters and actions via event propagation connections.

Figure 5 shows the specification of a simple software agent that automatically downloads and uploads files from a shared file server. When the Serendipity process stage "2. Design changes" is enacted (i.e. the user starts work on this stage), an event indicating this is generated and sent to all stages, filters and actions connected to this stage. The Serendipity filter and action model on the left specifies that when an enactment event is detected from this process stage, a "request stage artefacts" action should be run. This reusable component determines the files associated with the "2. Design changes" stage (specified in another Serendipity-II view) and downloads (checks out) these to the user's computer from the file sever. When the stage is completed, the files are automatically uploaded (checked in) back to the file server.

The illustration on the right in Figure 5 shows how components providing the tool integration between Serendipity-II and the shared file server work. When the user adds the "request stage artefacts" action, a JViews component (implemented with JComposer or directly in Java) is created which implements the Serendipity-II action's behaviour. The JViews component establishes a connection to the distributed file server. When the Serendipity-II stage is enacted, the enactment event propagated to the action by the filter instructs it to request all files associated with the process stage be downloaded.

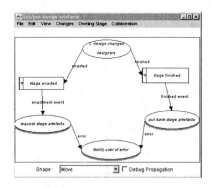

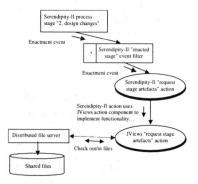

(a) Supporting external tool usage.　　　　(b) Intercommunication between tools.

Figure 5. Specifying the use of a third-party file server in Serendipity-II.

Another example of component-based tool integration is shown in Figure 6. In this example, a set of tools for planning travel, all independently developed, is being integrated. This tool set includes a reusable tree editor (used in this example to edit and browse a structured travel itinerary), a map visualisation, a chat tool, and a Web browser. The JComposer filter/action model shown in Figure 7 specifies interconnection between these tools, represented as components. This results in the map visualisation being dynamically updated whenever the travel route specified in the itinerary editor is changed, and a chat message is written when the map visualisation (and hence itinerary travel route) is updated.

The chat tool, map and tree browser/editor are third-party Java applets which have been "wrapped" with JViews component interfaces, with the Java events generated by these tools being converted into JViews change descriptions. A JViews action was written which parses the textual representation of the tree editor for city names and updates the map city route. Another action sends a chat message via the chat tool with parameters for user and chat message. JComposer was then used to create instances of each of these tool "components" and actions, and additional filters which detect itinerary item updates and map route property updates respectively. Connecting these components, filters and actions in JComposer results in the integrated environment illustrated in Figure 6.

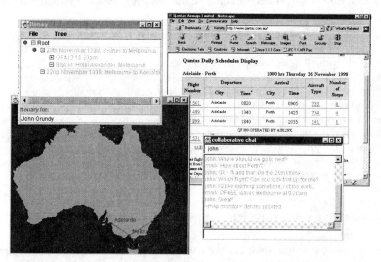

Figure 6. Integrating an itinerary editor, map visualisation and chat tool.

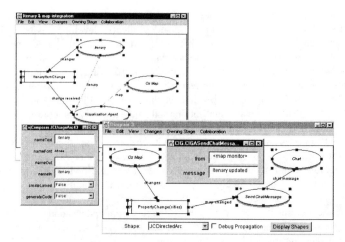

Figure 7. Serendipity-II filter/action models specifying tool integration mechanism.

Using JComposer to facilitate tool integration has been quite successful in the domains we have used it for. This has included Serendipity-II integrated with CASE tools, programming environments, communication tools and office automation tools, and several tools characterised with JViews components and then integrated. We have been able to successfully and very tightly integrate Serendipity-II, JComposer, a UML modelling tool and an ER modelling tool [14]. Limitations of this approach are encountered when having to "wrap" third-party tools that do not already have well-developed component interfaces. This requires the development of JViews components to communicate with these tools, often in a limited way, and the translation of tool events into JViews change descriptions. This can be a complex process [20][7][28], and one which sometimes can only provide limited interface solutions. We hope that as component-based architectures become more widely used, 3rd party tools will increasingly provide component-based interfaces we can leverage more effectively.

5. Collaborative work support

Supporting collaborative work has been an important aim in many of our component-based environments [11] [12]. Usually much effort is required to adequately architect an environment for collaborative editing, and to re-architect a single-user environment is very difficult and time-consuming. Our JViews-based environments were all originally single-user environments, and we used a component-based approach to seamlessly add flexible collaborative editing support, without necessitating changes to the environments or the components we used to facilitate this editing functionality.

Figure 8 shows a "collaboration" menu in use in Serendipity-II to configure the "level" of collaborative editing with a colleague (e.g. asynchronous, synchronous and "presentation" i.e. show editing changes to others as they occur but don't action them) [9]. The "change history" dialogue on the bottom, right hand side shows a history of editing events for the user's process model. Some changes were made by the user ("John"), and others by a collaborator ("Mark").

The illustration on the right in Figure 8 shows how these collaborative editing components were added to Serendipity-II (and can in fact be added to any JViews-based environment, with no change to these components or the components that make up the environment). A "collaboration menu" component is created when the user specifies they want to have collaborative editing of a view. This listens to editing changes in the view, and records these. If the user is in presentation or synchronous editing modes with another user, the changes are propagated to that user's environment. There they are stored and presented in a dialogue (presentation) or actioned on the other user's view (synchronous editing). With asynchronous editing, a user requests a list of changes made to another user's view and selects from a dialogue which they wish to have applied to their view.

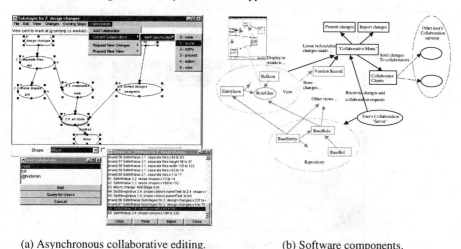

(a) Asynchronous collaborative editing.   (b) Software components.

Figure 8. Collaborative editing components in Serendipity-II.

JViews has abstractions supporting the replication of components (via object versioning), which are used to maintain copies of collaboratively edited views. Change descriptions generated in one view are propagated to another user's environment with component references translated appropriately. The change description propagation and listening support of JViews made it very easy to add collaborative editing components to existing JViews-based environments. It even allows fully synchronous editing, with locking, to be properly supported with no change to the original environment or the collaborative editing components [9].

Figure 9 shows another example of distributed components in Serendipity-II. In this example, a distributed software agent is being specified using reusable filter and action components. When artefacts (in this example, Java source files) are modified while stage "4. Modify code" is enacted, events describing these changes are sent to all components linked to this stage. The two filters note the modification of Shape.java or EditorWindow.java, and the action forwards the change descriptions it receives to a "remote" stage, identified by remote user and name properties specified for the sender action. The receiver action in the right hand view forwards all changes it receives to a store action, which records the change description in an event history artefact. The left-hand view is run by Bill's Serendipity-II environment, while John's runs the right hand view. The nett result is that changes made by Bill to either of the two classes are sent to John for later examination via the user interface of the history artefact.

Implementing and deploying JViews-implemented collaborative editing components for JViews-based environments has been successful. In general, however, it is difficult to distribute components and provide appropriate collaborative editing functionality for them if they have not been designed with this in mind. Often component-based systems use simple subscribe-notify patterns that broadcast component update events only after the event has been actioned. It is often very difficult to provide fully synchronous editing for such components. Propagation of events and replication of component objects across multiple machines requires component registration and identification mechanisms that are also hard to retrofit to software components designed for single-user use.

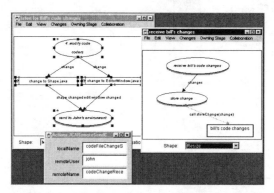

Figure 9. Specifying distributed software agents in Serendipity-II.

6. User interaction and configuration

Component-based software systems must provide consistent user interaction mechanisms across all components, and must allow users to modify the configuration of their application components in appropriate ways. A key implication of component-based software is the need to support extensible interaction mechanisms i.e. allow new components added to an environment to extend existing interaction menus, buttons, dialogues and windows.

We have developed a range of extensible interaction mechanisms and reusable components with human interfaces in our environments. For example, the change history dialogue (

Figure 1) and enactment history dialogue (Figure 8 (a)) are both human interfaces of the JViews "version record" component, used to record change descriptions. The collaborative editing component illustrated in Figure 8 extends the menu bar provided by the view editing panel component of JViews-based systems. The buttons and menu items of JViews components can be extended by other components e.g. actions can add extra menu items to Serendipity-II process stage icon pop-up menus to allow users access to extra functions they provide.

End-user configuration of components is supported in our environments by several mechanisms: "wizards" which guide users through component configuration, visual manipulation of component object representations, the use of plug-in actions, property sheets, and menus and buttons provided by components. Figure 10 illustrates a configuration wizard dialogue allowing a user to configure a simple change monitoring action and the visual configuration of an equivalent change monitor using filters and actions. Both of these techniques have been successful in our environments, with wizards useful for end-users with little knowledge of the component-based architectures behind the environment, and visual filter and action component composition useful for more sophisticated configuration by experienced users.

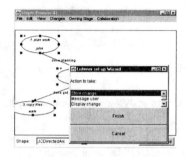

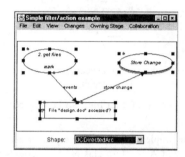

(a) Part of a simple configuration "wizard"   (b) Visual component configuration.

Figure 10. End-user configuration in Serendipity-II.

7. Advertising and using component aspects

End-user interaction and configuration are two common "aspects" of component-based systems and inter-component interaction that need to be carefully designed, implemented and used, to ensure appropriate mechanisms are supported and are accessible by both end-users and other components. For example, the JViews version record dialogue should provide the ability to disable and/or hide its undo/redo buttons, which are sometimes not used when this component is reused, e.g. as a Serendipity-II enactment history. Similarly, JViews editing panel components should provide methods allowing (or disallowing) other components to extend its menu bar, as done by the collaborative editing component.

Other aspects of component-based systems we have commonly dealt with include distribution and collaboration support, persistency, and inter-component linkage for tool integration. Each of these requires a component to advertise certain characteristics (such as unique identifier allocation, change locking and/or transactioning ability, and valid component types it can be linked to), so other components can effectively interact with this component.

We have been developing a design and implementation methodology, and appropriate support tools in JComposer and Serendipity-II, for representing and using such aspects of components. Figure 11 illustrates the publication of and subscription to such aspects in JViews, and how end-users can use these when configuring and using component-based systems. A component publicises information about aspects it supports and how these can be used e.g. a set of methods to allow extension/modification of its human interface aspects. Other components query it for these aspects and use them as necessary and appropriate.

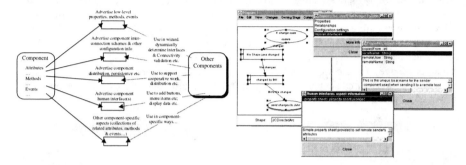

(a) Implementing aspects for JViews components

(b) Using component aspects in Serendipity-II

Figure 11. Describing and using component aspects in JViews and Serendipity-II.

Our implementation of component aspects in JViews uses a set of design patterns and associated AspectInfo classes and methods to provide an extensible set of characterisations of a component. JComposer and Serendipity-II allow component designers and users to access these aspects and check components are correctly linked and interacting by using aspect information. Automatic reconfiguration of components is also supported.

The example on the right in Figure 11 shows an end-user browsing the aspects of a "RemoteSendChange" action, which publicises four aspects (its parameters, links to other components, configuration constraints and human interface elements). The user can obtain extra information about these aspects as desired. Other components can also make use of these aspects, for example wizards, visual configuration tools and other components that want to reuse and/or extend the component. Aspects differ from low-level property, method and event descriptions JavaBeans publicise and COM type libraries, in that they describe responsibilities of sets of component methods, properties and events. Our JViews AspectInfo classes also provide methods allowing other components to use different kinds of aspects in "standard" ways, no matter what methods, properties and events are used to implement the aspect.

8. Discussion

Much recent work has been done in relation to component-based systems development. Various component-based software architectures have been developed, including JavaBeans [1], COM [18], and OpenDoc [1]. In addition, distributed object management architectures like OMG CORBA [22] offer capabilities for component modelling and distribution. Various tools have been developed for engineering systems with such architectures including JBuilder [4], Visual Age [15], Visual Javascript [21], and those for specialised application domains like 3D modelling [29]. All of these systems provide low-level support for component development. End-user configuration support is generally limited to simple component object linking. All component-based architectures provide mechanisms for publicising component properties, methods and events, but generally have no concept of higher level aspects encompassing collections of component features.

Tool integration approaches include federation [5], enveloping [28], middleware architectures [7], database and file-based integration [19], and message passing [23]. While these techniques have proved successful in limited domains, none has managed to provide an ideal solution. Enveloping, middleware and message passing architectures are the most similar to component-based tool integration approaches that we have used.

Workflow management systems and process-centred environments generally provide some support for task automation, tool integration and collaboration. Examples include ProcessWEAVER [8], SPADE [2], Oz [3], and Regatta [27]. These generally adopt low-level, macro or programming languages to support environment extension, or use a basic range of inflexible event-based triggers configured with Wizards. We have found the use of primarily visual notations to support environment extension to be more useful, although Wizards and property sheets provided by components are also important. It is difficult to design components for end-user configuration in advance as designers often do not know exactly how and where their components are to be deployed.

Computer-supported cooperative work tools and environments allow groupware tools to be constructed which support distributed workers and artifacts. Examples include GroupKit [24], Suite [6], COAST [26], and TeamWave [25]. TeamRooms and COAST adopt component-based approaches, but require systems to be designed with this functionality in mind from the outset. We have managed to re-architect JViews-based tools to support various forms of collaborative work without the need to re-implement existing components.

9. Conclusions

Component-based software architectures are becoming increasingly important as solutions for a wide range of software engineering problems. We have focused on the use of software components to support diverse tool integration mechanisms, collaborative work and object distribution, extensible human-interfaces, and end-user configuration of software applications. We have developed both software architectures that support component-based software development, and tools for design and implementation with these architectures. Component-based solutions for tool integration, collaboration, human-interfaces and end-user configuration have proved appropriate and useful in the domains we have worked.

We are developing JViews-based "wrapper" components for a variety of third-party components and tools, including standard JavaBeans, COM components and CORBA objects, and software development, office automation and database tools. The use of semi-automatic component interface and event generation tools in JComposer will make this easier and repeatable. Mapping components supporting complex inter-component event and method mappings are being developed, allowing both tool integration and collaborative work with components to be better-supported. We are working on techniques for designing extensible human interface aspects for components, along with automatic wizard generation for end-user configuration of components. The publicising of and subscription to component aspects, and a development methodology for components incorporating standardised aspect patterns, will enable more flexible combination of all aspects of software components.

312

References

[1] Apple Computer Inc., *OpenDoc™ Users Manual*, 1995.
[2] Bandinelli, S. and DiNitto, E. and Fuggetta, A., Supporting cooperation in the SPADE-1 environment, *IEEE Transactions on Software Engineering 22 (12)*, December 1996, 841-865.
[3] Ben-Shaul, I.Z. and Kaiser, G.E., A Paradigm for Decentralized Process Modeling and its Realization in the Oz Environment, *16th International Conference on Software Engineering*, IEEE CS Press, 1996, 179-188.
[4] *Borland JBuilder™*, Borland Inc, http://www.borland.com/jbuilder/.
[5] Bounab, M. and Godart, C., A federated approach to tool integration, *Proceedings of CaiSE*95*, Finland, June 1995, LNCS 932, Springer-Verlag, pp. 269-282.
[6] Dewan, P. and Choudhary, R. Flexible user interface coupling in collaborative systems, in *Proceedings of ACM CHI'91*, ACM Press, April 1991, pp. 41-49.
[7] Dossick, S. and Kaiser, G.E., Middleware architectures for workgroups, *Proceedings of IEEE Workshops on Enabling Technologies: Infrastructure for Collaborative Enterprises*, June 17-19, 1998, IEEE CS Press.
[8] Ferstrom, C. ProcessWEAVER: Adding process support to UNIX, *2nd International Conference on the Software Process*, Berlin, February 1993, IEEE CS Press, 12-26.
[9] Grundy, J.C. Engineering Component-based, User-configurable Collaborative Editing Systems, *Proceedings of 7th Conference on Engineering for Human-Computer Interaction*, Crete, September 14-18, 1998, Kluwer Academic Publishers. (in press)
[10] Grundy, J.C. and Hosking, J.G., Serendipity: an integrated environment for process modelling, enactment and work coordination, *Automated Software Engineering*, Vol. 5, No. 1, Kluwer Academic Publishers, January 1998, 27-60.
[11] Grundy, J.C., Hosking, J.G. and Mugridge, W.B., Supporting flexible consistency management with discrete change description propagation, *Software - Practice & Experience 20 (9)*, September 1996, 1053-1083.
[12] Grundy, J.C., Hosking, J.G., Mugridge, W.B. and Apperley, M.D., A decentralised architecture for process modelling, *IEEE Internet Computing*, Vol. 2, No. 5, September-October, 1998, IEEE CS Press.
[13] Grundy, J.C., Hosking, J.G., and Mugridge, W.B., Inconsistency management in multiple-view software engineering environments, *IEEE Transactions on Software Engineering*, Vol. 24, No. 11, November 1998.
[14] Grundy, J.C., Mugridge, W.B., and Hosking, J.G., Visual specification of multi-view visual environments, *Proceedings of 1998 IEEE Symposium on Visual Languages*, Halifax, Nova Scotia, September 2-4 1998.
[15] IBM Inc, *VisualAge™ for Java*, 1998, http://www.software.ibm.com/ad/vajava/.
[16] *Java Beans™ 1.0 API Specification*, Sun Microsystems Inc., 1997, http://www.javasoft.com/beans/.
[17] Linton, M. and Vlissides, J.M. and Calder, P.R., Composing User Interfaces with InterViews, COMPUTER, Vol. 22, No. 2, February 1989, 8-22.
[18] Microsoft Corporation, Component Object Model™, 1998, http://www.microsoft.com/com/.
[19] Meyers, S. Difficulties in Integrating Multiview Editing Environments, *IEEE Software*, Vol. 8, No. 1, January 1991, 49-57.
[20] Myers, B.A. et al, The Amulet Environment: New Models for Effective User Interface Software Development, *IEEE Transactions on Software Engineering*, Vol. 23, No. 6, June 1997, 347-365.
[21] Netscape Communications Inc, *Visual Javascript™*, 1998, http://www.netscape.com/compprod/products/tools/visual_js.html.
[22] *OMG CORBA*, Object Management Group, 1998, http://www.omg.org/.
[23] Reiss, S.P. Connecting Tools Using Message Passing in the Field Environment, *IEEE Software*, Vol. 7, No. 7, July 1990, 57-65.
[24] Roseman, M. and Greenberg, S., Building Real Time Groupware with GroupKit, A Groupware Toolkit, ACM *Transactions on Computer-Human Interaction*, Vol. 3, No. 1, March 1997, 1-37.
[25] Roseman, M. and Greenberg, S., Simplifying Component Development in an Integrated Groupware Environment, *Proceedings of the ACM UIST'97 Conference*, ACM Press, 1997.
[26] Shuckman, C., Kirchner, L., Schummer, J. and Haake, J.M., Designing object-oriented synchronous groupware with COAST, in *Proceedings of the ACM Conference on Computer Supported Cooperative Work*, ACM Press, November 1996, pp. 21-29.
[27] Swenson, K.D. and Maxwell, R.J. and Matsumoto, T. and Saghari, B. and Irwin, K., A Business Process Environment Supporting Collaborative Planning, *Journal of Collaborative Computing*, Vol. 1, No. 1, 1994.
[28] Valetto, G. and Kaiser, G.E., Enveloping Sophisticated Tools into Process-centred Environments, *Automated Software Engineering*, Vol. 3, 1996, 309-345.
[29] Wagner, B., Sluijmers, I., Eichelberg, D., and Ackerman, P., Black-box Reuse within Frameworks Based on Visual Programming, in *Proeedings of the. 1st Component Users Conference*, Munich, July 1996, SIGS.

Author Index

Notes

Notes